Studies in Historical Archaeoet

Volume 1

AFTER EMPIRE
TOWARDS AN ETHNOLOGY OF
EUROPE'S BARBARIANS

Studies in Historical Archaeoethnology

SERIES EDITOR: GIORGIO AUSENDA

Already published:

The Anglo-Saxons from the Migration Period to the Eighth Century: An Ethnographic Perspective
edited by John Hines

Franks and Alamanni in the Merovingian Period: An Ethnographic Perspective
edited by Ian Wood

The Visigoths from the Migration Period to the Seventh Century: An Ethnographic Perspective
edited by Peter Heather

Forthcoming:

The Scandinavians from the Vendel Period to the Tenth Century: An Ethnographic Perspective

The Continental Saxons to the Carolingian Period: An Ethnographic Perspective

The Ostrogoths from the Migration Period to the Sixth Century: An Ethnographic Perspective

The Langobards from the Migration Period to the Eighth Century: An Ethnographic Perspective

Forthcoming conferences:

Vandals and Suebi from the Migration Period to the Sixth Century

The Burgundians from the Migration Period to the Sixth Century

AFTER EMPIRE

TOWARDS AN ETHNOLOGY OF
EUROPE'S BARBARIANS

Edited by

G. Ausenda

THE BOYDELL PRESS

Center for Interdisciplinary Research on Social Stress,
San Marino (R.S.M.)

First published 1995
The Boydell Press, Woodbridge

Reissued in paperback 2002

ISBN 0 85115 634 7 hardback
ISBN 0 85115 853 6 paperback

The Boydell Press is an imprint of Boydell & Brewer Ltd
PO Box 9, Woodbridge, Suffolk IP12 3DF, UK
and of Boydell & Brewer Inc.
PO Box 41026, Rochester, NY 14604-4126, USA
website: www.boydell.co.uk

*This volume contains the papers presented at the first conference on "Studies in Historical
Archaeoethnology " organized by the Center for Interdisciplinary Research on Social Stress, which
was held in San Marino from 26th August to 1st September 1993, under the auspices of the
Department of Public Education and Culture of the Republic of San Marino.*

A catalogue record for this book is available
from the British Library

Library of Congress Catalog Card Number 95-44014

This publication is printed on acid-free paper

Printed in the Republic of San Marino

CONTENTS

INTRODUCTION

Center for Interdisciplinary Research on Social Stress, 6 Contrada S. Francesco, San Marino (R.S.M.)

Purpose of the Conference

Social stress is defined in this context as generated by the aggregate of forces acting on society and thereby producing change. One of the aims of the Center for Interdisciplinary Research on Social Stress is the study of social change, in particular the change undergone by societies at critical stages in their history. Among the most relevant changes experienced by European society was that which affected the Continent's populations during the transition from the Roman empire to the Middle Ages. This transition was accompanied by a shift from a Mediterranean polity at its twilight to the foundation of a Continental polity with a new sociocultural character and economic autonomy.

The purpose of this conference was to discuss a new approach to the recovery of the customs and beliefs of the populations which settled in Europe at the close of the Western Roman empire, an exercise considered useful better to understand the nascent stage of those traits and attitudes which are at the base of present-day Europe. A few examples of the attitudes which began to take shape during or just after the transition period are feudalism, the status level achieved by the merchant class, the beginnings of an ideology that led to the separation of Church and State, the demise of slavery as an inefficient mode of production, the origin of national identities, etc.

The approach to such a recovery must necessarily be interdisciplinary because no single discipline can supply all the data, let alone the know-how, to accomplish an aim of this sort. To find a suitable term for this new interdisciplinary approach it may be worthwhile briefly to review other programs of an interdisciplinary nature born in the area common to the disciplines of archaeology, history and anthropology represented in this symposium.

The first approach to appear, and an interdisciplinary one as its name implies, was *Ethnohistory*. Historians as far back as Herodotus occasionally wrote what today would be considered ethnohistory. However, the discipline came into its own shortly after World War II. *The Journal of the American Society of Ethnohistory* was first published in 1954 by the Texas Tech University Press. Perhaps the early beginnings at that university were prompted by the predisposition toward such an approach in the study of Mesoamerican and neighbouring societies, many of whose characteristics were recorded with a fair degree of accuracy because of the presence of Spanish colonial society.

Ethnohistory's purpose is to reconstruct the remote or proximate history of populations lacking a historical record. These may be either pre-contact societies, for which oral accounts, non-historical documentation, archaeology and network theories may supply a fitting historical framework, or small communities belonging to the fringes of historical societies, for which non-collated documentary evidence, such as parish or similar records, survives.

© C.I.R.O.S.S.
San Marino (R.S.M.)

Ethnohistory is written both by historians and anthropologists, but the feeling is that anthropologists outnumber historians, mainly because they are accustomed to work with non-documentary information.

Maxine R. Kleindienst and Patty Jo Watson's article (1956) *Action Archaeology: The Archaeological Inventory of a Living Community* is taken to be the manifesto of *Ethnoarchaeology*. In that article the two archaeologists advocated the study of the layouts and characteristics, including a careful description of all material objects (increasingly spurned by cultural anthropologists more inclined to study the symbolic aspects of societies), of what could be considered 'future' archaeological records in contemporary usage, as an aid to understanding pre-historic or pre-contact archaeological records.

The proposed methodology was extended to the recognition of ancient artefacts by contemporary descendants of the populations which presumably used them, and the study of disposal patterns in contemporary living sites as an insight to prehistoric ones, on the assumption that archaeological sites are mostly formed by disposal patterns.

Anthropologie historique was a French development and is better known by its name in that language. The relatively recent (1976) foundation of this new interdisciplinary venture was preceded by a long involvement of French historians with the socioeconomic undercurrents of historical developments. This trend gravitated around the journal *Annales, économie, société, civilization* founded by Marc Bloch and Lucien Febvre in 1929 (Biersack 1991:11). A further impulse in the direction of Anthropologie historique was given by the social historian Fernand Braudel who was interested in expanding history to embrace all aspects of society.

Anthropologie historique began its official career when Jacques Le Goff inaugurated the name in a seminar under the title of *Anthropologie historique de l'Occident médiéval*, given in 1976 at the École des hautes études en sciences sociales (EHESS) (Berlioz *et al.* 1991:270). The practitioners of this school are mostly historians also versed in the theoretical works of contemporary anthropologists. They look at traditional anthropological aspects of historical societies, i.e. kinship, the relationship of individuals and society to the human body both in health and sickness, symbolic life, and political history (Berlioz *et al.* 1991:272) with special attention again to "the material, economic, symbolic and imaginary aspects that had escaped the old political history" (Berlioz *et al.* 1991:287). Because their sources are mostly documentary, the practitioners of Anthropologie historique rarely venture earlier than the tenth century.

The seed was carried to the United States by Marshall David Sahlins who, in his *Historical Metaphors and Mythical Realities* (1981) on the discovery of Hawaii, attempted to apply a structuralist approach to history. In recent years the American version has grown into a full-fledged *Historical Anthropology* (cf. Biersack 1991), albeit more popular with anthropologists than historians, as those who are considered anthropological historians deal mostly with recent or contemporary populations.

For the sake of completeness one should mention *Historical Archaeology*, which is well summed up by the quotation:

> Historical Archaeology as a sub-discipline (rather than the journal) began formally, I suppose, in 1967, when the Society for Historical Archaeology was founded. It began as a very artifact-centered, antiquities-oriented field, and has only recently become modern, theoretical, and interesting in the 80's (Rothschild: personal communication).

In a recent comprehensive publication on various aspects of this sub-discipline, James Deetz defines Historical Archaeology as "the archaeology of the spread of European societies worldwide" (Deetz 1991:1 in Rothschild 1992:1009). In another essay Kathleen Deagan sees the aim of Historical Archaeology as increasing knowledge of the past in (1) understanding the reciprocal effect of colonial interaction, (2) reconstructing the landscape better to understand past ecology, (3) greater understanding of health and nutritional processes from archaeological remains, (4) focussing on accidents, and (5) highlighting the lives of the dominant strata of the population (Deagan 1991:97-112 in Rothschild 1992:1009). So far the new approach is dominated by archaeologists even though other disciplines have also been involved.

The common aim of the participants in this symposium was to try to recover knowledge of several aspects of the life style and sociocultural conditions of past populations, in this case those which settled in Europe between the fourth and the ninth century of our era. This endeavour should be capable of acquiring momentum from an interdisciplinary approach because of the complementarity of the disciplines that belong to the tripartite division of the field between: (1) historical disciplines that rely on documents, i.e. history, philology, and literature; (2) those that can shed light on long-forgotten customs and procedures by comparing them with examples from contemporary societies at similar levels of complexity, i.e. ethnology, folklore, and socio-cultural anthropology; and (3) archaeology and physical anthropology, the disciplines whose practitioners recover and interpret the actual remains of the past reality of the populations under study. In the process the practitioners of all the disciplines involved would certainly benefit from the cross-fertilisation and feedback inherent in such interdisciplinary encounters.

If this should become an accepted approach it may be defined, perhaps, by a combination of the names of the three disciplines involved: archaeology, history, and ethnology.

Synopses of Papers

Ten papers were presented at the symposium. Rather than by discipline, presentations were grouped by topic in a sequence ideally ranging from subsistence and material aspects to politics and religion. While there were none touching on subsistence and material aspects the first four presentations were dedicated to social structural aspects. They were followed by papers concerning the economy and relationship between cities and countryside. The last group concerned problems of politics and religion.

To the first group of four papers on various aspects of the social structure belong G. Ausenda's "The segmentary lineage in contemporary anthropology and among the Langobards", J. D. Richards' "An archaeology of Anglo-Saxon England", J. Hines' "Cultural change and social organisation in early Anglo-Saxon England", and D. A. Turton's "History, age and the anthropologists".

In his discussion of "The segmentary lineage in contemporary anthropology and among the Langobards" Ausenda takes his cue from the most recent critique of the concept of lineage among Germanic populations represented by A. C. Murray's *Germanic Kinship Structure*. Briefly stated, Murray dismisses the idea that Germanic social structure was based on agnatic lineages. He asserts that ancient sources were unreliable and he disproves the idea that the most often cited examples of an agnatic lineage, the Langobardic and Burgundian *farae*, were lineages at all.

Ausenda chose to discuss the 'segmentary lineage' believing that Germanic populations were also involved in an agro-pastoral subsistence similar to that of contemporary populations amongst which segmentary lineages in their many variations are the basic components of the social structure. The earliest recognition of a segmentary lineage structure is due to E. E. Evans-Pritchard and Elizabeth Bacon who first recognised a segmentary lineage system. They describes it as having two basic features: (1) a 'tribal genealogical' structure linking all lineages in a tribe, and (2) agnatic relationship between members. In one of the most important contributions to the study of pastoralist populations, R. L. Tapper recognises the widespread existence of two main structural levels: *A* communities, comprising a dominant lineage with temporarily resident affines, matrilateral kin and unrelated clients, having a strength between 20 and 50 households, or 100 to 300 individuals, and *B* communities at higher levels of aggregation, corresponding in many cases to clans. Agro-pastoralists are found in the Saharan belt across Africa, and from East Africa southward, in the Middle East and across to India and Pakistan, and from the Asian steppes to Europe. Ausenda describes the main cohesive structures amongst these societies, which are based on kinship, age and class.

When they first settled in Italy, the Langobards' subsistence was based both on agriculture and animal husbandry. Their original social structure was based largely on kinship. Tacitus and the *Origo* hint at the existence of a 'tribal genealogical' system comprising all Germanic groups.

Even discounting Paul the Deacon's statement that *farae* were "generations or lineages", Ausenda shows by documentary and philological proofs that the *fara* was a bounded group akin to a level *A* group as described by Tapper, comprising agnatic kin, affines, and clients, in addition to some slaves. Ausenda goes on to point out the topical reliability of ancient sources, confirmed both by 'internal' documentary and archaeological proofs and by 'external' parallels among contemporary societies at a comparable level of sociocultural integration. Ausenda believes he presents convincing evidence that the Langobards had corporate groups based on kinship and that they coincided with the *fara*. Contrary to A. C. Murray's suggestion that the concept of *fara* should be eliminated because it is a poor basis for a comprehensive view, Ausenda holds that it is dangerous to disqualify the concept of *fara*, but that one should take it into detailed account and understand all its implications if one wants to understand the social structure of the *Germani* at the time of migration.

The opening remarks in J. D. Richards' paper "Archaeology of Anglo-Saxon England" concern the limitations of archaeology in that both deposition and recovery are affected by non-random processes.

Artefacts have been interpreted by functionalists as "extra-somatic adaptations to the environment", while post-processualists considered them non-verbal forms of communication. Archaeological theories can be grouped into:

a) cultural historical, whose major proponent was V. Gordon Childe;

b) functionalism or processualism, influenced by structural functionalism in anthropology, where culture is seen as a society's set of customs and beliefs developed to adapt to a situation;

c) post-processualism generally sees culture not only as a passive response to the environment but as an active participant in the construction of society. In line with the attention to the role of symbols paid by post-processualists, Richards studied grave goods on the assumption that they: (1) denote needs of the dead in the afterlife, (2) codify age, gender, and status of deceased, and (3) indicate ethnic belonging.

Anglo-Saxon cremation burials are the most abundant data set for the pagan period: many thousand hand-made vessels with slight variations of size, shape and character within tightly defined boundaries. Within the urns, deliberately deposited unburnt items, such as 'girdle-hangers', tweezers, and combs are found whose correlations with urn decoration are statistically significant. Richards concludes that an interdisciplinary approach can provide archaeology with 'ethnographic' information. History could be useful if one remembers that documents are also artefacts. He argues that in non-literate societies pictorial symbolism is that more important. According to the symbolic domination corollary, the native population was quickly absorbed and became archaeologically invisible. In Anglo-Saxon mortuary practice the connection with heritage was emphasised: the élite employed material symbols to propagate the concept of a common mythical past and ritual to construct this new reality.

In "Cultural change and social organisation in early Anglo-Saxon England" John Hines, aware of the lack of statistical and behavioural data concerning Germanic settlers, proposes to treat the sociocultural process as independent of individuals. One could assume that the subsistence basis was mainly agricultural, while the more sophisticated features of Roman administration, based on towns, collapsed. There is some evidence of continuity in livestock husbandry, even though agriculture too appears to have been subject to decline in the fifth and sixth centuries. Certain crafts survived the late Roman period and were adopted by settlers who also brought in their own methods.

The author recognises the importance of the model as favouring a competition at individual level which appears to have transformed societies led by military élites by promoting new élites. Alongside this, the unifying factor of ethnic identity has become an area of considerable research. The fluidity of Germanic groupings shows up in the changes in names and even in tribal composition; while regional centres of wealth and cult and their boundaries are easy to determine, it is more difficult to detect the distribution of any group's distinctive material culture. Germanic grave finds west of the Elbe show the emergence of a Saxon material culture for which the chronology is still vague. A distictively Frankish style did not emerge until the burial of King Childeric in Tournai dated to 481. Beginning in the fifth century Germanic culture flowed unimpeded into lowland Britain. The Saxon areas there were distinctive from the outset. A distinctive Anglian-English culture was composed out of several sources within few generations.

Political units of the early period are difficult to classify. Reliable information reveals the existence of small groups like those with names ending in -*ingas*. Beginning in the later sixth century, political units in England could be recognised. From 650 the larger political units are clearly demarcated, and there are early examples of recognition in diplomatic letters from the pope. The issuing of coins was another sign of sovereignty. One recognises a supra-regional uniformity typified by the spread of a single dress style, even though differences in personal adornment persisted. Significant regional differences also appear in art. Thus boundaries were physically or symbolically demarcated as major political centres gradually matured. The largest kingdoms were in the West, probably because of confrontation with Celtic populations of pre-existing British kingdoms. In the smaller south-eastern kingdoms there is evidence of a syncretic development between Germanic settlement and Roman organisational structure. A tendency for cultural aggregations into larger groups is reflected in the emergence and symbolisation of a recognised English identity.

In conclusion, one observes that culture is a strong, unifying social factor, considerably wider than the boundaries of political authority. Cultural homogeneity spurs competition towards the consolidation of a new élite status in a process that debouched in forms of nationalism that are observable in the continuity between post-Carolingian kingdoms and modern nation-states in Europe.

In "History, age and the anthropologists", David Turton recognises the increasing recourse to an interdisciplinary approach in a context of growing specialisation. He thinks he can contribute to the advancement of knowledge about the populations which settled in the Western Roman Empire in two ways. In the first place he can present the most recent views of practicing anthropologists on various aspects of the relationship between anthropology and history. In the second place, by presenting a case study of the East African population which he has done fieldwork with, he can make scholars in other disciplines aware of the implications of age-based social organisation, with no presumption, however, that his conclusions will automatically apply to populations living in Europe some fifteen centuries earlier.

Turton notes that physiological ageing, like biological reproduction, can be regarded as a human universal. His fieldwork with the Mursi, in Ethiopia, leads him to believe that their age system is a 'male cult', dedicated to the ritualisation of violence and to the maintenance of Mursi identity in opposition to neighbouring groups. Turton goes on to analyse the relationship between history and anthropology. Among the theoretical underpinnings of modern anthropology there is a rejection of 'conjectural history' as an explanation of contemporary ethnographic data.

The model suggested by structural functionalists allows many insights but eventually causes widespread reactions because of its focus on social equilibrium and its inability to explain change. The author's own work has led him to see Mursi society as the "temporary product of large movements of population which had taken place gradually over hundreds of years, and which were remembered highly selectively and schematically in oral tradition". In the '60s and '70s anthropologists such as Clifford Geertz recognised that many categories were not only historically but also culturally constructed. It was recognised that the 'segmentary lineage', which had been defined in the '40s and '5Os as a system of groups linked by genealogical descent, was in many cases an ideological or mental costruct. In fact, the Nuer, who served as the basis for the theory, did not live in 'segmentary lineages' but in villages, with members of other lineages whether kin or non kin. Turton pursues his argument by showing that both kinship and age are biological realities which can be used as the basis of symbolic systems. The traditional view is that kinship systems reflect biological relationships, whereas the more recent view is that genealogy serves only as a metaphor, i.e. a communicational template. The same approach can be applied to the biological reality of age.

An age grade (a stage in the life cycle) should be distinguished from an age set (a named category of men who passed through the various grades). Turton describes the activities of age grades and age sets among the Mursi and more generally among East African populations. In parallel with the development of the understanding of kinship, the study of age organisation has highlighted the lack of correspondence between the supposed governmental functions of age sets and their actual significance in every day life. Their contemporary decadence is generally explained as a consequence of colonial rule. The dominant activity specific to age sets in Africa is male ritual activity and only by extension does it become political and/or military. They are similar to Men's Cults in Melanesian societies: their main purpose is ritually to usher males over the threshold of manhood.

Turton uses this case study to show how anthropology can help in the 'recovery' of the European past. Recognising that societies studied by anthropologists are as subject to history as any other and that their characteristics cannot be projected into the past, he suggests that they can be taken "as sources of comparative data to assist in the process of understanding and framing generalisations about historical and—although presumably with more difficulty—archaeological data". Having had to face intersubjectivity and interculturalism in their own discipline, anthropologists can assist historians by "inducing critical reflection on the culturally specific categories of historical understanding". Anthropologists are just as much prisoners of their own cultural biases as historians but the difference is that anthropologists are professionally dedicated to getting at 'the native point of view'. Anthropological accounts of other cultures can help historians and archaeologists to be aware of the pitfalls of ethnocentrism in their categorisations and assumptions and therefore to "hypothesise with greater boldness, inventiveness and daring".

A second group of three papers dealing with socio-economic relations comprised R. Balzaretti's "Cities and markets in the early Middle Ages", Dennis H. Green's "The rise of *Germania* in the light of linguistic aspects", and S. Schutte's "Continuity problems and the authority structure in Cologne".

In his paper on "Cities and markets in the early Middle Ages" Ross Balzaretti underscores the paucity of written documentation for Western Europe between AD 400 and 800 and recognises the need to make use of a multi-disciplinary approach. In his view, economic life in all its articulations is fundamental to the understanding of the transition period, the realisation of cities, the interaction between ethnic groups. In these contexts Karl Polanyi's views can be helpful. The author proposes to "challenge the importance of structure and system". He relies on anthropology, to produce "very useful" analogies for an analysis of early medieval economics.

Balzaretti recognises that there is no doubt that cities existed in Mediterranean Europe before 400 and after 900, although their character is disputed. While most contemporaries considered them as ongoing, many scholars doubt that they existed during the period under discussion and take their absence as evidence of underdevelopment. To the author this seems a mistaken position as contemporary anthropology shows that pre-capitalist economies can exhibit complex economic functions.

Three models of the end of the Roman empire are considered. Hendy's model takes coinage as a key indicator of change. Both Wickham and Hendy's emphasise the lack of integration of the economies of successor states, whose linkages are at most regional. Neither say much about markets. Hodges' gives priority to archaeology where exchange and trade have a more prominent position.

A decline in economic activity is taken as the greatest difference between late Antique and early Medieval. The reason for the decline could have been not necessarily economic. The economic change can be interpreted better by closer attention to the possibility that these societies operated in ways unnoticed in economic thinking.

Dennis H. Green's paper, "The rise of *Germania* in the light of linguistic evidence", is aimed at highlighting through the medium of language the import and stages of the encounter of the intersecting worlds of the late Roman empire, its successor, Christianity, and its heir *Germania*. Among the three disciplines which, largely independently of each other, are most concerned with this transition, the difficulty for archaeology is to relate its finds to a defined ethnic group, history's telescopic vision has had difficulties recognising the considerable changes that occurred from the inception of contact between *Germania* and the wider world, philology provides a third approach which could integrate and give more depth to the others. The main relevant avenues of study in philology are: loanwords, etymology, and semantics. The transition to the Middle Ages can be conventionally divided into three stages: a view of the *Germani* and their culture, their slow symbiosis with many aspects of classical Antiquity, and the final take-over by Christianity. In this development the Church found it expedient to appropriate some of the trappings of imperial structure, the *Germani* took over many features of the Roman model, and the Church made concessions, willingly or not, to Germanic mentality. Indeed, combinations of the three traditions are found in many transitional artefacts, customs, and beliefs.

The process can be divided into: an initial stage, most difficult to reconstruct, akin to what happened often during the colonising drive of the nineteenth century, the end of the process signalled by the entry of Germanic tribes onto the stage of history. The long-drawn out civilising process by which the *Germani* developed from a set of cultures marginal to the Roman world to a central position in medieval Christendom was punctuated: (a) by the adoption of loanwords mostly on a material level, and (b) by the construction of Christian religious and ethical concepts.

Often loanwords followed different paths especially military and educational usage. In Green's words: "Together, these two semantic spheres create the setting for the medieval conjunction of the *miles* and the *clericus* and demonstrate continuity between the process we have been following and the incipient Middle Ages".

In "Continuity problems and the authority structure in Cologne" Sven Schütte picks up the thread of his presentation contending that in AD 50 the city of Cologne, *Colonia Agrippina*, was already a thriving centre settled by a Germanic substratum and by veterans from all over the Empire. An anecdote shows the difficulty of trying to separate the Roman from the Germanic factor: envoys of Germanic groups tried to convince the 'Germanic' population of the city to conspire to overthrow the Roman authorities, but they were refused on the grounds that the population was an inseparable mixture of Germanic and Roman elements. The situation is also reflected in material culture whereby so-called Ubian ceramics were made according to Roman technique but to Germanic taste. In the fourth century Frankish groups, which were not only enemies but also trading partners, gradually settled in the city or its immediate vicinity. The view of classical archaeologists who contend that the city fell into ruins with the fall of the Empire and was resurrected only in later centuries contrasts with the results of recent work.

Cologne had been intended as the main city of the province of *Germania inferior* which was given up after Roman military reverses between the Rhine and the Elbe and became a border town. Even now the inhabitants of Cologne consider the eastern side of the Rhine as the negative side; they think of themselves as belonging to Western rather than Central Europe and in their eyes it lingers on as a kind of border city. The proof of continuity is also seen in the documents concerning property which was unchallenged and peaceful for long periods of time. A strong continuity is seen also in the excavations of the market place, in the sense that they testify to an uninterrupted activity. Even the population make-up did not radically change as the inhabitants of Cologne in the late Roman period had their roots there so that, apart from the top administration which left the city, even high ranking officials below the top level stayed on and so did the merchants.

Frankish coinage appeared soon after Roman coinage. When the Frankish petty kings, 'Kleinkönige', moved to cities in the West, Cologne was ruled by its bishops in constant struggle with the powerful merchant class. For some time the Merovingian kings minted gold coinage, later *Colonia sancta* coins were minted. A further proof of continuity is that the Roman walls were kept up and they must have encircled the whole city as no other special fortification was found. Churches and buildings inside and around the market attest to the importance of trade which seems to have surpassed the military role of the city. There was even a strong continuity in the relations with other cities, attested by the constancy of the borders of the diocese.

In conclusion, the former Roman border city became the richest central city in north-central and eastern Europe for that period. This wealth, which is readily observable at the beginning of the tenth century, has its roots in earlier times when trade was already quite important. Merchant houses in Cologne were still built of stone when in the rest of Europe they were made of wood. At the fall of the Western Empire Cologne did not become a deserted city but underwent continuous development. The question left open will hopefully be solved by multi-disciplinary work.

To the last group of three papers on problems of politics and religion belong D. N. Dumville's "The idea of government in sub-Roman Britain", M. Axboe's "Danish kings and dendrochronology", and I. N. Wood's "Pagan religion east of the Rhine from the fifth to the ninth century".

"The idea of government in sub-Roman Britain" by David N. Dumville considers the last phases of Romano-British *ciuitates* as they can be understood from the tract *De excidio Britanniae*, written in the mid-sixth century by Gildas, a British cleric. The process which saw the withdrawal of the Roman administration from the island, already divided in three areas, an independent one, a militarily controlled one, and one with Roman-style civilian government, began with a series of rebellions at the close of the third century.

In the South, city-states were affected by internal unrest, internecine conflicts, and barbarian invasion. In Gildas's account, civil wars and famine began concomitantly during the first half of the fifth century in societies now led by rulers or warlords whom Gildas called *tyranni*—'usurpers/tyrants'. A British fleet and army were active on the Continent, possibly as part of an effort to secure friendly territory for eventual escape, and some *ciuitates* survived into the sixth century as may be gathered by the romanising names still in use.

Gildas's writing style presupposes a romanised audience, even though nationalism emerges in his treatment of the Romans. In his interpretation, the Britons are punished for their sins and, in the tradition of biblical prophets, he calls his fellow *ciues* to repentance. In the wake of Roman rule came law, civilisation, Christianity and the Roman language, values which he commends to his countrymen for whom Latin was not a foreign language. In its stead an unusual culture had developed whereby rulers of both Church and State had become oppressors to their own people, and he sees them as usurpers marked by evil behaviour in office. Their authority was illegitimate because of their predecessors' rebellion against Rome and because of its current unjust exercise. He sets out the guidelines of good rulership by negative examples of excesses committed by contemporaries.

Gildas's attitude toward the Church, which he considers the sole representative of religion, is coloured by the activism of radical ascetic movements of the late Roman world and he points out the excesses of contemporary clerics: greed, hypocrisy, bad habits, lack of dedication, falsity, arrogance toward the poor and a servile attitude toward the powerful, miserliness, thirst for advancement, simony. Gildas's tract closes with an illustration of the liturgy of ordination to point out the contrast between the clerics' behaviour and their vows. Through Gildas's pessimistic account there emerges, however, the reality of the existence of some measure of administration and justice, and the presence of a pious and charitable laity dedicated to worship in a Church "securely anchored" in British society. In spite of the abusive epithets by which he characterises them, the barbarian threat is unspoken. A large portion of British territory was settled by the invaders during the second half of the fifth century, and they could have had treaty relationships with the *tyranni* mentioned by Gildas. Our understanding of the process of acculturation of the non-Britons who settled in England is still very limited.

Morten Axboe's contribution "Danish kings and dendrochronology" bears on the transition of the populations of the area, which later formed the medieval kingdom of Denmark, from barbarism to statehood. 'Danes' were noted historically as active raiders of former Roman territories in the sixth century and engaged in struggles with other Germanic populations. In the two centuries which followed there were few mentions of the Danes. In the first half of the ninth century, the annals of the Frankish kingdom show greater interest in the Danes as opponents of the Frankish rulers. But although some vague information can be discerned, the actual extent of Denmark and any possible political division of the area remains uncertain throughout the Viking period.

Dendrochronology can be used to throw light on the age of some large defensive works excavated in Denmark which can be connected with specific sociopolitical situations or, indeed, rulers. They tend to concentrate within certain periods: to the period between the third and the early fifth centuries AD are dated ramparts, navigation barriers and bog deposits of weaponry, to the eighth century are dated larger undertakings like the Kanhave Canal, major building activities on the Danevirke rampart system, and the founding of the trade and craft site of Ribe, and finally to the tenth century, close to the threshold of history, are dated ring-forts, walled towns and renewed construction on the Danevirke.

An interpretation of the archaeological finds from 500 BC to 800 AD by Lotte Hedeager attaches importance to rituals legitimizing the power of élites. Ritual in turn can be traced through prestige goods. In the early Iron Age uniform graves seem to characterise an egalitarian society. With the Roman period there was a considerable increase of prestige goods in the graves. In the Migration period furnished burials ceased and gold hoards with arm- and neckrings, bracteates and other jewellery are found instead. In the following Vendel period neither grave furnishings nor hoard deposits were found. The corresponding socio-political situation points to chiefdoms in the early Roman period, while kingship could have gradually emerged in the late Roman or Migration periods, possibly stimulated by a diffusion of Roman customs learned while serving in the Roman army.

Central places, of which Gudme was the most outstanding, present both unusually rich finds and a special layout of the settlement divided into large clusters of farmsteads. Possible cult functions of these centres are reflected by place-names and by finds of ritual deposits.

In the opinion of some scholars, pagan Scandinavia had a role as a counterpart to the Christian Merovingians who attempted to dominate Britain. Kingship in Denmark could have started about 700 or perhaps even earlier. From the late Viking age to the present-day Danish kings have all come from the same kinship group, and the Frankish sources can be interpreted as pointing to a similar situation in the ninth century. Royal power was possibly based on substantial land ownership, and religious legitimation, expressed as descent from Woden, could have been an important part of royal legitimacy.

In "Pagan religion east of the Rhine from the fifth to the ninth century" Ian Wood recognises the difficulty of writing a "religious history" of Germanic tribes before christianisation on account of the sometimes contradictory attitudes reported and the unreliability of sources which used earlier accounts probably modifying them. The best source on paganism is a tract written at the time of a Germanic council in 743 reporting the most common superstitions among Germanic populations. Descriptions, particularly that of the temple of Uppsala with sacrificed animals and humans hanging from trees, are suspect because they are often affected by the specific strategies and concerns of individual authors, while, up to now, archaeologists have not been able to contribute much to the understanding of paganism. Temples are mentioned for the eighth century but they are insignificant structures and accounts were not even clear as to whether they contained idols. Natural features such as trees and springs, on the other hand, were loci of worship. There is no mention of organised priesthood in the extant documents. Among religious rituals at shrines and holy places there were festivals with special fires, sacrificial meals and meals for the dead, and also human sacrifice. According to Tacitus, religious significance was attached to the drawing of lots, and also divination under the most varied forms was considered as belonging to the sphere of the religious. These 'superstitions' could not be ascribed only to Germanic populations as they thrived also among later Christian populations.

One should remember that some Germanic regions were already Christian while others, such as Saxony and Frisia, were still pagan. The difference in social structures could have paralleled that in beliefs. The strong resistance to Charlemagne's Franks by the Saxons led by Widukind could have made the traditional authority structure obsolete. Religion and worship may have varied quite consistently even among pagan areas. The author's conclusion is that there probably were several kinds of paganism based on the regional importance of various gods of the Germanic pantheon, on different geographical factors which constituted varying backgrounds, and on sociopolitical structures which varied in time. These variables explained the difference between Tacitus' description of religion among the *Germani* and the situation in the seventh and eighth centuries.

Christianisation saw the last phase in the development of Germanic paganism and finally destroyed the paganism of the populations east of the Rhine, while superstition, an individual rather than a sociopolitical aspect of belief, remained significant even after paganism.

Common Aims and Problems

A certain number of common threads and related problems inherent in the study of the early medieval period surfaced in several presentations. They were collated and grouped by topic and the topics arranged in a logical sequence so as to offer a synthesis of the state of the art with regard to the most common problematic.

An awareness of the *dearth of information* on the historical and sociocultural vicissitudes concerning the period under study was implicit in the presentations of most participants, and made explicit by Balzaretti concerning the paucity of written documentation and Wood on the limited contribution offered by archaeology towards an understanding of paganism.

Green proposed that three main groups of actors were involved on the European scene at the time of transition, the Roman imperial administration, the Church, and the Germanic populations. Among the latter the *fluidity and diversity of groupings* was seen as a difficulty for clear historical focussing, especially by Hines and Wood.

A corollary of the fluidity of the Germanic social structure was the *presence of small groups* noticed by Hines among English Saxons and by Axboe for the Southern Scandinavian élite, explained by Ausenda on the basis of the theory of 'segmentary lineages'.

The arrival of the Germanic invaders/immigrants accompanied a *decline of cities* within former imperial territory, noted by Hines through the collapse of the Roman administration, and Balzaretti who cited the common view that Germanic populations did not wish or could not adopt Roman ways of living, to the point that many cities appear to archaeologists as being deserted between the sixth and the eighth centuries, while Dumville pointed to the internal unrest which reigned in the *ciuitates* and their initial abandonment.

Concern with an explanation of the *subsistence basis* of the immigrant populations was expressed by Hines, who noted that this was mainly agricultural and that there was evidence for some continuity in livestock husbandry, while agriculture appeared to have been subject to decline, and Balzaretti who asserted the need to know economic life in all its articulations.

The decline of cities was accompanied by the *disappearance of Romano-native populations* from the archaeological record especially in Britain and other border regions. In noting it, Richards explained this with the quick acculturation of Romano-natives to barbaric customs, while Dumville maintained that even if reduced to a minimum they must have been present as the writings of authors of the time "presupposed a romanised audience".

In the case of *rural settlements*, Hines pointed out that what happened in the countryside was as yet little understood and Richards noted the discrepancy between the "heroic manner" of rural interments and the "egalitarian society" which lived in those settlements.

As to life styles and particularly *changes in technology*, Hines noted that some crafts survived the late Roman period and some even partook of improvements due to the adoption of mixed practices.

Since most production originated in the countryside, to understand the vicissitudes of cities one should understand the *relationship between cities and countryside*, as underscored by Balzaretti, especially concerning the locus of the élite and the function of cities in exchange and administration, while others were concerned with the proportional presence of members of the immigrating populations in cities during and immediately after the Migration period.

What was the *military organisation of barbarians*? Were they organised by kinship groups or by an age-grade structure seen in many contemporary societies, as explained by Turton? Barbarian populations outside the *limes* were active raiders, as noted by Axboe for the Danes, but, as pointed out by Dumville, once settled within former imperial territory they were mostly tied to Romano-native populations by treaty relationships.

There was a certain degree of continuity in cities even when mostly abandoned. Balzaretti pointed out that cities existed in the perception of contemporary people. Some cities, such as Cologne, which were border towns during the late Empire, became central with the advent of barbaric kingdoms and showed a high degree of continuity as indicated by Schütte.

In Dumville's interpretation, some *ciuitates* on the Empire's borders survived into the sixth century and had some administrative and judicial functions. Outside the Empire some central places were becoming prominent and permanent markets were appearing, as shown by Axboe for southern Scandinavia.

Nuclei for new cities may have been characterised by the presence of *ritual centres*, which, according to Axboe and Hines, were used by the élite to legitimize their own power. Wood pointed out that temples were mentioned from the eighth century onwards, but were insignificant. It could be possible to reconstruct the cult function of those centres by the study of place-names, as suggested by Axboe and Wood.

The end result of the settlement of Germanic populations within the territory of the Empire was their *acculturation*. According to Dumville, the understanding of this all important process was still very limited. According to Hines, within neighbouring Germanic settled groups culture represented a strong unifying social factor. Green reminded us that the interplay of the three traditions, the Imperial, the Christian, and the Germanic, was shown in many transitional artefacts in a process "by which the *Germani* developed from a set of cultures marginal to the Roman world to a central position".

Understanding this transition was also the end purpose of this project.

Acknowledgements—I am grateful to John Hines for his considerable help in editing parts of the Introduction and several points in the discussions, and for his advice on editing problems and assistance concerning information not readily available to me.

References

Berlioz, J., J. Le Goff & A. Guerreau-Jalabert
   1991   Anthropologie et histoire. In *L'histoire médiévale en France: Bilan et perspectives.* G. Duby (ed.), pp.269-304. Paris: Éditions du Seuil.
Biersack, A.
   1991   Introduction. In *Clio in Oceania: Toward a Historical Anthropology.* A. Biersack (ed.), pp. 1-36. Washington, D.C.: Smithsonian Institution Press.
Deagan, K.
   1991   Historical archaeology's contribution to our understanding of early Americans. In *Historical Archaeology in Global Perspective.* L. Falck (ed.), pp. 97-112. Washington, DC: Smithsonian Institution Press.
Deetz, J.
   1991   Archaeological evidence of sixteenth and seventeenth century encounters. In *Historical Archaeology in Global Perspective.* L. Falck (ed.), pp. 1-9. Washington, DC: Smithsonian Institution Press.
Kleindienst, M. R., & P. J. Watson
   1956   Action Archaeology: The Archaeological Inventory of a Living Community. *Anthropology Tomorrow* 5 (1).
Rothschild, N. A.
   1992   Review article on "Historical Archaeology in Global Perspective". *American Anthropologist* 94 (4): 1008-9.
Sahlins, M. D.
   1981   *Historical Metaphors and Mythical Realities: Structure in the Early History of the Sandwich Islands Kingdom.* (Association for Social Anthropology in Oceania: Special Publications 1). Ann Arbor: University of Michigan Press.

THE SEGMENTARY LINEAGE
IN CONTEMPORARY ANTHROPOLOGY AND AMONG THE LANGOBARDS

GIORGIO AUSENDA

Center for Interdisciplinary Research on Social Stress, Contrada S. Francesco 6, San Marino (RSM)

Introduction

Knowledge of the social structures of the barbarian populations at the time of migration is fundamental for the understanding of their motivations, values, and historical vicissitudes. On account of the scarcity of documentary evidence, historians looked to ethnological theory for insights. As a consequence they have felt, with a suitable time-lag, the changes in anthropological leanings from naif evolutionism to cultural relativism.

In this paper I shall endeavour to explain the features and functioning of a segmentary lineage-based social structure among contemporary pastoral populations and then, by using documentary and philological proofs, to show that barbarian and specifically the Langobard social structure was based on corporate groups akin to those common among contemporary agro-pastoralists and that the Langobard *fara* was such a kind of corporate group and was perceived as a lineage by the Langobards themselves.

Historians and the Segmentary Lineage

A repertory of historians' misgivings with the segmentary lineage may be obtained from a doctoral dissertation of 1976 by Alexander C. Murray, published in 1983 under the title *Germanic Kinship Structure: Studies in Law and Society in Antiquity and the Early Middle Ages*. There does not appear to be a more recent summa and, anyhow, this one is sufficiently comprehensive to serve for comments and clarifications.

In considering "theories of Germanic kinship structure" Murray points out how early historians believed the *Germani* to have agnatic "clan or lineage systems" which could be identified with the *farae* of some and the *genealogiae* of other populations (A. C. Murray 1983:12, 13). Those lineages were considered by most historians to be patrilineal, and some saw in them earlier matrilineal features (A. C. Murray 1983: 15).

The theoretical picture was complicated by terminological niceties whereby a kinship group called *Sippe* was seen as a closed or fixed structure corresponding to an agnatic lineage, or as an open and shifting one corresponding to the ego-centred 'kindred' (A. C. Murray 1983:16, 17). Early scholars quoted from Caesar in support of the theory that during the invasion of the Roman empire *Sippen* settled as residential units and, equating *Sippen* with *farae*, they considered as sufficient proof of their theory the existence of place-names formed with the term *fara* (A. C. Murray 1983: 19, 20).

The points common to those theories were: the division of early Germanic society into unilinear descent groups, the primacy of agnation in the constitution of these groups,

15

the highly corporate nature of the lineage or clan, its progressive disintegration during the historical period and gradual replacement by a bilateral kindred structure, the direct derivation of Germanic kinship from, and its essential harmony with, the alleged patrilineal structure of Indo-Europeans. Variations in these theories consisted mainly in the discovery by different scholars of matrilineal influxes in some features of a population's customary laws.

In trying to decide whether early Germanic society was indeed based on clans and lineages, Murray examines in sequence Caesar's *Bellum gallicum* and Tacitus's *Germania*, and supplements his analysis of those early sources by excursions into sixth-century barbarian laws, the *Pactus legis salicae* and the *Edictum Chilperici*.

Caesar's and Tacitus' reliability are summarily dismissed because "the *Germania* and *Bellum gallicum* were affected by the undesirable features of the long ethnographic tradition which lies behind them", i.e. the bias of Greek poets and geographers concerning "human history and the place of barbarian peoples within it" (A. C. Murray 1983:41). Neither Caesar nor Tacitus are considered eyewitnesses, even though Caesar in 55 BC campaigned across the Rhine for eighteen days, crossed it once more in 53 BC and was familiar with the Germanic populations on the Rhine's left bank, but probably was too busy with logistics to bother about their subsistence and economy.

Caesar's account of the *Suebi* in Book 6 of the *Bellum gallicum* is conceded not to be a "spurious interpolation", but considered "a literary expansion, intended for the reading public, of the official sketch of the Suebians originally given in the year end report of the fourth year (Caesar, *B. g.* IV, 1)" (A. C. Murray 1983:42). An erudite evocation of Greek sources purportedly shows that Caesar's account was influenced by those 'classical' views, not by his army's informers! (A. C. Murray 1983:47- 9).

According to Murray, Caesar's weakness lay in drawing:

...a sharp distinction between the Gauls and the Germans, and their respective cultures, on each bank of the Rhine. On one side stand the Gauls, sedentary and agricultural, on the other the far more primitive Germans not given to agriculture and private property, displaying the litany of primitive characteristics proper to the ancient conception of nomads and pastoralists. Archaeologically this distinction is completely false (A. C. Murray 1983:45).

Fault is also found with Caesar's account of the *Germani* changing their agricultural land and abodes yearly to sow and cultivate their staples (A. C. Murray 1983:49). Therefore, when Caesar wrote that land was distributed annually to the *gentibus* and *cognationibus* (Caesar, *B. g.* VI, 22), he did not know what he was writing about. In fact:

...the foundation of the clan theory inexorably leads back to a misinterpretation of Caesar's account and a misunderstanding of the [specious] value of his Germanic ethnography (A. C. Murray 1983:50).

Tacitus' *Germania* is discussed in a more even minded manner despite the fact that:

...it has its faults, notably a tendency to anachronism: it does not give a picture of Germanic society at one moment in time and some of the observations may be of varying value (A. C. Murray 1983:52).

According to Murray, nowhere does Tacitus in the *Germania* stress the existence of agnatic lineages. On the contrary, he points out the existence of a bilateral kindred where "cognation plays a critical role in the descent system" (A. C. Murray 1983:64-5).

Murray then deals briefly with the Langobard, Burgundian, and Frankish *fara* considered "one of the central supports of the unilineal clan theory" because "to many authors the agnatic clan or extensive lineage and the *fara* are synonymous" (A. C. Murray 1983:89). Murray quotes the deceptively clear passage of Paul the Deacon, the Langobard historian (*ca* 790), equating *farae* to generations or lineages, "*faras hoc est generationes vel lineas*" (Paul the Deacon, *Historia Langobardorum*, II, 9), commenting that Paul did not know what was going on at the time of the Langobard invasion of Italy to which the contested excerpt refers because:

> ...in describing the *fara* he is transferring the eighth-century conditions with which he was familiar onto the sixth-century occupation, and explaining, after the fact, the founding of the houses of Friuli nobility (A. C. Murray 1983:96).

Besides the dismissal of Paul the Deacon's testimony, Murray cites Gian Piero Bognetti, a noted historian who specialised in Langobard law. Bognetti accepted an "obvious" etymology of *fara* from Old High German *faran* (to travel). This gloss is based on a passage from the chronicle of Marius Aventicensis, a contemporary to the events, who wrote:

> *Alboenus...cum exercitu relinquens atque incendens Pannoniam suam patriam cum mulieribus vel omni populo suo in fara Italiam occupavit* (MGH, *Chronica minora*, II, p.238 in Bognetti 1967-III: 12).

Following German historians, Bognetti interpreted the *fara* as a military expedition or migration, but he reconciled this feature with the fact that the *fara* comprised natural families or agnatic groups (A. C. Murray 1983:90-1).

Taking that "obvious" etymology as the "necessary first step", Murray argues that the word *fara* can only refer "to the body of people who go with a person: train, followers, troops, *comitatus*; thus too, family, household, movables, livestock" (A. C. Murray 1983:91). With a sleight of hand trick Murray explains away Rothari's law 177 (*Edictus Rothari* 177) allowing a freeman to leave with his *fara* once he has given back to the lord with whom he lived all the latter's property, by limiting the meaning of *fara* to "some variation of family, in a relatively narrow sense, or household movables", where the comma between the words 'household' and 'movables' of page 91 (see above) has disappeared, and concedes it may "even, in part, constitute a very shallow lineage" (A. C. Murray 1983:95), a truism if the count is taken from the living ancestors, but not so true if the count is taken from the closest ancestor, whether living or not, common to all agnates in the *fara*.

The surprising aspect of this book lies not in its lack of balance, whereby all unfavourable sources are disqualified on the excuse of their scant familiarity with the events which took place two centuries before or their prejudices, in the improbable and unprovable etymologies that are taken as the basis of proof, and in the unclear interpretations all bent to the author's thesis, i.e. that the unilinear lineage never existed even in early Germanic society, which instead was based on bilateral kindreds with cognatic features. What is surprising is that Murray's book has become popular among many historians who consider it the last cry on Germanic kinship relationships.

The most probable reason for the book's popularity is the rooted antipathy historians with few exceptions have for ethnological models which are guilty of two main drawbacks: (1) they represent a source of knowledge outside the direct control of their discipline, in that they must rely on secondary sources to interpret those exotic rules (cf. Le Goff 1976:684) and, more generically and significantly, (2) they are ahistorical in that ethnology is essentially a synchronic discipline which builds models without concern about their change in time.

Taking into account these givens, in the following pages I shall attempt to place the discussion on a more critical level?

The Segmentary Lineage in Anthropology

Theory

Better to assess the fit of the various models of Germanic social structure implied by the sources of antiquity and the interpretations of contemporary authors, I shall describe the social structures of present populations whose economy and complexity are closest to the presumed economy and complexity of Germanic 'tribes' at an early stage and at the time of migration.

Reliable anthropological accounts of pastoralists came in the wake of Bronislav Malinowski's and A.R. Radcliffe-Brown's holistic approaches to the discipline which encouraged field workers to look for all possible aspects of populations. Nomadic pastoralist ethnographies were late comers for several reasons: (1) that nomadic pastoralists are more difficult to follow and live with, (2) that colonial governments became interested in nomadic pastoralists at a later date because of their relatively minor contribution to the economy, (3) that nomadic pastoralist populations were politically unpredictable because of their shifting habits, and better left alone.

The first major ethnography on African pastoralists, based on fieldwork carried out in the thirties, was *The Nuer: A description of the modes of livelihood and political institutions of a Nilotic people* by Everett Edward Evans-Pritchard, while fieldwork carried out at the end of the thirties by Elizabeth B. Bacon among the Hazara Mongols in Iran and Baluchistan saw the light in 1958 under the title *Obok: A Study of Social Structure in Eurasia*. These studies concerned populations which belonged to the two main types of pastoralists: on the one hand the African and Middle Eastern and on the other the Eurasian of the northern steppes.

Both studies identified a characteristic structure of these societies. For Evans-Pritchard (1940:192) a Nuer clan is the largest group of agnates who trace their descent from a common ancestor and between whom marriage is forbidden and sexual relations considered incestuous. It is not merely the undifferentiated group of persons who recognise their common agnatic kinship, as some African clans do, but it is a highly segmented genealogical structure:

> A clan is a system of lineages and a lineage is a genealogical segment of a clan. One might speak of the whole clan as a lineage, but we prefer to speak of lineages as segments of it and to define them as such. Alternatively one may speak of a lineage as an agnatic group the members of which are genealogically linked, and of a clan as a system of such groups, the system being, among the Nuer, a genealogical system (Evans-Pritchard 1940:192).

Elizabeth Bacon's definition is along the same lines:

> The Kazaks and the Hazara Mongols have a social structure which although essentially unilinear, differs in a number of respects from the clan as it had generally been defined. Since this difference had not been recognized at the time much of the present work was written, the author adopted the descriptive term "tribal genealogical" to designate the type and proposed the Mongol term *obok* as a shorter and more convenient alternative. In the meantime Evans-Pritchard's term "segmented lineage" came into use in referring to the structure which we have called *obok* (Bacon 1958:viii).

and further:

> Beyond the residential family unit there is a more extensive solidarity group bound together by ties of patrilineal kinship. The term *alághe* was used by the Jaghuri Seyyid Hasan to designate

a group from twenty to fifty families who "gave their daughters to each other". He went on to say that there might be from three to five *alághe* in a single village or that sometimes a rich *alághe* might have its own village. No other informant was familiar with the term *alághe*, but Ali Shefa, the Uruzgani informant, described a village containing some fifty or sixty families as constituting a group which gave their daughters to each other. It appears from the context that both informants were referring to a lineage or kin group, that is, a group of families related in the paternal line whose feeling of kinship and memory of descent from a common ancestor are strong. This lineage group might occupy a single village or a group of adjacent villages, or, in the case of large villages, it might share a village with several other lineage groups (Bacon 1958: 12).

In other words, a clan consisting of segmentary lineages based on a genealogical model differs from a unilinear clan in that the lineages which branch off at different genealogical levels from the clan's founding ancestor are in varying relationships to each other that depend on their genealogical distance.

One of the principles which was recognised as specific to segmentary lineages is that of *complementary opposition* (cf. Evans-Pritchard 1940:143-4; Salzman 1978:65; Spooner 1973:26). According to this principle, segmentary lineages at different genealogical levels interact, both peacefully or conflictually, at the lowest common level. This means that, when a tertiary section is in confrontation with another tertiary section belonging to the same secondary section, it will act as a tertiary section. However, when a tertiary section is in confrontation with another tertiary section belonging to a different secondary or primary section, the two lower sections will face each other at the level of their secondary or even primary sections.

Thus homicides within close genealogical distance are generally transacted through a reparatory action while feuds at greater genealogical distances may involve larger segmentary levels, variously called sections, or clans and sub-clans, or primary lineages, etc., and entail a greater intensity of response. At the top of the segmentary pyramid confrontation usually involves the whole tribe and takes on the aspect of out-and-out war.

In the case of the Nuer, as described by Evans-Pritchard, one should note that lineages are not coterminous with local communities and that these included individuals of lower status belonging to different clans. In his case segmentary lineage interaction must be seen as a model of political interaction rather than a model of kinship organisation.[1]

More recently several scholars, Barth, Cole, Cunnison, Peters, and others writing on nomadic pastoralists, described in detail basic communities of a more or less corporate nature whose organisation and interaction could not be accounted for by the models of 'tribal genealogical structure' or 'complementary opposition' put forward in the 1950s, while some scholars upheld the idea that there are nomadic pastoralist societies where, in some circumstances, the 'native model' of complementary opposition may fit the situation (Salzman 1978a:65).

Opponents of the 'complementary opposition' model argued that, even though the folk ideology might seem to conform to the model, in reality this was not the case because: (1) segments at the lower genealogical level are not equal in strength, nor do they come in couples, so that their complementary opposition is impossible, (2) because of the acephalous

---

[1]　For a more exhaustive treatment of the Nuer's segmentary lineage in Evans-Pritchard's interpretation see Turton's comments on pages 46-7.

character of higher level sections, it is impossible for them to take concerted action, and (3) because of affinal and matrilateral ties, individuals conform to a "bundle of roles" so that "pure" agnatic behaviour is impossible (cf. Peters 1967:272).

Scholars who upheld the model countered that: (1) many societies conformed to the 'complementary opposition' principle in their intragroup actions, (2) even with demographically unbalanced groups segment solidarity may be present, being reinforced by non-genealogical ties. The conclusion was that complementary opposition could be found among populations which were "associated with territorial instability" in such a way that the complementary opposition folk model was maintained as a "social structure in reserve" (Salzman 1978a:67-9; Salzman 1978b:627).

Notwithstanding these partial disagreements it is safe to conclude that agro-pastoralist communities conform to the residential corporate model or the 'complementary opposition' principle according to circumstances and in varying degrees in relation to their territorial fixedness. It is also true that the 'complementary opposition' principle is maintained as a social structure in reserve, as the principle is invariably tied to tradition and, as will be seen later, is made recourse to in cases requiring legitimation or confirmation.

In sum, a segmentary lineage structure has a considerable degree of flexibility and is eminently suitable to pastoralists whose very existence is tied to a careful balance between population and ecology in every area of the tribal territory, and to their ability to face up to confrontations in proportion to the opposing forces involved.

Distribution and demography

Before considering kinship and economic aspects of pastoralists one should look at the distribution of present agro-pastoralist populations and the relative strength of their constituent units.

Relevant to distribution is the question of the development of agriculture and pastoralism and their relationship. While the question has never been clearly solved, it appears that the beginnings of agriculture and animal domestication were closely related. The archaeological record of nomadic pastoralists is much less visible than that of settled agriculturalists, hence the uncertainties inherent in the problem. Population transfers from nomadic pastoralism to sedentarisation and back have been historically observed beginning with the Mesopotamian and Egyptian civilisations (Spooner 1971:201). These transfers are caused by ecological and political pressures which act at different times in each direction (Spooner 1973:5). From recent developments it is possible to infer that in Eurasia and Africa agriculture and pastoralism developed approximately at the same time, that the paths for the segregation of one type of subsistence strategy from the other were many and varied, and that the populations which held longest to the nomadic pastoralist subsistence strategy were those which inhabited areas least suited to agriculture (Spooner 1973:5).

The best studied were pastoralist groups in Africa and the Middle East, while until recently those inhabiting the Eurasian steppes were more difficult to approach. One can safely say that pastoralism was present at one time or another in most areas of the Old World, and that nowadays, even though it has been largely supplanted by agriculture and, therefore, shrunk to marginal territories, it is still spread over considerable areas of Africa and Eurasia.

Pastoral nomads are still found throughout the Sahel-Sahara belt of North Africa from Mauritania and Morocco across to Sudan and Somaliland. The pastoral complex followed the Bantu migration into South Africa. Many of those populations have become sedentary and rely more on agriculture than pastoralism while the opposite may have been true in the past.

Semi-sedentary pastoralists could be found until recently in Greece, Italy, Spain, and Yugoslavia, and they are still found in Turkey, and across the Middle East to Pakistan and India. There are still many pastoral populations from Mongolia to the Russian Federation, whilst their descendants, Tatars, Avars, and Hungars, have been absorbed into the urban populations of Europe.

A short excursus on the structural level of pastoralist aggregations will complete the picture. A survey of the extant literature pointed out several shortcomings related to the ethnological involvement with pastoralists. In the first place there is a certain amount of confusion among different authors concerning the terms by which they specify different population groups. The terms 'clan' and 'tribe' are used indiscriminately for population groups of similar size and level without adequate definitions.

Table 1.1

Approximate numerical strength of some pastoralist populations

Name	Country	Animals herded	Population	Source
Al Murrah Bedouin	S. Arabia	Camels	15,000	Tapper 1979
Shammar	N. Arabia	Camels	10,000	"
Saadi	Cyrenaica	Camels-Sheep	180,000	"
Humr Baggara	S. Sudan	Cattle	55,000	"
Kababish	W. Sudan	Camels-Sheep	68,000	"
Rufa'a al Hoi	Sudan	Cattle-Sheep-Camels	27,000	"
Jaf Kurds	S. West Asia	Sheep	60,000	"
Bakhtiari Lurs	Iran	Sheep	190,000"	
Basseri	Iran	Sheep	15,000	"
Qashqai	Iran	Sheep	125,000	"
Shahsevan	Azerbaijan	Sheep	75,000	"
Baluch	Pakistan	Sheep	60,000	"
other sources:				
Nuer	S. Sudan	Cattle	214,000	Evans-Pritchard 1940
Oulad Bini	Mauritania	Camels	8,000	Toupet 1963
Teda Tou	Chad	Camels-Goats	8,000	Capot-Rey 1963
Rgueibat	Mauritania	Camels	18,000	Monteil 1959
Karimojong	Uganda	Cattle	60,000	Dyson-Hudson 1970
Hazara tribes:	Afghanistan	Sheep-Horses		
Dai Kundi			52,000	Bacon 1958
Dai Zangi			60,000	"
Besud			100,000	"
Polada			45'000	"
Jaghuri			117,500	"
Uruzgani			65,000	"
Rgibat (Rgueibat)	Morocco	Camels	250,000	Hart 1962
Samburu	Kenia	Cattle	30,000	Spencer 1965

Some clarity in this matter was achieved by a survey of the literature concerning pastoral societies in the Middle East and North Africa. The suggestion was to recognise two basic aggregations defined as *A* and *B* (Tapper 1979:58). Type *A* corresponds to the lowest level of aggregation. In the author's words it is based:

> ...on a dominant lineage, with a greater or lesser proportion of temporarily resident affines, matrilateral kin, unrelated clients and herdsmen (Tapper 1979:58).

Type *A* communities correspond to the lowest level of segmentary lineages. Their average size was found to be quite uniform throughout the area surveyed. It was said to vary between 20 and 50 "tents-households, or 100 to 300 individuals" (Tapper 1979:58).

Type *B* communities are higher level groups characterised (in the Middle East) by a high degree of endogamy. They exhibit:

> ...considerable historical continuity, being found above the level of shuffling, fission, fusion, and structural amnesia in genealogies. Although sub-groups of these communities may be demonstrably and often admittedly not of common origin, there is usually a pretence that they are, and certainly a great degree of cultural (and biological?) homogeneity and distinctiveness among the members as a result of intermarriage and interaction patterns (Tapper 1979:62).

These groups are normally called *clans*, Arabic *qabila* (plur. *qabail*). Their strength varies between 1000 and 3000 individuals (Tapper 1979:61).

In general, tribes are formed by clusters of such *B* communities or sections thereof. An idea of tribal strength may be obtained from table 1.1 condensed from Tapper's survey and other sources.

Kinship and other social networks

Kinship is a primary structure among simple societies, i.e. pastoralists, because it represents a social cohesion system which is universal and can be easily understood in a 'biological' way. Thus, kinship is used by simple societies even to represent the relationship between groups which are said to stand as 'brothers', 'cousins', or some other kinship relationship with respect to each other. This fiction enables the individuals involved to follow well trodden patterns of behaviour in their peaceful and even conflictual exchanges: brothers also fight. I shall, therefore, explore some of the kinship aspects of pastoralists because they may be useful better to understand some features of those societies.

The first aspect I will consider is that of *lineality*, in this case the genealogical succession along which privileges, prestige, and wealth are transmitted to succeeding generations. Most authors concur that descent is regarded as being 'patrilineal' by most pastoralist groups with few exceptions (Barth 1954:168; Goldschmidt 1979:21; Hudson 1938:24; Krader 1955a:70; Lewis 1962:1; Pehrson 1966:33; Peters 1960:30; Salzman 1971:434; Salzman 1972:63; Spencer 1965:xxiv; Spooner 1973:27; Stenning 1957:58; N. Swidler 1972:116). The most notable exception are the Tuareg of the Sahara, both in Algeria and Niger (Nicolaisen 1963:137; Spooner 1973:26). It should be noted, however, that the Tuareg also have some patrilineal rules, especially concerning inheritance, probably adopted together with the Islamic religion from neighbouring populations of Arabic tradition (Nicolaisen 1963:137).

The prevalence of patrilineality can be explained by the subsistence strategy of nomadic pastoralists whose herding activities take them in small groups, or even alone, at considerable distances from their dwellings where they have to depend on their own resources in encounters with both animal and human predators. The following is a fitting description of the qualities pastoralists value:

> ..physical strength, endurance, and the ability to withstand hardship...requires attitudinal sets that give even young boys a capacity to control animals which are not by nature entirely docile (Goldschmidt 1979:21).

Several authors stress that the patrilineality of pastoralist societies is mainly *emic*, i.e. a 'subjective' picture held by the populations, whilst the *etic*, objective, on the ground reality is quite different.

In the previous section the corporateness of residential units was shown to transcend lineage boundaries. In fact, several authors point out that such residential units include also non-lineage members (Hudson 1938:24; Irons 1972:92; Sahlins 1961:330; Stenning 1959:38). Many of the non-lineage members of residential units are afffinally related and their presence and participation contribute to loosening up lineality in favour of a considerable degree of cognatic influence.

Another factor which contributes to the weakening of the patrilineal ethos of many pastoralist populations, or rather the strengthening of a substantive cognatic substratum is the *endogamic aspect of alliances* prevailing among many pastoralist populations, especially in the Middle East and North Africa.

Endogamous pastoralist populations are those belonging to the 'Arab sphere' (Bacon 1954:60; G. W. Murray 1935:35; Spooner 1973:30). These populations are considered endogamous because of their preference for patrilateral first cousin marriage, i.e. FBD marriage which, in fact, occurs with a very high frequency (Barth 1954:167; Cole 1975:92; Cunnison 1966:186 ff.).

Anthropologists explain such alliances in terms of the necessity of maintaining a close cooperation between an individual and his father and brothers for the benefit of the joint property, their livestock, and to further lineage stability (Irons 1972:92; Pehrson 1966:90; Spooner 1973:32).

Many authors stress the considerable importance that sons have for the furtherance of the household's pastoral economy (Asad 1970:36; Barth 1963:74; Black 1972:626; Irons 1972:91, 96; Spencer 1965:3; Stenning 1957:57). The endogamous practice stems from the fact that "the lineage group aims, primarily, at keeping a young woman to betroth her to one of its own young men" (Stenning 1959:38). The priority of a close kinsman's claim to a girl is so stringent that among most populations marriage requests must be approved by close kin to make sure that no closer relative with a claim to the girl may come forward later (Cunnison 1966:186 ff.; Peters 1960:44).

The 'pure' patrilineality of such alliances is misleading inasmuch as several authors noted, as expressed in Barth's words:

> The impression of a patrilineal core [in an endogamic group] is deceptive, since agnatic kin in no sense predominate on other ties of kinship. [The genealogical chart] could be redrawn to give an impression of a group built around matrilineages. The correct and complete picture reveals their characteristics as *bilateral* [emphasis mine], nearly self perpetuating kin groups (Barth 1961:41).

W. W. Swidler noted that the "spatial relationship" among tents can be better understood in the light of the affinal links which bring together tents of closely related women. In Swidler's words "affinal relatives may be viewed as weaving a fabric of ties between tent households within the agnatic group. The camp, in fact, is a group of affinally related agnates" (W. W. Swidler 1972:73).

Outside and bordering with the above areas some populations are exogamous, e.g. Central Asian nomads (Bacon 1954:53; Krader l955a:72), the Toubou of Chad (Baroin 1985:183 ff.), Somali nomadic populations (Lewis 1962:25). While the features of Middle Eastern and North African endogamy have been carefully studied, the exogamy of other populations has not received a satisfactory explanation. In these cases the prevalent type of marriage is with MBD, i.e. with women belonging to the Mother's clan, different from the agnatic one. Spencer pointed to this lack of explanation and ventured that the search for a mate outside one's own group may be due not only to demographic reasons, i.e. lack of a suitable bride in one's own clan, but also:

> ...for more positive considerations, such as the need to maintain reliable relationships with other groups in ecologically strategic places, both nomadic and settled (Spooner 1973:32).

I would add political to ecological reasons, and underscore the fact that herding in Central Asia is conducted by fewer individuals herding a greater number of animals, at times dividing the herd with an allied group to control young animals by exchanging them (cf. Vreeland 1954:35).

The same as individuals, lineages are subject to ongoing birth-life-death cycles. The visible mechanisms which punctuate the cycle are the processes of fission and fusion of encampments, i.e. lineages. *Fission* is mostly occasioned by the excessive growth of a corporate unit, such as an encampment, which makes its functioning unwieldy. The sizes of encampments are limited by several factors, both ecological and social. When an encampment's strength becomes excessive there may take place several triggering incidents which bring about fission. These may be classified as: competition for resources or livestock, for women, and for leadership (cf. Pehrson 1966:88). The dissident group may leave. When it is successful in going its own way a new lineage might be born.

Fusion is generally brought about by the reverse process, i.e. the dwindling of the strength of an encampment to the point that its members see fit to join close or distant relatives in other encampments. When the group so affected is the last surviving of a lineage, after its absorption into another encampment and lineage its former name will soon be forgotten.

Relevant to this discussion is how well *lineages* function as *military units*. Several authors recognise the military potential of groups consisting of segmentary lineages and underline their bellicosity in the face of the central government (Barth 1954:166; Cole 1975:85; Vreeland 1954:13). An important point with reference to the military viability of segmentary lineages is that there is no mechanism to suppress internal violence which is barely controlled by the feud and blood money compensation systems.

Cohesion among segmentary lineages in a clan is not very strong. While raids of short duration may be staged by temporary leaders, defensive action is more difficult to organise. The Swiss explorer and Khedivial high commissioner of the Red Sea territories in the 1860s, now Eritrea and part of eastern Sudan, Werner Münzinger, wrote:

> If a major danger threatens, the Beni Amer do not care to save their lands, they escape with their people and livestock in waterless lands where no enemy can follow them. In those circumstances, if they are encamped, they abandon these encampments with all their goods, and no one touches anything, everything is entrusted to public honesty (Münzinger 1890:260) [My trans.].

At the beginning of this century a high commissioner for Eritrea wrote:

> The usual dances [are performed].... Such warlike dances are not very appropriate to the nature of these tribes which are all but warlike, always ready to flee in the face of an enemy (Martini 1946-IV:100) [My trans.].

Even 'wars' are hit-and-run affairs. The recent (1941-1946) 'war' between Beni Amer and Hadendowa consisted of raids and counter raids during which the better armed Beni Amer succeeded in abducting several thousand head of livestock with no more than about fifty 'bandits'.

It follows that the unification of a considerable number of lineages for military purposes can be at best a temporary effort, as disrupting differences emerge fairly soon aided by centrifugal tendencies due to the independent stances of segmentary lineages (cf. Irons 1979:369). Thus, military units based on segmentary lineages are better for offensive thrusts based mostly on quick raids rather than defense. This disposition can be recognised in many occurrences in early medieval history. Networks more suitable for military organisation, viz. age grades and age sets, will be discussed below.

Kinship is the basic and universal network of interaction in simple societies. Other networks exist which act together or across kinship boundary lines, but, whereas kinship is always present, other networks need not be.

A cohesive network which is frequently found especially among East and South African pastoralists is that of *age sets* (Goldschmidt 1979:21; Spencer 1965:xxi; Spooner 1973:27; Turton, this volume). Age sets are consequent upon a system of age grades, minimally two (boyhood and adulthood), but usually three (boyhood, early manhood, and elderhood) or even more. Age grades are bounded by initiation ceremonies that are passed by individuals belonging to an age set at the same time and in the same ceremony. One can readily see how passing through initiation ceremonies and working or fighting together throughout a lifetime enhances the morale and esprit de corps of age mates. In fact, members of age sets are particularly suited to be enrolled for common, especially military, efforts, because of the relatively large number of age mates held together by bonds which transcend and add to those of kinship. Women usually do not belong to age sets even though, or perhaps because, they have two 'biological' age grades, girlhood and womanhood.

Class is a further cohesive network separate from kinship and fairly frequent among pastoralists, e.g. the Rgueibat of Algeria (Monteil 1959:575), the Tuareg (Rognon 1963:59), the pastoral nomads of Mauritania (Toupet 1963:67), the Toubou of Chad (CapotRey 1963:84), the Mongols (Vreeland 1954:11), the Pakhtun (Barth 1953:7), the Bedouin of Cyrenaica (Peters 1960:41; 1968:168), the Somali nomadic pastoralists (Lewis 1971:66-7), the Beni Amer (Nadel 1945:56). Classes are normally three, a dominant class of freemen who own the land, a lower status class of clients who are seen as having originated elsewhere and migrated into the area belonging to the dominant class (Ausenda n.d.b; Peters 1960:42), and slaves. In a developed client-patron system the former are more numerous than the latter (Nadel 1945:66; Paul 1950:227) because they supply services and gifts to their patrons, while slaves are few as they are more useful in sedentary conditions.

Until 1948 among Beni Amer there were client groups. The Beni Amer clients were between five times, in the Sudan (Paul 1950:227), and nine times, in Eritrea (Nadel 1945:66), more numerous than their patrons. For their patrons they performed services such as milking, and offered them gifts on ceremonial occasions. Patrons were duty bound to protect their clients and help them in times of need. While clients roamed with their livestock in search of pastures, patrons were more sedentary: they lived in semi-permanent villages, changing location twice a year between the cooler plateau or upper valleys in summer and the lowlands in winter, thus following the general transhumance pattern of their clients.

The village structure may be seen even nowadays. The village centre contains the market, mosque, and coffee houses, and the dwellings of the dominant clan, whilst former client clans live on the outskirts in single lineage clusters. In villages, lineages continue to be important as vehicles of tradition. They surface on ceremonial occasions such as in the case of contributions to other lineages for funeral wakes; these are meticulously recorded because politeness requires a slightly higher return gift. Lineage lore is probably stronger in villages than in the bush because people's status depends on their lineage.

Kindred is the kinship network from Ego's reference point and it comes to life on special occasions as in the case of giving or receiving blood money or participating in a feud. Relatives belonging to Ego's kindred may be also involved in Ego's succession albeit to different degrees depending on lineality and gender.

Following the kinship network to higher levels of aggregation one generally encounters clans. These may be considered the smallest politically autonomous units. While tribes "may be viewed as a reaction to the formation of complex political structures" (Fried 1967:170 ff.), so much so that often a term for 'tribe' does not exist in the language of the population affected, clans are well recognised by the populations involved. Among pastoralists, clans have the property of polarising marriage alliances: when the marriage rule is endogamic almost all alliances take place within the clan, when exogamic, the majority usually involve another specific clan.

Clans usually have a common brand for various species of livestock (Ausenda 1987:408; Hart 1962:67; Hudson 1938:31; Nicolaisen 1963:138 ff.). If one thinks of head of livestock, the traditional wealth of the population, as units of account for ceremonial transactions, it is as if each clan had its own currency. In fact, livestock exchanges, unless it is sold for slaughter, are most frequent within the clan.

As previously mentioned, tribes come into being in response to external pressures. One should observe that chiefs or elders belonging to an autonomous native hierarchy have quite limited power and functions (Irons 1976:365), mostly connected with the organisation of migrations. In contrast, those tribal chiefs who are endowed with considerable power owe their position to external, colonial or govermental, backing (Barth 1961:71-86, 129; Black 1972:616).

Even at higher levels of aggregation, i.e. of lineages within a clan, or clans within a tribe, the kinship language is used to determine the group's position within the larger unit. Genealogical maps are produced that contain the names of the founding ancestors of clans or lineages in positions which parallel the on-the-ground relations between said groups. When two clans or sections thereof are very close and have frequent interactions, they may be described as brothers, whereas in case this should not be so, their common ancestry is made to recede by a few generations so that they will show up as, more or less distant, cousins.

The demise of the tribal genealogical system among pastoralists is also due to the adoption of writing, whereby these genealogical maps, once so flexible that they could easily accommodate change, are now rigid so that development forces populations to gradually consign the tribal genealogical system to oblivion.

Pastoral economy

Relevant to the present discussion is a definition of nomadism especially concerning pastoralists. It is difficult to arrive at a clear-cut definition because no nomadic population can be typified in its entirety since it almost always comprises some sedentary groups. A definition proposed for nomadic populations is that they are characterised by a "lack of interest in fixed property" as the obverse among "ethnographically recorded societies" is considered a factor excluding nomadism (Spooner 1973:3).

There have been many discussions concerning a definition of nomadic pastoralism. It was clear that nomadism is not necessarily pastoral and vice versa. However, it is very difficult to give a satisfactory definition of nomadic pastoralism because this would imply arbitrarily cutting the continuum between total nomadism and total fixedness of pastoral populations and at the same time cutting the continuum between total engagement in herding or vice versa agriculture and other non-herding subsistence strategies. Since such continua apply to all pastoral populations and, furthermore, their positions on the continuum are constantly changing, one can readily see how difficult it is to arrive at a precise and satisfactory definition of nomadic pastoralism.

In our case the problem is easier because for the early Middle Ages we are dealing with populations which were at least partly dedicated to pastoralism but not necessarily nomadic as present-day 'pure' nomads, assuming that they still exist. I offer a definition suitable for the purpose of this discussion: "Populations may be considered pastoral when the wealth of individuals and households is accounted for primarily in terms of livestock". It follows that among these populations real estate has no commercial value (cf. Spooner 1973:3) as it is generally considered communal property. With this definition in mind I will set out to show what the situation is among present-day pastoralist populations.

To begin with, let us check how present-day pastoralists conform to the definition which presumes them to consider livestock their paramount form of wealth. Most authors writing about pastoralists endorse this position:

A young man's desire to be head of his own household depends for its realization on his capacity to command the necessary animal wealth and domestic labour (Asad 1970:55).

Humr keep most of their wealth in cattle: a man is wealthy only when he has cattle in camp to prove it (Cunnison 1966:28).

...a man...keeps all his animals, even culls, because he wants large numbers to give in marriage, rather than limiting his herds to good milking animals (R. Dyson-Hudson *et al.* 1970:121).

I want particularly to emphasize another aspect of pastoralist social order, the utilization of livestock as tokens in all essential nexuses (Goldschmidt 1979:21).

The [Samburu] emphasis in social values is placed on cattle, at times to the exclusion of small stock: "A man who has cattle is important," they say, "He can have many wives and many sons to look after his herds" (Spencer 1965:3).

Their [Fulani] subsistence and wealth derives solely from their herds of cattle supplemented with sheep, goats, or camels (Stenning 1959:4).

The Wodaabe themselves recognize that the maintenance of families and herds lies at the heart of their social system and is the criterion of a man's status in his lineage group and the status of his lineage group in the clan (Stenning 1959:55).

Most authors also point out that the exchanges for which livestock is paramount are ceremonial and social ones:

...livestock is given at marriage (Baroin 1985:91).

Marriage involves the giving of cattle to all the relatives of the bride (R. Dyson Hudson *et al.* 1970:121).

A second major use of livestock as social nexus is brideprice. Cattle are used as a token of alliance between affines and establish the bonds (Goldschmidt 1979:22).

...circulation of cattle seems to reinforce all social relationships (Horowitz 1972:111).

A man must acquire brides for his sons in the order of their birth using a portion of his livestock for each bridal payment (Irons 1972:91).

Wealth in livestock enables a man to pay bridewealth (Lewis 1962:8).

Marriage is the most visible occasion during which livestock is used as currency but, as Irons points out, it is used in all social nexuses in payment or sacrifice (payment to the supranatural) at naming ceremonies, circumcisions, weddings, and funerals.

Relationships of pastoralist societies to agriculture and settled life

The relationship of pastoralists to agriculture may be analysed from the standpoint of a group's direct involvement with cultivation and also focussing on the proportion of agricultural foods, however procured, in the group's diet.

Several authors suggested that pastoralism was secondary to agriculture and that pastoral societies were a variant of an agricultural subsistence strategy (Bacon 1954:47, 49; Spooner 1971:201). Despite the tendency of most fieldworkers to concentrate on the pastoralist activities of the groups they are studying, many concede that most pastoralists, even nomadic ones, are involved to a greater or lesser extent in agricultural activities (Bacon 1954:59; Bacon 1958:9; Barth 1961:9; Barth 1963:72; Bates 1972:49; R. Dyson-Hudson 1972:41; R. Dyson-Hudson *et al.* 1970:114; Horowitz 1972:108; Krader 1955b:315; Lewis 1962:1; Pehrson 1966:8; Salzman 1971:192).

When nomadic pastoralists do not practice agriculture they mostly obtain agricultural staples for their consumption through trade (Asad 1970:30; Capot-Rey 1963:82; Johnson 1969:11,164; Rognon 1963:63; Stenning 1959:4). Several authors point out that distance from markets is no deterrent to pastoralists in their pursuit of exchanges of pastoral goods or other trade items for agricultural produce: in some cases the distances they travel to reach markets are of the order of thousands of kilometres (Asad 1970:30; Capot-Rey 1963:82; Rognon 1963:63).

Sometimes the symbiosis between settled agriculturalists and pastoralists takes the form of an exchange for permission to graze stubble in fallow fields against the deposition of manure or a fee (Bates 1971:124; Stenning 1959:6). A synthetic analysis of the situation reads:

> Neither in the ethnographic nor in the historical record does any nomadic population appear that does not depend either directly or indirectly on the products of agriculture, with the exception of reindeer nomadism which is found in areas where agriculture is not possible (Spooner 1973:5).

The preliminary conclusion is that pastoralism, even nomadic, does not exclude agriculture and the converse is also true.

A further aspect of the relationship between pastoralists and agriculture concerns their dependence on agricultural foods even though:

> ...information about the non-pastoral portion of the diet of nomads tends to be difficult to find and incospicuous in the literature due to the high cultural value nomads themselves place on pastoral foods (Spooner 1973: 19).

The various degrees of dependence of nomadic pastoralists on agricultural staples, however procured, have been observed by many authors (Asad 1970:30; Bacon 1954:59; Barth 1961:9; Capot-Rey 1963:91; Cole 1975:27; R. Dyson-Hudson *et al.* 1970:118; Spencer 1965:2). Having scanned the literature I noted that some authors formed the hypothesis that there might exist some 'pure' pastoralists, namely the Masai of Kenia, and the Beja of Sudan and Eritrea (cf. Salzman 1971:190). Having carried out fieldwork among two Beja groups, Hadendowa and Beni Amer, and read about a third, the Bishariin

(Morton 1988:88 ff.), I can confirm that among those populations some groups practice agriculture. While I have no first hand information about the Masai, I consider it highly unlikely that they ever lived solely on the products of their livestock.

Even in pre-colonial days, when still completely nomadic, both Hadendowa and Beni Amer were heavily dependent on agriculture. The Hadendowa of the Gash Delta awaited the end of the floods in September and used digging sticks to sow sorghum. The Beni Amer traded dried skins and clarified butter for sorghum and millet. With the growing trend to sedentarisation many former nomads have moved to villages and taken up occupations including agriculture.

Nowadays sorghum or millet supply the main part of the caloric intake of both populations. A survey of food intake per household conducted in 1989 among a dozen Hadendowa encampments in the bush yielded the average food intake per household (Ausenda n.d.a):

Table 1.2
Average distribution of the caloric intake of a pastoralist population per type of food

Type of food	% of total caloric intake
Sorghum	75
Milk	18
Sugar	4
Oil	2.8
Onions	0.2
Meat	negi.
	100

Reliance on sorghum among bush-dwelling pastoralists is actually greater than that of settled populations (65%) living in the same area because the latter eat meat daily and consume more oil and sugar. There may have been an ongoing trend among the pastoral population toward an increasing consumption of agricultural staples, possibly due to the decreasing cost of agricultural products with respect to livestock products. Nevertheless, it is reasonable to assume that also in the past, even if in lower proportions, agricultural staples were important in the diet of pastoral populations.

At the beginning of the section I noted how most nomadic societies are placed at various points on a continuum ranging between fully nomadic and fully sedentary groups. The literature on pastoralists gives an idea of the proportions of nomadic and sedentary in various cases. About two thirds of the populations of the Algerian Sahara are sedentary (Monteil 1959:574), and the same holds for the Toubou of Chad (Capot-Rey 1963:85). Until recently the Yomut Turkmen of Iran were divided between "two occupational groups", agriculturalists and pastoralists. Both lived in tents but the agriculturalists made infrequent and short migrations (Irons 1972:144). The Rwala Bedouin of Jordan who live on the edge of the desert are sedentary; the sedentary portion of the population waxes and wanes according to ecological and political pressures (Musil 1928:45). Even the most nomadic groups comprise sedentary fractions representing them, so to speak, in market towns, because tribesmen prefer to deal with their own kin and a few must be present and on good terms with the central authorities.

Probably from the inception of nomadic pastoralism there was, and still is, a growing pressure towards sedentarisation (Bacon 1854:52; Spooner 1971:20). Pressure is caused mainly by ecological and political factors. Several researchers have pointed out how govemments mistrust nomads and try to force them to settle. Sometimes, as in the case of the former Soviet Union, the French Maghreb, and the Western Desert of Egypt, governmental suspicion is accompanied by the purported intention to "rationalize" the nomads' subsistence strategy considered wasteful and destructive (Abou Zeid 1959:553; Black 1972:619, 620; Muhsam 1959:540; Monteil 1959:581; Planhol 1959:529, 530).

The other basic pressure toward sedentarisation is caused by ecological variations affecting the health and numerical strength of the herd. The marginal habitats in which nomadic pastoralists live are subject to frequent droughts. There are also livestock epidemics which can reduce a household's herd to naught. The first type of contingency was often offset by migration, a solution which has become increasingly difficult on account of borders and political unrest. The only solution to a serious epidemic was to change subsistence strategy, hence one's life-style, by taking up agricultural labor or some other humble occupation in a village.

Several authors have pointed out how, in fact, poverty is the principal condition forcing nomadic pastoralists to become sedentary (Bacon 1954:59; Barth 1961:109; Barth 1963:78; Monteil 1959:580). However, a weaker trend towards sedentarisation can be found also at the other end of the social spectrum among wealthy nomads who are attracted to the village by the possibility of an "alternative investment" in land, and the security inherent in such a permanent investment as compared to the insecurity of having one's subsistence depending solely on livestock (Barth 1963:73, 77). Wealthy nomads may also settle as merchants and monopolise their kin as customers.

A survey conducted in 1988 and 1989 among Hadendowa living in encampments in the bush and settled agriculturalists living in villages in the same area showed that settled agriculturalists expend on average more energy over and above Basic Metabolic Rate than do nomadic pastoralists (Ausenda n.d.a). In other words, nomadic pastoralists are more leisurely and, in case they become settled agriculturalists, they must work harder. When the rains are good and there are no epidemics, there is little incentive for a pastoralist to change his way of life.

Summing up, there are two opposite pressures on nomadic pastoralists: a positive one, both ecological and political, driving them to sedentary life, and a negative one, based on the fact that nomadic pastoralism entails a lower expenditure of energy than settled agriculture, holding them to their traditional lifestyle. The progressive dwindling of marginal areas, taken over by agriculture, where nomadic pastoralists thrive will gradually force them lo become sedentary.

The Langobard *Fara*

In this final section I shall point out the analogies between the socioeconomic aspects of the Langobard population at the time of their migration to Italy and those of contemporary pastoral populations, and show that the Langobard, and by extension other barbarian *farae*, had many characteristics in common with the corporate groups of agro-pastoral populations described in the previous sections and that, to the Langobards, the term *fara* meant indeed a kinship structure closely akin to what present-day historians and social anthropologists call 'lineage'.

We know that the Langobards were dedicated to both pastoralism and agriculture as witnessed by the laws in Rothari's edict issued in 643 AD, about three generations after the invasion of Italy. Among the laws concerning indemnification for damages and crimes concerning all kinds of property, beginning with Ro.249 and up to and including Ro.357, slightly over 50% concern cases involving livestock, little over 25% concern cases pertaining to agri- and viticulture, and just about as many are dedicated to cases concerning the practice of hunting. From these proportions one gathers how important animal husbandry and pastoralism still were to the Langobards three generations after they had settled in Italy.

We have seen that most pastoral populations were also dedicated to agriculture and the Langobards were no exception. If we are to apply the criterion which considers populations pastoral when they reckon their wealth primarily in livestock, Tacitus' testimony concerning the *Germani* in general leaves no doubt:

> There are some varieties in the appearance of the country, but broadly it is a land of bristling forests and unhealthy marshes, the rainfall is heavier on the side of Gaul; the winds are higher on the side of Noricum and Pannonia. It is fertile in cereals, but unkindly in fruit bearing trees; it is rich in flocks and herds, but for the most part they are undersized. Even the cattle lack natural beauty and majestic brows. The pride of the people is rather in the numbers of their beasts, which constitute the only wealth they welcome (Tacitus, *Germania* 5. Trans. Page 1958b).

Tacitus' passage on the preferences of the *Germani* concerning livestock is almost the same as that by Rada and Neville Dyson-Hudson concerning the Karimojong (see page 27).

The *Germani*, hence also the Langobards, invariably paid blood money compensation in livestock:

> Lighter offenses have also a measured punishment, those convicted are fined a number of horses and cattle: part of the fine goes to the king or the state, part is paid to the person himself who brings the charge or to his relatives (Tacitus, *Germania*, 12. Trans. Page 1958b).

Five centuries later nearly all penalties in Rothari's Edict are stated in gold *solidi*.[2] However, it is likely that *solidi* were principally a unit of account and that transfers of wealth may have involved many kinds of valuables, including slaves and livestock. In fact, comparing Ro.332 with Ro.333 and Ro.334, one obtains the information that a cow was worth one third of the price of a mare, which in turn was worth one third of the price of a servant girl, valued at an average of 30 *solidi*, which made the price of a cow approximately three *solidi* and gave a ratio for compensations in mares and cows. A free born man's blood money was worth 80 solidi or approximately 25 cows, more or less the same as a Hadendowa's in eastern Sudan in 1840 (Werne 1852:238 in Ausenda 1987:290).

In addition to Tacitus' testimony, there is philological proof that in earlier times the wealth of a Langobard was reckoned in livestock. This is also attested in Rothari's laws by the terms *metfio* (*magd* = maid and *fio* = livestock) and *faderfio* (*fader* = father and *fio* = livestock) which refer to bridal payments. Langobardic *fio*, akin to modern German 'vieh', meaning 'livestock', leaves no doubt as to the unit of account utilised for those transactions during the pre-contact period. Moreover, the word *metfio* was used in Langobard laws as late as Li.129 (*Liutprandi leges* 129) issued by Liutprand in 731, shortly before Paul the Deacon wrote his *History of the Langobards*.

One can hardly believe that people familiar with the traditions pertaining to kinship and marriage had no idea of what *fara* meant to the point that, according to Murray, Paul the Deacon did not know what it was (A. C. Murray 1983:96).

That livestock was an important value in Langobard practice even in later times is proven by the surname Fiumberti (*fio* = livestock, *behrt* = splendid) which survives to this day among contemporary surnames in northern Lombardy.

---

[2]　*Solidi* were the standard gold currency of the Roman empire since Constantine.

We know little about the proportion of sedentary and nomadic among Germanic populations. Tacitus wrote:

> It is well known that none of the German tribes live in cities, that even individually they do not permit houses to touch each other: they live separated and scattered, according as spring water, meadow or grove appeals to each man (Tacitus, *Germania*, 16. Trans. Page 1958b).

One does not know the pastoral habits of these mostly sedentary settlements.

Tacitus' remark that men were not accustomed to hard work is in line with the observation concerning present-day pastoralists' attitude to work (see page 30):

> ...whence it comes that their physique, in spite of their vast numbers, is identical: fierce blue eyes, red hair, tall frames, powerful only spasmodically, and impatient at the same time of labour and hard work (Tacitus, *Germania*, 4. Trans. Page 1958b).

Despite the scholarly misgivings on Tacitus, I am inclined to trust Tacitus' ethnography in certain respects, fortified by the knowledge that many of the facts he described survived almost intact in Langobard tradition five to six centuries later, e.g. blood money compensation, the description of the wedding cortege with the war horse and weapons, the absence of cities and the dispersal of extended family compounds, worship in open-air sites rather than in temples, etc.

In the previous section I described some of the social networks that transcend kinship among contemporary pastoralists, mainly age sets and clientage. Stratification was present among the Langobards and probably among other Germanic populations. The Langobards had a three-tiered social structure dominated by free born men, i.e. free men born of free men and women, with an intermediate stratum of *haldii*, clients, whose patrons were specific free men, and a lower class of slaves.

Haldii were allowed to cultivate land belonging to their patrons; they could transmit the privilege to their legitimate heirs as long as their descendance lasted. In the absence of legitimate heirs, land reverted to their patron. It is probable, although not recorded in the laws, that there were some customary obligations vis-à-vis the patron and occasional gifts to be made to him. This coincides with Tacitus' description of the status of those whom he termed 'slaves':

> Each of them remains master of his own house and home, the master requires from the slave as a serf a certain quantity of grain or cattle or clothing (Tacitus, *Germania*, 25. Trans. Page 1958b).

It is quite probable that the Langobards had age grades and age sets. The institution of the *arimanni* (*hari* = army, *manni* = men) and their landed privileges, mentioned in Ahi.4 (*Ahistulfi leges* 4) issued in 750, calls to mind the East and South African organisations based on 'warrior' age grades. A confirmation of the existence of this institution, possibly a relic of earlier times, can be found in a passage of the *Chronicum salernitanum* written at the end of the tenth century and referring to a visit of Charlemagne's envoys to the Langobard duke of Benevento. The passage describes the progress of the ambassadors in the duke's palace past groups belonging to four successive age grades: *adolescentes, juvenes*, i.e. warriors, *cani*, white-haired, and *senes*, elders (Westerbergh 1956:18-19).

The fission of genealogically related groups is something that can take place only in a nomadic or semi-nomadic stage and becomes almost impossible when populations are settled. Indeed, the only clue to a possible phenomenon of fission comes from the early stages of the Langobard invasion. A letter by Pope Gregory the Great to a Byzantine commander requesting that four groups of warriors and their families be sent back to their erstwhile leader, which will be discussed in detail below, might be a clue to the elusive phenomenon.

No trace is found in Langobard laws and related historical documents of the importance of sons as herd boys. The importance of young men in herding may be gauged by the small difference between blood money compensation for 'master' herders, valued at 20 *solidi*, and their apprentices, valued at 16 *solidi*. One can infer that Langobard families which were not wealthy or powerful enough to own slaves banked heavily on male children to help them with their herding chores.

It stands to reason that during pre-migration times, and for the same reasons prevailing among contemporary pastoralist populations, Langobard marriage preference was prevalently endogamic. This tradition clashed with Christian practice strongly set against endogamy. The vestiges of Langobard endogamy can be traced in their laws and in an exchange of letters between Rome and a cleric of Pavia, the Langobard capital.

The laws in question are Ro.185, issued in 643, forbidding "incestuous" marriages with one's step mother, step daughter, and sister-in-law, and Li.33 (*Liutprandi leges* 33), issued in 723, extending the prohibition to the widows of patri- and matrilateral cousins. These laws prove that there was a strong tendency to keep wealth, if not within close agnates, at least within the kindred by the marriage of widows with related agnates or affines. The implication is that the tendency was even more pronounced in earlier times, i.e. preferential marriage was with Father's Brother's Daughter.

Documentary support for this inference comes from a letter addressed by Pope Zacharias (741-752) to Theodore, archdeacon in Pavia, probably during the reign of Ratchis. This text proves that, among Langobards, marriage between relatives linked at the fourth generation, that is, with the same great-great-grandfather, was still frequent in the eighth century. On the strength of a permission granted by Pope Gregory the Great to the Angles a century and a half before, Theodore had requested the pope's permission to allow such marriages among Langobards. The pope's letter bore a refusal stating that the practice had been permitted to "rough people and those who have come to Christ recently", whereas the Langobards were to be treated "as those who were raised from the cradle within the Holy Catholic Church" (*M.G.H. Epistolae* III, page 709-n.18; *Italia Pontificia* vi/1:174,n.3 in Bertolini 1960:477 and Bullough 1969:323).

Tacitus' description makes it clear that at the end of the first century of our era Germanic tribes were linked in a tribal genealogical system:

> Their ancient hymns—the only style of record or history which they possess—celebrate the god Tuisto, a scion of the soil, and his son Mannus, as the beginning and the founders of their race. To Mannus they ascribe three sons, from whose names the tribes of the sea-shore are known as *Ingaevones*, the central tribes as *Herminones*, and the rest as *Istaevones*. Some authorities, using the license which pertains to antiquity, pronounce for more sons to the god and a larger number of race names, *Marsi, Gambrivii, Suebi, Vandili*; these are, they say, real and ancient names...(Tacitus, *Germania*, 2. Trans. Page 1958b).

Tacitus' passage shows that Germanic populations consciously used a mechanism allowing everyone to be genealogically linked to the founding ancestral god. The paradigm used by Tacitus reminds one of the similar one described by Emris Peters for the Bedouin of Cyrenaica (Peters 1960:29-30). In line with similar customs of contemporary populations, there is no doubt that the genealogies continued within each tribe to embrace the founding fathers of all clans and lineages within them.

Indeed, clans or lineages are mentioned in a later source, the *Origo gentis Langobardorum*, the Langobard most ancient chronicle, probably written when Rothari's edict was issued in 643, with additions ending with Perthari, *ca* 671. In chronologically listing Langobard rulers, the *Origo* gives their names and *genera* (sing. *genus*), i.e. clans or lineages.

The *Origo*'s list of kings starts with Agilmund, the first historical chief of the Langobards, who was *ex genere gugingus*, and so was the following one. Then came a dynasty of *lethinges* which ended with Gualtari [Walthari] who died heirless. Audoin, the next king, who led (*ca* 526) the Langobards into Pannonia within the Roman empire, belonged to a different clan or lineage: he was *ex genere gausus*. When his son Alboin, who led his people into Italy in 568, was killed in a conspiracy, he was succeeded by Cleph *de genere peleos* or *beleos*, who was followed by his son Authari. The next dynasty was inaugurated by Agilulf, also called Agiluald, a Thuringian, *ex genere anauuat*. Rothari, son of Nunding, whose genealogy is also given, was *ex genere arodus*.

Without prejudice to the possible cognatic features of the Langobard kindred, explicitly recognized in Ro.153 as a *parentilla*, one must admit that for strictly genealogical purposes descent was agnatic and patrilineal, as indeed it remains, with few exceptions, in contemporary Europe for the registration of male and female surnames to this day.

That complementary opposition was a viable mechanism in certain situations is proven by the initiation ceremonies described in Langobard history. To be admitted to his father's table, Alboin had to ask the king of the Gepids to impart the initiation to him (Paul the Deacon, *Historia Langobardorum*, I, 24). During the eighth century Charles, maior of the Frankish palace, sent his son Pippin to Liutprand to be initiated by him (Paul the Deacon, *H. L.*, VI, 53). Thus, we know that the initiation of kings' sons was performed by kings, a form of legitimation based on the principle of complementary opposition. According to the same principle, sons of dukes must have been initiated by dukes in the same kingdom, and sons of lineage heads by other lineage heads in the same duchy. However, no record of lower level initiations has come down to us.

Now I will show that the *fara* was akin to the lowest level of aggregation in the pastoral social structure, as described in a previous section (page 22), i.e. a residential group consisting of agnates and related peoples, headed at critical moments, such as migrations or conflicts, by one or more elders. I shall discount the clear testimony of Paul the Deacon, who wrote that the Langobard *farae* were "*generationes vel lineas*" (Paul the Deacon, *H. L.*, II, 9), i.e. 'generations or lineages', because A. C. Murray maintains that Paul the Deacon, who lived two centuries after the events, had a nebulous idea of what a *fara* was. I will rely, instead, on earlier testimony, both of a documentary and philological nature, which clarifies the meaning of the term.

I refer to a letter written in 591, i.e. 23 years after the invasion, by Pope Gregory the Great to a Byzantine commander defending Byzantine territory against Langobard raids. The fact that some Langobards were on the Byzantine side fighting against their own people was normal, since the idea of 'national' unity was still a long way in the future. In his letter the pope asked the Byzantine commander to release some Langobard military groups serving under his orders so that they could rejoin the contingent to which they originally belonged.

The pope's letter calls these groups *familiae*, 'families', and lists them as *Maloin, Adobin, Vigildi*, and *Grussingi* (*Gregorii Epistolae* Reg. II in Bognetti 1967-III:39). It is obvious that those described were not nuclear families, since the pope would not have bothered to intervene for such small units, they were multi-family groups linked by agnatic kinship. In fact, three out of the four names are Langobard names of individuals, probably the founding ancestors of the *familiae* in question, and the fourth has the suffix *-ing* of patronymics (Bach 1978:82).[3] There can be no doubt that these were the *farae* mentioned by Marius Aventicensis as having migrated into Italy with Alboin, again a testimony discounted by A. C. Murray who, in this case, maintained, on the strength of a doubtful etymology, that *farae* came from Germanic *faran* and meant 'expeditionary groups', not 'lineages'. The pope (see above), a contemporary to the events, did not call them *farae*, for the obvious reason that he would have preferred the Latin version when available, so he called them *familiae*, even though they had military functions, thus laying to rest the idea that they were expeditionary groups.

These families, coinciding with Paul the Deacon's and Marius Aventicensis' *farae*, had traveled to Italy 23 years before, and were defending the accesses to Rome. They were not traveling and the groups corresponded to those that Tapper classes as *A* groups (see page 21).

This also clarifies the apparent obscurity of Marius Aventicensis' passage:

> Alboin, king of the Langobards, leaving with his whole army and having burned his fatherland [in] Pannonia, occupied Italy with the women and all his people in *fara* (*MGH, Chronica minora* II:238 in Bognetti 1967-III: 12) [My trans.].

If the *fara* had been a military expedition, as in the case of the Langobard contingent which had fought in Italy on the side of the Byzantines during the Gothic war in 553, the chronicler would have not taken the pain of specifying that Alboin had left Pannonia with his whole army and in *fara*, because a military expedition did not ordinarily include women, and the expression *in fara*, which was clear to contemporary readers, meant that he had led the population grouped by lineages, i.e. in its entirety. This interpretation is in line with contemporary anthropological theory which holds complementary opposition and segmentary lineage practice to be at their highest in times of "territorial instability" (Salzman 1978a:67-9, see page 20).

The same considerations as for Pope Gregory's *familiae* can be made in the case of the expression *faramannos* which appears in the laws of the Burgundians written some time after their migration to Burgundy. The law upheld the principle that one half of the area of forests and fields obtained by clearing them should be left by the *faramanni*, i.e. the 'men of the lineages', to the Roman inhabitants (Bertolini 1968:509). These *faramanni* had settled, they were no longer on a military expedition, and yet still considered as belonging to *farae*, i.e. corporate groups based primarily on kinship ties.

To complete the discussion of documentary sources, I should point out that, in support of his interpretation of the meaning of *fara* in Ro.177 (allowing a "free man" to depart with his *fara*, provided he gave back to the duke or any other free man with whom he had lived the property that the latter had donated to him) as "family in a relatively narrow sense or household moveables", Murray quoted the *Codex matritensis*, a tenth-century text kept in Madrid which glosses *fara* as "*rebus*", i.e. "property" (A. C. Murray 1983:95 n.21). Quite conveniently Murray forgot two more codices, besides the *matritensis*, which contain the texts of Langobard legislation and their glosses. These are the *cavensis* and *vaticanus* which, by the way, are more complete as they carry respectively 165 and 103 glosses to

---

[3] A tentative translation of the names: *Maloin*, from *mahl*, 'courage' and *win*, 'friend' or 'friendship'; *Adobin*, from *ado*, 'nobility' and *win*, 'friend'; *Vigildi* from *wig*, 'fight' and *gild*, 'reward'; *Grussingi* from *grauso*, 'gruesome' with the *-ing* suffix pertaining to descent groups. Prof. Green suggested *mahl*, 'legal assembly', and *ado* from *hathu*, 'battle' (page 46).

the 65 of the *matritensis*. The *Cod. cavensis* glosses the term *fara* as *parentela*, i.e. 'kindred', and the *vaticanus* glosses it as *genealogia, generatio*, i.e. 'genealogy', 'generation' (Bluhme *et al.* 1868:653). Both glosses support the concept of *fara* as a kinship group, while the *Cod. matritensis* is obviously wrong as it repeats the term *rebus* (Bluhme *et al.* 1868:651) which, in Ro.177, refers to the property, not the group which is separately termed *fara*.

That the co-residents in the group were patrilineal agnates is supported by the knowledge that post-marital residence was patrilocal. In fact, the bride was 'delivered' and escorted to the bridegroom's residence (Tacitus, *Germania*, 18; Ro.183; Ahi.15).

I will now make recourse to philological proofs, in my estimation even more indisputable than documentary ones, to show that *fara* meant 'lineage' to the Langobards.

The first philological proof may be obtained from the *Origo gentis Langobardorum*, whose unknown author or authors cannot be accused of ignorance because he or they wrote at the same time or shortly after Rothari's Edict was issued. In the sequence of Langobard kings the dynastic change from the *Lethinges*, who ended with Gualtari, to the *Gausi*, who started with Audoin (see above), is explained by the fact that Gualtari was *farigaydus* (Bluhme *et al.* 1868:644), literally 'the tip of the *fara*', i.e. the end of his *fara*, which meant that he had no legitimate agnatic descendants. There is no doubt that *gaida* means 'tip', 'arrow point', 'spear' (Bach 1978:216-7; Bruckner 1895:205) and, therefore, there can be no doubt that for the anonymous chronicler *fara* meant simply 'lineage', not "detachments or the migration of the whole army" (A. C. Murray 1983:90), nor "family in a relatively narrow sense or household movables" (A. C. Murray 1983:95).

To remain in the field of philology one should consider the meaning of Germanic names in general, and Langobardic ones in this case, which are made up with *fara* as the first part of the compound name. The most popular were: *Fareperga, Faripertus* or *Farabert, Farelmo, Faremannus, Farimundus, Faroald*, and *Fariulf* or *Farolf* (Bach 1978:222; Bruckner 1895:246-7). These names are found in documents written as late as the eleventh century (Bruckner 1895:246-7). Contrary to many Langobardic and Germanic names which survived to this day in remembrance of men or women who distinguished themselves in one way or another, compound names with *fara* are not mentioned after the eleventh century: they were used as long as they had a meaning for the people who gave them and they became obsolete when the term no longer had any social significance. Thus, the first part of the compound *fara* had a clear meaning for those who gave these names to their children well after the time of Paul the Deacon.

The meanings of the second parts of the compound names are listed below. Having changed little to their modern German form the meanings of these terms are unquestionable:

perga = rescuer (Bach 1978:224; Bruckner 1895:233);
behrt = splendid (Bach 1978:225; Bruckner 1895:234);
helm = helmet, protection (Bach 1978:216; Bruckner 1895:267);
man = man (Bruckner 1895:283);
mund = guardian, protector (Bach 1978:225; Bruckner 1895:286);
wald = ruler (Bach 1978:224; Bruckner 1895:317);
wulf = wolf (Bach 1978:212; Bruckner 1895:324).

I will let the reader decide which one of the three meanings of *fara* as the first part of those compound names mentioned, whether the disputed 'lineage', or those proposed by Murray: 'detachment or migration of the whole army', or 'household movables', fits the second parts of the compound names best, e.g. 'rescuer of the lineage', or 'rescuer of the detachment or migration of the whole army', or 'rescuer of the household movables', or again 'splendid lineage', or 'splendid detachment or migration of the whole army', or 'splendid household movables', etc.

I have not mentioned that both the above quoted philologists translated *fara* with 'Geschlecht' (Bach 1978:222; Bruckner 1895:87,246) which in modern German means 'sex, race, family, line, generation'. Should this version be discounted on the same grounds as those given for Paul the Deacon, i.e. that a long time has passed since *farae* were living social bodies and these scholars had little idea of what they really were like?

Summing up, by quoting Bognetti and others, Murray tries to demolish the social significance of the term *fara* to uphold the philologically doubtful etymology of *fara* from High German *faran*, 'to wander', because it sounds similar to modern German, *fahren*, 'to travel'. In its transitive form *faran* means *ziehen*, i.e. 'to pull', while in its intransitive form it means 'to travel', and the term for 'migration' is *fard*, akin to modern German *Fahrt*, 'voyage' (Bruckner 1895:247). There are Langobard names with *fard* as the first or second part of a compound, such as *Fardulfus, Guarifardus, and Gifardus* (Bruckner 1895:247), that leave one in no doubt that for the Langobards *fara* and *fard* were two different concepts.

A philologically and conceptually more viable etymology that, so far, escaped Germanists is the Old High German *pfarra*, the ancestor of the modern German *Pfarre*, 'parish'. The same root also gives the word *Pferch*, meaning 'enclosure'. Therefore, the ancient meaning might have been that of a 'bounded community', which is what a *fara* was, i.e. a group of relatives with their clients and slaves living in a bounded community.[4]

Before concluding, I would like to restore some credibility to Caesar as a fairly reliable observer of the surrounding socioeconomic realities, contrary to Murray's opinion which considers a "pastiche [what] he offers as a Germanic ethnography" (A. C. Murray 1983:48). Murray attacks the "extraordinary statement of Caesar that the Germans changed their lands and abode each year—'*neque longius anno rernanere uno in loco colendi causa licet*' (*B. g.*, IV, 1)" (A. C. Murray 1983:49).

Two thousand years before Murray, Caesar was struck by the same disbelief, but he was in a condition to verify with his informants. Indeed, on his second crossing of the Rhine in 53 BC during a raid against the *Suebi*, having described the same agricultural routine mentioned two years before, he related:

> No man has a definite quantity of land or estate of his own, the magistrates and chiefs every year assign to tribes and clans that have assembled together as much land and in such place as seems good to them, and compel the tenants after a year to pass on elsewhere (Caesar, *B. g.*, VI,22. Trans. Page 1958a),

---

[4]   I am not entirely convinced by Prof. Green's opposition to my proposed etymology of the word *fara*, i.e. that it is cognate with O.H.G. *pfarra*. Prof. Green held that it is unlikely that OHG [pf] could become [f], and that one needs to show some parallels (see page 45). He was fair enough to allow that one scribe had transcribed *pfarra* with [f], but presumably this example is not sufficient. Prof. Green also held that O.H.G. *pfarra* comes from Latin (ultimately Greek) *parochia* and that it is of Christian origin. 1 would contend that it is just as, or more, improbable that the [p] in *parochia* could become [pf] compared to the transformation from [pf] to [f], which is more natural because [p] is unvoiced. I would consider *pfarra* a Germanic word which was used to translate a Christian concept. Thus *pfarra* originally a 'bounded community of kinsmen' took the related meaning of a 'bounded community of fellow Christians', while losing its traditional meaning because of the gradual weakening of the kinship network superseded by the community of co-religionists. This is supported by the competitive stance of the Church against extended kinship cohesion, which was expressed in the prohibition of marriage between close kin (see page 33).

and having explicitly inquired into the reasons, he added:

> They adduce many reasons for that practice: the fear that they may be tempted by continuous association to substitute agriculture for their warrior zeal, that they may become zealous for the acquisition of broad territories and so the more powerful may drive the lower sort from their holdings, that they may build with greater care to avoid the extremes of cold and heat, that some passion for money may arise to be the parent of parties and of quarrels. It is their aim to keep the common people in contentment, when each man sees that his own wealth is equal to that of the most powerful (Caesar, *B. g.*, VI, 22. Trans. Page 1958a).

I do not wish to evaluate the objectivity of the explanations given by Caesar, I only wish to point out that he inquired and obtained the information 'in the field' from bona fide informants, not from Greek sources, and having observed the practices under discussion.

Furthermore, if one bears in mind the main subsistence and defense strategies of those populations in Caesar's time, one will also understand why they behaved like that and why Caesar's explanation was not too far off the mark. In other words survival, both in regards to their primitive agriculture and also to defence against attacks by overwhelming enemy forces, lay in mobility. This is why the elders upheld this paramount value for survival.

Tacitus described in greater detail the self same procedure (Tacitus, *Germania*, 26), except for the fact that one hundred and fifty years had gone by and Tacitus wrote that the *Germani* changed "arable land yearly", not necessarily their abodes. It is possible that in the meantime, and probably owing to the stabilising proximity of the Empire's borders, they had become more sedentary.

Furthermore, the statement is not so extraordinary in an anthropological context. In fact, the method is still followed by many contemporary societies. The same practice is followed by contemporary Pakhtuns who:

> ...do not own particular fields, and their tenure is subjected to a system of periodic reallotment, known as the *wesh* (division) system, related in conception to the *musha'a* system of the Near East (Barth 1959:10).

and:

> [Among the Marri Baluch] Communal ownership [of agricultural land] within lineage segments, associated with periodic reallotment, is regarded as the traditional form...(Pehrson 1966:8).

The above are only two examples which apply to pastoralists, but dozens may be found in the ethnological literature. Furthermore, the system of rotation of communal property by drawing lots, whence the expression 'allotment', was followed in the foothills of the Italian Alps for the yearly allotment of tracts of forest among the residents of mountain villages for wood cutting as long as it was economical to burn wood, i.e. until World War II.

Is it possible that Caesar who based his overwhelmingly successful campaigns on the careful appraisal of information about the populations, their motivations, interactions and movements, could have been so superficial, as claimed by Murray, in his evaluation of the differences between the Gauls and the *Germani* (see page 16)? Murray maintains, without quoting sources, that "archaeologically this distinction is completely false" (A. C. Murray 1983:45).[5] One

---

[5] This statement is also questionable; to date archaeology has not found bounded settlements in the territory of the early *Germani*:

> But according to the latest results of archaeology and ethnology it appears that until the first century AD, even within an inhabited area, great forests separated individual communities.

should bear in mind that nomadic pastoralists are almost invisible archaeologically, so that it would be virtually impossible to assess the pastoral portion of the population.

One does not have to make recourse to archaeology but only to pay moderate attention to contemporary histories to realise that there were differences between certain Celtic and Germanic groups. In his campaigns Caesar was often faced with Gauls in their *oppida*, 'fortified villages', to which he was compelled to lay siege or make recourse for his supplies, e.g. *Bibracte, Vesontium*, three *Noviodunum, Samarobriva, Lutetia Parisiorum, Cerrabum, Gergovia, Alesia*, and dozens more, whereas nowhere in Roman history is there any mention of the siege of an *oppidum* in Germania. One hundred and fifty years later on this matter Tacitus was unequivocal: "It is well known that none of the German tribes live in cities...." (Tacitus, *Germania*, 16. Trans. Page 1958b).

When Caesar for the second time built a bridge across the Rhine to launch a retaliatory raid against the *Suebi*, he was told that they had fled to the far reaches of their territory (Caesar, *B. g.*, VI, 10). This is the typical, and quite wise, strategy of a pastoralist population when menaced by overwhelming enemy forces. Their wealth consists of easily abductable livestock which can only be safe when led as far as possible from the enemy. It would be foolish and counterproductive to try to make a stand, since livestock, their wealth, would be easily plundered. Only a sedentary population, such as the Gauls, would try to defend their land and *oppida*, because they could not be moved.

As for the fault found by Murray with Caesar's comment that the Gauls sacrificed more than the *Germani*, I should recall that pastoralists sacrifice their livestock rarely, only at ceremonies occasioned by rites of passage, whereas city dwellers have a number of religious festivities connected with urban, regional, and 'national' cohesion several times a year during which livestock, and at times human beings, were sacrificed. We know from Caesar (*B. g.* VI, 22) that the *Germani* had a less stratified society, i.e., a lower level of complexity than that of the Gauls whose society was stratified with religious, wealth, and authority statuses (Caesar, *B. g.* VI, 13).

While we may question his interpretations, I believe some of Caesar's direct observations to be fairly factual, especially when plain descriptions are concerned, and those which may be gleaned from his short comments to be helpful when placed in the proper context. When Caesar writes about *gentes* and *cognationes*, we will never know the exact functioning of those structures, all we are entitled to conclude is that there were discernible kinship groups among the *Germani*.

Conclusion

I believe I have presented convincing evidence of the equivalence of a Langobard *fara* with a residential group comprising a lineage in its entirety or part thereof, with the possibility of affinal and even foreign admixtures, especially clients, as is the case among contemporary agro-pastoral societies.

---

and further:

Note 25: The Germani, instead, fortified individual strongholds where they could withdraw when in danger, but not adapted to a permanent stay. ('Ringwälle', i.e., 'circular walls') (Werkmüller 1976:649) [My trans.].

There is no need to do away with the *fara* as a kin-based group to make room for cognatic features, because these are satisfactorily explained by the *fara's* coincidence with the *A* level of aggregation, as previously discussed, while only descent and genealogical relationships between groups were reckoned along patrilines. The above features together with post-marital patrilocal residence are sufficient proof of the clustering of some agnatically related individuals, which is what I set out to show.

There is very little difference, as far as the presence of cognatic features is concerned, between my conclusion and Murray's except that, in his conclusion concerning the *fara*, Murray contends:

> ...that the word *fara* is a poor basis for any comprehensive view of the nature and development of kinship. It should be *eliminated* [emphasis mine] once and for all as evidence that in the ancient period Germanic society was composed of extensive unilineal and corporate clans and lineages (A. C. Murray 1983:97).

Eliminating evidence of any kind, even when confusing, is an indication of an absolutist and obscurantist attitude. In this case I wish to uphold the opposite conclusion, i.e. that a true desire for knowledge must give one the ability to cope with uncertainties and gradually bring them into focus even when they seem to be "a poor basis for any comprehensive view".

Concerning the *fara*, I would like once more to underscore the fact that there is no "comprehensive model" of segmentary lineage that applies to all pastoral societies whether past or contemporary. Each tribe and sometimes each clan has different types of segmentary lineages, in that the 'mix' between agnates and affines, clansmen and others, patrons and clients, changed both among social groups and in time; each one must be studied in its own right and compared with related ones.

However, the cohesion mechanisms of ancient residential clusters before and after migration and acculturation, especially when confronted with obstacles, such as an extended sea voyage, cannot be properly understood unless one patiently tries to reconstruct the salient features of the particular kind of segmentary lineage that existed, especially among the non-urban part of a population, during the period of transition from the Roman empire to the early Middle Ages.

Acknowledgements—I am grateful to Ian Wood for reading this article, correcting semantic mistakes and pointing out some weak points. I still claim full responsibility for the argumentation.

References

Textual sources:

Caesar
> *Bellum gallicum*: see Page 1958a.
Chronicon salernitanum: see Westerbergh 1956.
Edictus Rothari, Liutprandi leges, Ahistulfi leges: see Bluhme *et al.* 1868.
Origo gentis Langobardorum: see Bluhme *et al.* 1868.
Paul the Deacon
> *Historia Langobardorum*: see Bethemann & Waitz 1878.
Tacitus
> *Germania*: see Page 1958b.

Bibliography:

Abou Zeid, A. M.
  1959   The Sedentarization of Nomads in the Western Desert of Egypt. *International Social Science Jour.nal* 11: 550-8.
Asad, Talal
  1970   *The Kabahish Arabs.* New York: Praeger.
Ausenda, G.
  1987   Leisurely Nomads: The Hadendowa (Beja) of the Gash Delta and Their Transition to Sedentary Village Life. Doctoral dissertation, Graduate School of Arts and Sciences, Columbia University, New York.
  n.d.a   Physical Activity Levels and Complexity: A Comparison between Nomadic Pastoralists and Settled Agriculturalists in the Gash Delta in Eastern Sudan.
  n.d.b   Beni Amer and Habab: A Diachronic Ethnography (1890-1992).
Bach, A.
  1978   *Deutsche Namen Kunde, Band I, 1: Die deutschen Personennamen.* Heidelberg: Carl Winter - Universitätverlag.
Bacon, E. B.
  1954   Types of Pastoral Nomadism in Central and Southwest Asia. *Southwestern Journal of.Anthropology* 10: 44-68.
  1958   *Obok: A Study of Social Structure in Eurasia.* Viking Fund No. 25.
Baroin, C.
  1985   *Anarchie et cohesion sociale chez les Toubou: Les Daza Keserda (Niger).* Cambridge: Cambridge University Press.
Barth, F.
  1954   Father's Brother's Daughter Marriage in Kurdistan. *Southwestern Journal of Anthropology* 10: 164-71.
  1959   Segmentary Opposition and the Theory of Games: A Study of Pathan Organization. *Journal of Royal Anthropological Insitute* 89:5-21.
  1961   *Nomads of South Persia: The Basseri Tribe of the Khamseh Confederacy.* Boston: Little, Brown, and Co.
  1963   Capital investment and Social Structure of a Pastoral Nomad Group in South Persia. In *Capital Saving and Credit in Peasant Societies.* R. Firth and B. S. Yanney (eds.), pp. 69-81. London: Allen & Unwin.
Bates, D. G.
  1971   The Role of the State in Peasant-Nomad Mutualism. *Anthropological Quarterly* 44: 109-131.
  1972   Differential Access to Pasture in a Nomadic Society: The Yorak of Southeastern Turkey. In *Perspectives on Nomadism.* W. Irons and N. Dyson-Hudson (eds.), pp. 48-59. (International Studies in Sociology and Social Anthropology, Vol. XIII). Leiden: E. J. Brill.
Bertolini, O.
  1960   Le chiese longobarde dopo la conversione al cattolicesimo ed i loro rapporti con il papato. In *Le chiese nei regni dell'Europa occidentale e i loro rapporti con Roma sino all'800.* Settimane di studio del C.I.S.A.M., VII. Pp. 455-492. Spoleto: C.I.S.A.M.
  1968   Ordinamenti militari e strutture sociali dei Longobardi in Italia. In *Ordinamenti militari in Occidente nell'Alto Medioevo.* Settimane di studio del C.I.S.A.M., X. Pp. 429-607. Spoleto: C.I.S.A.M.
Bethemann, L., & O. Waitz (eds.)
  1878   *Scriptores rerum Langobardicarum et Italicarum, saec. VI-IX. Monumenta Germaniae Historica.* Hanover: Hahn.

Black, J.
    1972   Tyranny as a strategy for survival in an 'egalitarian' society: Luri facts versus an
                    anthropological mistique. *Man* 7 (4): 614- 634.
Bluhme, F., & A. Boretius (eds.)
    1868   *Leges Langobardorum. Monumenta Germaniae historica. Leges* (in folio), 4.
                    Hanover: Hahn.
Bognetti, G. P.
    1967   *L'età longobarda.* Vol. III. Milano: Giuffré.
Bruckner, W.
    1895   *Die Sprache der Langobarden.* Strassburg: Karl J. Trubner. [Reprinted in 1969 by
                    Walter de Gruyter & Co., Berlin].
Bullough, D. A.
    1969   I vescovi di Pavia nei secoli ottavo e nono: Fonti e cronologia. In *Atti del 4° Congresso
                    Internazionale di Studi sull'Alto Medio Evo.* Pp. 317-328. Spoleto: C.I.S.A.M.
Capot-Rey, R.
    1963   Le nomadisme des Toubous. In *Nomades et nomadisme au Sahara: Recherches
                    sur la zone aride.* Pp. 81-92. Paris: U.N.E.S.C.O.
Cole, D. P.
    1975   *Nomads of the Nomads: The Al Murrah Bedouin of the Empty Quarter.* Chicago: Aldine.
Cunnison, I.
    1966   *Baggara Arabs: Power and the Lineage in a Sudanese Nomad Tribe.* Oxford:
                    Clarendon Press.
Dyson-Hudson, N.
    1972   The Study of Nomads. In *Perspectives on Nomadism.* W. Irons &
                    N. Dyson-Hudson (eds.), pp. 2-29. (Intl. Studies in Sociology and Social
                    Anthropology, Vol. XIII). Leiden: E. J. Brill.
Dyson-Hudson, R., & N. Dyson-Hudson
    1970   The Food Production System of a Semi-Nomadic Society: The Karimojong of
                    Uganda. In *African Food Production Systems.* P. F. McLoughlin (ed.),
                    pp. 91-123. Baltimore: Johns Hopkins University Press.
Evans-Pritchard, E. E.
    1940   *The Nuer: A description of the modes of livelihood and political institutions of a
                    Nilotic people.* Oxford: Clarendon Press.
Fried, M. H.
    1967   *The Evolution of Political Society: An Essay in Political Anthropology.* New York:
                    Random House.
Goldschmidt, W.
    1979   A general model for pastoral social systems. In *Proceedings of the international
                    meeting on nomadic pastoralism.* Pp. 15-27. New York: Cambridge Univ. Press.
Hart, D. M.
    1962   The Social Structure of the Rgibat Bedouins of the Western Sahara. *The Middle
                    East Journal* 16: 515-527.
Horowitz, M. M.
    1972   Ethnic Boundary Maintenance among Pastoralists and Farmers in the Western Sudan.
                    In *Perspectives on Nomadism.* W. Irons & N. Dyson-Hudson (eds.), pp. 105-114.
                    (Intl. Studies in Sociology and Social Anthropology, Vol. XIII). Leiden: E. J. Brill.
Hudson, A. E.
    1938   *Kazak Social Structure.* New Haven: Yale Univ. Publications in Anthropology,
                    resprinted by H. R. A. F.
Irons, W.
    1972 .   Variations in Economic Organization: A Comparison of the Pastoral Yomut and the
                    Basseri. In *Perspectives on Nomadism.* W. Irons & N. Dyson-Hudson (eds.), pp. 88-
                    104. (Intl. Studies in Sociology and Social Antluop., Vol. XIII). Leiden: E. J. Brill.

Irons, W. (*cont.*)
1979   Political stratification among pastoral nomads. In *Pastoral production and society*. Proceedings of the international meeting on nomadic pastoralism, pp. 361-374. New York: Cambridge Univ. Press.
Johnson, D. L.
1969   *The Nature of Nomadism: A Comparative Study of Pastoral Migration in Southwestern Asia and Northern Africa*. Research paper no. 18, Dept. of Geography, Univ. of Chicago, Chicago.
Krader, L.
1955a   Principles and structures in the organization of the Asiatic steppe pastoralists. *Southwestern Journal of.Anthropology* 11 (2): 67-92.
1955b   Ecology of Central Asian Pastoralism. *Southwestern Journal of.Anthropology* 11 (4): 301 -326.
Le Goff, J.
1976   Les gestes symboliques dans la vie sociale: les gestes de la vassalite. In *Simboli e simbologia nell'Alto Medioevo. Settimane di studio del Centro Italiano di Studi sull'Alto Medioevo*, XXIIIP Pp. 679-779. Spoleto: C.I.S.A.M.
Lewis, I. M.
1962   *Marriage and the family in Northern Somaliland*. (East African Studies no. 15). Kampala: East African Institute of Research.
1971   From Nomadism to Cultivation: The Expansion of Political Solidarity in Southem Somalia. In *Man in Africa*. M. Douglas & P. Kaberry (eds.), pp. 59-77. London: Tavistock.
Martini, F.
1946   *Il Diario Eritreo*. Firenze: Vallecchi.
Montagne, P.
1947   *Les civilizations du désert: nomades d'Orient et d'Afrique*. Paris: Hachette.
Monteil, V.
1959   The Evolution and Settling of Nomads of the Sahara. *International Social Science Journal* 11: 572-585.
Morton, J. F.
1989   Descent, Reciprocity and Inequality among the Northern Beja. Doctoral dissertation in Sociology, Univ. of Hull, Hull.
Münzinger, W.
1890   *Studi sull'Africa Orientale*. Rome: Voghera, Carlo.
Muhsam, H. V.
1959   Sedentarization of the Bedouin in Israel. *International Social Science Journal* 11: 539-549.
Murray, A. C.
1983   *Germanic Kinship Structure: Studies in Law and Society in Antiquity and the Early Middle Ages*. Toronto: Pontifical Institute of Medieval Studies.
Murray, G. W.
1935   *Sons of Ishmael: A Study of the Egyptian Bedouin*. London: Routledge & Sons, Ltd.
Musil, A.
1928   *The manners and customs of the Rwala Bedouins. (*Oriental Explorations and Studies, no. 6). New York: Amer. Geog. Society.
Nadel, S. F.
1945   Notes on Beni Amer society. *Sudan Notes and Records* 26: 51-94.
Nicolaisen, J.
1963   *Ecology and Culture of the Pastoral Tuareg*. (Nationalmuseets Skrifter. Etnografisk Raekke IX). Copenhagen: The National Museum of Copenhagen.
Page, T. E. (ed. & trans.)
1958a   *Caesar: The Gallic War*. Cambridge, MA: Harvard University Press.
1958b   *Tacitus: Dialogue, Agricola, Germania*. Cambridge, MA: Harvard University Press.

Paul, A.
1950   Notes on the Beni Amer. *Sudan Notes and Records* 31: 223-245.
Pehrson, R. N.
1966   *The Social Organization of the Marri Baluch.* (Viking Fund Publications in
                   Anthropology, no. 43). Chicago: Aldine.
Peters, E. L.
1960   The Proliferation of Segments in the Lineages of the Bedouin of Cyrenaica.
                   J.R.A.I. 90: 29-53.
1967   Some structural aspects of the feud among the camel-herding Bedouin pastoralists
                   of Cyrenaica. *Africa* 37 (3): 261-282.
1968   The tied and the free: An account of a type of patron-client relationship among the
                   Bedouin pastoralists of Cyrenaica. In *Mediterranean Rural Communities and
                   Social Change, Contributions to Mediterranean Sociology.* J. G. Peristiany (ed.),
                   pp. 167-188. Paris: Mouton.
Planhol, X. de
1959   Geography, Politics and Nomadism in Anatolia. *International Social Science Journal*
                   11: 525-531.
Rognon, P.
1963   Problemes de Touaregs du Hoggar. In *Nomades et nomadisme au Sahara:
                   Recherches sur la zone aride.* Pp. 59-66. Paris: UNESCO.
Sahlins, M. D.
1961   The Segmentary Lineage: An Organization of Predatory Expansion. *American
                   Anthropologist* 63: 322-345.
Salzman, P. C.
1971a   Movement and Resource Extraction Among Pastoral Nomads: The Case of the
                   Shah Nawazi Baluch. *Anthropological Quarterly* 44: 185-197.
1971b   Adaptation and Political Organization in Iranian Baluchistan. *Ethnology*
                   10: 433-444.
1972   Multi-resource Nomadism in Iranian Baluchistan. In *Perspectives on Nomadism.*
                   W. Irons & N. Dyson-Hudson (eds.), pp. 60-68. (Intl. Studies in Sociology and
                   Social Anthrop, Vol. XIII). Leiden: E. J. Brill.
1978a   Does Complementary Opposition Exist? *American Anthropologist* 80: 53-70.
1978b   Ideology and change in Middle Eastern tribal societies. *Man* 13: 618-637.
Spencer, P.
1965   *The Samburu: A study of gerontocracy in a nomadic tribe.* Berkeley: University
                   of California Press.
Spooner, B.
1971   Towards a Generative Model of Nomadism. *Anthropological Quarterly* 44: 198-209.
1973   *The Cultural Ecology of Pastoral Nomads.* An Addison-Wesley Module in
                   Anthropology no. 45, Reading, MA.
Stenning, D.
1957   Transhumance, Migratory Drift, Migration: Patterns of Pastoral Fulani Nomadism.
                   J.R.A.I. 87: 57-73.
1959   *Savannah Nomads.* London: Oxford University Press.
Swidler, N.
1972   The Development of the Kalat Khanate. In *Perspectives on Nomadism.* W. Irons
                   & N. Dyson-Hudson (eds.), pp. 115-121. (Intl. Studies in Sociology and Social
                   Anthropology, Vol. XIII). Leiden: E. J. Brill.

Swidler, W. W.
  1972   Some Demographic Factors Regulating the Formation of Flocks and Camps
               Among the Brahui of Baluchistan. In *Perspectives on Nomadism*. W. Irons &
               N. Dyson-Hudson (eds.), pp. 69-75. (Intl. Studies in Sociology and Social
               Anthropology, Vol. XIII). Leiden: E. J. Brill.
Tapper, R. L.
  1979   The organization of nomadic communities in pastoral societies of the Middle East.
               In *Pastoral production and society*. Proceedings of the international meeting on
               nomadic pastoralism, pp. 43-65. New York: Cambridge University Press.
Toupet, C.
  1963   L'évolution de la nomadisation en Mauritanie saheliénne. In *Nomades et
               nomadisme au Sahara: Recherches sur la zone aride*. Pp.67-79. Paris: UNESCO.
Vreeland, H.
  1954   *Mongol Community and Kinship Structure*. New Haven: H.R.A.F.
Werkmüller, D.
  1976   Recinzioni, confini e segni terminali. In *Simboli e simbologia nell'Alto Medioevo*.
               Settimane di studio del C.I.S.A.M., XXIII. Pp. 641-659. Spoleto: C.I.S.A.M.
Werne, F.
  1852   *African wanderings: or, an expedition from Sennar to Taka, Basa and Beni Amer,
               with a particular glance at the races of Billad Sudan*. London: Longman, Brown,
               Green and Longman.
Westerbergh, U. (ed.)
  1956   *Chronicum salernitanum: A critical edition with studies on literary and historical
               sources and on language*. (Acta Universitatis Stockholmiensis. Studia Latina
               Stockholmiensia III). Stockholm: Almqvist & Wiksell.

Discussion

GREEN: Concerning the etymology of the word *fara* proposed by Murray. It is not possible to connect it with Old High German *faran* 'to travel'. There is too much of a jump from 'travel' to 'travel in an expeditionary force'. So far I am in agreement with you.

I am in disagreement when you relate *fara* to modern German *Pferch*. I agree that this is possible, but I am unhappy when you say that *pfarra* could be regarded as the origin. *Pfarra* is attested in Old High German and is transcribed with [f] instead of [pf] only in a text from Reichenau. You believe that the [p] was dropped by the Latin scribe, but to show this, one would have to come up with parallel cases.

Old High German *pfarra* is certainly of Christian origin (from *parochia*), probably of the sixth century. You would have to make a semantic jump from Christian and Merovingian to secular and Langobardic to establish your case.

Finally, while I agree with your contention concerning the meaning of *fara* as a corporate group of kinsmen, I should like to point out that Old High German *faran* means 'ziehen' [page 37]. This modern German verb has two meanings, in the transitive form it means 'to pull', while in the intransitive it means 'to move'.

WOOD: I would like to know whether there are possibilities of coming up with an etymology.

GREEN: I agree with the meaning but not with the proposed etymology.

HINES: The Danish scholar Lars Jørgensen has looked for discrete groupings in Germanic cemeteries (Jørgensen 1992a, 1992b). He presents a reasonable case that such groupings can be seen and has identified them as families. He has recently produced a substantial study of the Langobardic cemeteries of Nocera Umbra and Castel Trosino. He makes a confident identification of the *fara* with a family group, a unit of between ten and fourteen persons (1992a:55-6).

TURTON: Do other sources discuss what was actually meant by 'family'?

HINES: There is some analysis of these units. Jørgensen's paper suggests that they are rather larger than a nuclear family, comprising for instance unmarried sisters and affines. He does not believe that what he is saying is in contrast with what Murray suggests, but he relies more on Herlihy's studies (Herlihy 1969, 1985) than on Murray.

AXBOE: It is a relevant point to be debated. It is difficult to identify kinship on grave goods alone, one needs to know more about the DNA.

GREEN: On page 31, wealth in form of livestock. There is a parallel in Latin between *pecus* and *pecunia*, and between modern German 'Vieh' and modern English 'fee'. However, when you say that livestock was an important value even in later times we cannot argue from the presumed etymology of a Langobardic name: that only tells us what the name *once* meant, at the time of its coinage.

On page 35 there is a footnote with tentative translations of Langobardic names. *Mahl* in *Maloin* suggests 'legal assembly', not 'courage'. *Ado in Adobin* probably comes from *hathu* 'battle'.

I agree that fission and fusion are formative mechanisms for groups. The most helpful treatment is in the book *Stammesbildung und Verfassung* by R. Wenskus. I also agree that the presence of colonial powers helps in the formation of tribes.

DUMVILLE: Contact with hegemonic power can in certain circumstances help tribe formation. Secondly I do not agree with the idea that kinship-groups are not good as military units. In fact, raiding is a military activity within those types of society.

AUSENDA: I did not wish to infer that kinship related groups do not engage in military activities. I desired to point out that these groups are better suited for offense, consisting in quick raids, than in defence. In fact, their defence consisted in raiding other groups to keep them at a distance from their borders. In other words, offense was used also for defensive purposes, which implies a more limited set of available alternatives in warfare.

DUMVILLE: I am wondering whether there wasn't military activity within groups.

AUSENDA: Yes, it was possible to have military activities between clans belonging to the same ethnic group. However, these were limited in scope and in time and of a nature that one might call 'ritual'. There was a limitation in the types of weapons used, pointed sticks rather than spears, in the duration of the engagements, and in the consequences.

TURTON: I question the use of the word 'group' in the context of segmentary lineages. One must bear in mind that there is a difference between *categories*, created by means of the segmentary lineage principle, and *groups* that can do things 'on the ground'. I think one should make it clear that sections are *territorial* groups. In Evans-Pritchard's account, the segmentary lineage principle is a mental construct, used to organise the relations between territorial groups. The dominant clan is represented because it occupied the territory. Village A would relate to village B in the way that dominant clans behave toward each other. Thus, 'segmentary lineage' is a mental category. Evans-Pritchard was concerned with the problem of order, his is a political theory. 'Balanced opposition' is used as a basis of a political system. In acephalous society ordered relations were possible and they could group against outside aggression. Also European populations seem to have used the genealogical construct. One should think of the 'segmentary lineage' principle as a construct, as a way to organise things on the ground.

Further, anthropologists have counter-examples. Giorgio describes populations which are different from Evans-Pritchard's Nuer who are not as pastoral as Giorgio's people. The idea of 'segmentary lineage' is used to unite people who differ tremendously. Obviously groups organise themselves on the basis of clans. People he studied are genealogical groups without segmenting. It is good to recognise that variety of pastoralists and the way descent is used.

AUSENDA: The Beni Amer too had groups characterised by sections of a dominant clan and clients. They interacted according to the relationship between sections of dominant clans. In faet, households belonging to client clans were dispersed among sections of the dominant clan.

TURTON: Among the Nuer, the lineage is not a local group. The Langobards obviously had a descent construct but this could have had other uses apart from group recruitment. It would be wrong to assume that, because they had a descent construct, they necessarily had groups that were recruited by means of it. The *fara* may simply have been a local group of assorted kin and affines organised around an 'agnatic core'.

AXBOE: The Langobards were in a migratory situation. This may perhaps have made them cluster into groups and made lineages more important than they had been before.

DUMVILLE: How much anthropological work has been devoted to migration?

TURTON: Anthropologists—and I am thinking here of Africanists—have had a lot to say about labour migration, especially in southern and central Africa, but very little about the interpretation of traditions of origin. Rural-urban migration was one of the major preoccupations of the so-called Manchester School in the nineteen fifties and sixties— such authors as Max Gluckman, Clyde Mitchell and Bill Epstein. Later on David Parkin wrote about rural-urban migration by Luo in Uganda and Kenya. But anthropologists have not had much to say about the kind of movements which people describe in their oral traditions. This is no doubt because of the general anthropological assumption that oral history tells us more about present interests than past events. African historians have led the way here, notably J. Vansina who developed a methodology for interpreting traditions of origin (1965, 1971). A good example of an attempt to interpret the traditional history of a single group is J. Lamphear's The *Traditional History of the Jie of Uganda* (1976). Raymond Kelly, an American anthropologist, wrote a book called *The Nuer Conquest* (1985) in which he tried to use archival material to explain the causes and mechanisms of Nuer expansion in the nineteenth century. Gunther Schlee's *Identities on the Move* (1989), about what he calls 'interethnic clan identities' in northern Kenia remains one of the few examples I know of a book by an anthropologist which takes a long-term movement and migration as its prime focus of interest.

AXBOE: I would be careful about your linguistic arguments for the Langobards as pastoralists. The fact that Romans had the word *pecunia* for 'money' does not make them pastoral. In Iron Age southern Scandinavia, although the villages moved slowly through the centuries, they actually remained in each place for one or more generations, and their inhabitants were farmers. I do not know about Langobards, but of course their special situation may have made cattle more important.

GREEN: The relationship between cattle economy and money economy need not be unidirectional (from the former to the latter). The reverse process can be detected in the Gothic tvord for a coin, *skatts*: in going from Gothic to Slavonic it came to mean 'cattle'.

BALZARETTI: What is the evidence of the primacy of pastoralism in the early period? In reference to cattle one should take into account how many. Maybe there were very few.

Archaeological work tends to find only pigs. Cattle do not predominate. Large stock seems to consist primarily of horses.

AUSENDA: In my discussion on the importance of pastoralism among the Langobards at the time of migration I did not imply that their pastoralism was confined to breeding cattle. I referred to all types of livestock, cattle, horses, pigs, etc.

SCHÜTTE: Archaeology has shown that in northern Germany settlements moved slowly.

AXBOE: One should perhaps rely more on archaeology and not trust Caesar in every detail, he was influenced by the biases of classical ethnography concerning barbarians (Lund 1993:3-98).

AUSENDA: I agree that archaeology is important. However, I do not believe it can be used to prove the *absence* of given features, as it is quite possible that these features were not found yet. Regarding Caesar, I hope I made the point in my paper (page 37 ff.) that, in reference to the *Germani*'s custom of changing abodes for cultivation purposes, Caesar made express inquiries with local informants, so that his testimony can not be simply dismissed by saying that he was influenced by classical sources, as he also inquired with local individuals. One would have to go on to say that he did not understand the local peoples' explanations. Furthermore there are ethnological examples of contemporary societies using the same procedure.

WOOD: I wish to make a few points. First, concerning the term 'nomadic pastoralists', I am happiest when the qualification 'nomadic' is left out. While the ethnography of migrations is exciting, one should leave nomadism on one side.

Second, law-codes are difficult texts. Originally they were thought to describe Germanic society. More recently a Greek code has been used to argue that provincial law served as a guide for the drafting of Germanic laws. Thus, laws do not necessarily reflect the tradition that was brought in by the barbarians.

Third, in support of the consideration that Langobardic lineages had both agnatic and matrilineal features I wish to cite Fredegar who wrote about royal succession, showing how the Franks had an interest in matrilineal descent among the Langobard royal families, in particular with the descendants of Theodelinda, considered a Frankish-related princess.

Fourth, on *faramanni* in the Burgundian code, law 54 is problematical in terms of date. There must have been laws issued by Burgundian kings from the late fifth century onwards. The code itself, which includes earlier laws, was issued on March 29th 517 by Sigismund (I argued the case for the date in a volume called *The settlement of disputes in the early Middle Ages,* Wendy Davies and Paul Fouracre (eds.)). Almost immediately some laws were appended to the original collection, e.g. 52, which was promulgated on the same day that the law code was issued. Some time later, perhaps in the 520s, a final group of laws was added to the code (the so called *constitutiones extravagantes*). The fact that the law dealing with *faramanni* comes after law 52 could make it a law of 517 or later; though not much later, because it is not one of the *constitutiones extravagantes*. On the other hand law 54 may just have been omitted from the original collection. It cannot, however, have been issued by the first generation of Burgundian kings, since it refers to predecessors. Nor can it refer to the earliest period of Burgundian settlements, since it envisages earlier gifts by the legislator and by his predecessors. All you can say is that law 54 proves that there were *faramanni* among the Burgundians by *ca* 517, and it implies that they were one of the elements in the settlement of the Burgundians, which had begun half a century earlier. This neither helps nor hinders your case, but I hope the comments are of some use.

Fifthly, I found that your critique agrees more or less with Murray's. In his approach Murray is perhaps less precise than you are, but his is still a significant book, not least because he clarified what had become amongst historians a very muddled understanding of such terms as 'agnatic' and 'cognatic'.

AUSENDA: Concerning your first point, I believe I made it clear that nomadism was not particularly significant as pastoralism embraced the entire spectrum from total nomadism to total sedentarisation. The important feature in the discussion is pastoralism, not nomadism.

Concerning your second point, it is quite likely that there were laws concerning livestock in provincial collections; my point is that, in the earliest Langobardic collection, laws concerning livestock are twice as numerous as those concerning agriculture and hunting. It might be interesting to compare this with the proportions in Roman collections of provincial laws.

Concerning your fifth point I agree that my conclusions are similar to Murray's. However, I do not believe that because of its inherent cognatic aspects the concept of *fara* should be thrown out altogether. On the contrary, I believe that it should be studied in greater detail to arrive at a thorough grasp of its early significance and historical evolution which may prove to be quite interesting for the understanding of early site distributions, kinship, relations between free born men, clients and slaves, of the social structure in general and economics.

HINES: The concepts of nomadism and pastoralism should not be thrown out altogether. They may not exist in pure forms anywhere, but could still be real enough as dominant characteristics of cultures that provide informative analogies for the study of the early Middle Ages.

The apparent wealth of evidence for predominantly settled communities comes from northern Germany and Scandinavia, not from southern Germany. Further south the assumption of stable settlements is based on the archaeology dominated by evidence from burial sites that appear to be stable over several generations. Is that a phenomenon that is incompatible with nomadic-pastoral groups? Is there any anthropological study of the funerary behaviour typical of such peoples? My question is directed at the possibility of detecting some degree of nomadism.

SCHÜTTE: So far archaeology does not have an answer. The area in question is very widespread. Traces of pastoral subsistence might consist of single buildings or huts spread over wide areas in small groups, as their bones indicate. These were scattered types of settlements, not dense groups. Maybe these are the groups to look for.

TURTON: I suggest that the important points are (1) the recognition that corporate groups had cognatic features; (2) one should not worry whether the Langobards were pastoral or not since we can find segmentary lineages among sedentary populations; and (3) endogamy is not a necessary feature of the segmentary lineage.

AUSENDA: On endogamy, I hope I made it clear that endogamy was not a necessary feature of those societies as exogamy was also present in some (see page 23).

GREEN: A few differences in English language usage have come up today, for example the distinction between Germans and *Germani*. To use one for the other introduces ambiguities.

References in the discussion

Textual sources:

Fredegar
> *Fredegarii Chronica:* see Krusch 1888.

Bibliography:

Herlihy, D.

1969   Family Solidarity in Medieval Italian History. In *Economy, Society, and Government in Medieval Italy.* D. Herlihy *et al.* (eds.), pp. 173-184. Kent, OH: Kent State University Press.

1985   *Medieval Households.* Cambridge, MA: Harvard University Press.

Jørgensen, L.

1992a   Castel Trosino and Nocera Umbra: A chronological and social analysis of family burial practices in Lombard Italy (6th-8th century A.D.). *Acta archaeologica* 62: 1-58.

1992b   The early medieval family in Europe: Studies of family burial practices in North-Germanic, Merovingian and Lombard societies. In *Medieval Europe 1992, Death and Burial, Pre-printed papers* 4: 23-28.

Kelly, R.

1985   *The Nuer Conquest: The Structure and Development of an Expansionist System.* Ann Arbor, MI: The University of Michigan Press.

Krusch, B. (ed.)

1888   *Fredegarii et aliorum Chronica. Vitae sanctorum. Monumenta Germaniae Historica. Scriptores rerum Merovingicarum , 2.* Hanover, Hahn.

Lamphear, J.

1976   *The Traditional History of the Jie of Uganda.* Oxford: Clarendon Press.

Lund, A. A.

1993   *De etnografiske kilder til Nordens tidlige historie.* Århus: Århus University Press.

Schlee, G.

1989   *Identities on the Move: Clanship and Pastoralism in Northern Kenya.* Manchester: Manchester University Press.

Vansina, J.

1965   *Oral Tradition: A Study of Historical Methodology.* Chicago: Aldine.

1971   "Once Upon a Time": Oral Tradition as History of Africa. *Daedalus* 100: 442-468.

Wenskus, R.

1961   *Stammesbildung und Verfassung: das Werden des frühmittelalterlichen Gentes.* Köln: Böhlau Verlag.

Wood, I. N.

1986   Disputes in late fifth- and sixth-century Gaul: some problems. In *The Settlement of Disputes in the Early Middle Ages.* W. Davies & P. Fouracre (eds.), pp. 7-22. Cambridge: Cambridge University Press.

AN ARCHAEOLOGY OF ANGLO-SAXON ENGLAND

JULIAN D. RICHARDS

Department of Archaeology, University of York, King's Manor, York YOI 2EP

Archaeology can nowadays be defined as the systematic study of human material culture.[1] It should therefore be seen as a set of methods rather than either a programme for research or a body of knowledge. The discipline of Archaeology is defined by the source of its data rather than by its goals. Its techniques of data-recovery and analysis are applicable to the study of past societies, in the service of history, or to the study of contemporary societies, in the service of sociology and social anthropology. Its methods differ from those of History or Linguistics in that it is not normally concerned with spoken or written language; and from those of Anthropology or Sociology in that it is not able to make use of participant observation.

What Are Archaeological Data?

Archaeologists are therefore concerned with 'things', and the relationship of these 'things' to human behaviour. Where archaeologists are investigating past societies these things have normally, but not always, been buried underground. Such burials may have been deliberate or accidental. Graves and hoards are therefore intentional statements, although the latter may often have been buried with the intention of recovery, whereas collapsed buildings or rubbish middens are accidents of deposition. Standing buildings, stone sculptures and other works of art are also archaeological evidence.

In order to be able to say anything useful about the things which they study, archaeologists need to be able to identify the human activity which goes with them. However, this is a far from simple process, and any such statement will always be a theory rather than a fact.

First, only a small part of human activity involves physical things. In the basic human action of dying, only a small part of death-related behaviour stands any chance of being incorporated into the archaeological record (see Bartel 1982). Weeping, mourning, feasting, graveside vigils and other ceremonial actions will rarely leave material traces. Only burial is certain to have a physical consequence. Thus only a small and non-random subset of human activities will have a material result.

Secondly, of those artefacts used, only a small and non-random subset will be incorporated into the archaeological record. Most will be of sufficient value to be retained for future use. Of those objects discarded some may be re-used by others in a different context; others will be subject to animal, chemical and physical attrition before they are buried. Only in extreme cases, such as volcanic eruption or shipwreck, are the complete material-culture sets of a society or part of a society incorporated into the record.

---

[1]   Human material culture should be taken to mean anything made or modified by human action; it, therefore, includes artefacts, burials and structures, as well as ecofacts and the effect of human beings on their environment.

AFTER EMPIRE:
TOWARDS AN ETHNOLOGY OF EUROPES'S BARBARIANS

Thirdly, of those artefacts which make it into the archaeological record, only a small and non-random subset will survive to the present day for archaeologists to find. Chemical and physical processes will each act on the deposits, both immediately and through time. Survival rates will be subject to the speed of deposition and burial, the water content of the deposit, the chemistry of the deposit, subsequent animal activity, subsequent human activity, the material of the artefact in question and whether it is durable or non-durable, and finally, the length of burial.

Fourthly, of those artefacts which do survive to the present day, only a small and non-random subset will be recovered by archaeologists. Highly visible artefacts, such as burial mounds, may benefit from relatively high recovery rates, but hoards, post-hole buildings, and burials which leave no physical monument, will only be found by chance. Here the important factors will be the nature of subsequent land-use (quarrying, pasture, arable, etc.) and its susceptibility to archaeological-discovery techniques (aerial photography, field-walking, metal-detecting, etc.), as well as the geographical location and archaeological interests of those responsible for recovery.

Therefore, archaeologists have to deal with at least four stages of filtering of their evidence: behavioural, depositional, post-depositional and recovery-related (Schiffer 1987). At each stage in the process a biased sample of evidence is passed on to the next stage. This makes fairly depressing reading, and one may be left thinking that there is little justification for the expenditure of large sums of public and private money, except that it is fun.

However, the picture is not quite so bleak in that the filtering processes are non-random. Physical and chemical processes act on the data in a regular and quantifiable fashion, according to the science of taphonomy. Even animal attrition can be quantified (e.g. Binford 1981). Similarly the effectiveness of various recovery techniques is measurable, as are the interests and areas of work of archaeologists. Therefore it is theoretically possible to define a series of 'visibility templates' which indicate the direction and level of bias in the final three stages of bias in the filtering process (Carver 1990).[2] However, it is at the first stage of bias, at the level of the original human activity and its associated artefacts, that it is most difficult to develop scientific laws which govern human behaviour.

There is a complex relationship between human-beings and artefacts. The study of this relationship has led to major debates in the archaeological literature, ranging between those who see artefacts as simple extra-somatic adaptations to the environment (functionalists), and those who see artefacts as non-verbal forms of communication which may even be actively used in the construction and reconstruction of the social reality (post-processualists). Many archaeologists have fallen back upon the study of material culture in contemporary societies (ethnoarchaeology and garbage archaeology) as a means of observing the relationship between people and things, allowing them to develop what they term a 'middle range theory'.[3] Until such a theory can be defined then there is a major stumbling block or 'black box' in using archaeology to develop an understanding of human behaviour.

---

[2] Our own York Environs Project is attempting to define visibility templates for the archaeology around York as part of its study of the relationship between the Anglo-Saxon and Viking town and its hinterland. Geographical Information Systems (GIS) are employed to study the relationship of the distributions of archaeological finds and sites with those of soils, geology, archaeological work, urban development, and other potential biasing factors (Chartrand *et al.* 1993).

[3] The term 'middle range theory' was coined by Binford (1983) to cover research on material culture, depositional processes and the like, which he saw as independent of one's higher-level cultural theories.

What Does Archaeological Data 'Mean'?

The perceived relationship between human behaviour and material culture is therefore dependent upon the dominant theoretical stance, for which there have been perhaps three main contenders so far.[4]

Cultural historical archaeology

It was David Clarke (1968) who wrote that "Archaeology is Archaeology is Archaeology", implying that the discipline had a distinct method which differentiated it from related subjects. This method rests upon a single concept, which, although it can be traced to earlier writers, owes its clearest definition to Gordon Childe. The concept is that of the 'archaeological culture', which has been the basic building block, in one shape or form, in all subsequent archaeological research. Although rejecting any simple racial or linguistic interpretation of cultures, Childe believed that a culture represented what he called a 'people':

> We find certain types of remains - pots, implements, ornaments, burial rites, house forms constantly recurring together. Such a complex of regularly associated traits we shall term a 'cultural group' or just a 'culture'. We assume that such a complex is a material expression of what would today be called a 'people'. Only where the complex in question is regularly and exclusively associated with skeletal remains of a specific physical type would we venture to replace 'people' by the term 'race' (Childe 1929:v-vi).

The normative view of culture is that common patterns of behaviour, or 'norms', produce spatial regularities in material remains:

> Community of tradition imposes on all members of the society in question a common pattern of behaviour. This must result in the production of standard types, which, if they be artifacts, burial rites or remains of repasts, archaeology can identify (Childe 1956:9-10).

Similarities and differences between cultures were interpreted in terms of diffusion or population movement, allowing the writing of a rather limited 'cultural historical' archaeology.

Functionalism

A radical reinterpretation of the 'meaning' of archaeological cultures developed from the influence of anthropological structural-functionalism on archaeology, particularly in North America, where the disciplines were not distinguished. For functionalists, culture was seen as the means by which a society became adapted to its situation. Thus Radcliffe-Brown saw funerary ritual as an expression of group solidarity:

> A person occupies a definite position in society, has a certain share in the social life, is one of the supports of the network of social relations. His death constitutes a partial destruction of the social cohesion, the normal social life is disorganised, the social equilibrium is disturbed. After the death the society has to organise itself anew and reach a new condition of equilibrium (Radcliffe-Brown 1922:285).

Under extreme examples of the functionalist approach, such as ecological functionalism, such adaptation was seen purely in terms of adaptation to the environment.

---

[4] For a more detailed discussion of interpretative traditions in Archaeology see Hodder (1992) and Trigger (1989).

Functionalist interpretations in archaeology were linked with systems theory, processualism and the desire for scientific testability under the banner of the "New Archaeology". In the United States they were associated especially with Lewis Binford (1972), in the United Kingdom with David Clarke (1968). Culture was now seen as an adaptive system. Among the central tenets of the New Archaeology was the denial of any basic limitations to our knowledge of the past. Binford argued against the pessimistic view prevalent in the 1950s and epitomised in Hawkes' 'ladder of inference' (1954) that archaeologists could come to reliable conclusions only about the technology and economy of past societies, while social organisation was mainly beyond the limits of the data, and ideology and religion entirely so.

However, the role of material culture in the system was not always clear. In some designs it formed a separate sub-system, interacting with the economic sub-system, the social sub-system, and the ideological sub-system, with all the sub-systems being constrained by the environment; in other conceptions material culture was outside each of the sub-systems while environment was beyond the system altogether. In each case there were difficulties in explaining change, other than from external stimulus, and in defining system and sub-system boundaries, as well as basic theoretical objections to the perception of human beings as adaptive organisms responding to stimuli as if they were merely laboratory rats. The basic disagreement was whether the fundamental definition of humanity should be that of 'tool-makers' or 'language-users'.[5]

Post-processualism

It is more difficult to characterise post-processualist approaches in Archaeology, but most have in common the idea that material culture is not just a passive response to the environment but rather that it is an active participant in the production and reproduction of society. Structuralists have adopted a linguistic analogy for material culture:

> All the various non-verbal dimensions of culture, such as styles in clothing, village lay-out, architecture, furniture, food, cooking, music, physical gestures, postural attitudes and so on are organised in patterned sets so as to incorporate coded information in a manner analogous to the sounds and words and sentences of a natural language (Leach 1976:10).

In societies with a strong oral tradition material culture is frequently used to store and pass on information and, given its relative permanence, it may be used as an alternative to writing. In order to translate the message, one needs to understand the conventions which apply, although the 'grammar' of non-verbal communication is simpler than that of language. Like words, symbols do not occur in isolation: a symbol is always a member of a set of contrasted symbols which function within a specific cultural context.

Material-culture symbols are less logical and more dependent upon context than meanings in language. Symbols may also be appropriated by particular cultural groups. Material culture meanings are often ambiguous; speech and writing are both linear forms of communication; on the other hand, with material culture there is no fixed direction in which to read a message. The meaning of symbols can also change through time. A Roman object in an Anglo-Saxon grave may be used to evoke stereotyped images of an imperial past. The meaning of symbols are not intrinsic to them. They become established through cultural tradition; one reads meaning into, not out of, a text (Richards 1992).

---

[5] 'Language-users' in the sense that artefacts can be interpreted, adapting a linguistic metaphor to material culture, as tools for thinking about the world.

But symbols are not just a means of communication. As Bourdieu (1979) has noted, they also function as an instrument for knowledge and construction of the world. In other words, symbolic systems operate to categorise information as an aid to the regulation and direction of appropriate behaviour. Language is just one means by which the world is classified and made understandable and controllable. Artefacts are also tools for thinking about the world.

To this end, we may generate abstract ideas in our heads, such as the opposition between good and bad, and then give these abstractions manifest form by projecting them into the external world, for example by projecting them into the colour difference, black vs white. This is part of thinking. By converting ideas into artefacts we make them concrete and can manipulate them.

Finally, artefacts are not only a passive symbolic reflection of the world. They are used to constitute and change it. Bourdieu (1979) has written that symbolism establishes and legitimates the dominant culture.

> Material culture is thus an active participant in the construction of the social system, and its meaning is internal to that system (Barrett 1981:206).

> Reality is not reflected by language or material culture as much as actively produced by it (Shanks *et al.* 1987:98).

Thus Childean cultures are given new significance, not as passive reflections of the political geographies of their time, but as active weapons in the hands of those constructing those geographies.

The Role of Archaeology in Relation to the Early Medieval Period

The cultural-history model has dominated twentieth-century Anglo-Saxon archaeology, principally through the work of two men: J. N. L. Myres and E. T. Leeds. Both wished to contribute to the history of the period, for which a chronological and geographical framework became necessary. Therefore, both treated archaeological sites (principally cemeteries) which they used in two ways. First, grave-goods became the basis of typological dating, and secondly they served as dots on a distribution map. By comparing distributions of classes of grave-goods, the growth and spread of archaeological cultures could be traced, with the added advantage that these could be related to the historically named peoples of Bede's *Ecclesiastical History* (e.g. Leeds 1912, 1933; Myres 1969).

The impact of the 'New Archaeology' on the study of the early medieval period has been less, and later, than for Prehistory, perhaps because the close relationship of Archaeology and History in reference to the early medieval period has acted as a constraint on development. However, Anglo-Saxon archaeology in the 1980s has been characterised by an explosion in publication of both data (namely site reports) and interpretation. In particular, the development of alternative theoretical approaches has embraced Anglo-Saxon data, in a way in which it did not in the 1970s, so that the study of the period has involved a lively debate between 'cultural historians', processualists, contextualists, and structural Marxists (see, for example, Arnold 1980, Hines 1984, Pader 1982, Richards 1987, Saunders 1991). But there is no consensus and so no common platform for research, and, while new approaches involve asking questions in a new way and so lead to new types of data, their requirements often seem too demanding for field archaeology at present.

There has been a growing consensus on the extent of political and economic change in late Anglo-Saxon England, shown both territorially and institutionally and reflected in the written sources. We are also beginning to understand the 'Middle Saxon' period much better, but may have to accept that the early Anglo-Saxon period is *pre*-historic—a major methodological issue for long-term historical and regional studies of landscape units.

There have been few advances in answering the big questions in the early period. With characteristic understatement the English Heritage *Exploring our Past* policy-document of 1991 says:

> The nature of the Roman decline in the province of Britain is not well understood. Neither is the influx and settlement of immigrants from across the North Sea.

The continued lack of success in answering what are historical questions should perhaps prompt us to muse whether the questions are couched in the right terms, or whether they should be posed at all. My own position is that archaeological data are mostly unsuitable for writing traditional history and that it may be more fruitful to examine questions of beliefs and customs. Here I think that a post-processualist approach offers the most productive methodology. I shall attempt to demonstrate this with a case study.

Gender, Age, Status and Identity in Anglo-Saxon England

My own research has focused upon the role of symbolism in Anglo-Saxon burial (Richards 1987). An Anglo-Saxon burial can be interpreted as a complex piece of communication. On one level it signifies ideas of the afterlife and the needs of the dead. On another level, the grave represents the identity of the deceased. It might be said that the symbols indicate the status of the deceased, although this begs the question of how status is defined.[6]

It is the task of the analyst to attempt to identify those aspects of identity which are represented in the burial rite. These may include gender, age set, wealth, and kin group, as well as race and tribal and sub-tribal groupings. But it is important to remember that these are all cultural constructs, rather than natural categories. Mortuary behaviour reinforces cultural differences and helps classify Anglo-Saxon society. It is a means of describing and defining social identity.

The symbols may also be instruments of domination, asserting one group's view of the world. The 'message' put forward by fifth-century burial rites in England is of a homogeneous society practising Germanic forms of burial. On the basis of the cemetery evidence, one might be forgiven for accepting at face value the account given by Gildas (see Dumville, this volume) that the native inhabitants of sub-Roman Britain were massacred and that such survivors as there were sought refuge in the west of the country. There is still plenty of room for debate over the scale of the Anglo-Saxon settlement. Not all archaeologists would accept the minimalist view of the scale of migration (e.g. Arnold 1984, Higham

---

[6] The term 'status' is also potentially misleading because it can be taken to imply that society was hierarchical, and grave-goods have been used as reflections of status in crude wealth-score analyses in attempts to define social ranking (e.g. Arnold 1980). In fact there is nothing in Anglo-Saxon cremation cemeteries which would contradict the notion that early Anglo-Saxon society was egalitarian, although no doubt some people were more important than others. Nevertheless, it is also important to remember that grave-goods may reflect who you would like to be, rather than who you are.

1992, Hodges 1989) but few, on the other hand, would be prepared to accept that the indigenous population was completely wiped out. There is sufficient continuity in place names and land-holding patterns to indicate some survival, and there is also the suggestion that building types in Anglo-Saxon settlements owe much to native building traditions (e.g. Dixon 1982).

In England, there is nothing to suggest a substantial influence of urban populations during the post-Roman period, although some towns may have become the administrative centres of large agricultural estates. We are forced, therefore, to accept that the sub-Roman British population became archaeologically invisible in death, not through survival or recovery factors (see above) but because they adopted a Germanic burial rite (e.g. Hills 1979). The burial rite is asserting the domination of Germanic culture, not the annihilation of the previous inhabitants. In order to understand symbols, therefore, one must be as aware of what is missing as of what is present. Germanic burial takes its meaning from the absence of Romano-British burial.

Wherever possible, cemetery assemblages must also be viewed in the context of the objects in associated settlements. One clear contrast is the absence of tools, and the emphasis upon weapons, in Anglo-Saxon inhumation burials. Iron tools are found in domestic contexts but almost never in Anglo-Saxon inhumation graves. This does not mean that smithing and farming were unimportant to Anglo-Saxons, but rather that they did not choose to symbolise them in death. At West Stow, awls, spindlewhorls and other tools are rarely represented in the neighbouring cemetery, despite being common finds in the settlement. In the cemetery weapons and brooches are common, although bracelets are not. Clearly some items were appropriate grave-goods, and other were not. Artefacts were selected to symbolise some aspects of social identity, such as the warrior, and to ignore others. Heinrich Härke's study of weapon burials has revealed that many of those buried with weapons were unlikely to have been warriors; they include the old and the young, and even those suffering from debilitating physical conditions (Härke 1992). Again we see the symbol as instrument of domination.

Anglo-Saxon Cremation Burial

Anglo-Saxon cremation burials constitute one of the richest data sets for early Anglo-Saxon England. Most people dying in England from AD 400 to 650 could expect to be cremated. Although the inhumation cemeteries are numerically superior, the majority seem to have contained fewer than a hundred burials, while a cremation cemetery typically contains several hundred and frequently several thousand burials.

Cremation burial was common in Roman Britain, although it appears to have lost popularity towards the end of the Roman period, large late Roman cemeteries, such as Lankhills near Winchester, consist almost entirely of inhumation burials (Clarke 1979). However, the arrival of Germanic immigrants seems to have led to the reintroduction of the cremation rite in what is now England.

The sites of funeral pyres have rarely been clearly identified in England, although it has been suggested that there was one at Sancton, Yorkshire (Myres *et al.* 1973), and another at Snape, Suffolk (Carnegie *et al.* forthcoming). This has led to the suggestion that the bodies must have been cremated elsewhere and brought to the cemetery as a collection of ashes (Kirk 1956). This would certainly have been the obvious answer to the problem of transporting a body and fuel to a central cemetery site, which may have been some distance from the settlement of the deceased. A number of pyres, apparently one for each burial, have been excavated in the North German cemetery of Liebenau (Hässler 1990).

Cremation burial would, in fact, have been more labour intensive than inhumation, demanding the collection of considerable amounts of firewood. The most effective method of constructing the pyre would probably have been to erect a low platform of the more substantial timbers, upon which the body would have been placed. More timber, including lighter brushwood, would then have been heaped over and around the body. Given the amount of fuel required, it seems probable that, on occasion, more than one body may have been cremated at once. This may be one explanation for the fact that the remains of more than one individual are sometimes found in the cremation burial.

Once ignited, the pyre would fairly rapidly have reached a temperature of *ca* 800° C, the normal temperature for a substantial open bonfire. However, the evidence for the fusing of glass and the vitrification of sand suggests that considerably higher temperatures were sometimes reached, well in excess of 1000° C. Once alight the body would itself burn well, the body fats contributing to the heat of the pyre. A distinctive cremation clinker has been identified in many cremation burials, probably caused by the fusing of bits of burnt bone and other objects on contact with the sandy ground (Henderson *et al.* 1987).

It appears that once the ashes had cooled, the fragments of burnt bone and fused objects with which the corpse had been decked were deliberately and meticulously collected. Substantial pieces of bone would often have survived the cremation process, and recognisable fragments of the skull and leg bones appear to have been particularly carefully gathered. Examination of these burnt remains can often tell us the sex of the deceased, and sometimes provides a rough age as well. Careful study of the cremated bone from Spong Hill has revealed that the extremities of the body, particularly the feet, were less thoroughly burnt, suggesting that they may have been left sticking out of the pyre (McKinley 1989). Similarly, the shoulder blades are often not fully burnt, indicating that in such cases the corpse was lying flat on the ground, with the pyre built above and around it (Welch 1992).

The cremated bones from many sites also include the remains of a variety of animals. These appear to represent more than joints of meat from a funeral feast. Indeed, many are complete skeletons and appear to have been cremated on the same pyre as the human body. They most frequently include sheep and cow, but horse and pig are also common (Table 2.1). The remains of various wildfowl, as well as deer, dog and cat have also been identified. It seems to have been normal practice for a cremation to include just one class of animal. The animals appear to have been regarded as another class of grave-goods, as representatives of the possessions of the deceased.

Table 2.1
Numbers of animals included in cremation urns at Elsham

Species	Numbers
Sheep	49
Horses	37
Pig	15
Cattle	11
Birds	3
Deer	1

Once gathered together, the cremated remains were then generally buried in pottery vessels or cremation urns. Occasionally a glass vessel was substituted for a pottery one, and sometimes no container survives at all, the cremated bones apparently being placed directly in the ground. In order to bury a cremation, first a small pit would be excavated, generally only slightly larger than the urn itself. The pits were not deep, generally being found about half a metre below the surface, although erosion of the topsoil in exposed places has sometimes brought them closer to the surface, where they are vulnerable to ploughing. In fact, many cremation cemeteries have been located when the tell-tale potsherds have been brought up by the plough.

The urns were generally buried singly, but sometimes pairs of urns have been found in the same pit, and occasionally larger groups have been recorded, ranging up to seventeen urns in one pit from the cemetery at Spong Hill, Norfolk. Although these must have been buried together at one ceremony, this does not necessarily mean that the deaths occurred at the same time, as part of an epidemic perhaps. We may reasonably suppose that cremation must have followed shortly after death, but the cremated ashes could have been preserved for some time before being buried in their ultimate resting place. Similarities between the pottery vessels in paired burials, and combinations of male and female or of adult female and child, suggest that these grouped burials may sometimes represent family plots.

In most cemeteries the burials are found at least one metre apart, although they are rarely in rows or any other regular pattern, being apparently randomly spaced. However, they are rarely disturbed by later burials, and where this does occur it appears that deliberate care has been taken to avoid damaging the first burial, placing the later ones carefully over it or alongside it. This suggests, therefore, that the position of the cremations must have been indicated by some above-ground marker. There is rarely any archaeological trace of this, and although post-holes are sometimes identified in the cemeteries there is little to suggest that each burial had a marker post. The remains of cairns of stone and flint are sometimes recorded, although they have often been disturbed by ploughing. These would have formed miniature barrows over each burial plot, making them visible landscape features.

At some sites in southern England, such as Alton, Hampshire and Apple Down, East Sussex, there is evidence for the erection of wooden shelters over individual cremations (Down *et al.* 1990; Evison 1988). Square structures are also known in cemeteries of the late Roman and early Anglo-Saxon periods in North Germany and Holland. At Liebenau, where the preservation conditions were exceptional, evidence for burning suggested that these were platforms to support the funeral pyre (Cosack 1982). At Alton, however, the burnt material was confined to the central cremation pit, and the structures are more likely to have functioned as tombs or shelters.

The cremation urns appear to have been normally provided with a lid. Sometimes this was ceramic, of the same design as the pot, although one remarkable seated human figure has been found at Spong Hill. More often nothing survives of the lid, which must have been of some less durable material such as cloth or leather. As this decayed, the surrounding earth collapsed into the urn, as is shown by a layer of loose earth at the top of the vessel.

The urns are generally between half and three-quarters full of the remains of the cremation itself. These include the cremated skeleton, those dress ornaments such as beads and brooches which adorned the corpse on the funeral pyre, and sometimes a number of grave-goods, unburnt items which have been deliberately placed in the urn.

The cremation urns are themselves remarkable. Although somewhere approaching 10,000 vessels have now been excavated from England as a whole (with over 3,000 of these from a single site, Spong Hill), no two vessels have ever been found which are precisely the same. In some ways this is not surprising for the vessels are hand-made, being built up from coils of clay, and sometimes over a mould. Although we can never be sure who was responsible for making the pottery, most evidence from comparative ethnographies suggests that it is likely to have been women who were the potters, most probably producing individual vessels, to order, within their local residence groups. However, an important point is that the pots were produced to cultural norms which cross-cut such localised groups. On the one hand, there is considerable variation in the shape and size of the urns, which range from about 0.1 to 0.4 m. in height. Nevertheless, statistical analysis demonstrates that this variation exists within tightly defined boundaries of size, shape, and decoration, following certain rules or cultural norms. On the other hand, therefore, there is considerable conformity to a rigidly defined cultural model of the type of pot which could be produced, such as one might expect in a society in flux.

About 10% of the cremation urns are plain vessels but most are decorated. This is in contrast with pottery assemblages recovered from settlement sites which contain a higher proportion of plain vessels, as well as more obvious functional forms such as 'cups' and 'bowls'. Undoubtedly some cremation urns are simply reused cooking pots, and sooting around the base attests to their former use. However, it has been argued that most of the cremation urns were manufactured specifically for use in the funerary ritual (Richards 1987).

Care seems to have been taken when decorating these vessels to provide each with a distinctive design. Decoration was produced by a combination of incised lines, applied clay and stamped patterns, before the pot was fired. The incised lines frequently define horizontal bands, or fields, of decoration around the neck and shoulder of the pot, and may also form chevrons or arches on the sides of the vessel. Sometimes more complex patterns were produced, including runic or pseudo-runic designs. Extra clay could also be added to create a raised cordon, or frequently to produce raised bosses or lugs.

The incised fields and the bosses may then have themselves been decorated with stamped patterns. The stamp dies must have been made of wood or more usually bone. Some dies have been found, including examples from Lakenheath (Briscoe 1981), and one from a female grave (Hines, pers. comm.). These show that the desired pattern was cut, as a negative image, in the end of the bone tool. This was then repeatedly pressed into the surface of the pot before firing. A number of dies is often used in combination to produce quite elaborate patterns. The dies themselves exhibit a wide variety of patterns. Some appear to us to be purely geometric, although similar designs have a long tradition in the iconography of the north European peoples, having been traced back as far as Scandinavian Bronze Age rock carvings (Richards 1987). Others seem to carry some symbolic intent. These include the '*planta pedis*' motif, the imprint of a human foot, the '*wyrm*' or serpent motif, and runic stamps. Some common motifs recur in stamped and incised form. These include the swastika, frequently taken to be a symbol of the god Thor. Thus the decorated vessels can range from those with a single incised line to elaborate *Buckelurnen* combining stamps, bosses and lines in a complex pattern.

The use of distinctive dies has enabled the output of particular pottery workshops to be identified. These may be individual potters or schools of potters, but they frequently follow particular styles of decoration.[7] Some workshops were extremely prolific, and many

---

[7]   Microscopic analysis of fingerprints might throw more light on this problem, although in general the fabrics are too coarse to preserve such impressions.

examples of their work have been identified. At Spong Hill, for example, stamp group 7/12 consists of over 30 vessels identified in several areas of the cemetery (Hills *et al.* 1987). The output of some workshops, such as the so-called Sancton-Baston and Illington Lackford groups has been identified at a number of cemeteries, often spread over considerable distances (Green *et al.* 1981). It has been suggested that even where the same tools have not been used, particular care has been taken to create dies which would appear to be identical (Arnold 1983, 1988). Thus the form of the decoration was clearly important and it has been proposed that it might even have some heraldic significance.

Indeed, the whole cremation urn can be seen to be telling us about the deceased, in much the same way a Christian tombstone provides the name and age of the deceased, the family lineage, and sometimes details of the cause of death, as well as invocations for happiness in the 'afterlife'. Clearly it is infinitely more difficult to read an Anglo-Saxon cremation urn. Not only do we not understand the language, but the message has itself been distorted and fragmented in its transmission to us over the centuries. Nevertheless, by examining associations between the form and the decoration of the cremation urns and what we know of the deceased (from the grave-goods and skeletal remains), it may be possible to start to decipher the code (Richards 1987). Thus, the age of the deceased is reflected in the size of the cremation urn, although other factors should also be taken into account, with adult males with many grave-goods tending to be buried in larger vessels as well. Certain decorative motifs also appear to be saying something about the social identity of the deceased. Thus, for instance, the use of applied decoration, such as raised bosses, is linked with adults rather than children, males rather than females, and cows rather than sheep (Fig.2.1). Incised hanging

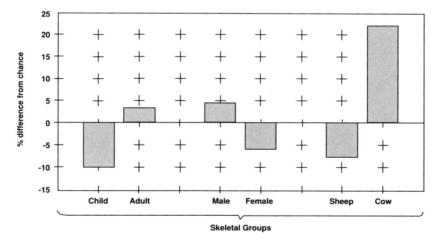

Fig. 2.1 - Use of applied decoration on Anglo-Saxon cremation vessels. Graph indicates percentage difference from chance for age (n=216), gender (n=70), and sheep vs cows (n=20).

arches are associated with children rather than adults, and females rather than males, while groups of diagonal lines are linked with adults and males. More work needs to be done before we understand the significance of all these symbols, but enough has already been done to demonstrate that the marks on the cremation vessels were an important component of the funerary ceremony and should not simply be regarded as decorative.

The implication of this work is that funerary vessels were probably manufactured with a particular individual in mind. This process may not necessarily have been a conscious one; it may be that certain designs were somehow considered suitable for certain individuals.

In all societies death is a traumatic event which destroys existing relationships and moulds new ones. Symbols were used in the mortuary ritual as statements, about the identity of the dead, which would have been understood by the Anglo-Saxon audience. They defined and maintained the structuring principles of Anglo-Saxon society, which rested partly upon biology but cannot be understood solely in those terms. Thus, while age and gender are the only aspects of social identity which can easily be correlated with other aspects of burial ritual, they do not provide a total explanation of the variability encountered. Gender appears to have been given primary importance, and age to a lesser extent, but neither of these factors can be seen to determine status.

The symbolic role of many of the grave-goods is also clear. Miniature tweezers and combs especially are generally unburnt and were, therefore, deliberately deposited in the urns. Frequently only token pieces are included, confirming that it is the symbolic presence which is important, not the functional use. So-called 'girdle-hangers' are common finds in female inhumations; they have been variously interpreted as symbolic copies of Roman keys, or as signifying the sexual act. Crystal balls are also found in female inhumation graves in Kent and the Isle of Wight, and have been associated with magical properties.

Grave-goods are also linked with aspects of decoration (Richards 1987). The differences from chance are not huge, but the sample size is large and they are statistically significant. Clear links cannot be expected given the element of noise and the difficulty of defining meaningful categories of decoration. Applied decoration is associated with bronze and iron tweezers, crystal beads and playing pieces (Fig.2.2). Stamped decoration is linked with glass vessels, but not with iron tweezers. In each case the same social groupings which are symbolised by particular grave-goods are also represented by the use of particular decorative styles.

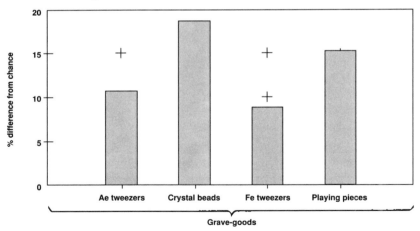

Fig.2.2 - Use of applied decoration on Anglo-Saxon cremation vessels (n=738). Graph indicates percentage difference from chance for four categories of grave goods.

I have suggested that the same symbolic motifs and grammatical rules used in pottery decoration are also found in bronze metalworking (Richards 1992). Superficially there appears to be little similarity between pots and brooches. This is despite the fact that at a micro-level there are some obvious similarities, for example in the selection of stamped motifs on pots and sixth-century annular and square-headed brooches. The problem is principally that of perception. It is conventional that Anglo-Saxon cremation vessels should be drawn in profile, as if they are symmetrical, with one side a repeat of another. However, by representing them in this fashion we make a nonsense of their intended appearance. The vessels were coil-built by a potter working from above; the need to lay out concentric circular fields of decoration demanded that they were decorated from above. And most importantly, when buried in a shallow urn pit as part of the mortuary ritual, they were designed to be viewed from above. Once the decoration is perceived as concentric bands of motifs then the parallels between pottery and metalwork become obvious. One can see, therefore, a transformation of a coded message from one medium to another, and in some cases a substitution of one medium for another.

Conclusion

The relationship between human behaviour and material culture is revealed to be extremely complex, and must be studied in context. The early Anglo-Saxon period provides an ideal testing ground in which to do this. Other disciplines can help provide archaeology with information of an 'ethnographic' character about the social and historical context of the period. As Driscoll (1988) has pointed out, if material culture can be read in complex ways we need a unified approach incorporating both archaeology and history. Written sources alone are incapable of providing complete social history, generally being too much the domain of the élite. Artefacts, being universal, provide the basis for an account which represents the majority of members of a past society. Neither artefacts nor texts alone can serve as a sufficient basis for constructing our image of the early historical past.

In non-literate societies, such as early Anglo-Saxon England, it is argued that pictorial symbolism may have played a particularly important role. The vacuum left by the decline of Roman power was filled by various competing groups, all emphasising their similarities or differences, both from each other, and from the Romano-British, with the aim of gaining cultural and political domination. The assertion of aspects of ethnic identity has frequently been documented in contemporary migrant contexts (e.g. Cohen 1974). The surviving native population was swiftly culturally subsumed and is archaeologically invisible. The newcomers were then left to fight it out among themselves in asserting their various cultural identities. In a society under stress social roles were also continually redefined and reinforced. One mechanism for asserting identity whether real or assumed was in mortuary behaviour. In Anglo-Saxon mortuary practices those connections with a non-Classical heritage were emphasised; Southern Scandinavian and other Germanic symbols abound in the ornamentation of the pottery and jewellery. Material symbols were employed to propagate the concept of a common past, and artefacts and mortuary behaviour were used to construct this new reality.

Acknowledgements—I am grateful to Giorgio Ausenda for the kind invitation to present this paper at the CIROSS seminar in San Marino in September 1993, and to the other participants for their constructive comments which I have endeavoured to incorporate.

References

Arnold, C. J.
   1980   Wealth and social structure: a matter of life and death. In *Anglo-Saxon Cemeteries
             1979*. P. Rahtz, T. Dickinson & L. Watts (eds.), pp. 81:142. (British Archaeological
             Reports, British Series 82). Oxford: B.A.R.
   1983   The Sancton-Baston Potter. *Scottish Archaeological Review 2* (1): 17-30.
   1984   *Roman Britain to Saxon England*. London: Croom Helm.
   1988   Early Anglo-Saxon Pottery of the 'Illington-Lackford' Type. *Oxford Journal of
             Archaeology 7* (3): 343-359.

Barrett, J. C.
   1981   Aspects of the Iron Age in Atlantic Scotland. A case study in the problems of archaeological
             interpretation. *Proceedings of the Society of Antiquaries of Scotland* 111: 205- 19.

Bartel, B.
   1982   A historical review of ethnological and archaeological analyses of mortuary practice.
             Journal of Anthropological Archaeology 1: 32-58.

Binford, L.
   1972   *An Archaeological Perspective*. New York: Seminar Press.
   1981   *Bones: Ancient Men and Modern Myths*. New York: Academic Press.
   1983   *In Pursuit of the Past*. London: Thames and Hudson.

Bourdieu, P.
   1979   Symbolic power. *Critique of Anthropology* 13 (4): 77-85.

Briscoe, T.
   1981   Anglo-Saxon pot stamps. In *Anglo-Saxon Studies in Archaeology and History 2*.
             D. Brown, J. Campbell & S. C. Hawkes (eds.), pp. 1-36. (British Archaeological
             Reports, British Series 92). Oxford: B.A.R..

Carnegie, S., & W. Filmer-Sankey
   n.d.   A Saxon Cremation Pyre from the Snape Anglo-Saxon cemetery, Suffolk (in press).

Carver, M. O. H.
   1990   *Digging for Data: Archaeological Approaches to Data Definition, Acquisition and
             Analysis*. Firenze: All'insegna del Giglio.

Chartrand, J., J. D. Richards & B. E. Vyner
   1993   Bridging the urban rural gap: GIS and the York Environs Project. In *Computer
             Applications and Quantitative Methods in Archaeology 1992*. T. Madsen (ed.),
             pp 159-166. Århus: Århus Univ. Press.

Childe, V. G.
   1929   *The Danube in Prehistory*. Oxford: Clarendon Press.
   1956   *Piecing Together the Past*. London: Routledge & Kegan Paul, Ltd.

Clarke, D. L.
   1968   *Analytical Archaeology*. London: Methuen & Co., Ltd.

Clarke, G.
   1979   *The Roman Cemetery at Lankhills*. Winchester Studies 3, Pre-Roman and Roman
             Winchester, Part 2. Oxford: Oxford University Press.

Cohen, A.
   1974   *Two-dimensional Man*. London: Routledge & Kegan Paul, Ltd.

Cosack, E.
   1982   *Das sächsiche Gräberfeld bei Liebenau, Kr. Nienburg (Weser),* Teil 1. (Germanische
             Denkmäler der Völkerwanderungszeit, ser. A 15). Berlin: Gebrüder Mann.

Dixon, P.
   1982   How Saxon is the Saxon house? In *Structural Reconstruction*. P. J. Drury (ed.),
             pp. 275-287. (British Archaeological Reports British Series 110). Oxford: B.A.R.

Down, A., & M. Welch
    1990   *Chichester Excavations 7: Apple Down and The Mardens.* Chichester: Chichester Civil Society Excavation Committee.

Driscoll, S. T.
    1988   The relationship between history and archaeology: artefacts, documents and power. In *Power and Politics in Early Medieval Britain and Ireland.* S. T. Driscoll & M. R. Nieke (eds.), pp. 162-187. Edinburgh: Edinburgh University Press.

Evison, V. I.
    1988   An Anglo-Saxon Cemetery at Alton. *Hampshire. Hampshire Field Club Monograph 4.*

Green, B., W. F. Milligan, & S. E. West
    1981   The Illington/Lackford workshop. In *Angles, Saxons, and Jutes: essays presented to J. N. L.Myres.* V. I. Evison (ed.), pp. 187-226. Oxford: Clarendon Press.

Härke, H.
    1992   Changing symbols in a changing society: The Anglo-Saxon weapon burial rite in the seventh century. In *The Age of Sutton Hoo.* M. O. H. Carver (ed.), pp. 149-165. Woodbridge: The Boydell Press.

Hässler, H-J.
    1990   *Das sächsiche Gräberfeld bei Liebenau, Kr. Nienburg (Weser), Teil 4.* Veroeffentlichungen der urgeschichtlicher Sammlungen des Landesmuseums zu Hannover. Hildesheim: Verlag A. Lax.

Hawkes, C. F. C.
    1954   Archaeological theory and method: some suggestions from the Old World. *American Anthropologist* 56: 155-168.

Henderson, J., R. C. Janaway & J. D. Richards
    1987   A curious clinker. *Journal of Archaeological Science* 14: 353-365.

Higham, N.
    1992   *Rome, Britain and the Anglo-Saxons.* London: Seaby.

Hills, C. M.
    1977   The Anglo-Saxon cemetery at Spong Hill, North Elmham, Part I. *East Anglian Archaeology* 6.
    1979   The archaeology of Anglo-Saxon England in the pagan period. *Anglo-Saxon England* 8: 297-329.

Hills, C. M., & K. Penn
    1981   The Anglo-Saxon cemetery at Spong Hill, North Elmham, Part II. *East Anglian Archaeology* 11.

Hills, C. M., K. Penn & R. Rickett
    1984   The Anglo-Saxon cemetery at Spong Hill, North Elmham, Part III. *East Anglian Archaeology* 21.
    1987   The Anglo-Saxon cemetery at Spong Hill, North Elmham, Part IV. *East Anglian Archaeology* 34.

Hines, J.
    1984   *The Scandinavian Character of Anglian England in the pre-Viking Period.* (British Archaeological Reports, British Series 124). Oxford: B.A.R.

Hodder, I.
    1992   *Reading the Past.* Cambridge: Cambridge University Press.

Hodges, R.
    1989   *The Anglo-Saxon Achievement.* London: Duckworth & Co., Ltd.

Kirk, J. R.
    1956   Anglo-Saxon cremation and inhumation in the Upper Thames Valley in pagan times. In *Dark Age Britain.* D. B. Harden (ed.), pp. 123-131. London: Methuen.

Leach, E.
   1976   Culture and Communication: *The logic by wich smbols are connected.* Cambridge:
                Cambridge University Press.
Leeds, E. T.
   1912   The distribution of the Anglo-Saxon saucer brooch in relation to the Battle of
                Bedford AD 571. *Archaeologia* 43: 159-202.
   1933   The early Anglo-Saxon penetration of the Upper Thames area. *Antiquaries Journal*
                13: 229-251.
McKinley, J
   1989   Spong Hill, Anglo-Saxon cremation cemetery. In *Burial Archaeology: Current
                Research, and Developments.* A. Roberts, F. Lee & J. Bintliff (eds.), pp. 241-248.
                (British Archaeological Reports, British Series 211). Oxford: B.A.R.
Myres, J. N. L.
   1969   *Anglo-Saxon Pottery and the Settlement of England.* Oxford: Clarendon Press.
Myres, J. N. L., & W. H. Southern
   1973   *The Anglo-Saxon Cremation Cemetery at Sancton, East Yorkshire.* (Hull Museums
                Publication No. 218). Hull.
Pader, E.-J.
   1982   *Symbolism, Social Relations and the Interpretation of Mortuary Remains.* (British
                Archaeological Reports, International Series 130). Oxford: B.A.R.
Radcliffe-Brown, A. R.
   1922   *The Andaman Islanders: A Study in Social Anthropology.* Cambridge: Cambridge
                University Press.
Richards, J. D.
   1987   *The Significance of Form and Decoration of Anglo-Saxon Cremation Urns.* (British
                Archaeological Reports, British Series 166). Oxford: B.A.R.
   1992   Anglo-Saxon symbolism. In *The Age of Sutton Hoo.* M. O. H. Carver (ed.),
                pp. 131-147. Woodbridge: The Boydell Press.
Saunders, T. S. A.
   1991   Marxism and archaeology: the origins of feudalism in early medieval England.
                Unpublished Doctoral Dissertation. York University.
Schiffer, M. B.
   1987   *Formation Processes of the Archaeological Record.* Albuquerque: University of New
                Mexico Press.
Shanks, M., & C. Tilley
   1987   *Social Theory and Archaeology.* Cambridge: Polity Press.
Trigger, B. G.
   1989   *A History of Archaeological Thought.* Cambridge: Cambridge University Press.
Welch, M.
   1992   *Anglo-Saxon England.* London: B. T. Batsford, Ltd.

Discussion

SCHÜTTE: Related groups of makers are probably related to certain family groups, and that means people working for the same workshop, the same people, the same chronological level. There is a new technique of searching for fingerprints in terracotta workshops to identify the potter. In Cologne we started to do this. I did not look inside the bottles of Anglo-Saxon oil, but I am convinced that there must be some fingerprints inside.

RICHARDS: It is an exciting idea. It is worth, perhaps, following up microscopically. Certainly, under a macroscopic examination it is unusual to find fingerprints preserved, mainly because of the nature of the fabric, the coarse clay, and the firing. Many vessels were burnished anyway.

SCHÜTTE: I mean from the inside, not from the outside.

RICHARDS: What has been done is to try to identify a group of pots made by the same person on the basis that the same tool may have been used for stamping the pot. However, work by Chris Arnold (1983, 1988) suggests that it is not an identical tool, but one that is very, very similar. This would reinforce the idea that certain stamps and designs are carefully selected, and that the reproduction of the same design is important, almost down to a microscopic level. If it is not the same tool that is being used then I think it must mean, nevertheless, that those pots represent, perhaps not the same workshop, but perhaps the same kinship group.

AUSENDA: I have a few remarks.

The first, concerns the following statement [page 57]:

> We are forced, therefore, to accept that the sub-Roman British population became archaeologically invisible in death, not through survival of recovery factors (see above) but because they adopted a Germanic burial rite (e.g. Hills 1979). The burial rite is asserting the domination of Gerrnanic culture, not the annihilation of the previous inhabitants.

In other words, you posit that the lack of differentiation in burial customs points to the fact that survivors of the Romano-British populations adopted Germanic customs. In your introduction you pointed out that archaeological distributions were non-random. Is it not possible that you have not found the Romano-British because you have not looked in the right places? According to Dr. Dumville's paper there still was a Romano-British population present in the sixth century, probably mainly in the cities. Is it possible that excavations conducted so far have not found their remains?

You say [page 60] that cremation vessels were hand-made. In the subsequent discussion there is no clarification as to whether the vessels were made by men, or by women, or both. When [page 62] you say that "...the same symbolic motifs and grammatical rules used in pottery decoration are also found in bronze metalworking", you seem to draw a parallel between pottery and bronze metalwork, undoubtedly a male activity. In my experience, amongst populations in eastern Sudan and Eritrea, hand-made pottery is manufactured by women following the widespread rule among non-literate populations that each gender manufactures the implements for its own activities. A man would never engage in pot making because pots are used mainly for cooking or storing food. Men take over when pottery making becomes a trade and is produced on the wheel or in moulds. Women potters belong to the same kin groups and make pots on request and without payment within the reciprocity network that characterises some of the exchanges in simple societies. It is quite likely that the same situation obtained among the Anglo-Saxons and that pots were made by women belonging to the kinship group of the deceased, and not made to specifications but according to the know-how and tradition of the potter belonging to the group affected.

You say [page 61] "...the use of applied decoration, such as raised bosses, is linked with adults rather than children, males rather than females, and cows rather than sheep", and in the course of your presentation you showed us charts with very evident correlations between age and gender on the one hand and related livestock bone deposits and funerary pottery decoration on the other. This is a very interesting observation. I would like to remark that, in my experience, at funeral feasts livestock is sacrificed and eaten. The value of the sacrificed livestock is related to the status of the deceased. Among both Hadendowa and Beni Amer men, have a higher status than women, and individuals who have come of age have a higher status than children. Thus, it seems obvious that you would find the bones of higher value livestock, such as cows and horses, associated with males, and lower value livestock, such as sheep or goats, associated with women or children. By the same token the more decorated vases would be associated with men, whilst the less decorated or plain ones would be associated with women or children. I think your observations are quite useful in showing the status situation with respect to gender and age among Anglo-Saxons, and I would relate it to this simple explanation.

RICHARDS: Concerning your first point, are you suggesting that the Romano-British were in settlements which are now under modern villages?

AUSENDA: No, I believe the Romano-British population were mostly in the cities, some cities.

RICHARDS: If they were living anywhere as Romano-British then, with the amount of archaeological work that has been carried out, they would have been found. The same applies to the towns, unless we are very wrong about the dating of the latest urban levels, and throw out a lot of the urban archaeology of the last twenty years, I think we would have found substantial remains of British people who were continuing to occupy towns. Now, there are a number of limited exceptions, but many of these can be explained in terms of localised villa-type centres of agricultural estates, with some cultivation within the former walled areas.

AUSENDA: When the Slavs came into Dalmatia close to present day Split, the Illyrian local population left Salona, some 20 km. inland, and sought refuge in Diocletian's fortified former palace (Nikolajevic 1983:809).

DUMVILLE: The problem is that in Britain the natives were in the countryside also to start with, they are not just urban.

AUSENDA: When the Slavs came into present day Yugoslavia, the natives left the countryside and gathered in cities along the seashore. I am not saying this is what happened in Britain.

GREEN: Your suggestion is that this flight from the countryside to the city did not take place in Britain?

DUMVILLE: I would rather support it the other way around, if anything.

RICHARDS: If anything, the evidence suggests that towns were being deserted as towns and that urban life was in decline from the third and fourth centuries AD.

AUSENDA: This discussion will not bring us closer to the truth. We must wait until the whole picture is clarified in positive terms by archaeology.

RICHARDS: There has been enough excavation in the centre of London and York to clarify it already.

AUSENDA: Have Saxon urns been found?

DUMVILLE and RICHARDS: They are abandoned.

AUSENDA: Are there no cemeteries?

DUMVILLE and RICHARDS: There is nobody.

AUSENDA: Another point. When missionaries came to Britain at the beginning of the sixth century, they established their centre in Canterbury, which is close to the sea, not in London. This suggests that there must have been a retreat towards the seashore. There must have been a demographic crisis and at the same time people trying to do as much as they could to maintain their independence. I believe the problem has not been solved. Just because you only find Saxon remains does not necessarily mean that there were only Saxons....

DUMVILLE: I would say that, but he is not.

AUSENDA: Or Britons assimilated with Saxons.

WOOD: Heinrich Härke has got some recent information. He and I are working on a paper on Wessex at the moment. What he has got is a very dramatic infiltration of tall people in cemeteries in the late fifth century, and you have a period of three generations when you have tall and small people in cemeteries. And he is arguing that the tall are Anglo-Saxons, the small are Britons and then after that period you get medium height, and it does look like intermarriage.

RICHARDS: It does sound too good to be true [laughter]. I prefer to remain sceptical about the interpretation of racial skeletal types.

WOOD: It is still very striking.

HINES: Actually, they shrank on baptism [laughter].

GREEN: As a sign of humility.

SCHÜTTE: I think body-height is not the one and only indicator. One should look very closely at inventories and physical anthropology could reveal more information; perhaps blood cells could be screened genetically to see what group they belong to, not just body height, that is too simple: blue-eyed and tall versus short and dark-haired British people.

A stronger argument.... I was most impressed by the quoting of Heinrich Härke with the variable *spina bifida*, which just reflects the burial rite.

WOOD: In fact the tall skeletons are the only ones that have grave goods. None of the others do.

RICHARDS: Could I deal with Dr. Ausenda's second and third questions very quickly? I do not see any problem with either of them. You say that pottery manufacture is often done by women within the kinship group to order. That fits exactly with the hypothesis which I have proposed. If it is so, then I do not see any reason why it should not be the women who preserve this cultural information in the case of pottery production, while the men preserve it in the case of metalworking. There is also the interesting idea that the urns were fired as part of the mortuary ritual on the same pyre on which the deceased was cremated. If so, then this might have interesting implications for female involvement in the funerary rite.

AUSENDA: Pottery firing is a very delicate operation: the pot must be dried a few days before firing, especially in a cold climate, and pots are not burned on top of a fire but resting on a cavity in the ground and enveloped by a mound of dry brush, with new brush constantly added.

RICHARDS: The temperature to which the pots were fired is identical to that which the cremated bones reached. It is possible to reach it on an open bonfire. It might be more economical in fuel if the same bonfire was used! You noted the differences between cattle and horses being proportional to status. I may have mislead you when I said that I did not think these animals were just the remains of funerary feasts. What I meant is that I do not think they were random collections of bones from the funerary feasts, rather that they were deliberately collected, and very definitely appropriate to the status of the individual concerned, just as aspects of the decoration were. In fact, you appear to be agreeing with my hypothesis that decoration is related to status. I do not believe that it is so obvious that it should be. The analysis provides a way of looking at status that would otherwise be observable from grave-goods; one can look at decoration instead. The meaning of status is perhaps a little bit more complicated; it is not just age and gender.

GREEN: You started off by linking your discipline of archaeology with anthropology. You will not take it amiss from me, I trust, if I link your discipline with mine on one or two points, where you refer explicitly to language—not in metaphorical use, when you talk about archaeological language, but in non-metaphorical use. I am not trying, as may at first appear, to pull down bridges between our two disciplines but, on the contrary, to establish what the nature of these bridges is and what kind of traffic they can bear.

First you have raised the age old question as to whether mankind is to be seen as comprising tool makers or language users. If the former, 'mankind as tool makers', falls within the scope of archaeology, can the same be said of the latter 'mankind as language users'?

RICHARDS: In a very simplified way I was trying to characterise the broad difference between what many people call the processualist approach in archaeology, which sees material culture as just an adaptation to the environment—that is, one makes tools in order to survive—, with the post-processualist view which sees the act of making the tool as a less passive response to the environment, more an active structuring of the world.

GREEN: In other words you are here using 'language' in a metaphorical application to archaeology. It looks a little bit ambiguous from the point of view of the philologist. Secondly, I noted your remark that "the grammar of non-verbal communication is simpler than that of written language". I am not convinced of that from the philological point of view and indeed from the literate point of view. I should add here that over the last sixteen years I have been working on orality and literacy. Therefore, I am doubly interested in this. As an example, consider Skaldic verse in Scandinavia, which is definitely of oral composition and of oral delivery, and the syntax of its language is phenomenally complicated. This shows that one cannot suggest that because linguistic communication is oral it must be syntactically simple.

RICHARDS: Yes, again it is my fault for not being precise. What I mean is that there is less scope—in that the decoration of a pot forms a very complex grammar in terms of what lines you can put on—than there is in the use of words.

HINES: Firstly, I would like to underline the point that Dr. Ausenda was making in his first question. I want to put the question of whether you have given enough attention to the possibility that all of the variables you are looking at reflect a simple situation in which—in quite a crude way—the people who are considered the more important are getting the more elaborate and the larger vessels. All of the examples you gave seem to me to be capable of explanation in this very simple way.

RICHARDS: If they are just related to status, then there is the onus on us to try and define what makes up that status.

HINES: Indeed it is, but the impression given is that the potter works with the explicit notion that "I am going to need a pot for a man of such and such a family, who is sufficiently old that he is probably going to get a cow burned with him, etc.". You have in fact referred to Chris Arnold, who has argued that these individual elements are individually responded to. I don't want to labour the point, but I do think that it should be paid more attention.

On the question of women making pots: I do know at least one Anglo-Saxon grave in which a pot stamp was buried as grave goods, and it was indeed a woman's grave (a cremation burial from Lackford, Suffolk). One should also remember that textile production is widely represented as a female activity in grave finds. If you examine the general distribution of artefacts concerned with craftwork, it seems to support the view that male and female are differentiated in this way.

On the question of the links between pottery decoration and metalwork, the point about the relation between pottery and annular brooches is, I think, a good one, though I would draw attention to certain limitations. There is other metalwork you can associate with pottery decoration. One of the most interesting examples, I think, is that of square-headed brooches, where one can certainly make a case that the linear forms of decoration that come to dominate on this prestigious form of brooch in the middle of the sixth century developed first on pottery. This raises an interesting point, because the square-headed brooches seem to be considerably more prestigious, expensive and exclusive artefacts. Annular brooches tend to be dated fairly late in the Migration period. They may have been around in the late fifth century but it is hard to prove the point. They are certainly much commoner as the sixth century goes on; as with the square-headed brooches, then, it may be some way into the sixth century that this relationship between pottery and brooches appears.

There are also some items of archaeological jargon that I believe would bear more explanation for a wider audience, for instance the notion of 'middle range theory'. I assume that 'middle range' implies some 'higher' and 'lower' or other such bracketing ranges. But I never see these other ranges referred to anywhere. What then is 'middle-range theory' in between, or is this in fact a theory of relationships between people and things—which is what you refer to when you introduce the term?

Elsewhere [page 53]: "Similarities and differences between cultures were interpreted in terms of diffusion...allowing the writing of cultural history". Some of us still call ourselves cultural historians, and indeed I would call what we are all gathered here together to do 'cultural history'. I would agree that diffusion and population movement can only be part oi cultural history and can be argued to be large and important phenomena with which cultural history can quite justifiably be pre-occupied, but I would not agree that cultural history is something that only explains things in those terms, which this sentence seems to suggest I would ask you to think about putting this another way.

Equally [page 54], the equation you seem to make between functionalism and processualism seems to me to be misleading. I understand processualism to be something quite different from functionalism, essentially in that functionalism is exclusively an analysis of synchronic and diachronic dimensions. I can see that there are both practical and theoretical connections but I do not think that they ought to be presented as the same thing.

RICHARDS: Perhaps I could respond to your points in reverse order. In broad term functionalists and processualists were part of the same school.

HINES: Certainly part of the same school. I agree.

RICHARDS: I agree there are differences in emphasis because functionalism is much broader. It is found in anthropology, while processualism was a term particularly adopted by a group of American archaeologists who were functionalists but were interested in process rather than in particularistic explanations. I take the point that it is worth clarifying.

I certainly did not intend to denigrate cultural history. I was talking about what people in the past had done with cultural history and criticised a sort of narrow approach that has been found most of the time.

HINES: Could I suggest that what you were talking about in that section might be better called cultural archaeology rather than cultural history?

RICHARDS: It may be, although the term cultural history has entered the archaeological literature to describe the Childean approach. It would be difficult to change the formula now.

DUMVILLE: But if you use that term as you were using it there, and speaking to a historian who called himself a cultural historian, he would not recognise what was going on.

RICHARDS: Right, certainly.

DUMVILLE: It seems to me that it is important to avoid the use of such ambiguous formulae, especially within an interdisciplinary readership context.

RICHARDS: Yes.

DUMVILLE: My concerns are with terminology and presentation, but (I hope) relating to some important issues.

I should like to start briefly on this question of British survival. I do not think that in my professional career I ever met a British archaeologist who thought at all in terms of what one may call genocide of the British population. Yet I have always been struck by how vehement the language is which is used by British archaeologists against that idea. I wonder why. Your insistence that the sub-Roman British population became archaeologically invisible in death because they adopted a Germanic burial rite seems to me to be part of that pattern. I think that, if that is going to be asserted so bluntly, it needs some underpinning. It seems to be fundamental to a lot of what you and others are talking about. It ties into your discussion of ideas of domination, and this word 'domination' meaning asserting one's group's view of the world. This seems to me to assume a rather feeble response on the part of those who might be, in that sense, the dominated. I take it that groups were asserting their view of the world in competition with one another. I am not quite sure that the act of assertion necessarily has much to do with domination. It is what follows from that assertion which would be critical and the context in which these actions are taking place.

Lastly, I recall that, in introducing your paper, you described ritual as being the sacred and not the profane. I was thinking of what David Turton said earlier about using the word 'ritual' which suggested to me that for an anthropologist it has a very much broader meaning than that. And I wonder whether there could be some interplay between the two of you—as representatives of your disciplines—helping us out and informing us about how to use that word. It is something which historians often react badly to, indeed it is a joke among those who are not archaeologists about the way in which 'ritual' is used as an explanation by archaeologists. And again, with a multidisciplinary audience in mind, I think it would be helpful to have some agreement on the use of such terms of art.

Finally, I should like to pick up and endorse your remark that comparative work is needed on contemporary migration and its results. You moved straight on from that to speak of the idea of Anglo-Saxon invasions as an origin-myth, which I can certainly see as an argument. I just wonder, however, where that origin-statement is coming from, because we have it first presented to us by the Briton Gildas. We have a further attestation of it in another British source. While we cannot rule out the possibility that Gildas was drawing on Anglo Saxon informants, if I dare use that word here, there is a question as to whose question that origin-myth was answering. Was it the Britons asking about how the Anglo-Saxons came to be established in the country? Or is this an origin-myth from the English for the English themselves? Or is it something which was picked up from British sources in a literate context and then developed? There may be a simple answer to that query, but I think that it has to be teased out somewhat and discussed more. The point about connections between Gildas and the English, being in this particular context, is his employment of the latinised word *ciula*, a usage which begins (as far as I know) with him and then develops some currency through reading of his text; he was here using a Primitive Old English word for ship. What is more, when referring to the Irish he used the primitive Irish word for ship. It is almost as if he had done some research in the vernaculars of the people who were attacking sub-Roman Britain. That might be something which would suggest that this story came ultimately from English sources to be picked up by Gildas and then recycled in a literary context. But those are questions which have to be asked not simply left open.

GREEN: Could I come in precisely at that same point? Not merely did you talk about an origin-myth in that context, but, just before, you observed that, "The Anglo-Saxon invasion represents a shared ethnic past and an oral tradition: it is an origin-myth emphasising valiant sea journeys and distinguished ancestors rather than post-Roman colonial images". You seem to have assumed that the literary material rests on old tradition. There is no Anglo-Saxon evidence for that.

RICHARDS: No, I was stating, I suppose, that the written reference to that has itself developed after an old tradition, but this may be a false assumption.

TURTON: Is it a risky assumption?

GREEN: No, but it needs to be stated that it is an assumption.

DUMVILLE: I should be inclined to say it is a risky assumption. In other words, there is room for dispute.

GREEN: Yes, there is a field open.

HINES: Bede talks about having received information from Kentish sources (*Historia ecclesiastica*, Preface). The precise term he uses is "*seniorum traditio*" (the tradition of old men). This certainly identifies a tradition, though it does not necessarily identify an especially old tradition. He also talks of "*traditio priorum*" (the tradition of earlier men) as a source of information on East Anglia. In both cases, in fact, these sources are apparently quoted with specific reference to the post-Conversion (i.e. seventh-century) ecclesiastical history of the regions concerned.

GREEN: That is the difficulty with such references, whether with Bede or with Jordanes, that they could refer to old tradition, they could refer simply to hearsay, or postulate.

AXBOE: You said [in draft presented at the symposium] that there was a need to show who was inside the urns, because there otherwise were few possibilities in cremation burials of displaying status. I think it would be just the other way around. At a cremation burial, the bereaved built a pyre and placed the deceased on it, with grave goods and so on. With an inhumation burial, they would dig a hole in the ground and place the body and gifts there. Then they set fire to the pyre, or earth on the grave. In both cases they would of course observe the proper rituals and ceremonies, of which only some can be traced archaeologically, and might of course mark the grave somehow, perhaps even with a barrow. So far the two burial rites run parallel, but with the inhumation that was that, while with the cremation they had the extra chance for ceremonies and display, with the collection of the bones and the burial of the urn. I am sorry, but I really do not like your whole idea [laughter]. In Denmark physical anthropologists are very, very sceptical about determining especially the sex of cremated persons. They find it much too uncertain. I know that it is done again and again but, well, I am afraid it should be used with much more care than you do.

RICHARDS: I agree that it must be used with care, and I have only made use of identifications that have been made with some certainty. The techniques have advanced recently, especially through work carried out by Jacqueline McKinley on the Spong Hill cremations. Whilst she would, I understand, throw out much of the earlier work that was done on this site, there is now general agreement on her identifications.

AXBOE: I would expect that it would be less risky to judge the age of a cremated person than to determine the sex.

RICHARDS: You cannot do it with every cremation, because it depends upon the preservation of those bones that can be used to sex the skeleton.

AXBOE: But, you know, even with inhumation graves it may be uncertain to determine the sex. As an example I would mention some of the rich late Roman-period graves from Skovgarde/Udby in southern Sjælland, which contained lost of beads and jewellery (Ethelberg 1991:178 ff.). The first anthropologist who examined the bones determined them to be male (Ethelberg 1989:6 ff.), but later the determination has been changed.

RICHARDS: This raises an interesting point. There have been similar instances of anachronistic burials from England. I believe that there comes a point when one should believe the physical anthropologist, rather than cling to ethnocentric assumptions about gender roles. I do not see any reason why you should say: "If the deceased wore jewellery he must have been a woman"!

AXBOE: But my point is that sex determination may give problems even with well preserved skeletons, because physical anthropologists have to sum up a number of criteria; there are no absolutely certain signs. Another problem is the relation between urns and household pottery. Don't you find the same ornaments on the fine tableware of the settlements?

RICHARDS: Well, there is not very much fine tableware.

AXBOE: Again, from our Iron Age, especially the Roman period, we have lots of fine pots in the inhumation graves, often several in a grave. And we do find the same types and the same quality in the settlements, but only in limited numbers. The coarse houseware, which is predominant in the settlements, was seldom used in graves, but the fine tableware was.

RICHARDS: I think I said that there was an overlap. I am not saying that every urn in a cemetery was made as a funerary vessel; in some cases a crude domestic vessel may have been selected as appropriate.

SCHÜTTE: If we look at a medieval painting we know everything had a meaning inside because of written sources. But if we work in a prehistoric context we do not know if anything we see has a meaning. There are two basic views: (a) it is all meaningless, it is just the tableware on top of the burned meal from the last evening of the dying grandmother; (b) or it is the urn made for the rich male with his high status cow! I think it is an interesting illustration of how archaeology may apply critical methods to this material.

References in the discussion

Textual references:

Bede
               Historia ecclesiastica gentis Anglorum: see Colgrave *et al.* 1969.

Bibliography:

Colgrave, B., & R. A. B. Mynors
     1969   *The Ecclesiastical History of the English People*. Oxford: Clarendon Press.
Ethelberg, P.
     1989   Skrålbanken. *Skalk* 2: 3-9.
     1991   Ein seelandisches Fürstengrab aus dem frühen 3.Jahrhundert. Skovgårde Grab 8. *Fundberichte aus Baden-Württemberg* 16.
Nikolajevic, I.
     1983   L'arte bizantina: ricettività e creatività locale. In *Gli Slavi occidentali e meridionali nell'alto medioevo*. Settimane di studio del C.I.S.A.M., XXX. Pp. 801-826. Spoleto: C.I.S.A.M.

CULTURAL CHANGE AND SOCIAL ORGANISATION IN EARLY ANGLO-SAXON ENGLAND

JOHN HINES

School of English Studies, Communication and Philosophy, University of Wales, P. O. Box 94, Cardiff CF1 3XB; now at Scool of History and Archaeology, Cardiff University, Cardiff CF10 3XU

Introduction

The challenge of reviewing the social and cultural situation in early Anglo-Saxon England, in the context of a wide-ranging discussion of the behaviour and mentality of people living through the radical historical changes of the end of the Roman period and the start of the Middle (or the Dark) Ages, is an intriguing one. For a single paper it is, no doubt, a preposterously large topic, although occasionally to lift one's eyes from the small detail in order to reconsider the overall picture is a practice that requires no particular defence. A comprehensive descriptive survey of the relevant evidence and views being impractical, I have chosen to focus on a particular area of considerable current research interest, namely the relevance of one special social phenomenon, *ethnic identity*, as a factor in cultural history. It can be argued that this is a factor of fundamental importance, and one that is involved in social relations right through the communities concerned here.

It is an easy matter to choose between the two basic topics identified as the foci of this discussion (culture and society) for the best starting-point. Drawing a picture of the people of this period we have to posit as an ideal outcome of the discussion. We know no more about the fate of the Romano-British population or the numbers and behaviour of the Germanic invaders and settlers than Gildas tells us—and he, in the middle of the sixth century, may well have written down everything he actually knew about this. The only practical way to begin is to impersonalise the subject, and to discuss the cultural processes that took place as a large part of Roman Britain became Anglo-Saxon England as if they functioned on their own.

This procedure implicitly respects the principles of Christopher Hawkes's famous 'ladder of inference' (Hawkes 1954): that economic and technical facts should be relatively easily discernible in the archaeological record, past social structures less easily so, and the mentality of the past barely attainable at all. Taking this approach, however, we rapidly run into the limits of what we know and understand of economy and society in post-Roman Britain, while by contrast the introduction of surprisingly tractable ideological considerations seems essential for us to make sense of what we see. Our reconstructions of past ideas and attitudes are of course inferences and hypotheses. We may be grossly deceived, even when modern researchers come apparently independently to similar conclusions. But relevant evidence, both historical and analogical, is there, and it is certainly possible to check on where modern fantasies go far beyond the empirical data.

The overriding cultural prerequisite for any human population is to secure the basis of its subsistence—its supply of food and other such essentials—and this basis, in the early

AFTER EMPIRE:
TOWARDS AN ETHNOLOGY OF EUROPES'S BARBARIANS
© C.I.R.O.S.S.
San Marino (R.S.M.)

Anglo-Saxon period, was overwhelmingly agrarian. While the more sophisticated aspects of the Roman economy and superstructure collapsed or evaporated in late fourth- and early fifth-century Britain—industrialised production, towns, an administrative apparatus, a professional army—the level of continuity in the rural economy may have been relatively strong. One of the more convincing symptoms of this is the fact that at several (though by no means all) early Anglo-Saxon settlement sites, the proportion of sheep to cattle detectable appears to be markedly closer to an earlier Romano-British norm than to the high preponderance of cattle suggested by excavated Continental settlement sites in and around northern Germany (e.g. Bell 1977:240; Davies 1980:177; West 1985:85-96; cf. Schmid 1978:131; van Es 1967:403-5; Zimmermann 1978:160). There is still quite considerable, and valid, disagreement over many other details: for instance over whether some Roman villa estates survived as units, and what it would imply if they had (e.g. Fowler 1975:132-5; Hooke 1981:89-90; Welch 1985); over the alleged persistence of a native timber-framed building-tradition (e.g. Higham 1992:123-6; reviews by Hamerow 1993b, Hines 1994); over the extent and significance of the reversion of agricultural land to scrub and the silting up of ditches in the fourth to sixth centuries (cf. Hinchcliffe *et al.* 1981: 110-11). In fact we are still embarrassingly ignorant of early Anglo-Saxon agricultural practices in respect of such basic issues as field-systems, and have to rely largely on common sense and probability to postulate the likely use of resources accessible to the identifiable settlements.[1] Generally, however, I think no one would dispute the claim that basic agrarian history in the fifth and sixth centuries is better characterised by signs of evolution than by evidence of radical disruption.

Some specialisation of labour remained in the system, however, both inherited from late Roman Britain and brought in by the settlers from their homelands. Since metal survives so well for archaeological study in comparison with organic materials, there is really no choice but to use fine metalwork as an example. One of the most tantalisingly evident but little understood facts of fifth-century material-cultural history is that several different parts of the Germanic world in north-western Europe adopted the techniques and motif-stock of late-Roman provincial metalwork—best-known from belt-fittings—for their own most artistic metalwork: hence the Nydam Style in Jutland, the relief style of the Saxon saucer and equal-armed brooches, and the Quoit-brooch Style in southern Britain (Haseloff 1981:3-17). The Quoit-brooch Style, really an amalgam of diverse techniques and motifs, and thus a style-group rather than a single uniform style, may have been the only form of specialised Roman-period craft that the Anglo-Saxon culture was either able or willing to maintain. The disappearance of the Roman pottery industry provides a stark contrast.

It is a tolerably safe assumption that the range of skills observable in early Anglo-Saxon metalwork is directly representative of a range of economic (manufacturing) specialisation existing in that period. At a relatively early period especially (the late fifth and early sixth centuries, when Style I was a relatively young means of decoration), and intermittently later on (for instance with the products of the Sutton Hoo jeweller), we can be faced with art of such rare quality that only a professional artist can reasonably be postulated as its producer (cf. Bakka 1958; Bruce-Mitford 1978:432-611). Other skills, such as the neglected topic of the production of the delicate and sometimes elaborate punches used for stamping

---

[1]   It is illuminating that in her recent publication of the early Anglo-Saxon settlement at Mucking, Essex, Helena Hamerow (1993a) scarcely troubles even to speculate on the agro-economic basis of the settlement.

metalwork, or the techniques of cutting and setting glass or garnets, equally cannot reasonably be attributed to exceptional talent alone but should imply some organisation by which such skills, as well as the necessary tools and materials, were acquired, nurtured and transmitted. From a detailed and comprehensive study of a single complex artefact-type, the Kentish square-headed brooch, David Leigh (1980) concluded that the techniques of manufacture used, overlapped sufficiently to link all of the known brooches together as products of what he called a single 'workshop'. That the fine metalworker could have a distinctive status in north-western Germanic Europe around this period is reflected by the appearance, from the late Roman period and especially around the late Migration period, of a small set of jewellers' graves: a feature which contrasts significantly with the much larger number of blacksmiths' or ironworkers' graves that appear after them (Müller-Wille 1977; Vierck *et al.* 1971). As a complementary topic, the history of Anglo-Saxon glass and enamelworking and beadmaking, and its relationship with the relevant Roman-period crafts, is crying out for thorough study.

From such evidence concerning metalworkers, together with my own studies of particular artefact-types such as the Anglo-Saxon great square-headed brooch (Hines n.d.), I have suggested that within the archaeological phase known as the Migration period (the later fourth to the later sixth century) there was a *necessary* period of great social and economic 'freedom' or 'openness'. The Migration period, according to this view, comprised a time in which at least some of society's producers—certainly the makers of prestigious, complicated, status-linked artefacts like the de luxe brooches—were possessed of considerable freedom and had the power to create at least their own fortunes by entering and satisfying extensive markets. This model contrasts quite strongly with a common, perhaps the dominant view of specialised craftsmen in this period as being firmly under the control of powerful patrons who belonged to the (military) social élite (cf. Hedeager 1992:120-1).[2] One strand in my argument is the inferrable pattern of changing levels of production of Anglo-Saxon great square-headed brooches through the seventy years or so they were made in sixth-century England. Production grew to a peak around the middle of this period, and then gradually declined, ending with an ultra-late phase represented by a group of brooches from northern England (Fig. 3.1). The growth of production is interpreted as having proceeded from the date at which the brooch-type and the associated manufacturing skills were introduced, in two places in south-eastern England, as fast as was practicable to meet the level of demand; the turning-point is where growing supply met the declining level of demand, which then gradually fell away over some thirty to forty more years. (There are geographical variations that complicate matters somewhat, without affecting the general validity of this summary.)

The second essential element in this reconstruction, then, is the market. It is suggested that around the middle of the Migration period, *circa* 475 AD, a generation or two after the

---

[2]   I am encouraged that what seems to me to be an unorthodox and minority view in the field of Germanic early Medieval Archaeology has been vigorously supported by analogies from other quarters, both in the discussion of this paper and in other contexts. Giorgio Ausenda has pointed out that in many cases in comparative ethnology, while craftsmen may be of client status, as amongst the Tuareg and some other nomadic groups, they are still 'free'. David Dumville has emphasised the partial agreement of Welsh and Irish law—the latter in particular—on this point, with their evidence of relatively complex relations of power and status between craftsman and patron {e.g. *Uraicecht Bec* ('Small Primer') (Atkinson 1901:90-7, 102-9)}. Heather O'Donoghue (pers. comm.) has further made the point that Irish folktale can characterise the craftsman in a congruent manner.

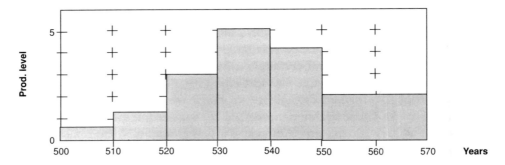

Fig.3.1 - The inferred production-levels of Anglo-Saxon great square-headed brooches in the Migration period.

Anglo-Saxon period can really be regarded as having begun in Britain, an era of competition for positions of social eminence reached a particularly intense phase. This was a situation that the postulated independent producers could prosper on, while the later Migration period decline in consumption and production represents the closing down of the competition. We recurrently find, in fact, that in 'jeweller's graves', in which the tools of the trade of the dead man are deposited, apparently as significant status symbols, the general social status of the deceased is also asserted in more familiar ways, through the inclusion of weaponry with the grave goods (Müller-Wille 1977:160-73). It is well known that England and Scandinavia see a great increase of expensive material production and deposition in the second half of the Migration period, with artistic creativity and a proliferation of types as well as a growth in output necessary to meet the needs for deposition. The argument that conspicuous consumption, *inter alia* in ritual deposition (graves and sacrificial hoards), is often a symptom of social competition need not be rehearsed here. What makes the social competition of this period particularly interesting is the widespread evidence for the breakdown of older élite groups and the appearance of rivalry at a more individual level. Up into the earlier Migration period, the Germanic societies concerned seem to have been headed by a military élite. Now, in Denmark for instance, group offerings of weaponry in hallowed bogs give way to individual offerings, of both men's and women's status symbols (Hines 1989a). In early Anglo-Saxon England, the proportion of weapon graves in cemeteries rises rapidly to a regular 15-20% of all graves (and considerably more in some cemeteries) in comparison with figures closer to 5% in the cultures from which the Anglo-Saxons had come (Härke 1989; Hines 1989b).

The uniquely fully excavated, large Anglian English cemetery at Spong Hill, Norfolk, offers a fine example of how, not long after a truly open competition like this could have started, its logical outcome, an end to competition with the emergence of a new élite, might be reflected in the material record (Hills *et al.* 1977-1987). The cemetery at Spong Hill is one of the earliest identifiable Anglo-Saxon sites, with its first burials datable to around, quite likely before, the middle of the fifth century. To begin with, all burials are cremations. At a later stage, a small group practising inhumation burial appears at the site, the earliest burials of this group apparently being marked out by the provision of small grave mounds (evidenced by surviving ring-ditches) with in one case especially rich grave goods with a sword in a fine scabbard. The latter supports a date of approximately 500 AD for the appearance of the inhuming group. Some 57 inhumation graves form a sequence from here down to the end of the Migration period: a burial-rate very roughly approaching one a year, which, multiplied by the probable mean life expectancy of the period, suggests (just as roughly) an inhuming group numbering some thirty persons: considerably more than a single nuclear family (cf. Jørgensen 1992). Throughout this period, inhumation graves are unquestionably outnumbered by cremations, probably by at least 10:1. After inhumation ceases, the pottery-types present suggest that cremation continued down to about the beginning of the seventh century. The special status possessed or claimed by the inhuming group is attested by the richness of some of their graves, not least the early sword-grave. This was not merely an alternative burial rite. Whether they emerged from the earlier cremating group or arrived from elsewhere, we probably see here the appearance of a wealthy group bidding for élite status. Their disappearance may represent their departure to a more special, reserved site as their position was consolidated, or their suppression by a successful élite elsewhere: the general implications are the same in either case. A teasingly similar situation can be glimpsed at the fifth-century cemetery site of Hammoor, Kr. Stormarn, Schleswig-Holstein, but the quality of information retrieved from here is unfortunately inadequate for an extended comparison (Hingst 1959:245-6).

Ethnic Identity

Even with the shared purpose that would-be élite groups as at Spong Hill thus apparently had to show, the picture of early Anglo-Saxon social development sketched above tends to emphasise rivalry and divisions within the population. For a balanced picture of the period, it is important to note that there is just as good evidence for certain powerful, unifying factors in the general culture that served other essential purposes and which profoundly affected material culture. The term 'ethnicity' is now widely used to denote an area of considerable research interest and activity: the analysis of ethnic identity, in which a historical (= diachronic) dimension seems to be practically indispensable. Although most emphasis in current archaeological theory concerning ethnicity is placed on ethnicity's role as an instrument of competition between different ethnic groups, it is reasonably clear that an 'ethnic' identity can also function in a regular way as a focus for group loyalty that overrides potentially alternative group-identification and interests within the single group, such as antagonistic grouping by social status and/or economic function, age or sex, religious sect or any other cultural difference (Barth 1969; Olsen *et al.* 1992; Shennan 1992). As such, ethnic grouping can be a unifying ideological instrument, serving the interests of a social élite as long as the élite benefits most from group efforts. But for that to happen, socio-political organisation and ethnic identification have to be integrated, and the post-Roman centuries offer a fascinating case study in the struggle to achieve this integration.

Ethnic identification was nothing new even in the barbarian world in the first millennium AD. I do not propose to digress into how far back in prehistory this process may be traced; in respect of the *Germani* there is solid evidence, for instance in the form of archaic elements preserved in place-names (*Himmerland* and *Thy* in Jutland), that it was not the needs of classical authors and audiences alone that gave group identities and, importantly, names to invading groups like the Cimbri and Teutons in the second century BC.[3] The fluidity of ethnic identity amongst the Germanic peoples is reflected by the changes in the name

---

[3] In this section, I acknowledge with gratitude Dennis Green's advice on various matters of early Germanic philology.

sets we see from such early records as Pytheas, Caesar and Cicero to Tacitus' ethnography of the end of the first century AD and then to the more frequent supply of historical references from the later Empire. It is precisely in this later Roman period (the late second to fourth centuries AD) that such historically important groups as the Goths, the Franks, the Saxons, the Thuringians and the Danes were apparently formed as new confederacies, with previously unknown names (Hedeager 1993; Wenskus 1961). The mysterious earlier Suebian group may be a now obscure prefiguration of this process (Tacitus, *Germania*, 38 46). That smaller, older groups could maintain their identity and independence down into the Migration period seems to be attested by the history of the Angles, and, more contentiously, the Jutes.

The question of how these new groupings are reflected in the material-cultural record is a delicate and as yet incompletely answered one. It is one thing to be able to identify (in some areas) plausible regional centres of wealth and power, regional cult centres, and even on occasion the physical demarcation or reinforcement of territorial boundaries (see Axboe, this volume). Such material reflects the *structure* of political entities and thus, importantly, helps to confirm the presence and character of such units. The adoption of a distinctive material culture—for instance in dress or pottery styles—to express or reinforce a particular ethnic identity is a very different matter. In whatever period one considers, it is necessary to filter out local peculiarities created, for example, by the apparently haphazard and probably purely pragmatically determined ranges of particular brooch-types, a phenomenon of which several plausible examples could be cited in northern Germany in the later Roman period (cf. Schulze 1977). We lack an agreed formula whereby the level of distinctiveness of individual cultures, either from one another or across time, can consistently be measured—and indeed we lack any exploration of the question of whether any such measure is possible. As a starting-point for discussion, however, it can be claimed that there is a valid *prima facie* case that, in northern *Germania*, in the crucial period from the late second to the end of the fourth century, material culture was used to symbolise identification with specific political units such as we should call a kingdom or a confederation *to a very limited extent.*[4] In later Roman-period Scandinavia, the diffusion of a new type of dress-fastener, a sleeve- and trouser-clasp, which was certainly used by the social élite although not apparently restricted to it, seems to offer us an illuminating insight (Hines 1993). These clasps first appear in the third century, in southern Scandinavia, possibly, perhaps even probably, within what was already the Danish kingdom but not certainly so. They soon achieve a wide range, from Gotland in the east to Jutland in the west; a range which, as far as certainty is possible, runs beyond the limits of the political territory of the Danes. From here, the clasps' range expands gradually, perhaps continuously, northwards into Scandinavia but in no other direction until the late fifth century, entering Norway at the beginning of the Migration period and then spreading quite rapidly up the west coast to the Arctic. With this, and several similar phenomena, we see a wide, regional cultural homogeneity effectively to be cultivated in a process that eventually becomes so intense, creating such marked contrasts between Scandinavia and north-western *Germania*, that it is reasonable to suspect it

---

[4] In the first draft of this paper, this was expressed as 'a remarkahly limited extent'. The word 'remarkably' was no more than a loosely selected intensifier. However, it was both instructive and welcome that David Turton could point out that, from a modern anthropological perspective, there was nothing particularly remarkable about this state of affairs at all.

has become conscious and deliberate. The major regional divisions that seem to emerge in this way are between a northern, a western and an eastern branch of Germanic culture.

Besides the methodological problems outlined above, however, we also still need such basic aids as more extensively comparable records and studies of the material across the whole Germanic area. That regional differentiation grows towards the end of the Roman period and is consequently characteristic of the succeeding Migration period is an accepted view. Horst Böhme's study of Germanic grave finds of the fourth and fifth centuries between the lower Elbe and the River Loire thus amply illustrates the emergence of a clearly focussed Saxon material culture (Böhme 1974). But the absolute chronology he is able to provide for this is unfortunately very vague. In southern Scandinavia, the chronology is very much clearer, but the optimum scale at which regionality should be studied has not been determined. Thus Hans Neumann and Jytte Ringtved consider late Roman-period Jutland, which has a distinctively different north and south and an intermediary middle part, in terms of three and two regional groups respectively (Neumann 1982; Ringtved 1989). Generally, recent work in Scandinavia has been focussed at a distinctly local level, to the effective exclusion of much appreciation of the development of a common Scandinavian culture. Eastern Europe too now has a thorough chronological scheme, but the evaluation and interpretation of regional groups is at an undeveloped stage. Kazimierz Godłowski, however, commented in passing on the homogeneity of his eastern Germanic groups in the middle of the late Roman period (Godłowski 1970:95 and *passim*). In the extreme west (in Continental terms), it is not until the burial of King Childeric in Tournai in 482 that we have evidence of the emergence of a distinctively Frankish prestige style (Ament 1977).

In the first half of the fifth century, Germanic settlers were arriving in Britain, and certainly from about the middle of the century Germanic culture flowed into lowland Britain apparently *in toto* and subject to little detectable restriction. A feature of this culture, therefore, was not just the notion that a particular material culture could reflect a certain area of origin and thus some sort of identity, but also a process-in-being whereby the link between group identity and material culture was strengthening. I have discussed elsewhere the way in which a new, consistent and distinctive Anglian English culture was rapidly—within a few generations—put together out of a remarkably diverse range of sources (Hines 1992). As earlier in Scandinavia, I suggest that the diffusion of a costume (here just for women) using sleeve-clasps exemplifies this especially well. Under this argument, the range of the dress-style is not simply a passive reflection of how far the Anglian group extended; the adoption of the costume was a means by which people could both claim their membership of the new group and promulgate the conditions by which membership was established. In Kent, we can see an equivalent process, with an adoption of mostly Continental models though an important Scandinavian element presumably related to early Jutish settlement survives. The Saxon areas, which, with the exception of the Essex coast, never seem to have been culturally very mixed as far as Germanic influences went, remain *de facto* distinctive enough, though with less dissemination of new, clearly marked identity-marking forms.

This means that the system of identities that Bede recognised amongst the English—Angles, Saxons and Kentishmen—existed by the beginning of the sixth century. It had not just always been there, in the sense that these were simply the groups the settlers had come from; in the case of the distinctly hybrid Anglian English group it had to be created by this early date. The particular problem that I wish to focus on now is the relationship between these known identities and social organisation—by which I mean, particularly, the establishment of political units. It is hard, in fact, even to find a satisfactory terminology for the political units we can imagine the early Anglo-Saxons to have had. *Tribe, petty kingdom* and *kingdom* are the terms most commonly used. A variety of reliable early historical sources show the widespread existence of small groups, such as those labelled *N-ingas*: 'the people of *N*' (e.g. the *Sunningas, Besingas, Woccingas, Feppingas*, etc.), which came to have at least some organisational and administrative character, being assessed in terms of hides in the Tribal Hidage or being possessed of some group cult centre, as at *Gumeninga hearh*, Harrow-on-the-Hill, Middlesex: the temple of the Gumeningas. Such, it is widely supposed, were the building blocks out of which the better known Anglo-Saxon kingdoms (e.g. the so-called heptarchy) were constructed (Bassett 1989; Yorke 1990:9-15).

We can put names to many different political units from later sixth- and earlier seventh-century England. In several cases we have a fair idea of the location and/or the extent of their territories. But what did the existence of these units mean for their inhabitants? I would suggest that we have little reason to suppose that they expressed in any consensual way the group-identity of most of these inhabitants, and that consequently a group-name like Hæstingas is not to be conceived of as representing some comfortably clannish system in which all the people of Hæst were one as if part of some extended family and thus united by their ethnic identity at least: it could rather be an administrative, possessive, imposed description—the people who belong to N. The evidence deployed by John Dodgson (1966) for the relatively late (i.e. late sixth- or seventh-century) emergence of the majority of place names in *-inga(s)* supports this view. Dodgson noted that a single historical explanation and function for the *-inga(s)* names was scarcely credible, although at the same time an important and substantial range of them have to be interpreted in terms of social power structures of the late sixth and early seventh centuries, when aristocratic rule was a fact. Such small political groups, then, would be units serving to feed some centre and élite through a system of hidation; an élite that in some identifiable cases reinforced its own mystique by establishing centres for pagan ritual such as the *Gumeninga hearh* (above). What archaeology shows in relation to these kingdoms, petty or larger, is overwhelmingly their structure; above all the sort of increasing stratification that produces a splendid burial for (presumably) a certain *Tæppa* at Taplow, Buckinghamshire.

If we look for the deliberate, distinctive marking of political units, by means of symbolism, we find that we only really have this in relation to the bigger kingdoms of the heptarchy, from about the middle of the seventh century onwards, and even then in far from blatant forms. The earliest concrete evidence that we have for the existence of the relevant kingships includes examples of formulaic international political recognition, in a language accessible to a wide European audience and to posterity, in diplomatic letters from popes to kings of Kent and Northumbria (copied from the Papal registry in Rome, one hopes *verbatim*, by Nothelm and preserved by Bede: *Historia ecclesiastica*, Preface, I.xxxii, II.x, III.xxix. Trans. Colgrave *et al.*). Fascinatingly, Æthelberht of Kent and Edwin of Northumbria are addressed here as *rex Anglorum* (= King of the English), while Oswiu of Northumbria is even more remarkably addressed as *rex Saxonum*, a title it is difficult to imagine Nothelm or Bede having created, in 655. From about the middle of the century, the issuing of coins provides an important medium for the assertion of royal authority—and of the distinctiveness—of the different royal domains, for we begin to see not only specific royal titles but also subtly different formulae in respect, for instance, of the use of runes and Roman lettering, and perhaps too the latinisation of names, to be characteristic of the different kingdoms (cf. Blackburn 1991:166, *passim* and fig.2; Grierson *et al.* 1986:271 and *passim*).

An Anglo-Saxon archaeologist, reviewing the general history of material culture in seventh–century England, would naturally and rightly emphasise the powerful spread of supra regional uniformity in personal adornment at that time, with, for instance, a single Mediterranean/Continental-derived female dress-style being widely adopted (Hyslop 1963). Yet differences survive, or persist, or may even be created. The still-Saxon southern Midlands saw a clear attempt to wed the new dominant *de luxe* brooch-type, the 'Kentish' garnet disc or composite brooch, with the traditional Saxon cast saucer brooch (Matthews *et al.* 1985:91-7). In East Anglia, and probably in Northumbria too, special connections with Celtic areas to the north and west in Britain, and Scandinavia across the sea to the east, were drawn upon to create subtle but crucially located differences in the outstanding artwork with which the culture marked its greatest treasures (Hines 1992). Was this a deliberate cultivation of difference, or the accidental result of historical connections and circumstances? With the constant presence and gradual entrenchment of this difference in the sharp contrast between the Roman style of manuscript art in the south and the Hiberno-Saxon style of the Midlands and North, in the ecclesiastical context that was otherwise so obsessed with orthodoxy, I find it hard to believe that deliberate cultivation was never a significant factor.

Slender and equivocal as such reflections of statehood are, they represent the range and substance of the earliest detectable linkage between known political units and material cultural symbolism in Anglo-Saxon England. A potentially important concurrent development is the reinforcement of a sense of territoriality—more than just a reflection of political structure—with the demarcation of boundaries, either by the location of conspicuous burials there or by the physical definition of a boundary line in the landscape, as with Offa's Dyke. It seems to make good sense for the process of consolidation of a political entity to proceed outwards from the centre. This sort of boundary focus could thus represent a regular stage in the maturation, or perhaps the life-cycle, of early political units.

Overall, however, the conclusion has to be drawn that the political division and organisation of early Anglo-Saxon England was not only smaller in scale but also of less impact on general material culture than a more deep-seated sense of ethnic identity in the population was. The early grouping of the Anglian English never corresponded to any political unit, yet Bede was acutely conscious of it, distinguishing these people as the *gens Anglorum* (a term that he could also use of the English as a whole, perhaps surprisingly with no serious ambiguity as the context practically always makes the implied meaning clear) and the speakers of a *lingua Anglorum*. Bede's sense of the English as one group, too, was not to be matched by a unified English kingdom before the tenth century; if, however, the appearance of a consistent Anglian English dress-style by *ca* 500 can be interpreted as the creation of Anglian English identity by that date, the post-Migration-period spread of a uniform dress style in late sixth-century England shows clearly that at least the conditions for the emergence of a conscious common English identity then existed.

Kingdom-formation in early Anglo-Saxon England was pursued by an incipient or reconstituted élite in their own self-interest. The role of a sub- or post-Roman political heritage in both lowland Britain and the Celtic west in this process ought not to be underestimated. The largest early Anglo-Saxon kingdoms appeared in the west, Mercia and Wessex, where both the direct annexation of British territory (for instance of the *Dornsǣte, Sumorsǣte, Pecsǣte* and *Wreocensǣte*) was possible, and the English communities bordered directly on the British kingdoms described by Gildas, a confrontation that must have been a stimulus to their internal political development. In many of the small south-eastern kingdoms, such as Essex, Surrey and Sussex, we find evidence of an early association between Germanic settlement and a Roman-period organisational structure; something which itself may have made these areas the more amenable to eventual Continental influence (Crummy *et al.* 1981; Welch 1983:217-28).[5] In East Kent, the administrative structure apparently reflected by four -gē centres (Eastry, Wester, Lyminge and Sturry) ought to be very early, reflecting a kingdom whose extent is still that of the brief and obscure phase of Jutish settlement in the second half of the fifth century (Brooks 1989; Hawkes 1982). Apart from a limited number of place-names, however, continuity from the Roman period in respect of East Kent is very elusive. From early in the sixth century, Kentish material influence was spreading over the south-east, through a variety of likely early 'political' units, penetrating the Essex coast, West Kent and Surrey, Sussex, Hampshire and the Isle of Wight.

It seems highly probable, then, that the political organisation of groups of people into any form that we can know of or could identify as a kingdom was essentially secondary to the cultural unification of areas within England in the Migration period itself. I have suggested that there were practical and largely psychological reasons for this first stage of, in effect, adaptation: in essence, that the adoption of a new local culture was concomitantly a cutting-of-ties with the area of origin and a means whereby the group could tell itself and others that it belonged where it was, and was not intrusive nor out of place (Hines 1992). The size of the groups thus created, however, may reflect the desirability of large effective alliances for both psychological and practical security.

Even when these 'popular' confederations start to be traversed by the boundaries of political territories, we can see a constant need for the élite producers and manipulators of material culture to ally in larger groups and to respect the existence of bigger entities of shared identity—entities that were too large for any possible political unification or central political control at that time. It is one of the axioms of cultural-historical theory that such early, rather small political groups will need to sustain one another by alliances via systems of trade, exchange and marriage (Renfrew *et al.* 1986). Most of the early kingdoms of the heptarchy seem to have actively cultivated their overseas connections—in some cases differentially, so as to accentuate their separation from one another, *if* the pro-Continental bias of Kent and eventually Wessex and the pro-Scandinavian leanings of East Anglia and Northumbria are correctly identified and interpreted. The great enigma in this respect is the slumbering giant of Mercia: it is tempting to speculate that careful research here, and to a lesser degree in Wessex too, will prove a western, British connection to have been important.

This discussion has drawn only on archaeological and historical evidence. A third, immensely important field of evidence is that of language. The way in which new linguistic varieties were created (Old English and its dialects) and the way in which the North-West Germanic language group develops through the Migration period and beyond is amenable to study, and seems indeed to be fully capable of integration into a single model along with the reconstruction of history and the analysis of historical processes outlined here. The details of this, however, will have to be developed elsewhere (cf. Hines 1990).

The only concluding observation that I would want to place any final emphasis upon is that the sense of community in the period and places under consideration was considerably

---

[5]   I have a paper on 'Suðri-gē: the foundations of Surrey', delivered to the annual symposium of the Surrey Archaeological Society in 1990, in an advanced state of preparation which it is hoped will appear in a future volume of *Surrey Archaeological Collections*. See also the discussion of Ross Balzaretti's paper in this volume.

wider than the practical limits of political organisation and authority. Culture, for the people involved, emerges as an intensely social and integrative matter, not something personal or idiosyncratic. This should not, however, be interpreted sentimentally as an image of early medieval Germanic society as a happy fraternity, even if, as claimed, practical and psychological security was one of the functions of this culture. Socially, another function fulfilled by the widespread unity—or at least similarity, or comparability—of material culture was to provide an agreed playing-field for competition for specific goals: the achievement and consolidation of élite status. This was how the ground was laid for continuous attempts by the political centres to make cultural phenomena—religion, language, ethnic identity—and the political unit coalesce.

That process of coalescence can be called nationalisation. The continuity that can be seen between the post-Carolingian 'unified' kingdoms and the nation-states of early Modern Europe suggests that it was in the ninth and tenth centuries that political units appear at an optimum size for this process to flourish. Yet there was still a bigger presence around to queer the pitch, producing, in the later medieval political map of middle Europe, the Holy Roman Empire and the Papal States and thus leaving the unification of Germany and Italy to be such major products of nineteenth-century European nationalism. While the little we can see of late Anglo-Saxon paganism shows us a partly politicised religious cult, the new religion, Christianity, with its eagerness to anoint kings and its absolutist claims, must have seemed a precious gift to ambitious early kings. The Roman Church was thus the effective heir to Roman imperialism in the West: it concurrently had its own universal claims; it wanted to keep kings in subjection; and volumes have to be written to survey the impact these objectives had on subsequent European political history. The world was already a big place for an early medieval king. Above, below and around him were large, social powers with which he had to struggle. So Garrett Mattingly opens his book on *Renaissance Diplomacy* by insisting on one crucial, underlying principle. At the end of the Middle Ages, "Latin Christendom still knew itself to be one" (Mattingly 1955:18).

References

Ament, H.
    1977   Zur archäologishen Periodisierung der Merowingerzeit. *Germania* 55: 133-140.
Anderson, J. G. C. (ed.)
    1900   *Cornelii Taciti Opera Minora*. Oxford: Clarendon Press.
Atkinson, R.
    1901   *Ancient Laws of Ireland*, Vol. 5. Dublin: His Majesty's Stationery Office.
Bakka, E.
    1958   On the beginning of Salin's Style I in England. *Bergen Museums Årbok* 1958, Historisk antikvarisk rekke 3.
Barth, F.
    1969   Introduction. In *Ethnic Groups and Boundaries*. F. Barth (ed.), pp. 9-38. Bergen: Universitetsforlaget.
Bassett, S.
    1989   In search of the origins of Anglo-Saxon kingdoms. In *The Origins of Anglo-Saxon Kingdoms*. S. Bassett (ed.), pp. 3-27. London: Leicester University Press.
Bell, M.
    1977   Excavations at Bishopstone. *Sussex Archaeological Collections* 115.

Blackburn, M.
    1991   A Survey of Anglo-Saxon and Frisian Coins with Runic Inscriptions. In *Old English
                Runes and their Continental Background*. A. Bammesberger (ed.), pp. 137-189.
                Heidelberg: Carl Winter.
Böhme, H.
    1974   *Germanische Grabfunde des 4. bis 5. Jahrhunderts zwischen unterer Elbe und Loire*,
                2 vols. Munich: C. H. Beck.
Brooks, N.
    1989   The creation and early structure of the kingdom of Kent. In *The Origins of Anglo-
                Saxon Kingdoms*. S. Bassett (ed.), pp. 55-74. London: Leicester University Press.
Bruce-Mitford, R.
    1978   *The Sutton Hoo Ship-Burial. Vol.2: Arms Armour and Regalia*. London: British
                Museum Publications.
Crummy, P.
    1981   *Aspects of Anglo-Saxon and Norman Colchester*. (Council for British Archaeology
                Research Report no.39). London: Council for British Archaeology.
Davies, S. M.
    1980   Excavations at Old Down Farm, Andover. Part I: Saxon. *Proceedings of the
                Hampshire Field Club and Archaeological Society* 36: 161-180.
Dodgson, J. McN.
    1966   The significance of the distribution of the English place-name in -ingas-, -inga- in
                south-east England. *Medieval Archaeology* 10: 1-29.
Es, W. A. van
    1967   Wijster. A native village beyond the imperial frontier 150-425 A.D. *Palaeohistoria* 9.
Fowler, P. J.
    1975   Continuity in the Landscape. In *Recent Work in Rural Archaeology*. P. J. Fowler
                (ed.), pp. 121 - 136. Bradford-on-Avon: Moonraker Press.
Godłowski, K.
    1970   *The Chronology of the Late Roman and Early Medieval Periods in Central Europe*.
                Cracow: Uniwersytet Jagielloński.
Grierson, P., & M. A. S. Blackburn
    1986   *Medieval European Coinage, 1: The Early Middle Ages (5th to 10th centuries)*.
                Cambridge: Cambridge University Press.
Härke, H.
    1989   Early Saxon Weapon Burials: frequencies, distributions and weapon combinations.
                In *Weapons and Warfare in Anglo-Saxon England*. S. C. Hawkes (ed.), pp. 49-61.
                (Oxford University Committee for Archaeology Monograph no.21). Oxford.
Hamerow, H. F.
    1993a   *Excavations at Mucking, Vol.2: the Anglo-Saxon settlement*. London: English Heritage.
    1993b   Review of N. J. Higham (1992). *Early Medieval Europe* 2 (2): 172-173.
Haseloff, G.
    1981   *Die Germanische Tierornamentik der Völkerwanderungszeit*. Berlin: De Gruyter.
Hawkes, C. F. C.
    1954   Archaeological Theory and Method: Some Suggestions from the Old World.
                American Anthropologist 56: 155-168.
Hawkes, S. C.
    1982   *Anglo-Saxon Kent c. 425-725*. In *Archaeology in Kent to AD 1500*. P. E. Leach
                (ed.), pp. 64-78. (Council for British Archaeology Research Report no.48). London:
                BAR.
Hedeager, L.
    1992   *Iron-Age Societies. From tribe to state in northern Europe*. Oxford: Blackwell.
    1993   The Creation of Germanic Identity: a European Origin-Myth. In *Frontières de
                l'empire romain*. P. Brun, S. van der Leeuw & C. R. Whittaker (eds.), pp. 121-131.
                Nemours: Mémoires du Musée de préhistoire de l'Ile-de-France, n° 5.

Higham, N. J.
    1992   *Rome, Britain and the Anglo-Saxons.* London: Seaby & Co.
Hills, C. M.
    1977   The Anglo-Saxon Cemetery at Spong Hill, North Elmham, Vol. 1. *East Anglian
                Archaeology* 6. Dereham: Norfolk Archaeological Unit.
Hills, C. M., & K. Penn
    1981   The Anglo-Saxon Cemetery at Spong Hill, North Elmham, Vol.2. *East Anglian
                Archaeology* 11. Dereham: Norfolk Archaeological Unit.
Hills, C. M., K. Penn & R. Rickett
    1984   The Anglo-Saxon Cemetery at Spong Hill, North Elmham, Vol.3. *East Anglian
                Archaeology* 21. Dereham: Norfolk Archaeological Unit.
    1987   The Anglo-Saxon Cemetery at Spong Hill, North Elmham, Vol.4. *East Anglian
                Archaeology* 34. Dereham: Norfolk Archaeological Unit.
Hinchcliffe, J., & R. Thomas
    1981   Archaeological Investigations at Appleford. *Oxoniensa* 45: 9-111.
Hines, J.
    1989a   Ritual Hoarding in Migration-period Scandinavia: a review of recent interpretations.
                Proceedings of the Prehistoric Society 55: 193-205.
    1989b   The Military Context of the *adventus Saxonum*: some continental evidence. In
                Weapons and Warfare in Anglo-Saxon England. S. C. Hawkes (ed.), pp. 25-48.
                (Oxford University Committee for Archaeology Monograph no.21). Oxford.
    1990   Archaeology, Philology and the *adventus Saxonum vel Anglorum.* In *Britain 400-
                600: Language and History.* A. Bammesberger & A. Wollmann (eds), pp. 17-36.
                Heidelberg: Carl Winter Verlag.
    1992   The Scandinavian Character of Anglian England: an update. In *The Age of Sutton
                Hoo.* M. O. H. Carver (ed.), pp. 315-329. Woodbridge: The Boydell Press.
    1993   *Clasps: Hektespenner: Agraffen.* Stockholm: Kungl. Vitterhets Historie och
                Antikvitets Akademien.
    1994   The Anglo-Saxons Reviewed. *Medieval Archaeology* 37: 314-318.
    1997   *A New Corpus of Anglo-Saxon Great Square-Headed Brooches.* (Society of
                Antiquaries of London Research Report). Woodbridge: The Boydell Press.
Hingst, H.
    1959   *Vorgeschichte des Kreises Stormarn.* Neumünster: Wachholtz.
Hooke, D.
    1981   *Anglo-Saxon Landscapes of the West Midlands: the Charter Evidence.* British
                Archaeological Reports. Oxford: BAR.
Hyslop, M.
    1963   Two Anglo-Saxon Cemeteries at Chamberlain's Barn, Leighton Buzzard, Beds.
                Archaeological Journal 120: 161-200.
Jørgensen, L.
    1992   The Early Medieval Family in Europe: Studies of Family Burial Practices in North
                Germanic, Merovingian and Lombard Societies. In *Medieval Europe 1992, Death
                and Burial.* Pre-printed Papers. Vol. 4, pp. 23-28. York.
Leigh, D.
    1980   The Square-Headed Brooches of Sixth-Century Kent. Ph.D. thesis, University
                College, Cardiff.
Matthews. C. L., & S. C. Hawkes
    1985   Early Saxon Settlements and Burials on Puddlehill, near Dunstable, Bedfordshire.
                Anglo-Saxon Studies in Archaeology and History 4: 59-116.
Mattingly, G.
    1955   *Renaissance Diplomacy.* London: Cape.

Müller-Wille, M.
    1977   Der frühmittelalterliche Schmied im Spiegel skandinavischer Grabfunde.
                Frühmittelalterliche Studien 11: 127-201.
Neumann, H.
    1982   *Olgerdiget - et hidrag til Danmarks tidligste historie.* (Skrifter fra Museumsradet for
                Sonderjyllands Amt, 1). Haderslev.
Olsen, B., & Z. Kobylinski
    1991   Ethnicity in anthropological and archaeological research: a Norwegian-Polish
                perspective. *Archaeologia Polona* 29: 5-27.
Renfrew, C., & J. F. Cherry (eds.)
    1986   *Peer Polity Interaction and Socio-political Change.* Cambridge: Cambridge Univ.
                Press.
Ringtveed, J.
    1989   Jyske gravfund fra yngre romertid og ældre germanertid. *Kuml* 1986: 95-231.
Schmid, P.
    1978   New archaeological results of settlement structures (Roman Iron Age) in the Northwest
                German coastal area. In *Lowland Iron Age Communities in Europe.* B. W. Cunliffe &
                T. Rowley (eds.), pp. 123-145. (British Archaeological Reports). Oxford: BAR.
Schulze, M.
    1977   *Die spätkaiserzeitliche Armbrustfibeln mit festem Nadelhalter: Gruppe Almgren, VI 2.*
                Bonn: R. Habelt.
Shennan, S.
    1991   Some current issues in the archaeological identification of past peoples.
                Archaeologia Polona 29: 29-37.
Vierck, H., & T. Capelle
    1971   Modeln der Merowinger- und Wikingerzeit. *Frühmiltelalterliche Studien* 5: 42-100.
Welch, M. G.
    1983   *Early Anglo-Saxon Sussex.* (British Archaeological Reports). Oxford: BAR.
    1985   Rural settlement patterns in the Early and Middle Anglo-Saxon Periods. *Landscape
                History* 7: 13-25.
Wenskus, R.
    1961   *Stammesbildung und Verfassung: das Werden der frühmittelalterlichen Gentes.* Köln:
                Böhlau Verlag.
West, S. E.
    1985   *West Stow. The Anglo-Saxon Village.* {East Anglian Archaeology 24 (2 vols.)}.
                Ipswich: Suffolk County Council.
Yorke, B.
    1990   *Kings and Kingdoms of Early Anglo-Saxon England.* London: Seaby & Co.
Zimmermann, W. H.
    1978   Economy of the Roman Iron Age settlement at Flögeln, Kr. Cuxhaven, Lower
                Saxony. Husbandry, Cattle Farming, and Manufacturing. In *Lowland Iron Age
                Communities in Europe.* B. W. Cunliffe & T. Rowley (eds.), pp. 147-165. (British
                Archaeological Reports). Oxford: BAR.

Discussion

TURTON: If I understand correctly what you have been saying, the same has been said in recent years by anthropologists about their appropriate unit of analysis—that it should be a regional system. There are two reasons for this: ethnic boundaries are 'emergent', not given, so we need to understand this process; and that there are tremendous economic interdependencies. To take one group on its own leaves you with all kinds of loose ends.

HINES: Indeed, I think that sums up very well what I believe I can see back in this period.

TURTON: What anthropologists now accept is that a 'cultural language' can cover a whole region. In the past they would assume that each 'society' had its own culture which fitted nicely on top of it.

HINES: This sort of 'regionality' is an important feature of the picture I think I can discern. I have tried using the term 'imperialism' to refer to it. This is influenced substantially by the use of the term 'empire' to refer to, say, the Celtic 'empire' of the last millennium BC, where one is indeed talking about just such an extensive cultural zone. I also think that there are useful analogies to be drawn between this sort of entity and a political empire of a more familiar form, such as the Roman Empire or the British Empire.

TURTON: There are ethnographic examples of peoples who can be distinguished from each other linguistically but who nevertheless have to be thought of as integral parts of a regional unit.

WOOD: Can I take up that point? Something struck me when you were talking about territoriality and group-formation. You may be aware of the debate about the 'personality of the law'. The point is that a Goth is subject to Gothic law and a Frank is subject to Frankish law, etc. A problem which then emerges is how you tell whether you are Gothic or not. There is a very clear statement in *Lex ripuaria* which says simply that a man's *gens* is determined entirely by where he is born.

HINES: That could be interpreted as a response to a particular, topical problem. It could have been the case that in western continental Europe around the year 600 a lot of people needed to worry about how they decided what *gens*, what group, an individual belonged to. And so a decision is made: "We select *this* variable: the place of your birth makes you a Goth, a Frank, or whatever".

WOOD: Yes, but much more important, presumably, is the issue of *how* you decide things. If you have different Ripuarian and Salian law codes, you do not want somebody to end up in one place being accused of a particular crime which gets a certain punishment and then saying, "No, no, I am not subject to that". What you are doing is to say, basically, that these groups do not move much—your aristocrats are always going to be outside the normal run of the law. They are always going to be tried before the king or whoever. What you are saying, therefore, is that the real issue is "to what local court is somebody likely to go?".

HINES: How is the rule actually formulated? Is it *ubi natus est*, or something like that? Is it absolutely precise as a criterion?

WOOD: It is absolutely precise.

HINES: Where you were born is likely to determine where you are brought up, and that in turn is likely to determine all sorts of habits and cultural features that you pick up. Some writing on ethnicity stresses the variability, the optionality, of ethnic identity, as if it were a purely voluntaristic matter. Now in South Wales, I know of one or two Englishmen who have successfully become 'Welsh' in a real sense, but of a lot more who would very much like to become Welsh but cannot do so because they cannot shake off some of those ingrained features they bring in from outside. Whatever the theory, I suspect that in practice ethnic identity can rarely be exchanged at will in an easy sort of way.

GREEN: [Made two points which have been incorporated into the main paper: see text, page 79, note 3]. My third point is really a tentative question. You have cited Godłowski on the homogeneity of the East Germanic groups. Do you think this really is a homogeneity, or do you think it is a matter of our inability to differentiate between them?

HINES: Here we have to evaluate the limited range of material culture that survives for us to study. Within that limited range of evidence I do not believe we are really faced predominantly with our own inability to identify differences because we can compare that particular period with different periods and see distinctions between sub-groups growing as one moves into later periods. However we could put important glosses on the very general statement that you query, for instance by noting that homogeneity is very much more marked in respect of metalwork than it is, for instance, in pottery—although even with the pottery one can realistically talk in terms of different 'circles', 'regions' and so on. For the most part, however, one would quite properly struggle to assert that any one of these 'circles' formed some unified entity on the grounds of the pottery alone.

GREEN: Can you be more precise as to what region you have in mind here, and then, in view of the fact that there are possible chronological differences, what period of time?

HINES: The whole region that Godłowski surveyed equates fairly closely to the old East Germany, Poland and Czechoslovakia.

GREEN: As far as that?

HINES: Yes, certainly including Bohemia and Moravia. Godłowski studies the period from the late second century through to about the middle of the fifth; I was referring here specifically to the period around the second half of the third and the early fourth centuries: the so-called period C2.

GREEN: I hear that with some measure of relief, because you place it in a region further south and in a later period. So I need not apply what you said to what I think.

HINES: You are really interested in the Baltic coast?

GREEN: The Baltic coast, where, as I read the evidence I have come across as an outsider, it is extremely difficult to differentiate between Goths in the first two centuries and the preceding Vandals and *Rugii*.[6] Would you accept that?

HINES: On the whole yes: one does not have such abrupt changes, and there is continuity.

TURTON: Is material culture the evidence you are using?

HINES: Yes.

TURTON: To what extent is material culture a useable way of distinguishing one group from another?

HINES: I would characterise it as a used way rather than a useable way.

TURTON: I was once sent some photographs of wooden stools/headrests coming from south western Ethiopia, by the late Professor Eike Haberland of the Frobenius Institute in Frankfurt. He had bought them in the market at Maji but had omitted to note the ethnic identity of the people he had bought them from. So he sent the photographs to me as someone who knew the area and asked me to identify the 'ethnic origin' of each stool. It proved impossible to do this, since all or none of them could have come from any of several different groups in the area.

RICHARDS: I found myself in total agreement with your interpretation of archaeological cultures. And whether you want to call it cultural history or not, I find it a much more sophisticated approach to the interpretation of cultures than what I think is the traditional Cultural History school. How you seem to be describing how people are using artefacts is more in accord with how Ian Hodder might write about it.

You tend though to talk about 'economy', 'society' and 'ideology' as if they were distinct spheres; this goes back to the point David made: it is like saying that everything is ritual,

---

6 *Rugii'* is the form used in Tacitus' *Germania* XLIV.

everything is ideology, everything is society—these are modern constructs. You cannot talk about economic behaviour and ideological behaviour: these are always intertwined aspects.

HINES: I accept that the classification, or taxonomy, is for modern convenience, to parcel things up within manageable compartments. I would certainly accept that all of these different forms of activity are likely to be (if indeed they are not always) interconnected in some way and that they affect one another. I would not think, though, that the division of remains from the past into those different categories is entirely unrealistic.

If we take evidence for textile production, pottery production, or the grinding of grain, etc., it is certainly possible to look at that data in purely economic and technical terms. That is not to say that there are not going to be ritual aspects involved in what people might have used particular types of pots for, when and how grain was ground, and so on, ideological aspects like that; and also social aspects in terms of who it was who was required or allowed to do certain jobs. But I do not think it is unrealistic to divide these things up in an analytical way as long as one realises that this is an analytical approach.

RICHARDS: I think it is perhaps dangerous if it leads us to try to categorise behaviour in that way. You say pottery production may not have been economic. In fact it may have been a very important social or religious activity; so indeed could almost anything you can think of, really.

HINES: Pottery may not have been an ideal example to choose. But one can certainly write a purely technical description of pottery.

RICHARDS: But that would be to look at it purely in modern terms.

HINES: But it would not be unrealistic; it wouldn't be misleading anybody to say "this, technically, was how pots were made". It might leave out a lot that you could say about pots, but you would not be telling anybody any lies about the subject. In an ideal world, one could offer some sort of factual answer to a basic question like "What did the early Anglo-Saxons eat?", covering basic facts of subsistence without being a culturally comprehensive view. A positive answer like "We know they ate such-and-such vegetables and the meat of these animals" could say nothing about possible ritual precepts or taboos concerning the consumption of some available foods. The point that a whole range of cultural phenomena are often intimately interconnected is one that I certainly accept.

RICHARDS: In terms of what they ate, subsistence might have been the least important factor.

HINES: I agree it might.

DUMVILLE: This was a wonderfully provocative paper, and I was excited positively and adversely all over the place. Positively, if you pursue Irish and Welsh legal material, particularly the Irish because of its earlier date, with reference to the craftsman as somebody with social mobility, you will find a lot of material which would both support that notion and quite consciously address the paradox which you were speaking about, in that a craftsman (which in Irish and in Welsh terms could mean somebody who is a craftsman with words as well as somebody involved with the technical production of something) is somebody who has considerable status. It is possible to rise to that status, but it is also possible for a patron of somebody working their way up to cut the development off. There is some rich material there which would help [see text, note 2].

Going off in a completely different direction, you talk about the absence of a politically unified England before the tenth century. I see exactly what you mean. If one starts to speak about politics and state-formation, that is obviously so, but my impression is that if we are talking in terms of what elsewhere you called 'an agreed playing field' as marked out by material culture and so on already in the seventh century then you are talking about England as a unit. It is not an artificial construct. We are also talking about a political playing field which seems to be recognised, although one remembers Eric John's argument that Northumbria constituted an *alter orbis* in the Anglo-Saxon view of its own world. Nonetheless, we have kings playing for dominance over the area, although there is the complicating factor that they are also playing for dominance over the Britons and the Picts.

HINES: That, I think, was the main reason that led me to put the case as I did: the fact that the earlier *imperium* that is referred to in Bede's *Historia ecclesiastica* is very clearly an *imperium* over Britons as well as the English, rather than a unification of the English.

DUMVILLE: I was not quite sure what you were getting at when you spoke of the end of Anglo-Saxon paganism as a partly politicised religious cult.

HINES: That was being deliberately provocative. I was drawing on views I reached in a paper (unpublished) I read to a symposium some years ago under the title of 'The Opium of the People? Anglo-Saxon Paganism in its Social Context'. It was an analysis of what evidence we have for the organisation of Anglo-Saxon pagan religion, putting that against what we know or think we know of its social context. Interestingly (for me), at this year's International Society of Anglo-Saxonists conference in Oxford, John Blair read a paper on Anglo-Saxon paganism and, quite independently, made many of the points that I had thought I had discovered in my review of the topic. Amongst these is the important point that nearly all of the evidence that we have for Anglo-Saxon paganism relates to a very late pagan period, just the time when Christianity is at the door if not actually over the threshold in some parts of England; and secondly that where we can identify pagan sites, pagan practices and so on there seems to be a linkage between these and the élite, the aristocracy of the period. To take just one example, I mentioned one of the pagan sites we can identify, which is Harrow-on-the-Hill, Middlesex, called in Old English *Gumeninga hearh*, 'the shrine or temple of the Gumeningas'. One of the few other early examples we have of a *hearh* (temple) name is again in this *-inga hearh* form: *Besinga hearh* in a famous seventh century charter dealing with land around Farnham in Surrey. Comparable in character is another form in this charter, *Cusan weoh*: the shrine that belongs in some way to somebody called Cusa, who has some sort of proprietorship over it. On this sort of evidence, and the geographical distribution of such place-names, one can mount an argument that many of the pagan sites we can identify have been integrated into either a hierarchical social structure or a structure of political units like the *-ingas* groups.

DUMVILLE: To what extent does that depend upon your assertion that the *-ingas* names are not 'comfortably clannish' but relate to possession?

HINES: It is very intimately associated with that particular interpretation of the *-ingas* groups, which I recognise to be far from proven and probably a controversial point. I do, though, think that there is a good case to be made for it. I would say, as a way of amplifying that particular argument, that what I am focussing on is the function of the *-ingas* groups in the late sixth and seventh century rather than what the function of any such named groups might have been around the year 500 if there were any then. I am not insisting that the late sixth century was when these names began to emerge, although it very well might have been; the famous work by John Dodgson would support the view that most *-ingas* names are fairly late forrnations in these terms.

DUMVILLE: How then does this relate to John Dodgson's idea that these names were connected to secondary settlement?

HINES: My real difficulty with this question is that I am not sure that secondary settlement is a realistic or pertinent concept to introduce. If most of these names are relatively late formations and were formed in a period when the anglicisation of areas beyond what one can call the area of primary settlement was going on, it is not surprising for them to appear in substantial numbers and marked concentrations in just those newly anglicised areas. I do not believe that the process of expanding anglicisation in that period would have required much population movement.

DUMVILLE: The reason why I asked the question is that to have accepted Dodgson's formulation of his argument would have allowed you to capitalise on the possibility that here you have somebody leading off new types of community from pre-existing settlements, perhaps formed on a different social basis.

HINES: Yes, it would, but I am not sure that that needs to have happened. Even if the names imply this, once again one can go back to the notion of an origin myth: that these names might have served *mythically* to provide an origin and an identity for these people when the reality, both historical and contemporary, was rather different. You can have a name that declares all are part of one 'family', but the whole group will not necessarily be treated like that nor would they all necessarily have come from that sort of single source or stock.

TURTON: I am beginning to get a picture of small politico-territorial units, with leaders, competing over a playing field that is not just geographical but also cultural, because that kind of competition presupposes some degree of cultural unity. It is the cultural rules that are important not the actual terrain. How much use has been made by archaeologists and historians of Marshall Sahlins's writings about chiefdoms?

HINES: They are widely referred to [laughter].

HISTORY, AGE AND THE ANTHROPOLOGISTS

DAVID TURTON

*Refugee Studies Centre, University of Oxford, Queen Elizabeth House,
21 St Giles, Oxford GB-OX1 31A*

Introduction

I am an anthropologist whose research experience is confined to a small population of around 5000 individuals living in the far southwest of Ethiopia. Known to outsiders as Mursi, they combine cattle herding with the eultivation of sorghum and maize and display many of the 'classic' features of East African pastoralism, ineluding an egalitarian political structure and a complex age organisation. I was invited to contribute to the conference which gave rise to this book on the grounds that the 'recovery' of the 'eustoms and beliefs' of European populations at the close of the Western Roman empire demands an interdisciplinary approach and that the use of age differentiation as a principle of social structure and military organisation may also have characterised certain 'barbarian' populations during the 'age of migrations'.

The call for an interdisciplinary approach is a common corollary of increasing specialisation in the organisation of academic research and teaching and seems sufficiently apposite in this case to require no special justification. On the other hand, the extent to which age organisation was a characteristic of 'barbarian' social structure is a matter for historical investigation which 1 am totally unqualified to undertake. The reader is therefore entitled to wonder what possible contribution I can hope to make to the project of 'recovery' which the conference was intended to advance. I can think of two ways of responding to this question .

Firstly, I can present a practising anthropologist's account of the ambivalent relationship between anthropology and history. The relationship is ambivalent because anthropology, as we know it today, established a separate identity for itself by rejecting historical forms of explanation and, despite a recent growing together of the two disciplines, anthropologists still bear the marks of this 'early up-bringing'. It is, furthermore, a paradox of interdisciplinary work that, to be productive, it must be undertaken by precisely those people who have erected the disciplinary boundaries in the first place: people who are in touch with the latest developments and most advanced thinking in their respective fields. Since it is virtually a contradiction in terms for one person to be a specialist, in this sense, in more than one discipline, there is a danger that, in turning to another discipline for assistance, we may turn to an outmoded version of it—to yesterday's science. My account of the relationship between anthropology and history will, inevitably, be subjective and partial, but it may at least help in the process of understanding each other's disciplinary perspectives and preoccupations; and this must be the first step in any productive intellectual collaboration.

Secondly, I ean present, as I was invited to do, a case study of one area of anthropological investigation with which I happen to be familiar—East African age organisation. I do not

© C.I.R.O.S.S.
San Marino (R.S.M.)

AFTER EMPIRE:
TOWARDS AN ETHNOLOGY OF EUROPES'S BARBARIANS

for a moment believe that it is, or could be, possible to 'read off' the social structure and military organisation of populations living in Europe between the fifth and ninth centuries from ethnographic accounts of twentieth century African pastoralists. To suggest this would be to deny some of the most enduring values and hard-won understandings of modern anthropology. On the other hand, the use of physiological ageing, like that of biological reproduction, to classify people and organise social action, is sufficiently widespread that we may regard it as a human universal. It happens also that my own work on the age system of the Mursi has led me to see this system as, essentially, a 'male cult' dedicated to the ritualisation of male violence, and as the institutional focus of Mursi political identity. It brings together, therefore, two other topics for investigation, warfare and the definition of political units, which have obvious relevance to the understanding of European society during the transition to the Middle Ages. It may not be fanciful to suppose—and whether it is must be for others to judge—that insights gained from the study of these topics in contemporary non-European societies may help to illuminate the 'other country' that was Europe between the fifth and ninth centuries AD.

History and the Anthropologists

Anthropology (by which I mean 'social anthropology' as it is called in Britain and 'cultural' or 'socio-cultural' anthropology as it is called in the United States) was born in the early years of this century as a reaction against the idea that all explanations, to be worthy of the name, had to be in terms of origins—for historians, the origins of the nation-state, for biologists, the origins of species, for philologists the origins of languages and for anthropologists the origins of 'civilisation'. Contemporary 'primitives' were assumed by nineteenth century anthropologists to provide us with a window through which we could inspect our own past. This assumption was based on two others: that it was possible to arrange all known societies in a single sequence, according to a 'law' of evolutionary development and that contemporary non-European societies had, for some usually unexplained reason, got 'stuck' at different stages of this sequence. The same historicist assumptions guided attempts to explain the 'customs and beliefs' of these societies. Take, for example, the approach of Lewis Henry Morgan described as the 'father' of kinship studies, to the understanding of non-European kinship systems.

According to Morgan, kinship systems—or, what was for him the same thing, systems of kin terminology—reflect knowledge of how people are genealogically related. This knowledge is a consequence of marriage practices. So, if you find that in society x Ego uses the same term for Father and Father's Brother, this must be because the marriage rules of the society are (or were) such that any male of the senior generation could have been Ego's biological father. Morgan called this system of terminology 'classificatory', and it did not worry him that, while it was widely represented in the contemporary ethnographic record (this was his 'discovery'), there were no known examples of marriage rules which could have given rise to it. His response was simply to assume that classificatory kinship was a 'survival' from a time when 'group marriage', of one sort or another, was the norm. As marriage practices become more 'advanced' (i.e. as they approximate more closely the European model) so kinship terminologies reflect more accurately the genealogical 'facts': they become more 'descriptive' and less classificatory.

The reaction against such 'conjectural history' in anthropology did not originate from a questioning of the overall evolutionary and historicist framework within which all branches of nineteenth century science and scholarship were conducted but from a new way of gathering data: the method of 'participant observation'. The classic statement of the new method was provided by Bronislaw Malinowski in his first monograph on the Trobriand Islands, *Argonauts of the Western Pacific* (1922), where he writes that the "final goal" of the anthropologist is "to grasp the native point of view, his relation to life, to realise *his* vision of *his* world" (p. 25). This meant "cutting oneself off from the company of other white men and remaining in as close contact with the natives as possible" (p. 6). This way of gathering data was to have profound implications for the nature of anthropological explanation and for the future of anthropology as an academic discipline—more profound, no doubt, than Malinowski (who had dedicated *Argonauts* to Sir James Frazer) at first realised.

Malinowski and his more theoretically minded contemporary, A. R. Radcliffe-Brown, were responsible, between them, for a devastatingly successful attack on the doctrine of 'survivals' and on the use of 'conjectural history' to make sense of contemporary ethnographic data. They presented themselves, at least initially, as pragmatists rather than as revolutionaries: they were not against conjectural history because it was history but because it was conjectural. This, of course, was disingenuous since, if one is specifically looking for historical explanations, then one may be forced to conjecture, if the evidence is not available to make firm inferences.

The fact is that Malinowski and Radcliffe-Brown, and the generation of 'structural functionalist' anthropologists whom they taught and influenced, were simply not interested in historical explanations. As it happened, the societies they studied generally lacked reliable historical data, at least of the written variety, but this was not really the point. The point was that they wanted to provide *sociological*, not historical explanations. They wanted to show—and indeed had great success in showing—how these societies could be understood in their own terms as 'working' systems. The aim was no longer to show how the apparently bizarre behaviour of 'primitive' people fitted into a grand scheme of social development, but to show how it fitted into a particular social context as part of a 'functioning' system. This entailed an assumption of both spatial and temporal closure: the unit of study was given a clear spatial boundary and assumed to have a time-depth so shallow that it could, for all intents and purposes, be treated as unchanging—unless externally influenced or 'disrupted'.

Reaction against the 'equilibrium model' of structural functionalism began in the mid to late 1950s with the work of Leach (1954), Turner (1957) and Barth (1959). Endogenous change, conflict and individual decision-making now came to be seen as legitimate and necessary subjects for ethnographic enquiry and analysis. A decade later, the ghost of conjectural history had been so well exorcised that the Association of Social Anthropologists of the Commonwealth could devote an annual conference to the topic 'History and Social Anthropology' (Lewis 1968). By now the use of the 'ethnographic present' had fallen out of use in anthropological writing and anthropologists were even beginning to forge working links with a new 'breed' of fieldworking historians. Like the members of the so-called *Annales* school in France (Burke 1989), these 'new' historians were more interested in writing the history of particular regions, using both written and oral accounts, than they were in tracing the development of nation-states. Recent examples of genuinely inter-disciplinary collaboration between anthropologists and historians in the East African region are the collections edited by Donham and James (1986), Johnson and Anderson (1988) and Fukui and Markakis (1993). As for my own work, if I have gained any insight into the behaviour and experience of the Mursi over the past 20 years, it has been by seeing Mursi society' as bounded in neither space nor time but as the temporary product of large scale movements of population which have taken place gradually, over hundreds of years, and which are remembered highly selectively and schematically in oral tradition (Turton 1979, 1988 and 1991).

It is to be expected, of course, that the anti-historicism which helped to give birth to modern anthropology will have left a permanent mark upon it, and this it certainly has. Malinowski saw indigenous historical accounts as 'mythical charters', justifying and legitimising contemporary institutions. This hypothesis proved as productive of new insights and understandings as the rest of the functionalist framework of analysis, even though it led to what J. D. Y. Peel has called with some justice "the blocking presentism to which anthropologists are so subject" (1989): the doctrine that indigenous historical accounts *can* only tell us about present interests and concerns and not about what actually happened in the past (see also Peel 1984). If some anthropologists are now ready to ask "How did the past create the present?" most are still far more comfortable asking "How did the present create the past?" (Tonkin *et al.* 1989). But there is no reason why these questions should cancel each other out. As the above reference to the Mursi suggests, one can look for a link between indigenous historical accounts and what happened in the past while recognising that these accounts are cultural products, reflecting present needs and interests. Having been guilty of throwing out the baby of time with the bathwater of conjectural history, anthropologists had better be wary of throwing out the baby of culture with the bathwater of presentism.

The 'constructed' nature of cultural categories and classifications became a central concern of anthropologists during the 1960s and 70s when they began to define their purpose as the 'interpretation' of 'symbolic systems' (Geertz 1963, 1975). In the protracted debate about descent and descent groups, for example, it came to be realised that descent groups are not groups because of descent, but because they are composed of people who live together and/or cooperate in some regular activity (Scheffler 1966). This explained why groups could look very similar 'on the ground' while having very different descent 'ideologies'. The classic case is that of the Nuer who, despite the fact that they have become famous in the anthropological literature for their 'segmentary lineage system', do not, in fact, live in segmentary lineages at all but in villages which are made up of a vast and motley array of kin (Evans Pritchard 1940, 1951). The segmentary lineage system is, at most, a mental construct, a conceptual framework and, from this point of view, it seems difficult to go on talking about societies 'having' segmentary lineages, or patrilineal descent, as though these were of the same order of reality as a particular kind of subsistence system or house design. Indeed, the very notion of 'societies' as bounded, discrete entities, which was a key theoretical assumption of structural functionalism, came to be seen as outmoded. Boundaries, and the way boundaries are 'constructed', became another central concern of 'symbolic anthropology'.

If the key anthropological questions of the 1970s revolved around the issue of cultural construction—how *'they'* created themselves—the key questions of the 1980s and 1990s have revolved around the issue of ethnographic authority—how *'we'* created 'them'. There are at least three worries here. Firstly, how can any anthropologist reach an adequate understanding of another culture when the data he or she collects will be greatly affected by his or her cultural and disciplinary assumptions? Secondly, is not this very attempt to 'understand' another group of human beings, from a position of supposed cultural neutrality, an act of objectification which diminishes the humanity of those who are thus 'understood' and objectified? And thirdly, does not this diminution of *their* humanity help to bolster our own? For our own, culturally specific, Western view of what it means to be human takes for granted that to extend our knowledge and understanding of the world is to realise more fully our potential as human beings. This assumption is well illustrated by the carefully rehearsed statement that Neil Armstrong delivered as he stepped onto the lunar surface in 1969: "a small step for man, but a giant leap for mankind".

The dilemma for the anthropologist as presumably for the historian, in seeking to extend our knowledge and understanding of other cultures is that objectivity in cultural comparison cannot be achieved except from a culturally neutral position which is, by definition, unattainable. As Evans-Pritchard is reported to have remarked: "There is only one method in social anthropology, the comparative method, and that's impossible" (Needham 1975). The structural functionalists were able to live with this dilemma because they saw themselves as getting on with the necessary but preliminary task of describing and analysing particular 'societies'. In today's 'postmodern' world, however, anthropologists make a virtue of not even aspiring to a culturally neutral position nor, therefore, to objectivity in the sense of getting 'once for all, one small thing right' (C. D. Lewis 1992). "In anthropology" writes Kirsten Hastrup "we have come to realise that we are part of the world that we study. The world is no less real for that, of course, and no less open for investigation and generalisation" (1993:734).

But what this realisation does entail is that the prime objective of the anthropologist must be to "make it new" rather than to "get it right" (Rorty 1991:44 in Hastrup 1993:734): to see the world, including his or her own world, in a new light and to make what had previously appeared natural into something strange. This must be the beginning of all knowledge and it is in this spirit that I now turn to the subject of age.

A Comparison with Kinship

We can assume that it is a universal feature of human social life to make use of distinctions based on physiological ageing for social purposes. Like biological reproduction, ageing is a 'fact of life' which is treated in a wide variety of ways by different societies and used to construct widely different symbolic systems. It may therefore be helpful to compare age, as a subject of anthropological study, to kinship especially since age is relatively under-researched by anthropologists, while kinship has been the central preoccupation of the discipline.

Anthropological writings on kinship revolve around this question: if kinship is a biological constant, how can we explain the cultural variation in the way it is used? How can we account for different 'kinship systems'? The way this question is answered depends on the assumptions one makes about what a kinship system is and about the nature of kinship as a social construct. This goes to the heart of what one understands by culture and what one sees as distinctive about human social life. There are two main views.

The first, chronologically, was Morgan's view that kinship systems are, at base, expressions or reflections of biological relationships. The ultimate determinant of a kinship system, according to this view, is the way people are, or are thought to be, related, genealogically. As we saw earlier, very briefly, the idea that kinship systems 'reflect' biological relationships—

or rather knowledge of biological relationships—made it possible for Morgan to construct a 'theory' to account for variations in kinship systems. Partly because of the obvious weaknesses of Morgan's theory, few if any anthropologists would now accept this kind of causal, or determining, link between biology and kinship.

The second, and today most widely accepted, anthropological understanding of kinship is that it is a system of communication; that is, a symbolic system, rooted in a genealogical metaphor. A kinship terminology, on this view, is a taxonomy, modelled on a genetic grid. The problem of understanding cultural variation in kinship then becomes one of understanding why societies employ one kind of *metaphorical* system, based on genealogical relatedness, rather than another. If you cut the link between biology and kinship in this way, it obviously becomes much more difficult to construct a universal 'theory' of kinship. What then are the implications of cutting the link between biology and age differentiation?

First, you will not expect a particular age system to be an expression of the facts of physiological ageing. You will therefore not find it problematic that the 'rules', as adumbrated by the members of a society, neither fit these facts nor *can* fit them.

Second, you will not be inclined to view the age system, however formally institutionalised and ritually elaborated, as the product of certain organisational necessities, whether economic, political or military. You will not, in other words, seek an explanation for the system in the practical tasks which are seen to be accomplished in its name or through its agency.

Third, you will not, therefore, see the task of analysis as beginning and ending with the elucidation of the properties and functions of the system itself and comparing and contrasting it with others. In other words, you will not see 'it' as a thing in itself, as a kind of sub-system of a larger system which can be separated out, analytically, from its social context for separate consideration.

Fourth, you will, rather, seek understanding by viewing age differentiation in its widest social context, not as an 'age system', in the sense of an institutional complex or bounded, self-contained structure of rules and activities, but as a system of communication which makes use of age as its dominant metaphor—that is, as a way of talking about and representing something else that cannot, for some reason, be talked about directly. The question then becomes, what is this 'something else'? According to this view it is a mistake and a diversion to spend one's time trying to make sense of the rules (i.e. trying to work out how and under what conditions they could be made to 'work', or could have 'worked' in the past) and elucidating the properties and functions of 'the system', except as a necessary preliminary to the real business of asking what is being said, what meanings are being communicated, by the behaviour in question.

Fifth, the conclusions you come to will not constitute an elaboration of, or a contribution to, a theory of age systems. That is, you will, in the course of following through your study, arrive at conclusions, questions and insights which do not, on the face of it, have any *necessary* connection with age, precisely because their connection with age is metaphorical. You will be led, that is, to the study of 'something else'.

Age and the Anthropologists

But first, you will be confronted with a paradox. On the one hand, age (together with sex) is the most 'natural' means of classifying human beings, allocating roles and organising social life. Every culture, we must assume, distinguishes separate ages in the life cycle for some purposes, while protests about the feckless and/or riotous behaviour of the young are probably also universal. On the other hand, when age differences are made the basis of a formally constituted hierarchical structure, such as is found in East African herding societies, we find what appears to be a highly complex, 'artificial' and even unworkable mode of social organisation. Before looking at the way anthropologists have sought to understand this paradox, it would be helpful to have in mind a particular ethnographic case and for this purpose I now present a brief outline of the organisation of male age sets among the Mursi.

A fundamental distinction needs to be made between an age grade and an age set. An age grade is a named, ritually demarcated stage in the life cycle while an age set is a named society-wide category of men who progress through the grades together. The two most basic male age grades among the Mursi are *lusa*, boys, and *zuo* adults. These are subdivided into four grades of boys and three of adults, the senior grade of boys being called *teru* and the junior grade of adults, *rora*. The process of physical maturation which is socially recognised by these terms is, of course, a gradual and continuous one for each individual. But social maturation is achieved suddenly, publicly and collectively by all the *teru* of a locality through a three-day ceremony called *nitha* which not only makes the *teru* into adults but also forms them into an age set. When a new set is formed, members of the immediately senior set move from the grade of *rora* to that of *bara* (elders). Each of the three main territorial sections into which the Mursi are divided, Ariholi, Gongulobibi and Dola, holds its ceremony in that order within the same year. The priority of Ariholi, which is in the south of Mursiland, is said to derive from the fact that the Mursi first occupied this part of their present territory when they crossed from the west to the east bank of the Omo about 200 years ago.

The span of an age set depends on the interval that has elapsed since the formation of the previous one. When the most recent set (Geleba) was formed in 1991, its members ranged in age from approximately 15 to 45, since the last set (Benna) had been formed in 1961. Some of the men who were 'given' adulthood in the 1991 *nitha* had married children and had been acting as adult members of the community for many years. This 30 year interval was said by the Mursi to be abnormal and was explained by a succession of crises and bad years which had apparently prevented the organisation of such an important ceremony. And yet, when the ceremony was finally held, in January 1991, the general situation of the Mursi could not have been more critical, most notably because their southern neighbours, the Nyangatom, who had recently acquired large numbers of automatic weapons, had driven them from half of their territory and were threatening to drive them from the rest of it.

The fact is that any attempt to use age differences to create a ritually defined and society-wide hierarchy of fixed categories is bound to create anomalies, which will then have to be explained away. There will be the problem, for example, that the progress of most individuals through the formal system of grades will be more of less out of step with their physiological ageing and with their social responsibilities. The people themselves usually bring forward *ad hoc* explanations to account for the anomalies—such as the Mursi explanation for the delay in holding their last *nitha*. Outside observers may attempt to establish an underlying 'structural pattern', showing thereby that what appear to be anomalies are in fact systematic and predictable (Turton 1978:122).

In East Africa, age sets occur, or at any rate are most conspicuous, in non-centralised political systems. This probably explains why they have generally been seen by anthropologists as serving political ends, especially in those societies where there was no highly developed 'segmentary lineage system'. In her book *Primitive Government* (1962), Lucy Mair, a student of Malinowski and one of the leading figures of structural functionalist anthropology in its heyday, wrote that "the division into sets" is "primarily important as a means of organising government". Over ten years later, Walter Goldschmidt, a distinguished student of East African pastoralism, described "the age set system in East Africa" as

> ...a sociological device which is highly adaptive to the functions of governance, the main tenance of order, and the protection of property in a predominantly pastoral situation (Goldschmidt 1976:349).

There is an interesting and ironic similarity between this approach to understanding age systems and Morgan's approach to understanding classificatory kinship. For when it was found, as it more often than not was, that the supposed governmental functions of age sets were not being performed, or were being performed in an arbitrary and half-hearted way, this was explained away with some such assertion as that colonial rule had 'undermined' the system. Age sets were therefore constantly represented as having fallen away from an earlier more active and efficient mode of operation. What we see today are the 'survivals' of a time when age set systems were more efficient in carrying out tasks which they do now only in a rudimentary manner, at best. In other words, and as Morgan asserted to explain the absence of 'group marriage' in association with classificatory kinship terminology, it was different in the past.

In attributing political and administrative functions to age set systems—or rather, in seeing such functions as their *raison d'être*—writers like Mair and Goldschmidt (and they were expressing a fair consensus of their colleagues) were ignoring one of the most basic injunctions of structural functionalism: to look for the contemporary functions of an institution rather than to conjecture about its past functions. If we look at age set systems with this injunction in mind, what do we find?

First, we find that age sets are not groups at all but society-wide categories of the male population. They are mental, not empirical realities. Of course, the locally resident members of an age set do form a group which does things together, but this is not an age set: it is an age group formed on the basis of age set membership. Dyson-Hudson expressed this well when he wrote: "The unity of an age set is a conceptual unity in the minds of the Karimojong, not the observable unity of, say, a company on a drill square" (1966:174).

Second, we find that neither age sets nor age groups own anything of any significance. They do not own or control stock nor any other means of material production. Rights in herds and cultivable land rest in families, not age sets. Rights to grazing and water are held in common or associated with particular clans and/or families (Baxter *et al.* 1978).

Third, we find that when the members of an age set assemble, *qua* members of that set, they do so for ritual, not political purposes. They are not political assemblies with executive, administrative or legal tasks.

Fourth, we find that even though age set members may be used as the agents of force on behalf of the community, they are only the *agents* of force—they do not control its use. They obviously have law and order and military tasks and, as in the case of Dingiswayo and Shaka, they can obviously be adapted to form highly effective 'regimental' organisations. But when one has said all that, there is more left over to explain: age set systems exist without such 'regimental' or even military (in the organisational sense) characteristics. When Evans-Pritchard wrote of the Nuer that "the age set system ought not to be described as a military organisation" (1940:253), he was noting something which he expected his readers to find odd and which he no doubt found odd himself. Now that it is more readily accepted that age systems cannot be understood simply in terms of the practical tasks performed by age set members, there is a recognition that anthropologists in the past overdid the attribution to them of military and political tasks. They may be *given* political and military tasks but this does not, of course, make them political and military necessities. "Sets are seized on, as it were, to perform the task, simply because they are there" (Baxter *et al*. 1978:19).

Fifthly, we find that the overwhelmingly dominant kind of activity associated with age differentiation in East Africa is male ritual activity. If we are concerned with the present, even with the present as a clue to the past, and with the people's own assessments and evaluations of their customs and beliefs, we will conclude that age systems among East African herders are, essentially, the focus of the ritual life of men and only by extension political and/or military organisations. That is, if they have political and military functions and characteristics, this is only as a consequence of their ritual role. They are the East African equivalent of what anthropologists have described as 'Men's Cults' in other societies, notably Melanesian ones. Their purpose, in the eyes of the people themselves, like that of Melanesian Men's Cults, is to make men into men, and this is why the Mursi, for example, consider their age system to be one of the few institutions which they must at all costs preserve.

A brief reference to Central Brazil is in order, because of the similarities between male ritual life there—focused on the so called 'men's house' where the men and boys of a village spend most of their time—and in Melanesia. David Maybury Lewis writes as follows:

> ...the belief that Central Brazilian age sets were 'originally' or 'mainly' military organisations stems from a misunderstanding of the way the Indians themselves talk about them. They stress that initiation, the men's house(s), and the age set or age grade systems train men to be men. These institutions define what it means to be a man in those societies. Warfare is also seen as an expression of manliness, but by no means the only one (1984:134).

Military activity is probably seen in all societies as "an expression of manliness"—it is certainly culturally valued in men rather than in women. So it is not surprising that age set systems in East Africa and Central Brazil, like Men's Cults in Melanesia, are very much connected with warfare.

The point I wish to stress is that the connection is ritual rather than organisational. It is not even, *pace* Baxter and Almagor, that age sets exist first and are made use of for military purposes afterwards. It is rather that male military activity is seen as ritualised activity from the start, not as a purely pragmatic activity which is given the stamp of legitimacy by ritual. On the contrary, warfare *is* ritual: not something which men engage in because they are by nature aggressive and competitive but which they can *only* engage in as a ritually transformed category of the population. If so, it would seem almost a truism that, the more warlike the society—and societies do differ in the degree of their "warlikeness" (Howell and Willis 1989)—the more evidence there will be of institutions devoted to the ritualisation of male violence. In seeking to understand age systems in East Africa, then, and in attempting to apply this understanding to the social institutions of early medieval Europe, we should look beyond the narrow confines of age systems themselves and consider the wider question, "Why should male violence be ritualised?"

The Ritualisation of Male Violence Among the Mursi

I take my lead in this section from a study of ritualised male violence at Avatip, on the Sepik River in Papua New Guinea, by Simon Harrison (1993). Harrison's argument, in a nutshell, is that the problem men have at Avatip is not how to control violence between already 'given' and politically independent groups, but how to carve out such groups 'in the first place'; how to 'extract' themselves, or rather the *idea* of themselves, as separate political units, from an all-embracing sociality.

Village communities are caught up in networks of 'normative ties'—of clanship, marriage, economic exchange, etc.—and, in order to create separate political identities for themselves, they have to find a way of 'overcoming' or denying these ties.

> ...peaceful sociality within and between communities is taken for granted. But because it is taken for granted, the only way that bounded groups can be created is by purposive action *against* that sociality (Harrison 1993:149).

The 'purposive action' in question is male violence and the institutional focus of this violence—and therefore of the community's political identity—is the Men's Cult. It is not just that men are trained in the tactics of warfare in the men's house—this would not require ritual means. It is rather that they are transformed in a ritual sense and that this ritual transformation is seen as necessary in order that the warfare they subsequently engage in should have the appropriate 'meaning' and thereby achieve the appropriate ends. It is this link between the ritualisation of male violence and the creation of a separate political identity for a group that I find so suggestive when applied to the Mursi case. I hope it might also prove suggestive when applied to historical societies, whether or not these may be said to 'have' age sets. I shall pursue the point by considering the circumstances under which the Arioli section of the Mursi held their *nitha* in January 1991.

I have already noted that the formation of a new set had been considered long overdue for several years by the Mursi and that they explained this by pointing to a series of crises that had affected them since the last set had been formed in 1961. The 1970s and 80s were certainly disastrous decades, beginning in the early 1970s with the worst famine in living memory. This was not a sudden event but the culmination of a long-term process of ecological degradation, falling crop yields and growing pressure on resources brought about by incorporation into the Ethiopian state. During the early 1980s about 20 per cent of the Mursi population migrated to previously uninhabited land in the Mago Valley where there were better prospects for cultivation but where tsetse flies made cattle herding virtually impossible (Fig. 4.1). Famine returned in the mid-1980s and then a new threat emerged as automatic weapons began to spread into the Omo valley from the war in southern Sudan. Among the first to acquire these weapons were the Nyangatom who used them against the Mursi for the first time in February 1987, killing at least 100 and possibly as many as 300 people in one day. The attack took place in the far south of Mursiland which the Mursi refer to as the 'stomach' of their country. Immediately following the attack they evacuated this area and had still not permanently re-occupied it when I last visited them in October 1992, although by that time they were beginning to acquire automatic weapons of their own.

Why then did the Mursi decide to form a new age set in 1991? It might be argued that they did so, in spite of the difficulties they were still experiencing, because of pressures internal to the age set 'system': on the one hand, some of the men who were waiting to gain adult status were well over 40 years old, with married children of their own and, on the other, those men who could 'hand on' adulthood to the new set were now very few in numbers, having become elders when the last set had been formed in 1961. Such pressures were certainly a factor, but there are also grounds for believing that the ceremony was held when it was not *despite* but *because* of the situation the Mursi were in at the time; that it was a kind of ritual reply to the Nyangatom attack of February 1987.

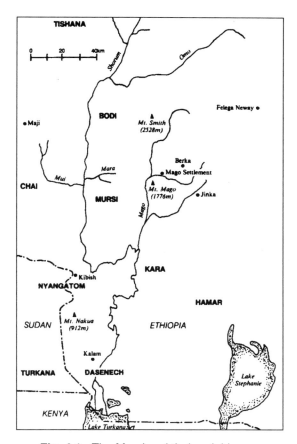

Fig. 4.1 - The Mursi and their neighbours.

Firstly, the Ariholi *nitha*, which was held virtually under the eyes of the Nyangatom as they sported their kalashnikovs on the other side of the Omo, could be seen as an assertion of Mursi ownership of the territory they had evacuated in 1987 and which they still considered too insecure for permanent occupation. One of the functions of public ritual is to establish *de jure* rights to territory (Turton 1979) and the locations of age set rituals in particular are used, in oral history, to mark the migratory routes of previous generations. Here we need to note some of the symbolism involved in the *nitha*. The main events take place in and around a specially constructed enclosure of branches with a tree at its centre and two openings, one opposite the other. The enclosure for the Ariholi *nitha* was built around a young tree, about 6 feet tall. This tree was chosen because, being young, it would 'grow up' with the members of the new age set. The symbolism therefore identified the members of the new set with the tree and, consequently, with the place where it was rooted. The fact that the *nitha* had been held there was concretely symbolised by the tree, which would be pointed to in future to validate Mursi claims to the surrounding territory.

Secondly, the *nitha* was an essential step in preparing the way for a *military* response to the Nyangatom attack. This was because it brought about a ritual transformation, no less real for being ritual, of the men whose task it would be, in due course, to make that response—those between the ages of 15 and 45. At the same time as they became jural adults they also became *rora*, that is occupants of the age grade which is formally associated with military activity. But of course, the majority of them already were adults and, for all of them, their new status would make no difference to the conduct of daily life. In becoming *rora* they did not become, overnight, more effective in military technique nor gain in physical ability. They *had* been transformed 'overnight', however, into a category of men whose 'official' role it was to engage in warfare, while those who died in the process would now die as jural adults rather than as 'boys'. This transformation did not even depend on participation in the ceremony. In fact only a very small proportion of those who became *rora* and members of the new set actually took part in the *nitha*. Those who did were mainly the younger boys who were of the traditionally 'correct' age—between about 15 and 20. Most of the older 'boys' (i.e. married men in their 30s and 40s) remained in the eastern grazing areas, ready to guard their cattle against possible attack by their traditional enemies to the east, the Hammar, and were present at the ceremony only by proxy.

It is important to recognise here that ritual *does* things: it is more than just a post facto 'expression' of, or comment on, what is already the case. To those in our secularised society who find this difficult to accept, two points can be made. Firstly, if this is how the Mursi and people like them think about ritual, as they certainly do, then their behaviour must obviously be understood from this point of view. Secondly, we can recognise the power of ritual to *do* things from our own experience of what J. L. Austin called the 'performative' function of language. Ritual, after all, is a kind of language, in the sense that it communicates meaning through symbols. We may therefore be tempted to think of it as essentially a descriptive medium, used to express or declare what is already the case. Austin pointed out that such a characterisation will not do, even for language. For one can think of sentences which cannot be true or false because they do not report or assert that something is or is not the case: rather they *make* it the case. These are sentences in which "the uttering of the sentence is, or is part of, the doing of an action," such as the words 'I do' when uttered during a marriage ceremony. "When I say, before the registrar or altar, etc., 'I do', I am not reporting on a marriage: I am indulging in it" (Austin 1962:5-6). To say that warfare is an activity of a ritually defined category of the population, then, is to say more than that a ritual 'stamp' must be given to what is already the case. The ritual definition *makes* it the case.

Anthropology and the Recovery of the Past

How, then, might the study of a contemporary non-industrial society, such as the Mursi, be able to help in 'recovering' the European past? We can dismiss at the outset any idea that anthropology can give us a kind of privileged access to the past, in the absence of hard historical or archaeological evidence. The societies anthropologists study are as much caught up in history as the societies anthropologists belong to: they are not available as time machines. But they surely are available, as sources of comparative data, to assist in the process of understanding, and framing generalisations about, historical and—although presumably with more difficulty—archaeological data. A number of anthropologists have already shown the value of applying the results of anthropological research to historical materials, thereby contributing to the creation of a kind of 'historical ethnography'. Examples that come to mind are Alan MacFarlane's study of witchcraft accusations in Tudor and Stuart England (1970) and of the origins of English individualism (1978), Marshall Sahlins' interpretation of the Hawaiian reaction to the arrival of Captain Cook in 1778 (1985) and the work of my Manchester colleague, David Rhuebottom, on marriage practices in fifteenth century Ragusa (Dubrovnik) (1988). What these various studies have in common is that they have brought to bear on good historical evidence insights and methods of analysis which have been the product of specialist research, central to the academic discipline of anthropology. They show that, while anthropology cannot 'recover' the past, in the sense of providing a convenient substitute for empirical evidence, it can provide striking insights into such evidence as exists, especially where this relates to topics which have been central to anthropological research.

A second way in which anthropology may be able to help in the recovery of the European past is by calling into question and inducing critical reflection on the culturally specific categories of historical understanding. One reason why anthropology cannot provide a window on the past is that it does not even provide a window on the present, in the sense of a transparent screen behind which the observer can remain insulated from what he or she is observing. I do not refer here to the fact that the anthropologist, unlike the historian, takes part in the daily lives of the people he or she is studying, but to the fact that, like the historian, he or she brings to this study such a baggage of taken for granted cultural assumptions that the 'reality' under observation is already a construction of the observer. Interpreted in this sense, Hastrup's comment, quoted earlier, that "we are part of the world that we study" applies as much to historians as to anthropologists. The only difference is that anthropologists are professionally dedicated, and prepared by their experience of fieldwork, to getting at what Malinowski called 'the native point of view'. Because of this, anthropological accounts of other cultures may help historians and archaeologists to recognise the ethnocentrism of their categories and assumptions and therefore to hypothesise with greater boldness, inventiveness and daring. It is not a matter simply of using contemporary ethnographic material to fill the gaps in the historical and archaeological record, but of loosening the grip of disciplinary and cultural assumptions which get in the way of what A. N. Whitehead called the process of 'imaginative generalisation' (1929:7). This, presumably, is the most productive way in which one discipline can hope to contribute to the project of another.

References

Austin, J. L.
    1962   *How to do things with words.* Oxford: Oxford University Press.
Baxter, P. T. W., & U. Almagor (eds.)
    1978   *Age, Generation and Time: Some Features of East African Age Organisations.* London: C. Hurst.
Barth, F.
    1959   *Political Leadership among Swat Pathans.* London: Athlone Press.
Burke, P.
    1989   French historians and their cultural identities. In *History and Ethnicity.* E. Tonkin, M. McDonald & M. Chapman (eds.), pp.157-167. (ASA Monographs, 27). London: Routledge.
Donham, D., & W. James (eds.)
    1986   *The Southern Marches of Imperial Ethiopia: Essays in History and Social Anthropology.* Cambridge: Cambridge University Press.
Dyson-Hudson, N.
    1966   *Karimojong Politics.* Oxford: Clarendon Press.
Evans-Pritchard, E. E.
    1940   *The Nuer: A description of the mode of livelihood and political institutions of a Nilotic people.* Oxford: Clarendon Press.

Evans-Pritchard, E. E. (*cont.*)
1951   *Kinship and Marriage among the Nuer*. Oxford: Clarendon Press.
Fukui, K., & J. Markakis (eds.)
1993   *Ethnicity and Conflict in the Horn*. London: John Currey.
Geertz, C.
1963   Religion as a cultural system. In *Anthropological Approaches to the Study of Religion*. M. Banton (ed.). (ASA Monographs, 3). London: Tavistock.
1975   Thick description: towards an interpretive theory of culture. In *The Interpretation of Culture*. C. Geertz (ed.), pp. 3-30. London: Hutchinson.
Goldschmidt, W.
1976   *Culture and Behavior of the Sebei: A Study in Continuity and Adaptation*. Berkeley, CA: University of California Press.
Harrison, S.
1993   *The Mask of War: Violence, Ritual and the Self in Melanesia*. Manchester: Manchester University Press.
Hastrup, K.
1993   Hunger and the hardness of facts. *Man* 28: 727-739.
Howell, S., & R. Willis (eds.)
1989   *Societies at Peace: Anthropological Perspectives*. London/New York: Routledge.
Johnson, D., & D. Anderson (eds.)
1988   *The Ecology of Survival: Case Studies from Northeast African History*. London/ Boulder, CO: Lester Crook Academic Publishing/Westview.
Leach, E. R.
1954   *Political Systems of Highland Burma*. London: George Bell & Sons.
Lewis, C. D.
1992   After an Encaenia, *The CompletePoems*, pp. 688-689. London: Sinclair-Stevenson.
Lewis, I. M.
1968   *History and Social Anthropology*. (ASA Monographs, 7). London: Tavistock.
MacFarlane, A.
1970   *Witchcraft in Tudor and Stuart England*. London: Routledge.
Malinowski, B.
1922   *Argonauts of the Western Pacific*. London: Routledge and Kegan Paul.
Mair, L.
1962   *Primitive Government*. Harmondsworth: Penguin.
Maybury-Lewis, D.
1984   Age and kinship: a structural view. In *Age and Anthropological Theory*. D. I. Kertzer & J. Keith (eds.), pp. 123-140. Ithaca, NY/London: Cornell University Press.
Needham, R.
1975   Polythetic classification: convergence and consequences. *Man* (NS) 10: 349-369.
Peel, J. D. Y.
1984   Making history: the past in the Ijesha present. *Man* (NS) 19: 111-132.
1989   The cultural work of Yoruba ethnogenesis. In *History and Ethnicity*. E. Tonkin, M. McDonald & M. Chapman (eds.), pp. 198-215. (ASA Monographs,27). London: Routledge.
Rhuebottom, D. B.
1988 '   'Sister first': betrothal order and age at marriage in fifteenth-century Ragusa. *Journal of Family History* 13 (4): 359-376.
Rorty, R.
1991   *Objectivity, Relativism and Truth*. Cambridge: Cambridge University Press.
Sahlins, M.
1985   *Islands of History*. Chicago: Chicago University Press.

Scheffler, H.
  1966   Ancestor worship in anthropology: or observations on descent and descent groups. *Current Anthropology* 75 (5): 541-551.
Tonkin, E., M. McDonald & M. Chapman (eds.)
  1989   *History and Ethnicity*. (ASA Monographs, 27). London: Routledge.
Turner, V. W.
  1957   *Schism and Continuity in an African Society*. Manchester: Manchester University Press.
Turton, D. A.
  1978   Territorial Organisation and Age among the Mursi. In *Age, Generation and Time: Some Features of East African Age Organisations*. P. T. W. Baxter & U. Almagor (eds.), pp. 95-130. London: C. Hurst & Co.
  1979   A journey made them: territorial segmentation and ethnic identity among the Mursi. In *Segmentary Lineage Systems Reconsidered*. Queen's University Papers in Social Anthropology, Vol.4, pp. 119-143. Belfast: Queen's University.
  1988   Looking for a cool place: the Mursi, 1890s-1980s. In *The Ecology of Survival: Case Studies from Northeast African History*. D. Johnson & D. Anderson (eds.), pp. 261 -282. London/Boulder: Lester Crook Academic Publishing/Westview.
  1991   Movement, warfare and ethnicity in the Lower Omo Valley. In *Herders, Warriors and Traders: Pastoralism in Africa*. J. Galaty & P. Bonte (eds.), pp. 145-170. Boulder: Westview Press.
Whitehead, A. N.
  1929   *Process and Reality*. Cambridge: Cambridge University Press.

Discussion

RICHARDS: What are the outward signs of belonging to an age set?

TURTON: There are no outward signs but they know precisely the age difference between one person and another. They do not 'know' how old they are. If I wanted to know how old someone was, in our sense, and there were two or three older men around, they would count off the years since the person was born, remembering events that occurred from one year to the next.

RICHARDS: Amongst the Mursi, are age sets an exclusively male institution? Is there no differentiation among women?

TURTON: Women take the age status of their husbands. So it is really a male cult.

RICHARDS: In general?

TURTON: Among East African pastoralists, yes. When the *teru* became *rora*, so did their wives, but their wives were not allowed at the ceremony.

RICHARDS: Have anthropologists considered what general principles there might be in defining the number of rungs on the age set ladder, and where the intervals are placed?

TURTON: There seems to be a general consensus that there are three basic grades which have been described as warrior, elder and retired elder. There seems to be a stage when men are no longer militarily active and become politically more important—they are married and have children, and take part in political assemblies. This stage, or 'grade', is usually described as elderhood. Of course, only a few men in the elder grade actually do have political influence but, unless you are in that grade, you cannot make your way politically. So, amongst the Mursi, you've got *rora* (warrior), *bara* (elder), and then a third grade, which they call *karui* (retired elder) who, as one man said to me, "can sit back and just listen". I think those three grades are probably found across the board.

RICHARDS: There is a fourth group of people, the infants, children....

TURTON: Amongst the Mursi, there are several grades of juniors. The senior grade of boys, called *teru*, is, in a sense, the most important, because it is the *teru* who are waiting to become adults.

HINES: Can a group of *rora* be supplemented, by holding a new ceremony which will add more *rora* to the existing group? Or, when you create a new age-set of *rora*, does this automatically push the previous set of *rora* up to the next category?

TURTON: The answer is yes to both questions. There is a period of, perhaps, three or four years during which the set is 'open'. During that period, other people can join it, but the minute a new set is formed it pushes the others up. This is probably one of the factors which holds back the formation of a new set, because the people who are handing on adulthood are the people who are going to be shut out from active political life in the future.

GREEN: I was reminded of the distinction between linguistics and philology: linguistics looking at language as it is, philology looking at language as it has become and is becoming. In other words, the distinction between synchronic and diachronic. How do you see the possibility of applying your anthropological approach, which I see as essentially a synchronic one, to the historic dimension and therefore to historical studies? How do you see the bridge from your discipline, from synchronic to diachronic?

TURTON: There are two ways of looking at it. One way is to ask whether an anthropologist needs to have an historical perspective. I certainly did not intend to suggest that being aware of the significance of time is unimportant in anthropology. Quite the opposite.

The other way of looking at it is to ask how an anthropological analysis like this can be of use to those who are directly looking at what happened in the past. I think I would have to say that anthropology is giving us, all of us, the opportunity to look at our data in a new light. Not in the sense that we should wonder whether they 'had' this or that institution but in the sense that the exercise of coming to terms with, and trying to understand, another culture helps us to bring into relief and therefore distance ourselves from certain assumptions we may have started out with. If one looks at history as the study of other cultures, then anthropology ought to be of help in the sense that it helps us in the process of looking at the world in a new way, making what is thought of as natural into something strange.

DUMVILLE: Are there scholars who would call themselves 'historical anthropologists' or would that be seen as a contradiction in terms?

TURTON: No, I think all anthropologists nowadays would have a lot of time for history. When I went off to study the Mursi twenty odd years ago, I was not interested in what they told me about their past; history was merely the projection of present interests. One of the things they most wanted to tell me about was "how we got here" but I listened in polite indifference. This was not what I had come to hear. But I later realised that this attitude to the past greatly impoverished my attempt to understand the present. I have only been able to understand what I have about the Mursi by focussing on this process of migration. In an article called "A journey made them" (1979), I argue that this was a huge movement of population which gave rise to individual political or ethnic units which then fell away and disappeared. As the Mursi tell the story, they started out from a certain place and moved on and on, gathering other groups as they went. One cannot, as one used to try to do, totally unhinge this kind of story from what happened in the past. So the problem is how are they related? My own understanding of the Mursi migration story is that it was a movement of people across the landscape, not of Mursi, but of people, which actually gave rise to different political groups, of which the Mursi are one. They have only been in existence about as long as the USA, for 200 years at most.

GREEN: What you just said constitutes a very illuminating parallel to Wenskus' theory about the formation of Germanic tribes in the process of migration.

WOOD: It would not only fit Wenskus, but it would also be a way of interpreting the whole migration story as told by Jordanes.

TURTON: The point is that they always talk as though they had made a journey, and one's initial reaction as a structural functional anthropologist is to say: "I do not want to know about that".

GREEN: What do you say about history being meant as a justification of the present, a mode of thought typical of almost any society which sees history as an attempt to explain the present? For that reason alone the anthropologist concerned with the present cannot cut himself off from that view of history.

TURTON: Absolutely. I presume, in a way, that all history is like that.

GREEN: We like to think that modern history writing is different [laughter]. But one has one's doubts.

TURTON: Well, it is not *only* like that, but present interests must influence our understanding both in anthropology and in history.

GREEN: Yes, but Clanchy, who has looked at the problem of written and oral history in medieval England over a very short period, has made the very interesting suggestion that the establishment of modern written 'objective' history has been bought at the price of sacrificing the relevance of history to larger numbers of people in Western society today.

DUMVILLE: I wondered about the places of these initiation-rituals. Is there any sense in which such places could become a focus of a hostile activity? Would the neighbours, seeing what had been done, come and profane the site as quickly as possible?

TURTON: I do not have any evidence to go on.

DUMVILLE: It was very much a feature of one of the medieval societies which I study. It was a kind of given that people would attempt such profanation.

TURTON: It would seem predictable in this case. The place where the Mursi held the age set ceremony had already been devastated by the Nyangatom. They had already burned a settlement there and they knew its significance in Mursi oral tradition—that they see it as symbolising their present political identity. So I suppose the Nyangatom could come back and destroy the place again and, in the process, destroy the tree—assuming they could recognise it as the tree where the ceremony had been held. It was certainly very important to the Mursi that the tree should survive.

GREEN: So, choosing a relatively insignificant looking tree had a double function [laughter].

TURTON: That is a thought.

WOOD: I found what you were saying about the destruction of a people not being the same as the destruction of individuals, in the sense that you do not have to have individuals destroyed to have a people destroyed, extremely interesting. Obviously one could apply that to another aspect of Wenskus' work: the question of tribes 'vanishing'. It might apply to Britain and might solve a lot of the problems that David and others are thinking about. Have you published anything on this? It would be very nice to be able to cite sources for the points you make.

TURTON: Something has just come out in *Nomadic Peoples* (1992). The title of the article is a quote: "We must teach them to be peaceful". I met an administrator once who, talking to me about the general lawlessness of the area, said: "Yes, yes. We must teach them to be peaceful". And that struck me as being a very interesting statement coming from a citizen of a country which then had the largest army in Africa and was absolutely riven by civil war.

The point about the political identity of the Mursi is that they see it as problematic. They are terribly worried about losing identity as Mursi, but they are not at all worried about losing identity as members of certain clans. Their clan identity, therefore, is much more fundamental and I see it as corresponding to what has been called ethnic identity, something you cannot actually lose. I think this is another important lesson for anthropologists who, in the past, have looked at groups like the Mursi as given, unproblematic. They have assumed that the world is made of politically independent groups 'from the start'. They have not made a problem of how those groups are created. For the Mursi that is precisely the problem. They do not take for granted the division of the world into separate political units.

DUMVILLE: What then is the nature of the relationship with their neighbours?

TURTON: They have two categories of neighbours. Firstly, there are those with whom they are in a state of what you could describe as permanent war. In pastoral societies this is seen in cattle raiding and is not terribly disruptive of daily life. You expect cattle raids just as you expect problems with the climate: you just have to cope with them. Then they have another category of neighbours, of whom the Nyangatom are one, with whom they are at peace for long periods. They have a lot of interaction of an economic kind, they understand each other's languages and individuals have particular friendships and associations with members of the other groups. And then, periodically, you get the most almighty bust-up. This is what happened in 1987. These events are much more destructive and disruptive than cattle raids and yet, for most of the time, the two sides are on the best of terms.

DUMVILLE: Is it obvious what triggers these explosions?

TURTON: It is not obvious but it is connected with movement. The Nyangatom are doing to the Mursi, from the south, exactly what the Mursi did to their northern neighbours, the Bodi, about 200 years ago. The Mursi evacuated the southern part of their territory following the Nyangatom attack. The Nyangatom did not come in and immediately occupy the territory, but if they do to the Mursi what the Mursi did to the Bodi, over the next hundred years or so you would expect to see the Nyangatom gradually taking over this no-man's land. And that is the threat the Mursi see, I think, and that is why they had to hold the age set ceremony when and where they did. In the early 1970s there was a war between the Mursi and the Bodi, and the Bodi were saying "This [northern Mursiland] is our territory...". And the Mursi replied "Nonsense: there are no broken Bodi pots here, no fire stones". So you have a war and then you have a peace-making ceremony which defines the boundary between the two groups in a legal sense. The relationship of the Mursi to their neighbours is characterised by violence of one sort or another, but in the case of the Bodi and Nyangatom it is violence and peace, not continuous war.

References in the discussion

Turton, D. A.
    1979   See references at end of paper.
    1992   'We must teach them to be peaceful': Mursi views on being human and being Mursi. *NomadicPeoples* 31:19-33.

CITIES AND MARKETS IN THE EARLY MIDDLE AGES

ROSS BALZARETTI

Department of History, University Park, Nottingham NG7 2RD

> It seems to me that the work of historians is unnecessarily impoverished when they are unaware that their living contemporaries still do things similar to what they describe in past societies (Christian 1989:190).

The economies of ninth-century Europe have received increased attention in the last two decades or so (Davies 1988; Devroey 1979, 1984; Fumagalli 1978, 1980a, 1980b, 1987; Hodges 1982, 1989a, 1990; Maddicott 1989; Montanari 1979; Nelson 1992; Randsborg 1991; Wickham 1984, 1988a, 1988b, 1989). Many of these studies have seen increased market activity and urban 'rebirth' in the period (Hodges 1988; Hodges *et al.* 1988; La Rocca 1986a, 1986b, 1989b, 1989c, 1992) perhaps emerging from a more intensive exploitation of the countryside. Our understanding of the rural economy, particularly the relations of churches and peasant producers, has been transformed as a result of detailed regional studies based on major ninth-century charter collections (e.g. East Brittany, Lazio, the Garfagnana Valley and Catalonia). Far from being obsessed with self-sufficiency the monks who preserved these charters were prime movers in the revival of economic exchange (Devroey 1984). Archaeologists have uncovered regional exchange networks (the North Sea, the Rhineland and perhaps the Mediterranean) and have highlighted long-distance trading in everyday items as well as luxuries whilst numismatists have seen ninth-century reforms of coinage, especially the introduction of the silver penny, as having facilitated local exchange and thus increased the pace of economic life (Grierson *et al.* 1986).

The emergence of a dynamic ninth century necessarily depends on a relatively stagnant earlier period (that of 'transition') for its explanatory force. In this paper it is suggested that this contrast may be more apparent than real and may have as much to do with deficiencies in the investigative methods employed by historians and archaeologists as with poor source material. Charters only survive in tiny numbers before the ninth century and therefore have not been used to portray a dynamic economy much before 750. The most common written texts of the earlier period (saints' lives, annals, letters and poems) provide only scattered 'economic' information. Similarly the archaeology of the period before 750 has concentrated on information which has been less studied in ninth-century contexts: burials, ethnicity and settlement (James 1989; Wood 1993). These simple facts may have resulted in an overvaluation of the innovations of the ninth century with respect to preceding centuries. It is probably not coincidental that such ideas have been put forward in a time of increased economic awareness across Europe, which has as its focus the single European market. Although no one has yet argued for a single market in the ninth century, many historians and archaeologists of the early medieval period have relied too readily on economic concepts which have been developed in the first instance with reference to capitalist formations when constructing models of the transition from late antique to early medieval (Balzaretti 1992b).

AFTER EMPIRE:
TOWARDS AN ETHNOLOGY OF EUROPES'S BARBARIANS

© C.I.R.O.S.S.
San Marino (R.S.M.)

Research Methods

> The process that is started when barbarism is brought into contact with civilization is not simple. The hitherto naked savage may at once assume some part of the raiment, perhaps the hat, of the white man. When after a while he puts these things aside and learns to make for himself clothes suitable to the climate in which he lives and the pursuits in which he is engaged, we see in this an advance, not a relapse; and yet he has abandoned some things that belong to the white man (Maitland 1960:270).

Western Europe in the transition period differed in many important respects from ninth-century societies. Most importantly it was, in general, less literate (hence less surviving documents). Verbal communication was dominant among the population. Writing was restricted mostly to clerical and secular élites. Ordinary social interaction in societies with limited access to writing tends to take the form of face-to-face contact:

> The development of writing greatly extends the scope of distantiated interaction in space as well as in time. In cultures which do not have writing, contact both within the cultural group as well as with other groups is perforce always of the face-to-face kind (Giddens 1979:204).

This restrictedness is embodied in the concept of *locale* (the regional concentration of particular social classes) and results in the *small-community*, "one in which there is only short distance in time-space separations" (Giddens 1979:206-7). These qualities can be seen in many of the early law codes which are directed at narrow social groups whose members are presumed to be in close contact: hence all those rules about violence towards the person (Balzaretti n.d.). This basic fact poses well-known methodological problems for early medievalists: written texts are few, often very corrupted by later accretions and frequently not helpful for answering the questions we should like to put to them. More seriously the activities of the majority of the population are hopelessly under-represented in the material and their interaction with élites will never be very successfully recovered if we simply stick to re-reading these texts (Moreland 1992).

Inter- and multidisciplinary approaches must lead the way ahead. When constructing models of the reproduction of 'barbarian' societies—in which the activities of the majority should surely play as large a part as possible—we have to bring ideas from elsewhere to bear on the problematic written material. In the context of economic life the choice of these poses considerable difficulty but must be confronted since it strongly conditions the sorts of possible models.[1] If it is admitted that historians face serious methodological problems in attempting to study the workings of early medieval economies this is only partly a question of evidence (and it is particularly not a matter of loss of documents). The usual methods of historical analysis, being dependent on written evidence, have not been able to study very effectively economic existence at the most local level. The types of written texts which have survived from the early Middle Ages only rarely contain the information which we would like to have about local economies because everyday processes which can be labelled economic are only exceptionally recorded in writing even in our own or other highly literate societies. Small-scale economic transactions, such as the bartering, buying or selling which goes on

---

[1] In this paper I have tried to be as multidisciplinary as possible, engaging in dialogue with as wide a range of comparative material from archaeology, economics and anthropology as possible. The advantages of such an approach heavily outweigh a more traditional historical concentration on the primary testimony of the written word over other forms of evidence: more so than usual given the economic slant I have chosen to challenge.

at a local market, do not need to be documented and therefore are not. Historians of economic life who rely solely on written texts will necessarily be observing exceptional rather than common trends, as can most clearly be seen in the numerous older studies of long-distance commerce and the disproportionate impact it was presumed to have had on local and regional economic systems (e.g. Lopez 1967; Luzzatto 1961:55-60; Pirenne 1936:16-39).

Archaeological evidence is potentially a better source for such information. Field surveys have altered totally our understanding of rural settlement and land exploitation in some areas (e.g. South Etruria, Farfa and the Biferno valley in Central Italy; East Brittany) by accessing material remains which may be derived from the mass of the population (Moreland 1992:121 ff.). However, finds of prestige or foreign objects, such as certain types of pottery (e.g. African Red Slip), tend to distract researchers from the mundane realities of local agrarian life (Wickham 1988a:140) in much the same way as a pocket of detailed charters can unbalance the written evidence. One result has been that local styles of pottery in some areas have proved almost impossible to identify (e.g. northern Italy), partly because isolation of local production is normally done by separating out the obviously foreign material first as being more interesting and useful. Similarly urban archaeology, which still has a tendency (at least in northern Italy with which I am most familiar) to concentrate on the transformations of the built environment (Balzaretti 1991; Brogiolo 1987; Brogiolo 1989; Panazza *et al.* 1988), tells us much less about the uses to which open spaces were put in this period. Almost no one has asked the question: "If cities were ruralised were they self-sufficient in food production?".

The ethnic approach, only rarely used to create economic data, is likewise a difficult and at times racist one (cf. Hudson *et al.* 1985) and has often tended to confuse the issue of the interaction of Roman and Germanic (in itself far too bald a question) because too many untenable assumptions are made about how to assign which artefacts to which ethnic grouping (Kiszely 1979). Finally, it is not a straightforward matter to detect human thoughts and motivation for economic activity from within the material context alone (although the great interest of contextual and post-processual ideas in this regard should be noted (Hodder 1986; Moore 1990; Moreland 1991; Moreland 1992:116; Tilley 1990)).

What use early medievalists might make of beliefs held by modern economists is a very debatable, if not much-debated, question. Mathematical economic theory and the many developmental theories of pre-capitalist formations are not appropriate because little statistical information of any value can be drawn from any type of early medieval evidence: even ninth-century polyptychs provide very small samples. Polanyi's views about reciprocity, redistribution and markets, terms which have been quite widely adopted in recent work (Haslam 1987; Hendy 1988:70 ff.; Hodges 1988:9-12, 52-5; Randsborg 1991) may be more apposite in early medieval contexts. His emphasis on the importance of social relationships in the transaction of economic business is perhaps the aspect of his economic theories most applicable. Although powerful critiques of Polanyi's overall approach exist (Godelier 1986:179-207) these critiques often pass over their own universalist assumptions.[2] But as this paper challenges the exaggerated importance of structure and system in some explanations there has been less cause to use economists' work than would otherwise have been the case.

---

[2] "In fact, it seems to me, there exists in all societies an empirical knowledge—which is often very advanced—of society's productive capacities, together with rules for a reasoned use of these resources so as to ensure their reproduction, and with it the reproduction of social life" (Godelier 1986:198), which is close to a general law behaviour.

From anthropology and ethnography comes a questioning of the whole economic viewpoint: "Is it right to look at magic, religious beliefs and conceptions of the human essence through the eyes of the economic historian?" (Gurevich 1992:14). Anthropological interpretations of economic life ('anthropological economics'), particularly that in so-called underdeveloped contexts, can provide very useful analogies (Hill 1986; Hugh-Jones *et al.* 1992). This work is valuable because it has exploited oral testimony and direct observation to show how major social formations can exist which go completely unrecorded in writing (except the anthropologist's). Economic transactions are one such formation. As will become clear, some recent anthropological work has demonstrated how economic transactions can be very complex even in societies where money is rare and where cities are not the dominant mode of settlement. Conversely, in modern Western contexts participation in market exchange may be very restricted and depend as much on social custom as on economic considerations, as Christian found in several Spanish valleys in 1968-69 where only male heads of household and widows normally went to markets (Christian 1989:17). Comparisons with such work may allow historians to envisage economic situations which are not documented textually in the early Middle Ages (for example explicit links between local rural markets and the support of urban life).

Economic Models of the End of Rome

Wickham, Hendy and Hodges have provided major politico-economic explanations of the ending of the Roman world in which ideas drawn (explicitly or implicitly) from recent economic and geographical work are important.

Wickham has adopted Marxist terminology to argue that two modes of production—the ancient and the feudal—co-existed in the late antique period and that the transformation of the Roman world was essentially a process whereby the feudal mode came to dominate over the ancient. The ancient mode was characterised by massive state spending which was possible because of an effective and heavy taxation system based on the cellular unit of the city and its territory. The city is given an important place as "the state in microcosm" (Wickham 1984:15). This system continued to dominate all the while that the aristocracy felt it to be beneficial for them, largely in terms of profits gained from state office-holding. These immensely rich landed aristocrats were at the same time extracting rent from their tenants (the feudal mode). The ancient mode was replaced by the feudal when these aristocrats abandoned the state in favour of their private resources, indicated by the fact that the successor states hardly ever raised tax (Wickham 1984:19). Landowning became the key mechanism for obtaining power, aristocrats had trouble in extracting surplus from free peasants and the relative material poverty of these aristocrats can be observed as a result. Even so these men still lived in cities and the exploitative link between city and countryside was thus maintained after Roman collapse (Wickham 1988a:144).

Hendy has studied coinage as a key indicator of these sorts of changes. Like Wickham he has argued that the dialectic between the state and private individuals was the crucial dynamic force in the far-reaching changes of these centuries (Hendy 1988:72 ff). The coinage of the late Roman empire was predominantly fiscal in purpose: there to collect tax and pay state servants (Hendy 1988:29-30). When private individuals began to abandon the state, coinage became less fiscal and state control of it weakened, even though the Carolingians attempted to bring about the use of coin as a medium of exchange. There were, of course, varieties of response among the barbarian kingdoms. The Ostrogoths maintained Roman state structures in northern Italy better than the others. But even here coin became an archaism and it was particularly weak economically-speaking (Hendy 1988:41 ff.). Reciprocity characterised the economic relationships of early medieval states and for this money was not necessary (Hendy 1988:70-1).

Wickham and Hendy have both emphasised the lack of integration of the economies of the successor states. This is important as all economies operate at various levels (local, regional, individual, group) and the linkages between these levels determine how integrated a given economy can be said to be. In the successor states such links were weak or non existent which resulted in a re-enforcement of the cellular character of economic relations. Surplus continued to be extracted by the powerful from those poorer than themselves by force or by agreement in the form of rent payments and labour-service.

Neither Wickham's nor Hendy's model is at all archaeologically-driven. Indeed Wickham has argued that the concentration by archaeologists on pottery analysis has caused them to under-represent agriculture in their models (Wickham 1988a:140). Both use archaeological evidence but they do not give priority to it in the way that Hodges has. In most archaeological models of the 'transition period' exchange and trade have a much more prominent place.

For example Hodges has stated that:

> ...competitive markets servicing the regions of Late Roman Europe disappeared in the fifth and sixth centuries. A far more primitive network of exchange systems took their place. This network was barely more than aboriginal in character, and focused upon the small royal, baronial and monastic nuclei of the seventh and early eighth centuries (Hodges 1989a:59).

Hodges has argued strongly that the control of exchange more than production was responsible for the power of élites and that where we observe powerful élites (e.g. in ninth-century *Francia*, the Rhineland or Wessex) this is an indicator of control of exchange at strategic places: emporia, gateway communities and markets. The emphasis remained on prestige goods rather than on local agricultural production (although in some places the latter was important) precisely because ruling élites deliberately exploited regional and even larger economic systems (Hodges 1988:83-6, criticised by Astill 1985; Balzaretti 1992b). His view of the Anglo-Saxon economy has been supported recently by Haslam and Kelly who have both argued for Offa's interest in establishing and controlling markets at fortified sites (Haslam 1987; Kelly 1993).

Cities, Markets and Models

> The economy was underdeveloped, as measured by the poverty of the mass of the people, the predominance of agricultural labour, the backward state of technology, the importance of land as a source of wealth and power, and, the dominance of the value system of the landed aristocracy (Garnsey *et al.* 1987:167).

Twenty years ago Garnsey and Saller's minimalist characterisation of the imperial Roman economy would have been impossible. Cities, trade, commerce and money were significantly more important in explanations of the ending of the Roman world (Jones 1964). As we have seen recent over-arching attempts to model late Roman collapse have convincingly given priority to land and its exploitation over trade and commerce as the principal explanation for economic change in the late Roman period and indeed as the

defining characteristic of early medieval economic life (Wickham 1984, 1989). As it has
become clearer that the motivations behind monumental city construction were much
more complex than a simple economic motive would allow (Ward-Perkins 1984), it has
been possible to suggest that the creation of towns as economic units "...went beyond the
frame of conscious thought of the people of the Classical world" (Jones 1987:50). We
have now reached the point where it is possible to see the great monumental cities of
Rome, Milan, Verona and the like as aberrations and to look much more closely at what
happened to small towns (Jones 1987:53). Nonetheless, for the late Roman period
Wickham and others have continued to emphasise cities as centres of consumption rather
than of production and distribution (Wickham 1988a).

The arrival of various Germanic groups in the heartlands of the old Roman world (where
most of these cities were) of course complicates the analysis. A good example is the impact
made on the Lombards by their encounter with urban life and settled agriculture on reaching
Italy. This is still very much disputed, largely because the accounts of contemporary
narrative sources and recent archaeological work often disagree (Harrison 1993). The
Lombards were long seen as especially barbaric and their time in Italy as essentially non-
urban (Bognetti 1966; Hodgkin 1895; Menghin 1985; Wallace-Hadrill 1952). Recently the
opposite view has come to the fore: the Lombards placed the city at the very centre of their
state (Harrison 1993; La Rocca 1992; Wickham 1988a). Again this is a question of emphasis
with many of the arguments initially dependent on considerations of ideology and mentality
(Frugoni 1988) but potentially supported by economic facts.

If no one has seriously doubted that flourishing cities existed in Mediterranean Europe
before AD 400 and after AD 900 (although their character is greatly disputed) the emphasis
changes as we pass to early medieval cities. Even those who believe in the long-term
continuity of urban life admit that cities of this period were much reduced in size and
generally scruffy places compared with Roman antecedents. Where cities are presumed to
exist arguments tend to have concentrated on *mentalité* and on concepts. Some recent work
has suggested that cities existed in the minds of those clerics who wrote annals and the like
and that it is likely that such images bore some resemblance to a real situation (Balzaretti
1992c; Frugoni 1988; La Rocca 1992). Others have doubted the continued existence of
many urban sites and argued that this discontinuity stands as an index of under development
(Brogiolo 1987). Most scholars have shied away from the detailed analysis of the economic
functions of such sites because the evidence is either very problematic or simply absent.
Cracco-Ruggini (1961) tried to, largely from written sources.

It seems to me that much recent writing on early medieval Italian cities rests implicitly on
economic points but has failed to consider these explicitly. The fact of economic
relationships between urban sites and the countryside cannot be assumed in the period
between 400 and 800 any more than it can at any other. The fate of cities is irrevocably
linked to the successful exploitation of the poor by the rich and to issues of production and
consumption. The important debates about the scale of urban decline, generally thought to
have been massive even by those who believe in substantial urban continuity, the arguments
about continuity and discontinuity, the quality of material life, the functions of urban sites,
all can be made to rest on what was happening in the countryside. This, at least in northern
Italy, is as yet poorly understood, although important recent excavations at Sirmione, Monte
Barro and Trezzo d'Adda may help (Brogiolo *et al.* 1989; Brogiolo *et al.*1991).

Relations between city and countryside and especially whether and how city and country
people interacted needs further investigation. This is an issue where we may be helped by

anthropological comparisons. Anthropologists have shown repeatedly that societies where land holding and agricultural exploitation predominate over urban consumption can be just as complex and varied economically as those where the opposite is the case. We must be clear that all pre-capitalist economies (like those of early medieval Europe) can exhibit complex economic formations and that we do not need to rank societies as superior and inferior (Crone 1989:17 ff.). This still needs stating in the light of the commonly expressed view that urban culture in the fifth to ninth centuries was a very debased version of Roman modes, largely because non-Romans did not adopt Roman ways of urban living without changing them. Inspired by anthropological accounts we must try to understand (rather than merely assume) the realities of this. I have tried recently to do this in a late ninth century context based on charter evidence (Balzaretti 1994). How to do it earlier remains a problem.

Many of these points apply to markets. Markets (and The Market) have often been regarded as the peak of economic sophistication as if other types of transaction were unimportant (Godelier 1986; Hill 1986:54 ff.; Hodges 1988; Luzzatto 1961:26, 29-30; Polanyi 1957). Societies where gift, barter and theft dominate as redistributive mechanisms (as in the justly famous 1959 article of Grierson) are by comparison 'underdeveloped' and somehow lesser. Recent anthropological work would support the suggestion that this view is wrong. Bartering for example, which is likely to have been widespread in most of early medieval Europe where money was rare or only available in large denominations and where surplus production was a luxury in much the same way as imported pots were, is a much more complicated activity than many historians have supposed (Hugh-Jones *et al.* 1992, Ch. 1).

It is to be ranked alongside market and gift exchange as a means of redistribution and is as worthy of historical study as these have been. Although activity of this sort remains rarely evidenced in written texts and may be impossible to detect archaeologically, its potential importance in explaining the functioning of early medieval economies should not be ignored, as it generally is. Further, the adoption of market, barter or gift exchange may be predominantly a cultural rather than an economic choice. Therefore, whilst explicit evidence for the existence of markets (rural and urban, local and regional) before the ninth century remains difficult to find, it is arguably the Eurocentric outlook of scholars who have not been able to believe that 'underdeveloped' agricultural systems could support complex economic transactions which were not focused on market sites which has made some reluctant to investigate other ways of redistributing wealth in the early medieval world.[3]

Modelling the Po Valley

In many models the region has taken on an important explanatory power. Regions are seen as forming coherent economic systems whose dominant character, while partly dependent on natural conditions, is subject to the organising impact of human activity, for example the direction or exploitation of long-distance exchange by kings (Hodges 1988:xiii, 8, 80 ff.). Again this is an idea derived from geographical or economic studies which is not necessarily appropriate to historical analysis.

---

[3]   Not all of course. Reuter (1985) is a classic demonstration of alternative 'economic' modes for the ninth century.

Northern Italy does play a part in the models of Wickham, Hendy and Hodges. Wickham argues for urban continuity (albeit on a much reduced scale), for the maintenance of the link between city and hinterland (because rural rents came into the city), and for the existence of local markets (Wickham 1988a:147). He regards the Lombard state as relatively sophisticated in spite of its inability to raise tax, in contrast with Ostrogothic taxation which demonstrates the continued use of coin as a fiscal instrument (Hendy 1988:41 ff.). The devastation of the Gothic Wars and the subsequent late arrival of the Lombards did not remove cities and markets from reality or from the minds of contemporaries, even though production may have been reduced to bare subsistence levels and taxation rendered impractical. For Hodges the Po plain, like the Rhineland, was "the heart of a smaller territorial entity" (Hodges 1988:86), at least from the mid-ninth century when more extended trading systems began to collapse. Hodges argues that it was only from the tenth century that this area revived as a result of Venetian trading and that, therefore, the economy of the preceding period was relatively static.

The interpretive problems are harder when we turn to the period prior to the ninth century. Before the eighth century charter documentation for the Po valley is sparse (with the important exception of Ravenna). We are forced to rely on law codes, chronicles (especially Paul the Deacon's *Historia Langobardorum*) and saints' lives (especially Jonas' *Vita Columbani*), which contain some useful but hardly extensive information about economic life. As a result the extent to which ninth-century patterns can reliably be traced back remains an open question and it is all too easy to see the Lombard period as economically static simply by default.

One possible solution is to turn to archaeology and, as we have seen, this has been done with great success in parts of central Italy (although even here seventh-century developments remain very obscure). The Po Valley is a much more difficult region from an archaeological point of view: massively altered in recent centuries and prone to hostile environments (Pearce *et al.* 1992). Few major rural excavations of early medieval date have been completed and even fewer field surveys (which may never be done for this area). Although fortified and cemetery sites (Castelseprio, Sirmione, Monte Barro, Trezzo d'Adda, La Torre) have begun to alter our understanding of what disruption in the Dark Ages meant in this region as yet they have yielded little in the way of this type of information. How or indeed if these sites were connected to agricultural production and the local population is most unclear.[4] Consequently the archaeological 'testing' of hypotheses derived from written texts is very difficult to do, even for the ninth century let alone before and at the moment comments about the north must remain very hypothetical (Balzaretti n.d.). Quite reasonably, therefore, archaeologists have argued for a more rudimentary economic picture than any of those which have been proposed from written texts.

An examination of the levels of urbanisation and market organisation observable in the Western Po valley (the heartland of Lombard Italy) allows us to test these hypotheses.[5]

---

[4] Castelseprio (Brogiolo *et al.* 1980; Carver 1987); Monte Barro (Brogiolo *et al.* 1991); Sirmione (Brogiolo *et al.* 1989); La Torre (Bougard 1991).

[5] It will be appreciated, in view of the complexity of the primary sources and the controversy with which these have been surrounded in recent years, that this paper is intended merely to propose a very general model which is almost certainly not applicable to all local and regional contexts. But it has seemed to me an appropriate occasion to attempt such a model rather than a narrower (or indeed wider) study.

Most characterisations of economic change in the transition period have, with the exception of Wickham's, neglected the Po Valley. This contrasts with work (based very largely on the evidence of ninth-century charters) on the ninth and tenth centuries which has proposed an economic system, agriculturally rich, varied and heavily exploited, whose flourishing cities were nodal points in a thriving trading network radiating from the river (Fasoli 1978; Montanari 1979:289-95; Violante 1974:3-49). Yet, there is not much evidence that such cities were central places within an integrated system of production, distribution and consumption in economic terms, even in the ninth century. To demonstrate this we need to examine in more detail those elements which are essential to such a system: production and consumption, exchange and communication, and the availability and use of money.

Production and Consumption

The exploitation of the natural environment of this region for food and other necessities has been the subject of exhaustive research, based largely on ninth-century charters (Fumagalli 1978, 1980a, 1980b, 1987; Montanari 1979). Montanari in particular has drawn a very complex picture, an enormous catalogue of products derived from agriculture, pastoralism and the management of marginal environments (Montanari 1979; Racine 1986; Squatriti 1992). From the late eighth century on it is clear that here, as elsewhere in Italy, monastic houses provided much of the impetus for increased production levels (Wickham 1988a:148). While some of these communities were in rather isolated places (e.g. Bobbio and Nonantola) many more developed in or near the major towns (notably in Pavia, Milan, Brescia, Piacenza, Bergamo and Verona) and some of these (especially Santa Giulia di Brescia, Sant'Ambrogio di Milano and several Ravenna churches) made determined efforts from the late eighth century onwards to exploit the hinterlands of the towns in which they were sited (Balzaretti 1989:248-86; Pasquali 1978; Vasina 1985).

This is important as the extent to which monasticism was an urban phenomenon with important economic consequences in this region has been rather overlooked. In addition to increased agricultural surplus this expansion included mineral extraction (predominantly iron) from some Alpine valleys (Menant 1987) and salt in the delta area (Squatriti 1992:12-3). Clearly there were parts of this region, such as the delta, where exploitation was very much determined by natural conditions, where agriculture was not very systematically organised and where agrarian activity remained marginal (Squatriti 1992:9). Nevertheless, the production of even this area arguably supported the monumental city of Ravenna, salt and glass production on a seemingly considerable scale at Comacchio and Venice and intellectual life in a thoroughly urban atmosphere.

Craft production can be an important part of a complex economic system. The volume and diversity of products made must be linked to levels of consumption, surplus and waste and allow some comment on the extent to which economic transactions were happening at more than a very local level. The problem here is the fairly rudimentary state of pottery studies in the area and the great problems involved in identifying local pottery styles. The contrast with our knowledge of central Italian production is huge and, should a major site turn up such material, interpretations could rapidly change.

However, there remains the problem of what to do with some very important written texts which demonstrate that Pavia, Milan, Verona and Brescia continued to be major political (and arguably consumer) centres, particularly in the later Lombard and early Carolingian period. The well-known praise poems for Milan and Verona which date to *ca* 739 and *ca* 810 respectively do suggest that the desire to live in towns persisted amongst political leaders and other great landowners. Town life was conceived as the highest form of organised life: legal business was done there and major churches were built there. All these qualities were perhaps more pronounced in northern Italy than in any other part of the West by virtue of its place as political centre of the Roman empire in the fourth century and its continued contact with Byzantium when that empire fragmented. The case for the continued existence of cities such as Milan, Pavia, Verona, Ravenna and Brescia throughout the early Middle Ages (Balzaretti 1992c; La Rocca 1989b, 1989c; Wickham 1988a) has remained more convincing to historians than to archaeologists who have generally preferred more catastrophic viewpoints (Brogiolo 1987, 1989).

It is perhaps worth pausing briefly to give detailed consideration to the example of Brescia. Paul the Deacon, writing at the end of the eighth century about the rebellion of Duke Alahis of Brescia against King Perctarit in 678-680 notes that, "*Brexiana denique civitas magnum semper nobilium Langobardorum multitudinem habuit*" which might be translated as "Therefore in the city of Brescia there had always been a great multitude of Lombard nobles" (*Historia Langobardorum*, 5, 36). Throughout his history Paul regards the city as a peopled space. This impression has been disputed in recent years by Gian Pietro Brogiolo whose excavations in Brescia, notably those at the monastic site of San Salvatore/Santa Giulia, have been conducted in order to trace what he has recently termed the "building transformations of a Lombard city" (Brogiolo 1989). It is clear from his work, in which he has sought to establish the mutations in the character of the built environment of this part of Brescia between the fifth and the eighth centuries, that he conceives of the urban space (he has sometimes phrased this as the 'urbanistic organisation') of Brescia primarily in terms of buildings and the deliberate alterations which were made to these over the centuries:

> Roman buildings destroyed by fire, collapsed masonry left *in situ* to encumber streets and private spaces, blocked drains, the continuous and random growth in street and habitational levels, makeshift houses in wood or the requisition of abandoned rooms of the *domus*, burials scattered haphazardly amid the houses, and the reduction to cultivation of large areas of the urban fabric (Brogiolo 1989:156).

In summary his proposed sequence for the Santa Giulia site is as follows:
1. A *domus* of fifth to sixth century date with some well-preserved mosaic floors, in continuous occupation in this period. At the same stage some floors given over to beaten earth, with hearths and slag present.
2. Also fifth to sixth century, but subsequent to stage 1: some new buildings in the eastern part of the *domus* which reutilised the external wall, remaining walls were new. The building was internally partitioned with wood. In the western part of the *domus*, existing floors disappear, replaced by rubble and refuse overlay. Then "a complete reorganisation of the structures of the *domus* then took place" (Brogiolo 1989:159): some single-room "makeshift" dwellings, with three burials present inside these.
3. Late sixth to seventh century: wooden huts with small posts and wattle and daub walling were built. "That the Santa Giulia huts were used as dwellings can be inferred from the presence of the two burials" (Brogiolo 1989:161). Perhaps these huts were of prehistoric type.

4. Seventh to eighth centuries: the area was reorganised with an aqueduct, solid masonry, bath and hypocaust built as the direct result of royal interventions (Desiderius and Ansa).

Although Brogiolo is careful to stress the provisional and local character of his conclusions they do, nonetheless, suggest that Gothic and Lombard Brescia was not urban: "The evidence from Santa Giulia thus shows clear contrast between the sharp fall in the quality of urban life in the initial Lombard period and the subsequent transformations" (Brogiolo 1989:164). It seems to me that from this evidence Brogiolo has a very clear conception of what constitutes an urban space and what does not. What he is less good at is conveying to us the motivations behind these transformations. For this he still relies on the gloom and doom of the Gothic/Lombard wars as related to us by Cassiodorus, Procopius and Paul the Deacon. Brogiolo is shy of arguing from his wealth of material about the concepts which those who deliberately changed this urban fabric must have had about what they were doing. This is important for we can be reasonably certain that Paul the Deacon (and the educated clerical classes in general) will not represent to us the views of those who built on and lived at the Santa Giulia site before the eighth century.

When we find—as we do at Brescia—a variety of building types within a relatively confined area in a context where it is probable that these types were deliberately chosen preferred types, we may be encountering evidence for the complexity of changing social relations over the centuries. Not necessarily the progressive simplification of such relationships which Brogiolo envisages. Brogiolo is correct, I think, to argue, from his precise observations of the changes in the structures which existed on the San Salvatore/Santa Giulia site over these four or five centuries, that we can extract information as to whether or not people lived in this area, at which times it was abandoned and which physical forms their habitation took. This in itself has proved an interesting discourse of material culture and one which has added much to our pre-existing discourses derived from the texts. His picture can be made more exciting if we view these buildings and the space which they ordered as distinctive products of an essentially non-literate culture which reflect the resourcefulness and adaptability of those people, whoever they were.

These arguments about the Brescia case may suggest that these societies were more complex than the minimalist position holds. Even so it must be admitted that at the present time many issues remain open. Whilst it must be the case, as Wickham has argued, that some economic consequences flowed from the mere fact of continued aristocratic habitation in cities (incoming rents, consumption of luxuries) there is no need to assume that this had a deep impact on the countryside or that the impact was the same everywhere. It may have been the case that the urban aristocracy were supported by food which was grown within the old walled circuits. Perhaps they extracted food by force (Balzaretti n.d. discusses power relations at the site of the *curtis*).

Exchange and Communication

Having established that there were a wide range of products available in northern Italy throughout this period which could have been exchanged and that there was demand from aristocrats for the necessities as well as the luxuries of life we now need to think about (a) how such exchange could have operated and (b) the degree to which it did. Gift, theft, tax, barter and monetised formal market exchange are all possibilities. We have seen that these usually do not operate in isolation in pre-capitalist contexts and that social and cultural customs often deterrnine how items are exchanged in face-to-face societies and that supposedly rational economic decision-making is of lesser importance. These notions can be used to explain why there was no need to document economic transactions in writing and why archaeological evidence of such activities is likely to be hard to find. These ideas also explain why such evidence as there is has often been misinterpreted.

The crucial north Italian text is the famous Comacchio pact of AD 715-730 (Montanari 1988:147-63; Violante 1974:3-5) which has been seen as evidence for a re-awakening of river traffic after the dire impact of the Lombard invasions (Racine 1986:10-1) and for a flourishing trading network along the entire length of the River Po (Fasoli 1978:583 ff.).[6] Gina Fasoli summed up established views of trade in the Po Valley in a lengthy contribution to the 1978 Spoleto conference based on the surviving written evidence from late Antiquity to the later Middle Ages. She argued that the Comacchio text evidenced an entire trading system within which the cities operated as nodal points each serviced by ports (*portus*) and bounded by the delta settlements in the East and Pavia "the most important market in the kingdom" in the West. She was less convinced than Bognetti had been that this sort of system existed much before the eighth century.

According to the text, the ports were Mantua, '*Capo Mincio*', Brescia, Cremona, '*Parmisano*' (Parma), '*ad Addua*' (Bergamo), '*Lambro et Placentia*' (Piacenza). The key to understanding this unusual text depends on two things. First, our interpretation of the word *portus* (Niermeyer 1966:816-17). This is a word with many shades of meaning ranging from a landing stage for ferries (*Edictum Rothari* 265-268) to a toll booth, to a larger merchants' trading settlement like that of Dorestad (Hodges 1988:85-6). Whichever it means here (and it seems from the context most likely to involve toll-taking) we must remember that the text does not indicate how frequently traffic passed through. Second, some understanding of why the text was made. The fact that this written agreement was made at all is important. Very few charters or memoranda survive from this part of northern Italy before the mid-eighth century. We may assume that the production of such texts was largely a royal monopoly and that they were made to regulate royal dealings with other aristocrats.

The travelling 'merchants' evidenced in this document (and in *Liutprandi leges* 18, *Edictum Aistulphi* 3 and 6) were most probably closely associated with the royal court at Pavia and doing business for the kings, 'axial traders' (Hodges 1988:40), perhaps operating out of Comacchio and Venice as emporia. There were probably not many of them and their activities did not therefore have much impact on local agricultural practice. Any products they transported were luxuries destined for the court rather than for wider diffusion.

As yet there has been little sustained archaeological investigation of these sites. We cannot tell therefore how typical the Comacchio evidence is of a wider situation. We cannot say how integral these 'merchants' were to any economic systems which may have operated along the length of the River Po.

The Availability and Uses of Money

Coin is a mystifying if important category of early medieval evidence. In spite of the many advances in modern numismatic study we still know little about how money was actually

---

[6] The text of this document is reproduced (from Fasoli 1978) in the Appendix to this paper. I have not seen the manuscript.

used in the early Middle Ages and it is all too easy to assume economic functions which it did not often have.

The types, quantities and distribution patterns of coin in early medieval northern Italy are now well-established. Coins in all metals (gold *solidi* and *tremisses*, silver *siliquae* and base metal *nummi*) continued to be minted in the fifth century although the mints of Milan, Ravenna and Aquileia, in common with others across the Empire, concentrated on gold (Carson 1990:6 ff.; Randsborg 1991:132-3; Spufford 1988:8). Few low denomination base metal coins were produced leading Grierson and Blackburn to conclude that, "...it is difficult to see how the commerce of the Empire can have been in a flourishing condition with such an inadequate means of exchange" (Grierson *et al.* 1986: 10).

Studies of Ostrogothic coinage, while noting the continued availability of both silver and base coins, tend to suggest an essentially similar pattern (Spufford 1988:910). Importantly the minting of coin remained a state monopoly focussed on the towns (Hendy 1988:41 ff.). Lombard coinage is a much-discussed issue (Bernareggi 1960, 1983; Harrison 1993:119-22; Lopez 1953:5 ff.). Famously the Lombards continued to mint the gold *tremissis* at a few centralised mints (Treviso, Lucca, Piacenza, Milan and Pavia) retaining its weight and fineness until the early eighth century. Minting seems to have remained in royal hands (*Edictum Rothari* 242) and prior to 680 minting was probably restricted to Pavia. However, we should at no point forget that only some 300 Lombard coins actually survive (Grierson *et al.* 1986:57). Charlemagne maintained gold minting in the Lombard kingdom at existing minting sites until 781 when the silver *denarius* was introduced there as elsewhere. Locally-produced coins were not the only ones circulating in Italy as Byzantine gold coins continued to be available for centuries after the administrative split of West and East.

Older studies tended to associate the presence of coin with trade and commercial activity (Luzzatto 1961:28 ff.) and to regard coiners as of especially high social status (Lopez 1953), a view taken up by Hodges (1988:115) with regard to tenth-century England. In some quarters this view is still current: "The prime function of a copper coinage is to provide for the enormous number of extraordinarily small payments that are a natural part of urban living, and play so much smaller a part in a thoroughly rural society" (Spufford 1988:10). Or "Coinage is surely one of our best witnesses to the intensity of market activity and the retail trade" (Fulford 1978:90). Peter Spufford's assessment of the importance of base metal coinage as an indicator of flourishing urban life represents a widely held view of late Roman urban collapse, "no money economy, no towns".

Many scholars have linked the eighth-century creation of the silver penny with the need for its use in local and regional peasant markets (Hodges 1988) and assumed that markets were rare where low denomination coin was unavailable. Other scholars have been much more hesitant. Hendy comes down firmly, as we have seen, in favour of fiscal interpretations: "Any suggestion that by 750—whether with regard to England or to the Continent—the economy was already monetised, *even in the countryside and at quite ordinary levels of society, represents the purest fantasy*" (Hendy 1988:73. My emphasis).

At all the periods discussed above it is possible to find those who doubt the commercial significance of money (Cameron 1993:115-16; Grierson 1976:608; Grierson *et al.* 1986:10; Harrison 1993 122). Hodges, drawing on anthropological analogies, has properly highlighted the importance of barter (Hodges 1988:123). The view of Grierson in 1959 that, "...the alternatives to trade were more important than trade itself..." (Grierson 1959:140), still sums up fairly the prevailing view about money in this period although Dick Harrison's view that, "You could use coin as payment, even if it is highly possible that there did exist other forms of payment as well" (Harrison 1993:123), is equally valid. We can conclude that, although the argument that money had economic importance in this period and region is supported by the consistently evidenced siting of mints in urban places and the presumed facility of coin as a medium of exchange, it is possible for markets to exist without readily available cash.

Conclusions

It can be argued that the general patterns which have been deduced from a consideration of environmental exploitation, craft production, the nature of exchange relationships and the use of money, point, in the case of the Po Valley, to a region able to support some non-agriculturalists living in cities and perhaps trading in markets. That rural markets are not mentioned by name in the written sources until the end of the period does not mean that these did not exist: they exist in many other ill-documented societies. However, the view that the existence of a flourishing *system* of market-based exchange is necessary to support urban life remains unconvincing.

The arguments of Wickham, Hendy and Hodges have properly been very influential and as models they seem to me as good as any which have yet been proposed for explaining late Roman collapse. Nevertheless, it may be that the search for overarching economic systems has followed too much an economic line and that too much power has been attributed, in post-Roman contexts, to ruling élites (especially kings) to determine the nature of significant economic transactions rather than simply benefit from them. The intricate patternings of the surviving documentation must not be ignored. It is not accidental that most of the surviving written documentation (and in a sense much of the archaeological evidence too) is heavily weighted in favour of kings and the Church and that matters of little direct interest to the document makers (such as local bartering arrangements or the day-to-day activities of peasant farmers) may pass almost entirely un-evidenced.

Many economic actions today go unrecorded and important people's lives are still much better documented than those of the rest of us. Control of the means of communication may have been crucial to the effective material as well as ideological exploitation of the majority by élites. In a face-to-face society this was done in person: hence the importance of state officials in creating and maintaining links between kings and ordinary men and women. We do not know if such officials kept themselves informed about small, local economic transactions. We cannot be certain that they attended markets or if they supervised transactions there. We can guess that such local transactions happened and that very probably they were more important to those who took part in them than the outside interventions of state agents. We cannot say (certainly not before the eighth century) if kings deliberately exploited rural, or any other, production, although we may assume that the aristocracy consumed whatever it could obtain by theft and plunder also. We may wonder if the presumed inability of 'barbarian' rulers to raise tax and generally to exploit the producers with the efficiency of the late Roman state did not stem from huge communication difficulties, linguistic as well as practical. For all such issues comparison with anthropological work seems to me the way forward.

This essay took as its starting point the idea that men and women met together for purposes now called economic which were generally not perceived in that way in the early

Middle Ages (cf. Hendy 1988:77).[7] It has asserted the importance of such face-to-face social contact relative to the more general (and supposedly deeper) structures and systems which have come to dominate recent analyses of early medieval economic life. Its impetus has come from the impression that a great deal of written and archaeological evidence records unusual economic situations at the expense of the commonplace and repeated transactions through which early medieval societies survived and reproduced. This repeatedness is important as a substantial decline in the volume of 'economic activity' has long been taken as the greatest difference between late antique and early medieval economies. Put another way if there were far fewer economic transactions in AD 600 than there had been in AD 400 it was not necessarily for economic reasons. Models of economic change between *ca* 400 and *ca* 900 which rely on concepts derived from economics may be improved by a closer attention to the possibility that these societies operated in ways unnoticed in economic thinking.

Acknowledgements—I am very grateful to Larry Epstein, John Moreland, and Chris Wickham for numerous comments which have much improved my text, even if I have not incorporated all of them.

Appendix

Capitulary of Liutprand in favour of the men of Comacchio (May 715 or 730).

IN NOMINE domini dei saluatoris nostri Jesu Christi die X, mensis magii indictione Xlll Ticino, tempore Lihutprandi regis.

Capitolare porrecto a nobis cunctis fidelibus Longobardorum [sic], *vobis Lupicino, venerabili viro presbitero, simulque Bertarene magistro militi, Mauro et Stephano comitibus et per uobis cunctis habitatoribus Comaclo, qualiter debeatis vestrum peragere negotium homines uestri in partibus nostris seu in modiis quamque in preciis simulque ripatico pro eo quod antiqua consuetudo ab auctoribus nostris praeferam. Judicia homines uestri pararunt; nunc quidem deo auxiliante remota sunt, ut pacis temporibus pars parti perfruamur. Inprimis porto Mantuano praeuidimus confirmare riparios tres, et quicquid miles habuerit ad uescendum, hoc et riparii cum eis commedere debeant; modio uero pensato libras triginta, cum quod suum peragat negotium; decimas uero dare debeant sale modios XVIII, et tremisse uno palo soluendum tantummodo. Item in Capo Mincio transitura debeat dare binos tremisses per singulas naues; scamaritico uero nichil praeuidimus dare, sed libenter transire praecipimus. Item in porto Brixiano riparios IV instituimus secundum antiquum; decimas uero dare debeant sale modios quindecim, et palo soluendum tremisse uno et modio pensato de libris triginta cum ipsa decima dare debeant. Item in porto qui uocatur Cremona praeuidimus confirmare duos riparios; decima uero dare debeant sale modios XV, et tremisse uno palo soluendum. Et qui uult sursum ascendere, det transitura solido medio; si uenumdauerit ad quatuor, det pro medio tremisse modia dua, et si uenumdauerit ad sex, modia det III nam amplius non detur, nisi quod precia posita fuerit. Et cum quale modio uenumdauerit, cum ipso decimas detur, tantum est. Item porto qui appellatur Parmisiano praeuidimus duos confirmare riparios; ripatico uero et palo solitura simul in unum dare praeuidimus solido uno, oleo uero libra una, garo libra una, piper uncias duas. Item porto qui dicitur ad Addua riparios confirmare praeuidmus duos; decima uero dare debeant sale*

---

[7] I have argued the case against economic rationality elsewhere (Balzaretti 1992b).

modios duodecim et tremisse palo soluendum. Simulque porto qui dicitur Lambro et Placentia qualiter Adda habuerit, hoc et ipsi consentire debeant seu in ripariis quamque in decimis tantummodo.

References

Textual sources:

Capitolare tempore Lihutprandi regis: see Hartmann 1904, also reproduced in Fasoli 1978.
Edictum Rothari, Liutprandi leges, Edictum Aistulphi: see Beyerle 1962.
Jonas
     Vita sancti Columbani abbatis discipulorunque: see Krusch 1902.
Paul the Deacon
     Historia Langobardorum: see Bethemann & Waitz 1878.

Bibliography:

Astill, G.
  1985   Archaeology, economics and early medieval Europe. *Oxford Journal of Archaeology* 4 (2): 215-231.

Balzaretti, R.
  1989   The Lands of Saint Ambrose: the acquisition, organization and exploitation of landed property in north-western Lombardy by the monastery of Sant'Ambrogio Milan, c.780-1000. University of London, PhD Thesis.
  1991   History, archaeology and early medieval urbanism: the north Italian debate. *Accordia Research Papers* 2: 87-104.
  1992a   The Creation of Europe. *History Workshop Journal* 33: 181-196.
  1992b   Debate: trade, industry and the wealth of King Alfred. *Past and Present* 135: 142- 150.
  1992c   Images of Dark Age Milan. *Medieval World* 4: 48-54.
  1994   The monastery of Sant'Ambrogio and dispute settlement in early medieval Milan. *Early Medieval Europe* 3 (1): 118.
  1995   The *curtis*: the archaeology of sites of power. In *La Storia dell'alto medioevo italiano (vi-x) alla luce dell'archeologia*. R. Francovich & G. Noyé (eds.), pp. 99-108. Rome: L'École française.

Barker, G.
  1989   The Italian Landscape in the First Millennium. In *The Birth of Europe*. K. Randsborg (ed.), pp. 62-73. Rome: L'Erma di Bretschneider.

Bernareggi, E.
  1960   *Il sistema economico e la monetazione dei Longobardi nell 'Italia superiore*. Milano: Ratto.
  1983   *Moneta Langobardorum*. Milano: Istituto Editoriale Cisalpino-La Goliardica.

Bethemann, L., & O. Waitz
  1878   *Historia Langobardorum. Monumenta Germaniae historica, Scriptores rerum Langobardicarum et Italicarum saec. VII-X.* Hanover: Hahn.

Beyerle, F.
  1962   *Leges Langobardorum*. 2nd, edn. Witzenhausen: Akademie fur deutsches Recht.

Bognetti, G. P.
  1966,   Longobardi e Romani. In *L'età longobarda*, vol. 1, pp. 83-141. Milano: Giuffré.

Bougard, F.
  1991.   La Torre. Relazione preliminare delle Campagne di Scavo 1989-1990. *Archeologia medievale* 18: 369-379.

Brogiolo, G. P.
  1987   A proposito dell'organizzazione urbana nel medioevo. *Archeologia medievale* 14: 27-46.
  1989   Brescia: building transformation in a Lombard city. In *The Birth of Europe: Archaeology and Social Development in the First Millennium A.D.* K. Randsborg (ed.), pp. 156-165. Roma: L'Erma di Bretschneider.
  n.d.   La città tra tarda antichità e medioevo. In *Archeologia urbana in Lombardia*, pp. 48-56. Modena: Panini.
Brogiolo, G. P., S. Lusuardi Siena & P. Sesino
  1989   *Ricerche su Sirmione longobarda.* Firenze: All'insegna del giglio.
Brogiolo, G. P., & L. Castelletti
  1991   *Archeologia a Monte Barro.* Lecco: Editrice Stefani.
Capograssi Colognesi, L.
  1986   Grandi proprietari, contadini e coloni nell'Italia romana. In *Società romana e impero tardo antico*, vol. 1. A. Giardina (ed.), pp. 325-366. Bari: Laterza.
Carson, R. A. G.
  1990   *Coins of the Roman Empire.* London: Routledge.
Carver, M.
  1987   S. Maria Foris Portas at Castelseprio: a famous church in a new context. *World Archaeology* 18: 312-329.
Christian, W. A., Jr.
  1989   *Person and God in a Spanish Valley.* Princeton: Princeton University Press.
Cracco-Ruggini, L.
  1961   *Economia e società nell'Italia annonaria: rapporti fra agricoltura e commercio dal 4° al 6° secolo.* Milano: Giuffré.
Crone, P.
  1989   *Pre-Industrial Societies.* Oxford: Blackwell.
Davies, W.
  1988   *Small Worlds: The Village Community in Early Medieval Brittany.* London: Duckworth.
  1990   *Patterns of Power in Early Wales.* Oxford: Clarendon Press.
Devroey, J.
  1979   Les services de transport à l'abbaye de Prum au IXème siècle. *Revue du Nord* 61: 543-569.
  1984   Un monastère dans l'économie d'échanges: les services de transport à l'abbaye Saint Germain des Près au IXème siècle. *Annales* 39: 570-589.
Duby, G.
  1974   *The Early Crowth of the European Economy.* London: Weidenfeld & Nicholson.
Fasoli, G.
  1978   Navigazione fluviale. Porti e navi sul Po. In *La navigazione mediterranea nell'alto medioevo*. Settimane di studio del C.I.S.A.M., XX. Pp. 565-607. Spoleto: C.I.S.A.M.
Frugoni, C.
  1988   *A Distant City: Images of Urban Experience in the Medieval World.* Princeton: Princenton University Press.
Fulford, M.
  1978   Coin circulation and mint activity in the Late Roman empire: some economic implications. *The Archaeological Journal* 135: 67-114.
Fumagalli, V.
  1978   *Coloni e signori nell' Italia settentrionale, ss. 6-11.* Bologna: Patron.
  1980a   Strutture materiali e funzioni dell'azienda curtense, Italia del Nord. *Archeologia medievale* 7: 25-90.
  1980b   Introduzione del feudalesimo e sviluppo dell'economia curtense nell'Italia settentrionale. In *Structures féodales et féodalisme dans l'Occident méditerranéen (Xème-Xlllème siècles)*. Rome: L'École française.

Fumagalli, V. (*cont.*)
  1987   *Le prestazione d'opera nelle campagne italiane del Medioevo.* Bologna: Cooperativa
            Libraria Universitaria Editrice.
Garnsey, P., & R. Saller
  1987   *The Roman Empire.* London: Duckworth.
Giddens, A.
  1979   *Central Problems in Social Theory.* London: Macmillan.
Godelier, M.
  1986   *The Mental and the Material.* London: Verso.
Goffart, W.
  1972   From Roman taxation to Medieval seigneurie: three notes. *Speculum* 47: 165-187,373-
            393.
  1980   *Barbarians and Romans, AD 418-584.* Princeton: Princeton University Press.
  1989   *Rome's Fall and After.* London: The Hambledon Press.
Greene, K.
  1986   *The Archaeology of the Roman Economy.* London: Batsford.
Grierson, P.
  1959   Commerce in the Dark Ages. *Transactions of the Royal Historical Society* 9:
            123-140.
  1976   Symbolism in early medieval charters and coins. In *Simboli e simbologia nell'alto
            medio evo.* Settimane di studio del C.I.S.A.M., XXIII. Pp.601-630. Spoleto:
            C.I.S.A.M.
Grierson, P., & M. Blackburn
  1986   *Medieval European Coinage, vol. 1, The Early Middle Ages.* Cambridge: Cambridge
            University Press.
Gurevich, A.
  1992   *Historical Anthropology of the Middle Ages.* Cambridge: Cambridge University Press.
Harrison D.
  1993   *The Early State and the Towns. Forms of Integration in Lombard Italy 568-774.*
            Lund: Lund University Press.
Hartmann, L. M. (ed.)
  1904   *Zur Wirtschaftsgeschichte Italiens im frühen Mittelalter.* Gotha: Friedrich Andreas Perthes.
Haslam, J.
  1987   Market and Fortress in England in the Reign of Offa. *World Archaeology* 19: 76-93.
Hendy, M.
  1988   From Public to Private: The Western Barbarian Coinages as a Mirror of the
            Disintegration of Late Roman State Structures. *Viator* 19: 29-78.
Hill, P.
  1986   *Development Economics on Trial.* Cambridge: Cambridge University Press.
Hodder, I.
  1986   *Reading the Past.* Cambridge: Cambridge University Press.
Hodges, R.
  1982   *Dark Age Economics.* London: Duckworth.
  1988   *Primitive and Peasant Markets.* Oxford: Blackwell.
  1989a   Emporia, monasteries and the economic foundations of Medieval Europe. In
            Medieval Archaeology. C. Redman (ed.), pp. 57-72. New York: State University of
            New York at Binghamton.
  1989b   Archaeology and the Class Struggle in the First Millennium A. D. In *The Birth of
            Europe.* K. Randsborg (ed.), pp. 178-187. Rome: L'Erma di Bretschneider.
  1990   Trade and market origins in the ninth eentury: an archaeological perspeetive *Charles
            the Bald.* M. Gibson & J. Nelson (eds.), pp. 203-223. London: Variorum.

Hodges, R., & B. Hobley (eds.)
>   1988   *The Rebirth of Towns in Western Europe*. (C. B. A. Researeh Report, 68). London: Council for British Archaeology.

Hodgkin, T.
>   1895   *Italy and Her Invaders*, vols. 4 and 5. Oxford: Clarendon Press.

Hudson, P., & C. La Rocca
>   1985   Lombard Immigration and Its Effects on North Italian Rural and Urban Settlement. *British Archaeological Reports, International Series*, 246: 225-246. Oxford: B.A.R.

Hugh-Jones, S., & C. Humphrey
>   1992   *Barter, Exchange and Value*. Cambridge: Cambridge University Press.

James, E.
>   1989   Burial and status in the early medieval West. *Transactions of the Royal Historical Society* 39: 23-40.

Jones, A. H. M.
>   1964   *The Later Roman Empire*. Oxford: Blackwell.

Jones, P.
>   1965   L'Italia agraria nell'alto medioevo: problemi di cronologia e di continuità. In *Agricoltura e mondo rurale in occidente nell'alto medioevo*. Settimane di studio del C.I.S.A.M., XII., Pp.57-92. Spoleto: C.I.S.A.M.
>   1974   Il crollo e la ripresa: il primo medioevo (500-1050). In *Storia d'Italia*, pp. 1590-1681. Torino: Einaudi.

Jones, R.
>   1987   A False Start? The Roman urbanization of western Europe. *World Archaeology* 19: 47-57.

Kelly, S.
>   1992   Trading privileges from eighth-century England. *Early Medieval Europe* 1: 3-28.

Kiszely, I.
>   1979   *The Anthropology of the Lombards*. British Archaeological Reports, (International Series, 61). Oxford: B.A.R.

Krusch, B. (ed.)
>   1902   *Passiones vitaeque sanctorum aevi Merovingici*. (II) *Monumenta Germaniae Historica. Scriptores rerum Merovingicarum, 4*. Hanover: Hahn.

La Rocca, C.
>   1986a   "Dark Ages" a Verona: edilizia privata, aree aperte e strutture pubbliche in una città dell'Italia settentrionale. *Archeologia medievale* 13: 31-78.
>   1986b   Città altomedievali, storia a archeologia. *Studi storici* 3: 725-735.
>   1989a   Le fonti archaeologiche d'età gotica e longobarda. In *Il Veneto nel medioevo*, pp. 81-164. Verona: Banca Popolare di Verona.
>   1989b   "Plus ça change, plus c'est la même chose": Trasformazioni della città altomedievale in Italia settentrionale. *Società e storia* 45: 721-728.
>   1989c   Trasformazioni della città in "Longobardia". *Studi storici* 4: 993-1011.
>   1992   Public buildings and urban change in northern Italy in the early medieval period. In *The City in Late Antiquity*. J. Rich (ed.), pp. 161-180. London: Routledge.

Lopez, R. S.
>   1953   An aristocracy of money in the Middle Ages. *Speculum* 28: 1-43.
>   1967   *The Birth of Europe*. London: Phoenix House.

Luzzatto, G.
>   1961   *An Economic History of Italy*. London: Routledge & Kegan Paul.

Maddicott, J.
>   1989   Trade, industry and the wealth of King Alfred. *Past and Present* 123: 3-51.

Maitland, F. W. [1897]
>   1960   *Domesday Book and Beyond*. London: Collins.

Menant, F.
1987   Pour une histoire médiévale de l'entreprise minière en Lombardie. *Annales* 42:
            779-796.
Menghin, W.
1985   *Die Langobarden. Archaeologie und Geschichte.* Stuttgart: Konrad Theiss Verlag.
Montanari, M.
1979   *L'alimentazione contadina nell'alto medioevo.* Napoli: Liguori.
1988   *Alimentazione e cultura nel medioevo.* Bari: Laterza.
Moore, H. I.
1990   Paul Ricoeur: Action, Meaning and Text. In *Reading Material Culture.* C. Tilley (ed.),
            pp. 85-120. Oxford: Blackwell.
Moreland, J.
1991   .   Method and theory in medieval archaeology in the 1990s. *Archeologia medievale* 18:
            7-42.
1992   Restoring the dialectic: settlement patterns and documents in medieval central Italy.
            In *Archaeology, Annales and Ethnohistory.* A. B. Knapp (ed.), pp. 112-129.
            Cambridge: Cambridge University Press.
n.d.   Production, distribution and consumption in the early medieval town. Unpublished typescript.
Moreland, J., & M. Pluciennik
1992   Excavation at Castel San Donato, Castel Nuovo di Farfa (RI), 1990. *Archeologia
            medievale* 18: 477-490.

Nelson, J.
1992   *Charles the Bald.* London: Longman.
Niermeyer, J.
1976   *Mediae latinitatis lexicon minus.* Leiden: E. J. Brill.
Panazza, G., & G. Brogiolo
1988   *Ricerche su Brescia Altomedievale*, vol. 1. Brescia: Ateneo di Brescia.
Pasquali, G.
1978   La distribuzione geografica delle cappelle e delle aziende rurali descritte
            nell'inventario altomedievale del monastero di Santa Giulia di Brescia. In *San
            Salvatore di Brescia. Materiali per un Museo*, 1. Brescia: Grafo edizioni.
Pearce, M., E. Calandra & M. Diani
1992   Riso amaro-recent field survey in the Lomellina (PV). In *Papers of the Fourth
            Conference of Italian Archaeology, 3.* E. Herring, R. Whitehouse, & J. Wilkins
            (eds.), pp. 119-122. London: Accordia Research Centre.
Pirenne, H.
1936   *Economic and Social History of Medieval Europe.* London: Routledge & Kegan Paul.
Polanyi, K.
1957   The economy as instituted process. In *Trade and Market in Early Empires.*
            K. Polanyi, C. M. Arensberg & H. W. Pearson (eds.), pp. 243-270. Glencoe, IL: The
            Free Press.
Racine, P.
1986   Poteri medievali e percorsi fluviali nell'Italia padana. *Quaderni storici* 61: 9-32.
Randsborg, K.,
1989   *The Birth of Europe.* Rome: L'Erma di Bretschneider.
1991   *The First Millennium A.D. in Europe and the Mediterranean.* Cambridge:
            Cambridge University Press.
Reuter, T.
1985   Plunder and Tribute in the Carolingian Empire. *Transactions of the Royal Historical
            Society* 35: 75-94.

Roffia, E. (ed.)
  1986   *La necropoli longobarda di Trezzo sull'Adda.* Firenze: All'insegna del giglio.
Sawyer, P. H.
  1977   Kings and Merchants. In *Early Medieval Kingship.* P. H. Sawyer & I. N. Wood
            (eds.). Leeds: Leeds University Press.
Schmiedt, G.
  1978   I porti Italiani nell'alto medioevo. In *La navigazione mediterranea nell'alto
            medioevo.* Settimane di studio del C.I.S.A.M., XX., Pp.129-258. Spoleto:
            C.I.S.A.M.
Spufford, P.
  1988   *Money and Its Uses in Medieval Europe.* Cambridge: Cambridge University Press.
Squatriti, P.
  1992   Marshes and mentalities in early medieval Ravenna. *Viator* 23: 1-16.
Tilley, C. (ed.)
  1990   *Reading Material Culture.* Oxford: Blackwell.
Toubert, P.
  1973   L'Italie rurale aux VIIIᵉ-IXᵉ siècles: Essai de typologie domaniale. In *I problemi
            dell'Occidente nel secolo VIII.* Settimane di studio del C.I.S.A.M., XX. Pp. 95-132.
            Spoleto: C.I.S.A.M.
  1985   Il sistema curtense: la produzione e lo scambio in Italia nei secoli VIII, IX e X. In
            Storia d'Italia, Annali 6: 5-63. Torino: Einaudi.
Vasina, A. (ed.)
  1985   *Ricerche e studi sul "Breviarium Ecclesiae ravennatis"* (Codice Bavaro). Roma:
            Istituto storico italiano per il Medio Evo.
Verhulst, A.
  1966   La genèse du régime domanial classique en France au haut moyen age. In
            Agricoltura e mondo rurale nell'alto medioevo. Settimane di studio del C.I.S.A.M.,
            XII., Pp. 135-160. Spoleto: C.I.S.A.M.
  1991   The decline of slavery and the economic expansion of the early Middle Ages. *Past
            and Present* 133: 195-203.
Violante, C.
  1974   *La società milanese nell'età precomunale.* Bari: Laterza.
Wallace-Hadrill, M.
  1952   *The Barbarian West.* London: Hutchinson.
Ward-Perkins, B.
  1984   *From Classical Antiquity to the Middle Ages.* Oxford: Oxford University Press.
Whittaker, C.
  1983   Late Roman Trade and Traders. In *Trade in the Ancient Economy.* P. Garnsey,
            K. Hopkins & C. Whittaker (eds.), pp. 163-211. London: Chatto & Windus.
Wickham, C. J.
  1984   The Other Transition. *Past and Present* 103: 336.
  1988a   *The Mountains and the City.* Oxford: Clarendon Press.
  1988b   L'Italia e l'alto medioevo. *Archeologia medievale* 15: 105-124.
  1988c   La città altomedievale: una nota sul dibattito in corso. *Archeologia medievale* 15:
            649-656.
  1989   Italy and the Early Middle Ages. In *The Birth of Europe.* K. Randsborg (ed.),
            pp. 140-151. Rome: L'Erma di Bretschneider.
  1992   Problems of Comparing Rural Societies in Early Medieval Western Europe.
            Transactions of the Royal Historical Society 42: 221-246.

Wood, I.
  1993   *The Merovingian Kingdoms.* London: Longman.

Discussion

WOOD: I would like to see whether I can make links between what is happening in Gaul and Italy. The first point I would like to make is about documentation: I would slightly disagree with your point that writing was associated with the clerical élite. Before 700 in *Francia* the clerical and the secular élite are having the same education. The fact that that education is being done by clerics does not alter the fact that secular people are being educated.

Second, the most interesting set of documents that I think exists for Gaul are the wills which people have not looked at in an economic context. We have twelve Merovingian wills. If you start mapping them out you start to get what might be the foundations of a rural community, because they are dealing with rural estates rather than urban houses. You can also add for the Merovingian period the extraordinary Tours fragments, and then in Spain you can add the slates as well. Working from there you might be able to begin to explain why toll stations are important. It may not necessarily be merchants who are being hit by toll stations: it may actually be aristocrats who are moving their produce from one estate to another.

Another point would be to take the archaeology of Dorestad which can be studied decade by decade because of dendrochronology. Dorestad grows, at least in the pre-Carolingian period when Frisian or Merovingian power is weak. In other words, you might well have a very good case for saying we are not dealing with something which is royally led. This must have implications for the *sceattas*. I think that suggests an economy which is in origin non-royal, but which the kings deliberately exploit. But it does not begin with them, and I would agree with you there entirely.

I think the second area I would want to consider in terms of parallels is the interesting question of cities. Whereas most people have tended to emphasise the importance of cities in Italy, they have not in Gaul. One of the interesting things about Gallo-Roman cities is that from the literary evidence we know that aristocrats are moving out of cities. I would have thought that is also true of Ennodius of Pavia's letters, which have a lot to say about rural estates. If it is not aristocrats who are living there, then one comes back to the point that some people have argued that cities exist, but they are merely ecclesiastical cities. But if you look at the numbers of monks who are in some of these big urban institutions you have, in Vienne for instance, monks in their thousands, and if you add to that the people who are provisioning them, that seems to me to look rather like a city. Where people say: "It's only an ecclesiastical city", it seems to me this would turn the point around. So, I wonder whether Gaul does not suggest in urban terms two different ways of getting at cities. One is re-evaluating the question of the ecclesiatical city and the other is considering to what extent the aristocracy may already have deserted the cities before or during the fifth century.

BALZARETTI: Certainly the point about the ecclesiastical cities is very helpful because, as you know, one of the issues is where these churches get their properties from, since by the ninth century bishops have thousands and thousands of acres of property all over the place. Where did it come from? Well, the answer is: they had it for a very, very long time. For example, the archbishop of Milan has estates as far away as Sicily in the sixth century. I agree that if we are dealing with a society where the Church has got hold of political power in many places, then it is going to be important in cities. "Are aristocrats still living there after 400?" I am sure they must have lived in the countryside, but I think they had urban palaces as well. That would be my inclination, but I cannot demonstrate it because there is not enough material to say that with certainty. But they live in towns, they have a town house. The point is: do they do business in an economic sense in those towns between themselves? The point I would like to know more about is this business of aristocratic tolls being levied on stuff being moved by aristocrats which is very interesting.

WOOD: The wills begin in the late sixth century and would also help you as a parallel to endowments of churches, because Bertrand of Le Mans gives 300,000 hectares in his will, largely to the church of Le Mans.

BALZARETTI: The problem that comes next is: how were these estates being worked? I gave a paper on that not too long ago, which came to a similar conclusion: that to actually find out *in detail* what is going on is not easy. One of the questions I asked on that occasion was: how do you actually find out about renders and rents, agricultural rents being taken by aristocrats from peasants, slaves, or whatever they were, in an archaeological context, how do you observe that? Can you observe that? That is an important thing to think about, because, if we could observe it, if we could say that the agricultural world is archaeologically visible that would answer really important things that historians would like to know about.

AXBOE: In your paper you stress the archaeological problems in the Po Valley. It seems to me very strange that you haven't found any rural settlements, either villages or farms, for the main part of the populations. Even estates must need many 'ordinary people' to be run: did they live in towns and walk for hours and hours to do their job?

BALZARETTI: The question of where people lived is an old chestnut of Italian historiography. Were there villages in the late Roman period and were they the same ones we have evidence for? Villages do not start being evidenced in documents until about the middle of the eighth century in the area of Lucca, elsewhere really a little bit later. So, it is pretty late.

AXBOE: Does that mean, according to that evidence, there were no villages? You have no evidence concerning rural settlements? Then I would of course say: "Go out digging and find it!"

BALZARETTI: No, quite, no negative evidence, I agree with you. What sort of archaeology there has been is cemeteries, but most of them were done a long time ago, which is a problem.

AXBOE: But those cemeteries *are* in the countryside

BALZARETTI: And the ones that have been recently dug, for example Trezzo d'Adda, have not revealed much in the way of what you could call consolidated settlement. The question remains open. I think the assumption is: "Yes, there were lots of them". That is the assumption that has been always made in Italian historiography. There have been some very recent, very important excavations. For example, Monte Barro, not far from Lecco, which has been excavated by Brogiolo. He has apparently found a fortified villa. Some quite interesting artefacts, weapons and things of some quality were found, which lead him to think that perhaps this was the residence of some sort of military leader, somebody quite important. What they have not been able to do is what would be really interesting: to field survey the area around it to see if they could pick up any indication that that villa is exploiting the land in a particular way at that period. And the problem is that it is not going to be easy to achieve this in northern Italy, because the countryside is so very much settled now and to get permission to dig is not easy. The intensive nature of the agriculture in Lombardy has certainly destroyed a lot of what we would like to know. Yet, it is precisely the hinterland of the biggest cities now, that we want to find out about and it is always those that are most difficult to find out about. In the vicinity of Milan the suburbs have just about destroyed everything. So, all the villages that are first evidenced in the ninth century are no longer villages. They are all suburbs of Milan and who knows what might be there. Where there has been substantial excavation, say at Milan, to be fair to the archaeologists, they have found very, very little of early medieval date. Almost nothing.

AXBOE: That is an interesting point.

BALZARETTI: Indeed, yes, yes. I did not include that because I have written on this elsewhere. One of the problems is that they find very little from the seventh to the tenth century. There are finds in the eleventh century and finds in the fifth century and late fourth century. Usually there is dark earth, rubbish everywhere. And they say: "Yes, it is abandoned". So, it is like Brogiolo's excavations in Brescia, nice Roman town house completely decayed when, in the late fifth century, people move in, they pull down walls, they build huts all over it, and it stays like that for a couple of centuries with these, as Brogiolo says, prehistoric huts. Then we get to the eighth century where documentation starts and lo and behold, yes we get buildings. Now, it is actually quite coherent, if you want to see it like that. The problem I have with that scheme is that some documents, poems and chronicles imply that cities were still important as places where people lived. Lombards lived in Brescia, and they always lived in Brescia. And this is precisely the period when the archaeologists find nothing. So, that is the problem.

DUMVILLE: The evidence for this period also is still documentary rather than literary.

BALZARETTI: One of the things that worries me is that I am not sure that this is a good way of dealing with literary material.

DUMVILLE: I am sure it is not....

BALZARETTI: Then, what I don't like to do is to go in and say: "Yes, we will read these saints' lives, and we'll find what economic information we can drag out of that context. I much prefer to study important collections of charters, where there is a body of material which you can make certain statements about.

DUMVILLE: In principle you can do the same with hagiography.

BALZARETTI: Yes, you could, but the trouble is that is nothing like the *amount* of early hagiography in northern Italy. Turning to the poems, the famous one is the *Praise of Milan* which is almost contemporaneous with the Comacchio document, dated probably 739, which is one of these late Roman *laudes*. It praises the city for being wonderfully made of stone and all the rest of it. Usually people say: "Well, that is all it is, it is a copy. It is somebody in the earlier part of the eighth century, probably a cleric, saying: 'Yes, this is what our city should be like, because we are trying to be Romans'". But the church of San Lorenzo, that fifth-century church in Milan, is still there, and if it is still there now, it was there when this poem was written, and it is referred to, and it is described, and it is accurately described. So, why is the rest of it not accurately described? This is a debate which is going to be almost impossible to resolve. I think it is just a choice. You choose, you say: "Yes, I think there was something like a city and it must be serviced in an economic sense as a city in order to maintain it. But, if you do not think it was there, the problem you have to explain is why it starts again. And, to my mind, people have not explained why it starts again in the ninth century, certainly not in northern Italy or anywhere.

SCHÜTTE: I see a situation quite comparable to the central Rhine Valley, especially Cologne. In some of your sentences one could just replace some of the cities with Cologne, which would be the same, because we have the same problems. One can see that it is highly dependent on the situation of archaeology. As well I can say the suburbs of Cologne have destroyed lots of the hinterland and limited much the possibilities of doing research here. But it is interesting to see that now, with the development of urban archaeology or medieval archaeology itself, in the last twenty years this problematic has come up more than before, when one concentrated on the older layers in these cities and in the countryside itself. We have absolutely parallel developments in Germany and here in northern Italy. The Rhine Valley could be replaced with the Po Valley and vice versa. I will stress in the late afternoon many of these points you have pointed out today.

The created image is very dependent on what is done for research recently. Nobody did concentrate on urban settlement and its development too closely because nobody was looking for it. Because the prejudice against all the Germanic groups was that they were basically oriented to the countryside, and nobody did look for them in the cities, because you do not expect them. If you read some of the books about Cologne, they are full of prejudices against the Franks as being basically people who hated the city and they tried to remodel the city into an agrarian area. But this is positively wrong. In fact, one has to see both sides, a more nuanced picture in this.

DUMVILLE: Could I ask about tax? Twice you were talking about barbarian successor states hardly ever raising tax. I wonder whether you can give me a sense of where your line of definition would fall between tax and tribute and whether there is a sense in which tribute is being collected in this area, in this period, and the means of raising it would effectively be taxation, or what one might describe as taxation? I realise that we may be getting into a terminological bind here.

BALZARETTI: The way I would use the word, is that tax is something very regularly levied and institutionalised, and you have governmental officials to do it, whereas tribute is something that is not just so institutionalised, it is done in a military sense. The two words are very close. What I meant there, however, that late Roman taxation is very well studied, all the various grades of it. Although that goes on in Ostrogothic Italy, it was nothing like it was. By the time you get to the Lombards there is none.

DUMVILLE: I take that point well. I just wondered to what extent settled tribute relationships could be seen, and whether they would provide any kind of basis for what you could describe as a taxation system, for the future. Certainly in the Insular world that is one of the ways by which one would explain the origins of taxation?

BALZARETTI: This is one of the areas where money might come into it. Where money is being coined as a way of gathering together resources, much could be given as tribute. Which might explain why it is often gold. The tribute could then be substantial. This may explain why there are not thousands of silver pennies in northern Italy before Charlemagne's time. But, in terms of actual tribute taking, it is not something about which there is much evidence from what I read anyway.

DUMVILLE: Thanks. This is something for both of us to ponder.

WOOD: I would like to make a point about coinage, or one of the peculiarities of Merovingian coinage. There are three types of coins: one which has the king's name on, one which has an ecclesiastical site named, and one which has neither. I have argued that they are distinct coinages. We know from one saint's life that the ecclesiastically stamped coin is actually an alms coinage. It is fairly clear that if you paid tax you paid it in royal coinage. Most historians see the non-royal coin as an invasion of royal rights. To my mind they are wrong. The coins are earmarked for different purposes. Moreover, that does not mean that once they are in general circulation they do not become general cash in the pocket, but at the moment they are minted they have a very precise function.

DUMVILLE: I was tempted to ask whether there were three economies on that basis.

WOOD: It is fairly clear from the alms coinage. It is very specifically said in a vision, that a man should go and pay alms with coins stamped with the name of a saint.

BALZARETTI: There are some very early Carolingian coins in Italy, probably the first ones that were coined, with images of cities on them. This might be something to do with: "Do you pay a toll in and out of a city?" and "Do you have to use this which says 'Medio-lanum' on it?" There is also a sense in some of the sources that some coins were not equivalent. So, when there were some coins minted in Milan and minted in Pavia, you might not be able to match them.

DUMVILLE: You are talking about different economies, presumably.

RICHARDS: With respect to Anglo-Saxon England, the problem of where seventh- and eighth-century cities were seemed as difficult a problem until the last four or five years when further assessment of archaeological work in York, Canterbury, and London, has shown that they fit into a broad pattern of the *wic* being established outside the Roman town walls. There are various possible models for what is going on there, but one possibility is that there is some sort of royal control from within the walled cities. A trading site is established at arm's length to keep it under control, but is not fully integrated. Certainly, I think it dangerous to worry about the absence of something in a particular period until you have much more complete excavation that shows that it is just a pattern of shifting settlements.

HINES: A question has been directed at me, as to whether I think agricultural history can be discovered through archaeology. I have a few points to make that have seemed to me to become more relevant, and more worth making, as the discussion has proceeded— leading up, in fact, to this issue of taxation.

On the question of past agriculture, I would say that one is very lucky to get more than scattered glimpses of what was going on. If very lucky, we might discover fossil field systems, droveways and so on that could allow us to postulate particular agricultural practices. To go beyond what they would tell you leads you into landscape history, an area that has put forward many interesting ideas but in my range of experience has rarely proved very much.

Coming back to the situation in northern Italy and the apparent near impossibility of discovering settlement sites: even if you could find such sites, they might very well still not tell you a lot. But I would not be too dismissive of what you might learn from cemetery sites. In respect of Anglo-Saxon England, we are beginning to see in a substantial way what can be done by studying the distribution of artefacts (such as are regularly deposited as grave goods) in association with close technical studies; we are beginning to understand not only what information this can provide but what methods this requires, and what needs to be invested in terms of research.

Useful inferences can also be drawn from the distribution of cemeteries, assuming that the cemeteries were not far removed from whatever communities used them. What are large problems in Italy are fairly minor problems in England, where we have quite a lot of excavation within the towns and the great benefit of Anglo-Saxon cemeteries all over the place, giving a very good overall picture of what is going on. But of course there are still gaps in England, and one of these is the area around London. Some recent work on early Anglo-Saxon Surrey is producing a number of interesting observations. Not the least of these is that the earliest Anglo-Saxon cemeteries seem likely to be sitting right on top of a ring of Roman *mutationes* (collection points) at regular distances to the south of the Roman town of London: at Ewell, Mitcham, Croydon, Orpington. All of these sites are ideally located relative to London for this purpose and you can read Roman archaeologists, who are not in the least bit interested in the Anglo-Saxon sites and maybe don't even know that they are there, postulating that these are where the Roman collection points were. Going later too, Nicholas Brooks, discussing the late tenth-century coin hoard from Croydon, suggested that this was the collection point for supplies for London (Brooks *et al.* 1986).

What that actually means about what was going on in London and whether London had anything more than a purely conceptual existence for the people living in the area at the time, I would not pretend to know. One can at least see that there is evidence here that is going to contribute to the discussion of this particular question.

BALZARETTI: What is the current thinking on urban cemeteries? This is always a problem in Italy as there are so few. Actual cemeteries rather than the isolated or odd burial.

HINES: I would not want to speak for the world at large and say what *the* current opinion is. I suspect there isn't one. We do indeed frequently find small numbers of early Anglo-Saxon burials in what were the late Roman urban cemeteries. It is quite usual now to find a fleeting Anglo-Saxon presence in the last observable phase of real life at late Roman sites, but this is not a link in a continuous history. More curious is the situation you have, for instance, at Derby, where a small number of Anglo-Saxon burials on a late Roman urban cemetery site seem to belong well into the sixth century. I do not know how widely this is repeated elsewhere, though I believe it is not unique. Overall, there is not a lot of evidence from urban cemeteries that one can start to use to build hypotheses.

SCHÜTTE: The same situation prevails in Cologne. Before they vanish, late Roman grave fields have a reasonable number of later graves. But this is just the phase before they vanished and then came complex urban cemeteries. Recently, two weeks ago, there was a publication of several grave fields with several thousand graves, more than 2400 pages of catalogue, which makes it very very complicated to see what really happened. Most are old excavations, since the end of the nineteenth century and the last ones in the 1960s, not excavated with modern techniques. So, it is just as you said, it is very complicated to say. This is the reason why there is not one page of interpretation of these grave fields: it is so complicated!

AUSENDA: I have a few remarks to make.

First, in your presentation [page 116] you wrote: "...some recent anthropological work has demonstrated how economic transactions can be very complex even in societies where money is rare and where cities are not the dominant mode of settlement", and later [page 119] you wrote: "...all pre-capitalist economies (like those of early medieval Europe) can exhibit complex economic formation and that we do not need to rank societies as superior and inferior".

You seem to be drawing a parallel between the complexity of economic transactions in simple societies and the general complexity of societies. I would like to point out that these two magnitudes are not comparable. You may have extremely complex economic transactions in simple societies, e.g. the *potlatch* of the Northwest Coast populations, or the *kula* ring of the Trobrianders. These transactions took years to prepare and days to be completed. They were in fact very complex. But that does not make the societies that practised them any more complex. You should separate these concepts in your presentation.

Second, you discussed [page 118] "...the reduced size of early medieval cities", and in subsequent pages you seem to question the hypothesis of a dramatic depopulation of cities during that period. I would like to comment that this is not an unnatural phenomenon by drawing a parallel with modern economics. Even in contemporary industrial society, during an economic crisis, the tendency for modern corporations is to 'decentralise', because one does away with the higher costs of centralisation, so it is not surprising that a similar effect was taking place as a result of the economic crisis in the Roman empire.

Third, you wrote [page 118]: "The fate of cities is irrevocably linked to the successful exploitation of the poor by the rich and to issues of production and consumption". On this point I would like to make the following remarks: in the first place, a clear dichotomy between rich and poor does not exist in *real* society, because wealth distribution is more like a continuum; in the second place, both poor and rich serve a function in society, as there is always some reciprocity between the 'contributions' the 'poor' give to the rich and the material and symbolic 'services' the 'rich' render in exchange. In many cases the 'rich' are more exposed to decline and more vulnerable than the 'poor'. Among Beni Amer and Habab, former dominant clans have almost disappeared as a result of the recent war, while client clans are stronger than before. Even in contemporary democracies there is a constant turnover: the 'poor' become 'rich' often more successfully than the 'rich' succeed in holding on to their privileges and wealth.

I disagree, therefore, with the assumption that exploitation of the 'poor' by the 'rich' may be a valid explanation for political vicissitudes. The picture is much more complex and will be finally clarified only when all variables are known and accounted for. In other words, it is the socio-political vicissitudes that must explain who and why they become 'rich', not the other way around.

Fourth, concerning the impact of urban life on the Langobards which you discussed [page 118] by noting: "The Lombards were long seen as especially barbaric and their time in Italy as essentially non-urban", I would like to mention an example from recent fieldwork in eastern Sudan. The Rashaida Bedouin, who came from the Arabian peninsula to eastern Sudan during the second half of the nineteenth century, still live in their own quarters some eight kilometres from the town of Kassala, and the same is true of another group living in an area not far from the town of Tokar near the Red Sea coast. The reasons for this are basically two: the first is that they tend livestock, mostly camels, goats and sheep which, for obvious reasons, not the least of which are pasture and watering, cannot be easily or comfortably kept in towns, and the second is because they prefer to keep to themselves as they, and especially their women, have different habits from those who live in the nearby towns, where they visit when they go to market.

As far as the Langobards are concerned, even when, right after the invasion, they established a garrison in Pavia, this was quartered "astride the walls" in a place called to this day Foramania (from *fara* and *magna*, 'the great *fara*'), and the same was true for Bergamo, where they settled on the hill above the Roman town, still called 'Monte della fara' (Bognetti 1966-I:66).

These remarks concern especially the period following their migration. It is quite certain, in fact, that eventual segregation would gradually die out depending on socio-economic circumstances and time.

Conversely, townspeople are wary of living outside the city when the countryside is populated by ethnically different agrarian or pastoral populations. Again, during my fieldwork I saw this to be the case in eastern Sudan, in a village which has a mixed population of peasants coming from the Nile river, Haussa from Nigeria, Borgu and Bornu from Chad, and a few Abyssinians. During the agricultural season they would walk as much as thirty kilometres to farm their allotments and slept near them in makeshift shelters at weeding and harvesting time, but they kept their families in the village. The countryside was the domain of Hadendowa nomadic pastoralists who lived in encampments located a few kilometres from each other. Some Hadendowa, who made up about 30 percent of the village population, lived in the village and were mostly acculturated, in that they had stores, or official positions in the administration, or were landowners, or had humbler jobs.

A similar situation obtained until not long ago in Istria and Dalmatia where the countryside was inhabited almost solely by Slavs.

Fifth, you wrote [page 119]: "Bartering for example, which is likely to have been widespread in most of early medieval Europe where money was rare... is a much more complicated activity than many historians have supposed. It is to be ranked alongside market and gift exchange as a means of redistribution...". Again, you imply that barter could sustain a complex economy. I believe that you should not draw a parallel between the 'complication' of a means of redistribution, such as barter or gift exchange, and the complexity of society. In fact, barter is a fairly rigid system of exchange. It is based on several types of interaction. One is the equal volume exchange of different quantities of different goods measured by the same volume, e.g. three bowls of sorghum for one bowl of milk; this was practised also among the Langobards as proven by the term *scutella de cambio*. Another is the exchange of goods for materials that can be divided in halves, quarters, eighths, etc., such as cloth. A third is the exchange of goods against valuable staples, e.g. cocoa beans, or pieces of ornamentation, such as beads or cowrie shells. All these interactions are less flexible than payment in coinage, which in turn is less flexible than payment in paper money, and so on. In conclusion, the lesser flexibility of barter should be kept in mind when evaluating its capability of sustaining an economic system. However, I agree with you that barter may well have been an important form of redistribution in early medieval society and should become the object of careful study.

On the same topic of redistribution I would like to bring to your attention a fairly important form of redistribution in the countryside that I have never seen mentioned in the literature and was followed until not long ago, amongst other places, in the Italian Alps. This was the giving away of old clothes and old furnishings to dependents and acquaintances with lesser means.

Sixth, you mentioned Hendy's model of the early medieval economy [page 117] as asserting that: "Reciprocity characterised the economic relationships of early medieval states and for this money was not necessary". While I agree on the given that there was very little money in circulation, I think reciprocity was not the only pattern characterising the economy, self sufficiency was another very important factor, and it is attested that Langobard kings and dukes were endowed with *curtes* which produced enough for their needs and those of their households. The kings and dukes might have moved with their retinue from one *curtis* to another.

WOOD: *Curtes* move in *Francia*.

BALZARETTI: In Italy courts do not move. In all references we have, the kings are in Pavia. The dukes lived in other towns.

AUSENDA: But they had their *curtes*, so it is possible that the overseers, *ovescarii*, brought the produce to their town residences.

BALZARETTI: Oh yes. I agree with that. Concerning the initial absence of Lombard settlers from cities, historians tend not to discuss where the Lombards lived when they arrived. I am not so sure that they did not live in cities.

We do not know for certain who lived precisely in cities in very late Roman times. They could have been abandoned for centuries before. It is quite possible that the Lombards moved into the *forum* in Pavia. Perhaps there were places where those people could move into.

DUMVILLE: When St Ambrose did his rabble-rousing, was there any rabble?

BALZARETTI: I agree that the collapse of the Roman government coincided with a period of 'decentralisation'.

AUSENDA: A system of tolls becomes necessary to raise tax when people are dispersed over the countryside and hence difficult to control. It is very difficult to raise tax in the countryside because you have small hamlets where it would be problematic to enforce collection. I know that in the colonial context you cannot get easily at people living in the bush for the purpose of obtaining tax. In this case it is simpler to collect tax at protected nodal points, i.e. city gates, hence the rationale for tolls, and I do not think they paid with pieces of cloth. Maybe they used fractional Roman coinage which still had legal course at the time. In fact, the toll system, *dazio*, was still in force well into the 1950s at the city limits on all roads entering Milan.

References in the discussion

Textual sources:

Ennodius of Pavia
        Letters: see Vogel 1885.

Bibliography:

Brooks, N. P., & J. A. Graham-Campbell
    1986   Reflections on the Viking-Age silver hoard from Croydon, Surrey. In *Anglo-Saxon Monetary History*. M. A. S. Blackburn (ed.), pp. 91-110. Leicester: Leicester University Press.
Vogel, F. (ed.)
    1885   *Magnii Felicis Ennodi Opera. Monumenta Germaniae Historica. Auctores antiquissimi, 7.* Hanover: Hahn.

THE RISE OF GERMANIA IN THE LIGHT OF LINGUISTIC EVIDENCE

DENNIS H. GREEN

Trinity College, Cambridge University, Cambridge CB2 ITQ

Introduction

The aim of the book on which I am engaged is to illustrate, on the basis of language, the encounter between the world of *Germania* and the Roman empire as well as Christianity. This can only be done highly selectively, because of both the richness of the material available and the chronological spread of the encounter, ranging from prehistory through the age of migrations down to the early Middle Ages.

The disciplines concerned with this field of inquiry are archaeology, history, and philology, although they have not always been ready to take account of each other's findings. How necessary this is, can be seen most clearly in the case of archaeology, which notoriously has difficulty in relating its finds to a particular tribe to which it can give a name and thereby connect them with our historical sources. Moreover, although it has proved possible to distinguish Gothic archaeological finds in the Lower Vistula area from those of the Balts, no such success has accompanied the attempts to distinguish these Gothic finds from those of other Germanic tribes which settled in the same area earlier. In other cases archaeological evidence leaves us even more in the lurch, for although it constitutes the most informative source for our knowledge of Germanic military equipment it lets us down, for example, when the Goths in the Black Sea area did not include this gear in their grave goods. In a case like this we have no choice but to fall back on the evidence of the Gothic language, on what we can learn from what even the restricted lexis of Wulfila's Bible translation hands down to us (e.g. *brunjo* 'breastplate', *meki* 'sword', *wepna* 'weapons').

Of much greater use to the philologist, because it confronts him with verbal evidence and not the testimony of objects, is the information conveyed by historical sources, starting, as far as *Germania* is concerned, with the classical historians and geographers who first reported about northern Europe. Even their written evidence presents its own problems, however, as when these sources at first confuse the *Germani* with the Celts or equate them with the Scythians or refer to the Goths as if they were *Getae*, in all such cases seeing these hitherto unknown tribes in terms of established classical geography. False equations of this kind are no prerogative of classical historians alone, however, for modern scholarship has often been prone to an oversimplified view of *Germania* at large, applying to one tribe features which are attested only of another. Thus, the Cheruscan Arrninius has been compared with the Gothic Athanaric, which ignores both the time-gap of three and a half centuries separating them and also the vastly different acculturation processes to which a West Gerrnanic tribe was exposed after its encounter with the Celts and Rome, and an East Germanic tribe also influenced by the nomadic peoples of the steppes. The relevance of this historical dimension is true even on a smaller scale, for if we confine ourselves to evidence coming from the western borders of *Germania* we need no longer regard differences

AFTER EMPIRE:
TOWARDS AN ETHNOLOGY OF EUROPES'S BARBARIANS

© C.I.R.O.S.S.
San Marino (R.S.M.)

between what Caesar reports in the middle of the first century BC and what Tacitus says at the end of the first century AD as contradictory and therefore needing to be explained away. Instead, we acknowledge that the *Germani* of Tacitus are no longer those of Caesar over a century earlier, that the differences are largely the result of their historical encounter with the Roman world.

This encounter is one of my concerns as a philologist whose discipline provides a third approach, with its own problems and promises of supplying information unavailable from other sources. There is no need for a Germanist to apologise for focussing on the evidence provided by Old High German, for even though other Gerrnanic dialects must be taken into account, this is largely with an eye to what they can tell us about the position in German. In our period Germany was as central to *Germania* as it is today to Europe at large. It was after all the area where the earliest contacts were made between the Germanic tribes and the Celts, the Romans, and the Christian religion. It was on German soil, too, that the contrasts in Christian vocabulary between Old English and Gothic were largely played out. To deal with our problem from the point of view of the German language is therefore to take up a central position. My approach involves three main problems of methodology: loanword studies, etymology, and semantics. Discussing these will open the way to looking at wider problems which form the context in which our specialist concerns must be placed.

Loanword Studies

Loanwords we may regard as the most obvious reflection of the loan of cultural goods from one society to another. This was already clear in the sixteenth century to Beatus Rhenanus, for whom any language was a mixed language, incorporating terms from other languages which accompanied the adoption of cultural goods from abroad, such as trading goods, plants or fruits. Such a remark agrees with the results of modern loanword studies on the influence of Latin on German in the first centuries AD (before the rise of monastic written culture introduced a wholesale Latin influence of quite a different nature). In these earliest centuries the novelty is almost always something concrete, the word accompanies a thing or object (e.g. 'wine', 'cellar', 'pillow'). What is largely true of these Latin loanwords also applies to earlier Celtic loanwords into Germanic; in both cases the novelties of a more advanced civilisation explain the loanword traffic.

To be sure that we are dealing with loanwords (and therefore with cultural influence from without) we have to be able to distinguish them from native words. This is generally simpler with loans from Latin into Germanic (and more so from Greek into Gothic), but less so with loans from Celtic into Germanic in a period when the language groups were still more closely akin. In view of this we need a criterion by which to determine a loanword from a native word, such as a positive agreement between the two languages in question which however differs from what is to be found in other relevant languages. An example generally accepted by Germanists (although doubts have been expressed by Celticists) is the agreement between Germanic and Celtic in the case of Gothic *reiki*, German 'Reich': no other Indo-European cognates show a long *i*, which is moreover a regular development in Celtic, but not in Germanic, so that a loan from the former to the latter seems uncontested. For converse examples, however, we can turn to other terms from the same lexical sphere (German 'Eid', 'Erbe', 'frei'), for which Indo-European cognates again exist, this time without the semantic specialisation found only in Celtic and Germanic. However, in these cases there is nothing about the Germanic terms (as there was with the long *i* in *reiki*) to suggest that they must have been loaned from Celtic. These three words could equally well be native Germanic terms, so that the most we can say is that in this context Celtic and Germanic form a common cultural group, distinct from the rest of Indo-European, without it being clear that there was cultural influence from one to the other.

The question of the direction of a loan occurs elsewhere. For example, in the case of the Old French adjective *estoult* ('brave', 'arrogant', 'foolish') it is still contested whether this is a native word (< Latin *stultus*) or a loanword (cf. German 'stolz'), so much so that recourse has been had to the theory of a crossing between both possibilities. Loans in each direction can also be established when we consider the various categories into which Latin loanwords into Germanic, but also Germanic into Latin fall, for in each case the most numerous concern trade and warfare, two areas in which traffic was understandably two-way. An example from trade is provided by Latin *ganta*, a word of Germanic origin meaning 'wild goose' (cognate with English 'goose', 'gander' and 'gannet'). The word is used as a loanword into Latin by Pliny who remarks that the down or feathers of Germanic *gantae* were sought after by Roman traders for their quality. That this loan betrays a reciprocal trading encounter is brought out by the converse phenomenon, the presence in Germanic of a number of early Latin loanwords from the same context. Thus, Latin *pluma* produces Old High German *pflûma* (German 'Flaumfeder'), *pulvinus* is loaned into Old English as *pylwe* ('pillow', German 'Pfuhl'), *coxinus* survives in Old High German *chussîn* ('cushion', 'Kissen'), whilst *piluccare* ('to pluck feathers') is loaned as 'pflucken'. That this last example could also have been loaned in the context of viticulture does not tell against this, for the word could have been adopted, like others, in different contexts and at different times.

This brings me to another problem in loanword studies, the question whether a particular loan is the result of monogenesis or polygenesis, which can be regarded both geographically and chronologically. The need to differentiate loanword traffic geographically can be illustrated from the names for the days of the week, borrowed from Latin into Germanic. We can be reasonably certain that this adoption took place in or before the fourth century, but equally that it occurred in at least two frontier areas under different conditions: in the North West (the area of the Lower Rhine in particular) and in the South East (the Lower Danube as the frontier between the Goths and the Empire), the former still within the context of paganism, the latter under the auspices of Christianity. Even if we narrow our focus more drastically and concentrate on one Germanic dialect alone we still have to reckon with different directions taken by loanwords from Latin: for German across the Rhine frontier, but also (if to a smaller extent) across the Danube, for Gothic across the Lower Danube in the fourth century, but also much earlier as the result of trading contacts from the West penetrating the Germanic hinterland and reaching the Goths in Poland before their migrations in the direction of the Black Sea.

This last geographical example also implies, of course, a chronological differentiation, which must be taken into account when we consider, this time, Gothic loanwords into Finnish and Slavonic in the course of their movement towards the South East. For both these encounters it has proved possible to establish three separate periods: pre-Gothic or Primitive Germanic (which may be no more than Gothic before it had undergone the changes characteristic of Wulfila's language), then Gothic itself as the originating language, and finally post-Gothic (in the case of Finnish possibly Gothic remnants left behind in northern Poland, in the case of Slavonic the so-called Balkan Germanic). Leaving on one side the linguistic omniscience which such possibilities presuppose, we may illustrate loanword traffic at different points in time from cases nearer home. The Latin word for 'cook', *coquus*, Vulgar Latin *cocus*, must have been taken across on two separate occasions, an earlier one producing Old High German *koch* with a short *o*, a later one yielding Old English *cōc* where the long *o* is the result of a (later) Vulgar Latin lengthening of a short vowel in an open syllable. The repeated loan process which this implies need not be spread over two different dialects, it can also occur in one dialect only, as can be shown, with regrettable oversimplification of a complex situation, with German 'impfen', originally a viticultural term meaning to 'graft a shoot', taken from Latin *imputare*. The difficulties presented by the Old High German form *impfîton* (alongside *impfôn*) could be resolved within German if we could assume a Vulgar Latin form **impudare* (cf. *catena > cadena*) whose *d* would have become t in German regularly as a result of the second sound shift. Solving our German difficulty in this way, however, creates a new difficulty elsewhere, for the assumption of **impudare* conflicts with French 'enter', where the *t* has been retained. Instead, French 'enter' is regarded as a regular development in Central French, whereas the phonological changes for Eastern French produced forms which, loaned into German at different times, resulted in, first, *impfitôn* and then *impfôn*. Only on the assumption of a double loan process can all the variant forms, in French as well as German, be accounted for.

A last point concerns the degree of novelty in the thing or object which the loanword designates. In many, even most cases what was conveyed was something quite new to *Germania* ('iron' as a loanword from Celtic, 'wine' from Latin), but we should avoid the assumption of absolute novelty in every case. In several examples it can be shown that the object whose introduction into *Germania* the loanword accompanies may have represented a technical advance on what was already known in a simpler form, not something completely unknown beyond the imperial frontier. Two examples may illustrate this. Latin *puteus* found its way early into Germanic, where it is attested in a number of dialects in the sense of a 'well' (built of stone or brick) as distinct from a native word (German 'Brunnen'), meaning a 'natural spring'. Similarly, the Latin word for 'mill', *molina*, found its way into Germanic, eventually displacing a native word (Gothic *qairnus*) which denoted simply a hand-mill, as opposed to the technically more advanced Roman model, operated by water or by a donkey, an animal likewise introduced to northern Europe by the Romans. Whether the novelty of the Roman imports was absolute or not, the cultural advance they represented is clear.

Etymology

Whenever we depend on etymological evidence to reconstruct the original meaning of a word and therefore the cultural standing of the language which employs it, we do well to keep in mind that etymology is not an exact science. In his discussion of the role of nomadic peoples of the steppes such as the Alans and Sarmatians in the migrations of the East Germanic tribes in that direction Vernadsky is at many points, perhaps unavoidably, dependent on etymological hypotheses, and the same is true of Birkhan's book on the cultural contacts between Celts and *Germani*. The use of etymology is legitimate when we lack written evidence, but its hypothetical and often contested nature means that an argument based on it cannot be fully conclusive. Reservations of this kind, however, fade into insignificance in contrast to the criticism called for when Scardigli in his book on the Goths maintains without more ado that a number of words in Wulfila's Gothic vocabulary for which no etymological cognates in other Germanic dialects or in Indo-European have been established are technical terms of shamanism taken over by the Goths from peoples of the steppes. I have no wish to deny in principle the possibility of shamanistic influence on Germanic in this region (the word 'hemp' may well belong here, derived possibly from Thracian in the sense of '*cannabis*' and used in shamanistic practices). However, to argue along these lines we need a positive pointer of some kind, not just an inability to find an alternative etymological explanation.

Behind these points there lies a much more fundamental difficulty in using etymology to throw light on the early culture of the Germanic tribes. Even if we were in a position to accept the claim of etymology to establish the original meaning of a Germanic word, that still tells us nothing about how long this meaning remained in force or whether it was subsequently subject to historical change. In other words, the (established) original meaning may not be identical with the meaning in force at the time when the language in question found its way into writing. To determine whether this is so we need a pointer other than etymology and where, as in many cases, this is not forthcoming we are left in doubt. What is involved here can be illustrated in the sphere of Germanic house-building. Gothic possesses a verb for 'to build', *timrjan*, which is cognate with English 'timber' and suggests that house-building was originally in wood, as borne out elsewhere in *Germania*. Thus, Old High German uses *zimbar* in the sense of 'building', but *zimbarâri* to mean 'carpenter'; the Gothic word for 'wall', *waddjus*, has cognates meaning 'willow' or 'to bind', 'twist' and suggests a construction with wattle and daub; the Old High German noun with the same meaning, *want*, suggests a similar origin by its kinship with the verb *wintan* ('to twist, plait') and the English noun 'wand' in the sense of 'rod, stick'. All this suggests that the *Germani* originally built in wood, but leaves it unclear how long they continued this technique or whether they supplemented it by another method of building. If the Christian vocabulary of Gothic and Old High German can use the stem corresponding to 'timber' metaphorically of 'religious edification', is it not possible that, independently of Christianity, they also used it metaphorically to denote building with any material, not just with wood? In this particular case we are not left in any doubt where they may have learned this new technique and when they began to employ it alongside building in wood. Although Tacitus in the first century AD says that the *Germani* use wood and are unacquainted with cement and tiles as building materials, Ammianus Marcellinus, referring to the year 360, reports that they build their dwellings "more carefully in the Roman manner". In the period covered by these two dates some *Germani* must have begun to build more permanently, using stones, bricks and tiles, a fact which is borne out by the Latin origin of German words taken over in these earliest centuries and referring to this new method of building (Vulgar Latin *mura* > *mûra, calx* > *kalk, mortarium* > *mortâri, tegula* > *ziagala*). In this period in which two methods of building coexist the old word for building in wood expands its meaning to imply building at large, so that it is no longer permissible to use etymology as a guide to contemporary practice. This example, where we are assisted by the fortuitous presence of external evidence, serves as a warning against using etymology as a reliable guide in the many cases where we have no such further evidence.

Semantics

Under this heading we return to the question of linguistic loan-traffic which we have so far considered only with regard to loanwords, a more obvious form because the foreign nature

of the word more commonly stood out as recognisable to us. Now we must consider two
other forms of loan-traffic where the task of recognising examples is made more difficult
by their employment of native word material in imitation of the Latin model.

The first form of loan-traffic we now have to look at is the so-called loan-formation
('Lehnbildung'), the imitation of a foreign model, generally part for part, with native
material, producing a word which had hitherto not existed in the recipient language and
whose creation arose from the wish to find a vernacular equivalent for what the Latin
language already possessed. A commonly quoted example may serve our purposes. The
Christian Latin word *conscientia* (itself a semantic development from a pre-Christian term
but under the influence of Christian Greek *syneídesis*) has proved particularly productive in
European languages as a central term of moral theology. It was taken over into Old High
German by Notker about AD 1000 in the form *gewizzenî*, constructed in the same way as
the Latin model: collective prefix (*ge-* = *con-*) + the verb 'to know' (*wizzen* = *scient-*) +
abstract suffix (*î* = *ia*). Although this pattern has been repeated in different ways throughout
Europe (Gothic *mithwissei*, Danish *samvittighed*, Swedish *samvete*, Russian *sovjestj*, the
point in including it under the heading of semantics is the suspicion that in each case the
new loan-formation (meaning literally something like 'withknowingness') must have been
largely unintelligible to a native speaker with no knowledge of the originating language and
that it must have required considerable time and constant repetition in varying Christian
contexts before the coinage acquired the same force as the original.

This is also true of the second form of loan-traffic, what has been termed the 'loan
meaning' ('Lehnbedeutung'), where a new word is not created artificially on the foreign
model, but instead an already existing word shifts its meaning or acquires an additional
meaning under the influence of another language. The advantage of this method (it avoids an
artificial construction and the difficulties in understanding which this involved) is bought at a
price, however, for now the semantic problem lies in showing that the old word with its
traditional meaning had acquired a new meaning. We can illustrate this briefly with the
Christian Latin *anima*, rendered into Germanic by such terms for 'soul' as Gothic *saiwala*,
Old High German *seula*, Old English *sâwol* . The difficulty in rendering this concept lies in
the fact that for the Christian the soul is the spiritual focus of a living human being, but is
also endowed with an eternal future in the life to come. By contrast, the Germanic languages
possessed two distinct terms: **ferh* (attested in various forms) denoted the spark of life, the
animating spirit in a living being, whilst **saiwala* stood for the spirit of a dead person.
Whichever of these Germanic terms was chosen to convey the Christian concept, difficulties
would be bound to arise in showing that its scope was now much wider, embracing this life
and the life to come. The problem is a complex one, but one reason why the attempt was
made throughout *Germania* with **saiwala* may well have been the overriding importance of
the soul's fate after death. How to convey that this word also applied now to a living being
and that his temporal existence had a bearing on his life to come was a problem which could
only be solved by a long period of pastoral instruction in the new religion.

Because these two forms of loan-traffic make use of native word material or even an
already existing native word, it is more difficult to tell with them than with loanwords
whether we are in fact dealing with loans at all. If it was necessary to seek for criteria to
distinguish loanwords from native words, this type of confirmation will be more than ever
necessary in establishing loan-formations and loan-meanings. From various points of view
a number of criteria have been proposed (e.g. a loan can be assumed when the word is in
one way or another exceptional in the recipient language, but not in the originating language)

and conversely indicators which disprove a loan-process. In most cases no single criterion is sufficient to make a loan probable, so that we need instead a variety of them pointing in the same direction.

How this works out in practice can be seen in the case of the Christian concept of obedience: Latin *oboediens* (< *obaudiens*) 'listening, paying attention, obeying' and Old High German *horsam* (verbal stem 'to hear' + suffix indicating a quality of character). A number of features suggest that the German word is no independent creation, but ultimately dependent on the Latin. First, the vernacular word is unique in German of this period in adding the adjectival suffix *-sam* to a verbal stem (suggested by *oboediens* as a present participle), for all the other examples add it to a nominal stem. Secondly, the German examples are confined to a geographically restricted area in South West Germany (Weissenburg, Reichenau and Freising). Thirdly, the richest lexical differentiation (adjective, abstract noun, verb, all in positive as well as negative forms) is to be found in one of these three monuments, an interlinear translation of the Benedictine Rule, which suggests that the word's function was developed in German to express the idea of monastic obedience in particular. Fourthly, this concentration on literature of translation (where the Latin model exerts constant pressure on the vernacular) is confirmed by the probability that the German translator of the Benedictine Rule was here dependent on a similar solution already found in Anglo-Saxon with a similarly wide lexical spread. To these linguistic features can be added a general observation which, whilst inconclusive by itself, certainly confirms what we have just seen. From their first encounters with them the Romans were struck by the lack of discipline shown by the *Germani* in warfare, a fact borne out for Christianity by the way in which the obedience owed to God by the worshipper was for long misconceived in terms of loyalty (*triuwa*), implying that God had commitments to man as much as man to God. That the concept of obedience (military or religious) was initially foreign to *Germania* underlines that *horsam* is quite unlikely to have been an independent native creation. A number of quite distinct criteria combine to suggest this conclusion.

Especially of loan-meanings, where native words are given a new function or, in the case of religious vocabulary, pre-Christian words are baptised and become part of Christian terminology, we have to ask the same critical question as of etymology. How far can we be certain that the original (pre-Christian) function is still in force when we first encounter these terms written down in texts which for the most part belong to Christian literature or are at least composed under clerical auspices? Too often uncritical assumptions have been made, informed by a wish to lower the barrier of Christianity and trace pagan continuity. For example, a bias of this kind is betrayed when it is argued that, because Old English *os* had originally denoted a pagan god, therefore the syllable "rang bells in a seventh-century Northumbrian head that it does not in ours", or that, because *Frea* had been the name of a god, therefore "connotations of this deity may well have been present in the use of *frea* as a common kenning for an earthly lord and for the Anglo-Saxon king" (Chaney 1970:23, 50). As the hesitant wording reveals, this is pure surmise, but no amount of surmises adds up to anything more than a hypothesis.

Even this wishful thinking, a readiness to assume pagan survivals where they have to be proved (a possibility which I have no wish to contest in principle), is not so bad as a line of thought pursued in German scholarship in the thirties and even earlier, summed up in the term 'Germanisierung des Christentums' and amounting to the deliberate retention of a pagan or at least pre-Christian meaning in a Christian context. For understandable reasons not much has been heard of this approach of late, but for us it illustrates in accentuated form the problem of semantic shift presented by loan-meaning. Applied to a particular work (the Old Saxon *Heliand* has often been exposed to this kind of treatment), this method assumes the survival of earlier Germanic modes of thought and grants them priority over Christian theological ones. What is now stressed, in conformity with the monastic origins of this work and the biblical and exegetical sources on which it is dependent, is the need to proceed from this Christian starting-point and to ask how far linguistic and conceptual accommodation to the needs and powers of comprehension of the audience was unavoidable if the author was to get his message across at all. To proceed the other way round by searching for 'pagan' content in a monastic work is to conflict with the missionary intention (in the widest sense of the word) of the author, whose task it was to bring home to the Saxons the Christian message. If accommodation was unavoidable at times in this process, this was not because of a misplaced wish to protect pagan antiquities, but rather because linguistic facts often allowed no other procedure and also because the Church had itself long conceded the right to accommodation in the context of its mission. Unsurprisingly, the direction in which semantic analysis takes us is forwards, into the Christianity of the Middle Ages, not backwards into Germanic paganism.

Three Constituents of the Middle Ages

This move forwards into the Middle Ages means seeing *Germania* first in its encounter, then in its slow fusion with classical antiquity and Christianity. These three factors (where for *Germania* we need to substitute tribal Europe at large, to find room for the Celts and Slavs as well) have commonly been seen as constituting the Middle Ages, so that our philological problem reflects on the small scale this overall historical development. We may consider now a few selected examples of how these three factors fused together, regarding them as the background to the similar process to which our linguistic evidence points.

Despite a long-lasting enmity between Christianity and Roman paganism there were numerous points where the Church found it politic or unavoidable to adopt aspects of classical antiquity for its own purpose. The pre-Christian cult of the divinity of the Emperor, imported from the East and applied to Caligula, Nero and Domitian, represented a challenge to the new religion which it met not simply by contesting it, but more polemically by applying titles at home in pagan divine kingship to Christ as the ruler of the world to whom they truly apply. Where the Emperor Domitian bore the double title *Dominus et Deus*, the gospel of St John gives a twist to this by having the apostle Thomas address the risen Christ as 'my Lord and my God'. Other terms appropriated with the same polemical purpose include titles which were so thoroughly christianised that it still comes as something of a shock to learn where they were originally derived from, e.g. 'saviour', 'epiphany', 'lord'. On quite a different plane of influence Roman imperial practice was followed as a model for papal registers: the imperial rescript for the form of papal letters and the imperial *commentarii*, organised by years and arranged chronologically, for the registers themselves. Not merely in administrative, but also in legal matters the language of papal authority owes much to imperial precedent. The language and decisions of Leo the Great depend largely on Roman law, the early bishops of Gaul recognise in the Popes the *auctoritas* not merely of St Peter, but also of the City. This last point was not lost on the Visigoths of southern France who distinguished Gallic Catholics (as well as Gallo-Romans) from themselves by calling them Romans. Again on quite a different plane the concept of *imperium* lives on not merely in the political pretensions of the barbarian kingdoms, the successor-states of Rome, but also in the liturgy.

This last point brings us to the possibilities of symbiosis between two other constituents (classical antiquity and *Germania*), for however much the former may have looked down on the latter as barbarians beyond the pale of the civilised oecumene, the impression made by Rome on the *Germani* was so overwhelming that, despite isolated conservative rejections of a foreign culture, Rome was the model to be followed in *Germania*. This is true not merely of the physical luxuries of an advanced civilisation which the earliest Latin loanwords suggest, but also of the new religion once the Church came to be identified with Rome after Constantine, and of the double authority, political and ecclesiastic, which Rome now signified. Thus, not merely the papacy, but also the new Germanic kingdoms imitate forms of imperial law: here written Germanic law codes such as that of Euric and the *Liber Constitutionum* of the Burgundians are eloquent. Roman pretensions are made for a barbarian ruler when Chlodwig, after a victory over the Goths, receives from the Emperor Anastasius I a diploma granting him the title of consul (*et ab ea die tamquam consul aut augustus est vocitatus*). Clothed in a purple tunic and chlamys, with a diadem on his head, Chlodwig rode from the church through the streets of Tours, scattering gold and silver among the crowd like a latter-day Roman ruler, but the shouts of *Augustus* by the crowd suggest that, if not officially, then at least for some the political claims may have been pitched even higher. In history-writing, too, it is above all the Franks, but not only they, who set themselves up alongside the Romans by fabricating a prehistory which parallels the Romans' claim to Trojan origins: Rome is now the criterion of history writing, by comparison with which a native oral *origo gentis* fades into official insignificance. In the seventh century Fredegar therefore claims a Trojan origin for the Franks and hints that Xanten was founded by Franks driven from Troy (and therefore parallels Rome), a wild claim based on bowdlerising the second-century *Colonia Trajana* into *Colonia Trojana*. With Otfrid von Weissenburg in the ninth century a variant claim, also reconcilable with Fredegar, is made in the vernacular: in arguing the military and political claims of the Franks (and in hoping to contribute to their cultural ones himself) he places them alongside the Romans and maintains their kinship with Alexander and the Macedonians.

The third fusion of traditions of disparate origins concerns Christianity and *Germania*. The Church could have as little truck with Germanic as with classical paganism, but here too it was ready to make compromises to achieve long-term ends, partly because this was by now established practice, partly because it had little choice, whilst on the other side of the religious divide a Germanic king could accept with caution a new God who could be useful to him in a variety of ways. The most obvious and recurrent way in which the new God could be useful to a king was to grant him victory in battle, especially after this had been vouchsafed to Constantine at the Milvian Bridge. Of Chlodwig, facing a similar situation in battle, it has been said that his throwing in his lot with the Christian God for the sake of victory was no total conversion, but that he regarded the new religion as an additional cult, as a supplement rather than a substitute. Not simply in this particular case, but in regard to Germanic conversions at large in this early period we may reckon with acceptance of an additional God joining the pagan pantheon, not with a wholesale abandonment of the latter. Thus, it is reported expressly of King Theudebert's troops, again in the context of battle, that they sacrificed Ostrogothic victims as the first fruits of victory, but that they did this, nominally at least, as Christians. Procopius comments: "These barbarians, though they have become Christians, preserve the greater part of their ancient religion". This may be the result of ignorance, but also what the new convert, still uncertain, could regard as prudence taking the form of a twofold allegiance. Bede tells us, for example, that Redwald, king of the East Angles, sought to get the best of both worlds by setting up a pagan and a Christian altar in one and the same building. We come across the same attitude, expressed in a different medium, in the Anglo-Saxon helmet from Benty Grange, whose raised crest is surmounted by the multi-metalled figure of a boar. The association of a boar with a helmet is well attested in *Germania*: one passage in *Beowulf* speaks of a boar "above the helmet" (as in the freestanding figure from Benty Grange) and another of the animal standing guard over the life of the warrior who wore the helmet (by warding off sword blows, but also because of the magic power attributed to the boar). The protection afforded by this boar-helmet is therefore well and truly *Germanic*, but it is more than that since the nasal also has a silver cross on it, perhaps because the cross reflects the faith of the wearer (at a time when conversion was still recent), but that need not exclude a talisman function as a symbol of victory. Boar and cross, paganism and Christianity, work together here at a time when both mingled: like Redwald, the wearer of this helmet appears to have taken out a double insurance policy.

To divide up the unity of the incipient Middle Ages in this way into three constituents might seem excessively analytic, but my aim has been not to separate these elements from one another, but to specify what ones combine with one another: Christianity with antiquity, antiquity with *Germania*, and Christianity with *Germania*. This makes it necessary to go one step further and consider examples where not just two, but all three constituents come together in a unity. The fortuitous nature of what has come down to us means that my examples come from Anglo-Saxon England, but that their significance is not confined to this country.

The Ruthwell Cross combines these three traditions in an impressive way. The *Germanic* past is adapted to new ends in the use of runes to inscribe part of the vernacular Christian poem, the *Dream of the Rood* (they are also used to inscribe some Latin words, as also on the coffin of St Cuthbert). Christianity is present in the shape of the cross itself, the incorporation of a poem dealing with the crucifixion, but also in the themes of some of the sculpture panels: e.g. Christ in Judgment, Mary Magdalene, the Annunciation, and the use of Roman letters for inscribing passages from the Vulgate. As regards classical tradition, the Cross sculptures have been described as a supreme example of realistic figure-work in that tradition, their programme is ultimately Byzantine, and the inhabited vine-scroll ornament is directly inspired by classical models. Even though we are far from an overall understanding of its meaning, these three traditions come together again in the Franks Casket. *Germanic* tradition is again represented by the use of runes to record vernacular (and occasional Latin) words, and in the scenes depicted from the legend of Weland the Smith and also concerning Egil (named as such). Christianity is present in depictions of the Adoration of the Magi and of the capture of Jerusalem by Titus. This last scene could equally be interpreted as belonging to Roman tradition, which is in any case present in the theme of Romulus and Remus. Whatever this thematic conjunction may add up to, it represents a 'heady mix' of the three elements whose slow fusion we are tracing.

For a third example of this fusion we consider another Anglo-Saxon helmet, found in the Coppergate at York. Its *Germanic* affiliations are clear: the helmet is of a type otherwise known only in England (Benty Grange, Sutton Hoo) and in Sweden (Uppland), a protective animal (if not a boar) is carved between the eyebrows, facing the interlace of the nasal. From the burial evidence this helmet and its parallels must have been the treasured possessions of a warrior class. This need not exclude Christianity in this case, which is suggested more conclusively than at Benty Grange by a Christian Latin prayer on a metal strip running from the back over the crown to the nasal. Finally, Roman influence is present in the prototype for this kind of helmet: a late Roman parade helmet of a general, as attested by two examples, one from Holland and another from Suffolk. Even where, as in this impressive example, we seem to stand closest to the warrior world of *Germania*, it has long been exposed to and penetrated by Rome and Christianity.

What we have followed through in these three examples illustrates in visible, concrete terms (in stone, whale's bone, and metal) what can be argued in regard to language. To analyse selected terms from Germanic vocabulary under three headings (reflecting Germanic society, but then its encounter with the Roman Empire and with Christianity) is as justifiable as when we exemplified the three constituent traditions which make up the Middle Ages, but only so long as we avoid an artificial separation and see them instead in their gradual merging. No one heading can therefore be treated in isolation from the others. Germanic, even specifically pagan vocabulary cannot be divorced from Christian usage when we consider terms such as *got, heil, heilag, ôstarun* in Old High German, for their pre-Christian usage created problems, but also provided opportunities which the Church could not ignore. Germanic terms for warfare cannot be discussed without attention being paid to words which they passed on to the Romans and words which they borrowed from them, and the same is true of trade, for these are the two areas where the encounter was most marked. Finally, Germanic, Roman and Christian aspects must all be considered together in connection, say, with the names of the days of the week (*Germania* takes these over from the Roman model, substituting pagan Germanic deities for the Roman gods whose names occurred, which created problems later for the Church). The same is true of the vocabulary of writing: runic terminology combines with a vocabulary acquired from Rome and then from monasticism, so that all three forces have to be seen in their interplay. In all this we face a mixture of linguistic factors comparable to what was more tangibly visible in the Ruthwell Cross, the Franks Casket, and the York helmet.

The Entry of the Germani on to the Stage of History

On the admittedly narrow basis of linguistic evidence we have been concerned with the emergence of *Germania* from a tribal culture on the margins of the classical oecumene to occupying, with the Merovingians and above all the Carolingians, a central position within medieval civilisation. In political and cultural terms the initial relationship between the *Germani* and the Roman Empire was one repeated frequently on a world scale in the nineteenth and twentieth centuries: the confrontation between a tribal culture and a highly organised state. This state may have collapsed in time, largely but not exclusively because of the assaults of these tribes on its territory, but its eventual resuscitation in the form of the Carolingian Empire is a measure of how far the Germanic tribes had acquired more settled forms of state organisation from those whom they had defeated.

Moving from beyond the frontiers of the Roman Empire to what became the heartland of medieval Europe means that the *Germani* entered on to the stage of history and now played a central part, but this is true in another sense, for they become an acknowledged entity in historiography, too. When the classical world first heard of these tribes it was not at first as a distinct novelty, for they were initially confused with the Celts or Scythians and acquired a separate identity only as they crossed further the horizon of the classical world, whose historians begin to take more accurate note of these newcomers and register their doings in their written (and therefore largely datable) historical records.

The emergence of the *Germani* from prehistory to history can be plotted better with the Goths than with many other tribes, largely because of what we are told of their origins by Cassiodorus, Jordanes, and Isidore of Seville. What is reported of the Goths' origins (their homeland in Scandinavia, migration across the Baltic to the region of the Lower Vistula, and trek southeastwards to the area of the Black Sea) may be geographically largely peculiar to them (even though this may rather reflect our lack of similar information about other tribes), but in one respect it is typical of what we learn elsewhere in *Germania*. These earliest origins are shrouded in uncertain myth whose connection with historical fact eludes us or is highly dubious (e.g. they crossed the Baltic in three boats, they were subjected to slavery "in Britain or in some other island"). Such unreliable details are unavoidable in any *origo gentis*, for they refer to an early period where the only knowledge available even to a trained, highly literate historian of antiquity came to him from tribal informants who themselves depended on oral tradition. If they are to include the origins of the tribe with whom they are dealing these historians have no choice but to make use of this oral tradition, as Jordanes makes amply clear in referring to *fabulae*, to what the Goths "remember" (*memorantur*), to what "is said" to have happened (*dicitur, fertur*), to their *prisca carmina* and to "the deeds of their ancestors sung in song" (*cantu maiorum facta*). However, Jordanes also makes it clear how, as a literate historian, he views sources of this kind for, in connection with the myth of the Goths in Britain, he says pointedly that he prefers to believe what he has read, rather than put his trust in old wives' tales. His doubts about the historicity of events transmitted only by oral tradition, before the existence of reliable written records, mean that for Jordanes the origins of the Goths belong to prehistory and that their history proper began only with the commencement of written records.

Written records and therewith a reliable history of the Goths could only become possible once the Goths came into contact with writing, not runes (which were rarely used for a pragmatic purpose or for longer texts), but writing as practised in the Roman empire. Isidore is quite clear about this origin of a historical tradition about the Goths: "For many centuries the Goths were united in one realm under the leadership of kings. But because the kings are not recorded in the chronicles, nothing is known about them. They entered into the historical sources only from that time when the Romans began to feel their martial ardour". Seeing Gothic history in this context means that Isidore could only write with the help of and in the context of Roman historiography, a conclusion which is also applicable to Cassiodorus' remark: *Originem gothicam historiam fecit esse romanam*. Grafting Gothic history in this way on to Roman history as a fixed framework meant accomplishing for historiography what the Franks were to do in pseudohistory by tracing their origins, like the Romans, back to Troy.

How important it was to integrate Gothic (which we may take as typical of Germanic) into Roman history can be seen in the way in which Jordanes concludes his history of the Goths, transforming an *origo gothica into a historia romana*. He describes how Mathesuentha, the grand daughter of Theoderic the Great and the last of her distinguished dynasty, was given in marriage to the Roman Emperor's nephew, himself of the stock of the Anicii, an ancient Roman family of renown. In this marriage Jordanes sees a union of Gothic with Roman, but as a Christian author he also calls down the Lord's blessing on it, seeing this combined Gothic-Roman history in terms of Christian history as well. The development followed in his pages is not merely one from myth to historiography, from oral tradition to writing, but also an integration of Gothic into Roman and Christian history.

We may conclude by seeing this development, not merely for the Goths but for the Germanic tribes at large, in one further respect, as a long drawn-out civilising process. This was early apparent on a purely material level, where Latin loanwords entered *Germania* accompanying the novel or technically more advanced cultural goods imported across the imperial frontier. It was also more profoundly true, if much more difficult to grasp, of the two other types of linguistic loan-traffic (loan-formation, loan-meaning), where the terms affected largely concern Christianity and religious or ethical concepts which had not been included in the introduction of loanwords. The difference between these two types of loan (even though it is certainly not an absolute one) can be illustrated in regard to two Latin terms which were borrowed twice into German, admittedly as loanwords only, but on the first occasion in a non-Christian, then later in a Christian context. The different functions which the two occasions serve indicate the civilising process which is at work.

The first word is Latin *magister*, loaned into Old High German as *meister* (and into other dialects). In the period of the Roman republic the word was used in a technical military sense (*magister equitum*) to denote the officer in charge of the cavalry squadrons of the legions, but Constantine introduced the office of *magister militum*, designating a general in the Roman army, but normally in charge of a formation within the army, not of the whole. A number of such generals were in fact Germanic mercenaries of high rank, even kings (Theoderic was given this honorary title), so that there is every reason to assume that *magister* in this military sense was known in *Germania* in the fourth to sixth centuries, even though its existence as a loanword with this specific function is not attested until Middle High German *scharmeister*, denoting like its Latin model someone commanding a formation within the army. Alongside this, however, another meaning of *magister* ('schoolmaster, teacher') is loaned into German and attested first in the translation of the Benedictine Rule in the context of monastic schooling, a meaning which there is certainly no reason to assume was taken over earlier together with the military meaning.

This differentiation of semantic function resulting from a twofold loan can be paralleled in the same two semantic contexts by another word, Greco-Latin *schola*, designating from about 300 the Emperor's bodyguard (in which many Germanic soldiers served, so that acquaintance with the word in this military usage can be assumed without difficulty). The word is attested with this meaning in Germanic: Old English *scolu* ('band, troop'), *handscolu* ('retinue'), Old Saxon *skola* (generalised in meaning to 'crowd, group'). The form *handscolu* in particular seems to retain much of the original meaning. With this word, too, we must reckon with a second loan introducing another meaning of the Latin word: Old High German *scuola* in the sense 'school', again attested for the first time in the Benedictine Rule. In this case, however, we can be even more sure of a twofold loan than was possible with *meister*, for the Old High German *scuola* with its diphthong presupposes an earlier form with a long *o*, whereas the Old Saxon term must go back to a form with a short *o*. This alternation between short and long vowel we have come across before (Old High German *koch* alongside Old English *cōc*): it presupposes the regular lengthening of a short vowel in an open syllable in Vulgar Latin and suggests that one form was loaned into Germanic before this lengthening, the other after it.

With both these words a military meaning has been not ousted, but supplemented by an educational one, so that this development by no means removed the problem of warfare, but rather introduced the cultural dimension of literacy, the hallmark of Benedictine education. Together these two semantic spheres create the setting for the medieval conjunction of the *miles* and the *clericus*, and demonstrate continuity between the process we have been following and the incipient Middle Ages.

Acknowledgements—I have to thank other participants at San Marino for suggestions and corrections made in the course of discussion. Where these have been adopted they are not included in the record of the discussion, but have been incorporated in the revised text of my paper.

References

Betz, W.
   1949   *Deutsch und Lateinisch. Die Lehnbildungen der althochdeutschen Benediktinerregel.* Bonn: H. Bouvier Verlag.
   1974   Lehnwörter und Lehnprägungen im Vor-und Frühdeutschen. In *Deutsche Wortgeschichte.* F. Maurer & H. Rupp (eds.), pp. 135-163, third edition. Berlin: Walter de Gruyter.
Birkhan, H.
   1970   *Germanen und Kelten bis zum Ausgang der Römerzeit.* Sitzungsberichte der Österreichischen Akademie der Wissenschaften in Wien, Phil.-hist. Kl. 272.
Campbell, J. (ed.)
   1991   *The Anglo-Saxons.* Harmondsworth: Penguin Books.
Chaney, W. A.
   1970   *The cult of kingship in Anglo-Saxon England. The transition from paganism to Christianity.* Manchester: Manchester University Press.
Hagenlocher, A.
   1975   *Schicksal im Heliand. Verwendung und Bedeutung der nominalen Bezeichnungen.* Köln: Böhlau Verlag.
Heiler, F.
   1959   Fortleben und Wandlungen des antiken Gottkönigtums im Christentum. In *La regalità sacra. Contributi al tema dell'VlII Congresso Internazionale di Storia delle Religioni (Roma, Aprile 1955)*, pp. 543-580. Leiden: E. J. Brill.
Kuln, H.
   1972   Das römische Kriegswesen im germanischen Wortschatz. *Zeitschrift für deutsches Altertum* 101: 13-53.
Müller, G., & T. Frings
   1968   *Germania Romana*, II. Halle: VEB Max Niemeyer Verlag.
Noble, T. F. X.
   1990   Literacy and the papal government in late antiquity and the early Middle Ages. In *The uses of literacy in early medieval Europe.* R. McKitterick (ed.), pp.82-108. Cambridge: Cambridge University Press.
Rathofer, J.
   1962   *Der Heliand. Theologischer Sinn und tektonische Form. Vorbereitung und Grundlegung der Interpretation*, pp. 51-194. Köln: Böhlau Verlag.
Scardigli, P.
   1973   *Die Goten: Sprache und Kultur.* Munich: Verlag C.H. Beck.
Schmidt, K. H.
   1986   Keltisch-germanische Isoglossen und ihre sprachgeschichtlichen Implikationen. In *Germanenprobleme in heutiger Sicht.* H. Beck (ed.), pp. 231 -247. Berlin: Walter de Gruyter.
Swanton, M. (ed.)
   1970   *The Dream of the Rood.* Manchester: Manchester University Press.

Vernadsky, G.
    1951   Der sarmatische Hintergrund der germanischen Völkerwanderung. *Saeculum* 2: 340-92.
Wagner, N.
    1967   *Getica. Untersuchungen zum Leben des Jordanes und zur frühen Geschichte der Goten.*
                Berlin: Walter de Gruyter.
Wallace-Hadrill, J. M.
    1962   *The long-haired kings and other studies in Frankish history.* London: Methuen.
    1971   *Early Germanic kingship in England and on the continent.* Oxford: Clarendon Press.
Webster, L., & J. Backhouse (eds.)
    1991   *The making of England. Anglo-Saxon art and culture AD 600-900.* London: British
                Museum Press.
Wolfram, H.
    1975   Gotische Studien I, II. *Mitteilungen des Instituts für österreichische
                Geschichtsforschung* 83: 1-32, 289-324.
    1976   Gotische Studien III. *Mitteilungen des Instituts für österreichische Geschichtsforschung*
                84: 239-261.
    1987   *History of the Goths.* Berkeley: University of California Press.

Discussion

WOOD: On page [150] you say: "This last point was not lost on the Visigoths of southern France, who distinguished Gallic Catholics from themselves by calling them Romans". That sounded to me as if the Visigoths were the first people to come up with that, but the Gallo-Romans were calling themselves "Romans" already. I just wondered whether it was worth slightly rephrasing that.

GREEN: Thank you for that suggestion.

WOOD: There has been a lot of discussion about this strange passage on the Emperor Anastasius, and the most recent thing is an article by Michael McCormick. He deals with it in his book *Triumphal Rulership*, but he also has an article on it.

RICHARDS: Could I ask a naive and innocent question. Being totally ignorant of philology, I am wondering why I am so ignorant of it, because it seems to have a tremendous potential where you are dealing with contact between societies, and you demonstrate it with loanwords and trade words and the contexts in which societies were involved. But I have seen very little use of it by historians and certainly by archaeologists. I just wondered, in complete innocence, why that was.

GREEN: I think the answer to that must be supplied from beyond the frontiers of my discipline. What I should like to ask, though, from historians and archaeologists is whether they themselves react to this kind of linguistic evidence as being at all useful to them or not, even if in the negative sense, marking out what is not possible on the basis of linguistic evidence.

AXBOE: I, too, find it very interesting, and I would like to hear more of the names of the days of the week, and also about the wine trade. In Scandinavia we have found hundreds of Roman glasses and bronze buckets, ladles and strainers, and it would seem possible that the wine had followed as well; only it cannot have come in amphorae, for we have not found one single sherd of them.

GREEN: First, if your evidence belongs to the third century, it is too late for my purposes. The main body of the Goths is down in southeastern Europe by that time.

AXBOE: The import started already in the first century, and with some very beautiful things, too. But it is true that the culmination of the trade came in the third century.

SCHÜTTE: Wine is not transported in highly uneconomical amphorae, but in normal wooden barrels. It is quite likely that barrels vanished from the archaeological record, if they are not buried as well.

GREEN: When I use the word 'amphora' as the origin of modern German *Eimer* I am not arguing that the word, once loaned, still denoted the same kind of object as was in use by the Romans. It now denoted, as the modern German word meaning a 'bucket' already implies, any kind of large-scale container, not necessarily of the same type as that used by Romans, but adapted for sub-Roman or barbarian use. The word was taken over, but not necessarily in every case the same kind of object. So that the lack of amphorae in Jutland, or the use of barrels, need not argue against the containers in Jutland or the barrels in Germany being denoted by a word which once denoted an object of quite a different kind, but which served the same purpose as a wine container.

What I would stress here about loanword traffic is that this exchange rarely takes place in the sense of introducing something completely new, but there is generally some degree of overlap in usage, in material, in shape, or in function between the new word and an old word or an old object. It is this degree of overlap which provides the bridge for loan traffic.

AXBOE: How can you date the transfer of the names for the days of the week from the Romans to the *Germani*?

GREEN: The names for the days of the week are taken over into Germanic in two areas quite independently of each other, one in the West and one in the East. If one looks at the evidence for the various names which can be located in modern northwestern Germany and the Low Countries, it suggests this area for an early contact. The Latin words contain the names of pagan Roman gods and the fact that the Germanic names operate technically as an *interpretatio Germana*, finding rough Germanic equivalents for the Roman pagan gods, suggests that these names were taken over in the pagan period in this area. The dating which is put forward for this group is some time in the fourth century or before, but not later. And I find it inconceivable that one name for one day of the week would have been taken over independently of the others. If you are going to name the days of the week, you are going to take over the whole lot, so that if two or three of these names come over in this area, then it is likely that all come together in that area as part of the same loan process.

The other area where the names of the days of the week were taken over into Germanic is the lower Danube, now in contact with the Goths, not from Latin but Greek. This time the Greek Christian move towards driving out the names of pagan gods was much more firmly advanced than with the Western Church, with the result that still in modern Greek you refer to the names of the days of the week by saying 'the first', 'second', etc. But in Gothic, too, you have traces: unfortunately the Gothic names are not attested, but what we have is, as part of the 'Gothic mission', loans of these Gothic names of the days of the week into southeast Germany, above all into Bavaria. The feature of these, especially by contrast with the northwest group, is that they all avoid, by one means or another, a reference to pagan divinities. Whereas the northwest group had Wednesday, referring to Woden, the southeastern area had *mittawecha*, modern German *Mittwoch*, the 'middle of the week'. Where the northwestern group had 'Thursday', the southeastern group had *Pfinztag*, in Bavarian, which goes back via Gothic to Greek *pempte* (*hemera*). One has these two areas operating under different principles: one still making use of pagan names of the days of the week, whether or not the Church got to work in trying to excise them, and the other already operating under Christian censorship. This example of the days of the week is one of the many examples of contrast between Gothic and Old English.

DUMVILLE: May I draw your attention to an article by D. O. Cróinín on the Irish names of the days of the week? The article is in *Ériu* 32, 1981. There is a comparable change in Irish.

WOOD: Can I come back to the point that you are making about loanwords, that some Greek words get into Gothic via Latin. What strikes me about that is that it ties up very nicely with some of the new work that has been done on Wulfila. I am thinking particularly of Peter Heather's recent work. He has shown the amount of imperial backing to Wulfila, and particularly he has pushed the notion of the Goths being converted as one aspect to their entry into the Empire. The way in which that works very nicely from your point of view is that, however much the Church of Constantinople may be significant in the Balkans, all the emperors in question are Latin-speaking emperors, Constantius II and Valens. Obviously that fits very nicely: one is dealing with a Latin political world in the background to what Wulfila is doing. Basically Constantius and Valens would have had Latin-speaking clerics in their households.

HINES: It is an irresistible temptation for me to take up the question of why archaeologists do not use philological evidence, such as loanwords, more. One of the major problems is the dating of the loanwords. You made the case for dating the borrowing of the word for 'wine' particularly early. This, however, contrasts with a number of cases, where, for instance, the first record of a loanword may be an attestation in Anglo-Saxon no earlier than the eighth century. We may then see that the word has gone through some sound-changes that took place in the previous couple of centuries—it could, however, perhaps have been borrowed just before that, or five centuries earlier.

GREEN: That is true, but not always. Let me put in a word of defence for philological dating. Obviously, in many cases the field is wide open, running over centuries. But with many sound changes one can home in on a century or two centuries at the most. As indicated by the case of *vinum* where the change *w* to *v* is quite closely datable and the loss of the flexional endings extends at most over a couple of centuries.

DUMVILLE: That is precisely the point that would worry me. How precisely, in geographical terms rather than purely chronological terms, is this change of *w* to *v* attested? We had a case made 40 years ago that in the Vulgar Latin of Roman Britain that change did not take place. What about other places in the Empire? Is this such a straightforward matter? You have implied a general development but I assume that a particularised approach is always necessary in dealing with Vulgar Latin.

GREEN: I wholly agree on the need for a particularised approach, but it is precisely this which, in the areas where Latin and Germanic first made contact, leads us to assume that this change took place early in Vulgar Latin.

TURTON: How do you actually know that there has been a change in the pronunciation of a word?

GREEN: Because Latin grammarians concerned with faulty pronunciation or faulty grammar, by being datable themselves, help to date the various changes which they are castigating.

TURTON: Grammarians working at that time?

GREEN: In fact, in dating sound changes in Germanic, apart from arranging a relative chronology which is entirely based on internal Germanic evidence, one can convert that into an absolute chronology only if one has written testimony from outside, from Greek or Latin, which is datable testimony.

HINES: I wanted to make the point that there is a range of problems, and that in some cases there are much greater difficulties in pinning the transfer of a word down to a particular context than in others.

Where you introduce the issue of loanwords, you make a clear statement of the classic *Wörter und Sachen* case, that new words come in with new things—and in some cases, like 'wine' and 'cellar' this is nice and clear. With several of the loanwords appearing in Old English discussed by Alastair Campbell (1959) one is struck by the apparent fact that it is not necessarily an entirely new thing that is coming but rather some new, or finer, gradation in how similar things are distinguished that is being marked with loanwords: not some new item the borrowing language-users had never previously heard or conceived of. There are for instance new words for 'shirt' (*chemise*) and 'mantel'; for 'dish' and 'knife'; even a word for 'spider'.

GREEN: I should agree that in more cases than people have been prepared to recognise in the past what the new loanwords convey is not something completely new, but a new style, or a better production of a similar object already in use.

HINES: You note that the word for 'cook' must have been borrowed into Germanic on two separate occasions, producing a German *Koch* and an English *cook*. One has to consider the possibility that if the form with a long vowel [o:] appears only in Old English—and I do not know whether or not that is the case—it could have been borrowed in Britain.

GREEN: Yes, but that would still confirm my point about loans repeated at different times and in different places.

HINES: On the question of building: the idea "...that words suggest that house-building was originally in wood and this possibility is borne out elsewhere in *Germania*..." is unduly cautious. If you look at the archaeology, it tells you that early building in anything other than wood here is practically inconceivable.

AXBOE: You are right that this 'primitive' way of building with wood and wattle-and daub was used in *Germania*: in Denmark we have used it right up into the nineteenth century!

GREEN: Certainly one can talk about something being primitive without saying that it did not continue in use after the primitive period.

AXBOE: Yes, but perhaps you should re-phrase it, not to offend more Scandinavians!

HINES: The final point I wish to raise is that of the difficulty of identifying Goths in the archaeological record. I discovered on a recent visit to Poland that Polish archaeologists currently have strong views on where the Goths were or were not, implying that they also have strong views on their identifiability. A Professor Okulicz has also been discussing the possibility of identifying the Gepids in a particular area between the traditionally supposed Gothic lands in Pomerania and the Baltic area, in the hinterland of Elbląg. It seems to be possible to distinguish groups within the Germanic culture area there, and also to distinguish Germanic from Baltic cultures. What seems to be a wide open question is just which, if any, of these groups can properly be labelled 'the Goths'.

GREEN: When I said "other Germanic groups", I should have been more specific, namely the difficulty of distinguishing from finds Goths from the Vandals and the *Rugii* (see note 6, p. 90). I am particularly concerned with the predecessors of the Goths in this region, not with their successors.

HINES: I think it probably is just a matter of rewording.

TURTON: My question is really about who the Goths are. What period are we talking about?

GREEN: We are talking about a period towards the end of the second century and then down to about 240.

TURTON: Is there any linguistic evidence, not from loanwords but from linguistic change of other kinds? I'm thinking of a group splitting off from another and this leading to linguistic differences as, for example, between American English and British English.

GREEN: One has an absolutely fascinating example of that in Gothic, but one extremely difficult to interpret, as all these things are. Namely the fact that what I have been concerned with, the loanword traffic of Latin words into Gothic, is the first step along the path to the complete linguistic and cultural romanisation of the Goths and east Germanic tribes at large. I say complete romanisation, but that concerns only the Goths who from the Black Sea area subsequently moved southwards and westwards. One group remained behind in the Crimea, and a Flemish merchant of the sixteenth century in Istanbul came into contact with a merchant from the Crimea and they discovered that they had a number of words recognisably in common. He made a note of these words, and they establish beyond all reasonable doubt that at the time Gothic was still being spoken in the Crimea. That has led, of course, to a flood of literature arguing about changes within Gothic between Wulfila and the sixteenth century.

TURTON: Are there sound changes associated with the movement of people? Just to give a quick example: there are people living to the west of the Mursi whose language is mutually intelligible with Mursi but there are certain differences in pronunciation. The word for 'leg' in Mursi is *jare* and in this other language it is *jagare*. In Mursi, 'I cross [the river]' is *kogoi tanno*, and in the other language *kogoi tando*. So there is a dropping away of sounds in Mursi. I have always assumed that this is linguistic evidence that the Mursi split off from this other group.

GREEN: I gathered from your initial remark that you saw linguistic change as tied up with geographical movement. What one cannot say is what Wulfila's Gothic, had it remained spoken, would have become. But, as far as Crimean Gothic is concerned, one is dealing with a language group which has remained static, which has not moved. So that if, *impossibile dictu*, one could find out what Wulfila's Gothic was like, had it remained in spoken parlance, it is likely that the changes would have been either from movement of the Goths westwards, or because of the conservative retention of older forms in the static society of Crimean Goths.

TURTON: Would there be any evidence that a group that moves away from another group suffers some kind of linguistic change?

GREEN: Or (this is a feature which dialect geography has constantly come back to) a group which moves from a centre towards a periphery becomes, by that fact alone, more conservative. The argument has been made frequently that features distinguishing American English from British English are conservative features, not innovatory ones.

HINES: The point is that we do not have surviving records of the 'East Germanic' left behind on the north coast of Poland with which we could compare what we have got recorded of Gothic—which is post-migration—in order to say how much the language changed in that period of migration. There are allegedly one or two 'East Germanic' words in the early runic inscriptions in Denmark.

GREEN: The problem then becomes distinguishing East Germanic from North Germanic.

HINES: Absolutely. But this is as much as you could possibly have of so-called East Germanic left behind in that area.

GREEN: I talked yesterday about possible links between East Germanic and North Germanic. Some hotly contested work has been done by Ernst Schwarz on the correlations between East Germanic and North Germanic.

DUMVILLE: One last question. Four times at least in your written presentation, when speaking of ecclesiastical loan-traffic, you spoke of monasticism as being a source. I do not understand why monasticism as one particular form of ecclesiastical organisation has been singled out rather than any other form or, better, ecclesiastical culture as a whole?

GREEN: Your question may have been prompted by the respective roles of monasticism and other types of ecclesiastical culture in your own specialist field. In Germany (to which your four references apply, as far as I remember) the position is clearcut, or at least is accepted as being clearcut: our earliest written texts (in which loanwords are attested) come overwhelmingly from monastic scriptoria. By contrast, other centres such as episcopal courts play a very minor part, at least in the Old High German period.

AUSENDA: What do you mean by ethnogenesis? Is it the literal interpretation and explanation of texts, or the interpretation of texts as mythological?

GREEN: I refer you again to this enormous tome by Wenskus.

References in the discussion

Campbell, A.
   1959   *Old English Grammar*. Oxford: Clarendon Press.
Cróinín, D. O.
   1981   The oldest Irish narnes of the days of the week? *Ériu* 32:95-114.
McCormick, M.
   1986   *Eternal Victory: Triumphal Rulership in Late Antiquity. Byzantium and the Early Medieval West*. Cambridge: Cambridge University Press.

CONTINUITY PROBLEMS AND AUTHORITY STRUCTURES IN COLOGNE

SVEN SCHÜTTE

Stadt Köln Archäologische Bodendenkmalpflege, Roncalliplatz 4, 50667 Köln

The Character of Roman Cologne

The distinction between an antique, Roman, and a medieval Germanic Cologne is an unrealistic one. At the end of the first century BC the Romans founded *Oppidum Ubiorum* to accommodate Ubians who had been moved from the eastern bank of the Rhine for protection. During the first century AD its strategic position was such that it was upgraded to a Roman *colonia* with the aspicious name of *Colonia Agrippina*.

From the first century onwards the city had a Germanic substratum and the veterans quartered there afterwards came to an already blossoming and very vital, expanding city. The members of the town council regarded themselves as non-Romans. When, on one occasion, a Germanic mission came across the Rhine, went to the town council and said, "Why don't you kill the Romans? You are our Germanic brothers", the people in charge answered, "We cannot do this because we cannot kill our families; we have been mixed with the Romans for generations; although we regard ourselves as Germanic people, we are not able to do this", and they sent them back to the right bank of the Rhine: I mean the eastern part.

This shows one complication in the develoment of the city. We find this as well in the material culture. The terminology is complicated. The so-called Ubian wares are syncretic products. They are wheel-thrown ceramics, which means they are made by a Roman technique but in Germanic shapes. Who is responsible for this we do not know and this shows the whole dilemma which extends even to the transition period later on.

The inhabitants of the city were a multi-cultural group and as early as the fourth century the first Frankish groups infiltrated the city; they were not only enemies, but always trading partners too. Much of what I say is highly hypothetical because the methods applied to detecting the relevant features have varied a lot in recent years. So I have to be rather diplomatic because there have been radical changes in the image of the city and in the attitudes in history and archaeology: it was dominated, some years ago, by classical archaeologists who had a different attitude towards the city and its surroundings from that which I or my colleagues now have.

Two images of the periods of transition are confronted: one is that the good period, the antique city, ended and everything fell into ruins; eventually, in later centuries the splendid medieval city rose from the ashes. But what we think, after the work which has been done in the last two years, is that this is much too simple. The same is true of the historical approach: looking anew at the written sources, we have found that they have been exploited like a quarry: you take the things which are useful and leave all the rest aside; this is nol supportable any longer, and what was published in the early '80s, for example by Heiko Steuer, has to be changed very much.

During the whole period the administration in the city was well connected with persons of Germanic origin; these may not have been the absolutely leading people, but there may have been merchants who were members of the town-council who quite probably also came from families of Germanic origin. The anecdote I quoted relates to the century when these struggles started between the Franks and the Romans leading to two severe conflicts. In the fourth century the Franks had several military successes around the city and so it happened that the *uilla rustica* and all the hinterland went down: all the great monuments were taken from the cemeteries and used in the fortifications thus emptying the area around the city, but, despite these military events, it was quite a peaceful period as far as we see it now from recent archaeological finds.

The last officials left in the mid-fifth century. However, almost a hundred years before, this process of transition had started; so our impression is that there was no fracture, but a gentle movement. If a Roman noble woman had to work for a Frankish household, it does not mean that this was an agrarian household and she was living in the countryside, it only means that she belonged to the former nobility and she had to take up some work only for financial reasons. In contrast with the views of Heiko Steuer, I think that the infiltrating Franks did not pull Roman palaces down to convert the sites to agrarian use, but still used the buildings.

What Helen Kaemper and others called a 'continuity of ruins' is not proved by archaeology. We find a lot of sites where the buildings have obviously been used for several centuries: the layers containing what I call 'dark-age material' outside, where the rubbish was Iying, but the houses were kept relatively clean inside. We do not find that the abandoned sites have wooden buildings inside. That process starts, but very, very late. We have sites like that, but they can be dated to the ninth or the tenth century when substantial parts inside large Roman building complexes were demolished and then rebuilt, always with wooden structures, always simple buildings completely remodelled or demolished. An example is the *forum* where underneath the collapsed Roman vaults big layers are found, but these layers do not contain Frankish material, they contain late Pingsdorf pottery. So these buildings were still standing at least into the tenth century and they were not demolished earlier than that. From the historians' point of view, many names which are not medieval, like *forum Julii*, survived: not only the names but the buildings themselves continued and the remodeling of the city did not start earlier than the powerful bishops (even before Bruno and Anno) in the tenth century. As far as we can see, there was no Frankish remodeling of the city. For example, we have found that very close to Sankt Maria Lyskirchen Roman floors are painted, but the painting was applied in the early Middle Ages: the red-painted floors were in use till the eighth or ninth century. This is quite different from what we read in the scholarly literature.

The city itself was intended to be the centre-point of the planned *Germania inferior* up to the River Elbe, but it was left as a border-city on the River Rhine. This border has, in effect, remained intact until now. I do not want to refer to Adenauer, who drew the curtains of his compartment in the train when he crossed the Elbe, because for him the Russian plains started there, but even in modern times the eastern bank of the Rhine belonging to the modern city of Cologne was known as 'Schalsick', meaning the negative side.[1] Even today for the inhabitants of Cologne there is a very real borderline and they regard themselves as

---

[1] 'Schälsick' derives from 'schielende Seite', lit. 'squinting side' or 'less meaningful side' where 'true' citizens of Cologne did not live (Editor's note).

part of Western Europe. For them, the border cities between Western Europe and Central Europe are Aachen and Cologne. And if, for instance, they say: "We have one of the largest archives of Western Europe", this is, I think, one of the traditions which shows that they regard themselves even now as being on the border. In its advertising for the modern business centre the city of Cologne today says: "We are the centre of the West", they do not say, "We are the centre of the Centre". It remains to some degree a border-city in the minds of its people.

This might explain why the Roman bridge, built in the time of Constantine, was demolished under the powerful bishops. Had it remained intact it could have been very useful for trade; even in a bird's-eye view of the sixteenth-century the remains of the bridge are still visible, but it was not used. They used boats for communication, and the north-south river trade had the most important role, not the east-west one. I shall come to the triangle Trier, Mainz and Cologne later on. The orientation of the city remained towards the west and north-west, not to the east, and remained so for a very, very long time. The only connection with the eastern part is the *castellum Deutz* which existed for a very long time, until the late Middle Ages when it was demolished. Today some remains survive. It had a military function as a bridgehead to the east, but not an economic function as a connection for trade, alas; but, of course, trade did go on, even with the east.

In the reigns of the Frankish 'Kleinkönige', the petty kings, Roman law was gradually replaced. This is shown by Marianne Gechter, our urban historian, who studied the property structures in the city, and she could trace back large areas which formerly belonged, for example, to a *temenos* complex, which was a completely closed area in the Roman city, then belonging to one family. This means that somebody must have granted this space in the city to someone in a process of transition of this property. There was no anarchy; but there was, I think, quite an orderly process for each block. This is a very strong argument for considerable continuity. Also the fact that no layers of Frankish ceramics have been found inside, for example, the church of Gross St. Martin, does not mean that this complex of the former *horrea* was not in use, because fifty metres to one side we have very thick market layers of the fifth, sixth and even the seventh century, which show that there was a lot of activity. This can only mean that this was in use, because they do not deposit any rubbish layers in an intact church. The problem of having two churches of Sankt Martin's could, therefore, mean that this is the church in the middle the Frankish market, and that the king was sitting about sixty metres away from there, behind the old Roman city-wall.

Economic Activities

What we found in this market-place indicates that there were very intensive activities where the intrusion of heavy metals (copper, lead, and so on) show that metal was produced in very substantial quantities, because this can only be washed in by rain and air. This site is so polluted that, were it functioning today, it would be declared dangerous and ordered to be removed. We also have glass and ceramic production very early. We only have a keyhole view of the market place, but this indicates that there was no interruption and no crisis of production, which also means no crisis in the short distance trade around the city, because somebody must have bought all the things produced there.

Concerning long-distance trade, the story is much more complicated because the Lower Rhine area suffered much more than the area from Cologne up to Mainz. Unfortunately we cannot trace any good parallels between Cologne and Mainz, because urban archaeology in Mainz concentrates on Roman history just as it has in the past in Cologne. The situation is very problematic and only some grave-find could indicate, of course, that a lot of activity was going on in these places; how it went on, where it was, or how the city was affected in these times by Trier and Mainz is, therefore, very difficult to say, but we know that they suffered destruction. All that is said about Cologne is that it was full of enemies. And if we look to see who wrote this, we find that this means only a very small group of persons who were regarded as enemies, while the populace itself did not move; they were there for centuries. Where should they go? They could not go back to Rome, because they did not come from there. Their families had been living in Cologne for centuries; so we think that the majority of the population remained in Cologne, and even groups of merchants and the lesser nobility, but not the upper nobility (which was replaced). These groups were still ruling or trading and, as we heard from Ross Balzaretti, there was a relationship between the kings and the merchants which we do not wholly understand; but we can guess that this was a very complicated one. If you want to finance warfare or even, for example, if you want to buy a silk dress or something very valuable, you need the merchants because these goods are only available through the hands of the merchants. They probably had quite a strong role, but we know no details.

Frankish coinage appears quite soon after Roman coinage. Afterwards, after the rule of the Frankish 'Kleinkönige' was removed from Cologne to western centres, the bishops or, later, the archbishops stood in the same role, ruling the city but never stamping their authority directly on the market. We can see this because there were so many struggles between the merchants and the bishop. We have a gap of one hundred and fifty years in the bishops' list. But the first one to appear after this gap has a Romance name, not a Germanic one. Probably we have a loss of written sources which may have been caused by raids in 881 when the Cathedral library survived, but a lot of other archival material was lost. But that can only be a guess.

I refer to the question of coinage in Cologne. For a short period in Merovingian times gold coinage was issued; this demonstrates that they regarded themselves as more important than in fact they were. The coinage used first shows the emperor or the king, and in later centuries it is the *Colonia sancta* type. This means that the bishop won complete control when the kings moved away from Cologne.

Another strong argument for continuity, in addition to the evidence of the continuous production or issue of coins, is that the Roman city-walls were not used as a quarry, but were maintained. This can only mean that the walls had to protect a considerable group of people. Too small a group of individuals would not have been able to maintain the Roman walls encircling an area of one square kilometre; and they are still there, as are some of the towers. They have not been quarried, which indicates that the theory of a moat-and-bank fortification around the Cathedral as the seat of the bishop is wrong: there is no archaeological evidence for this *Domburg*. We have just completed work and there is really no trace of any fortification there. We are convinced that the city-wall itself encircled the whole city: it was not a case of just a small settlement being left while all the rest was abandoned.

If there were existing and working churches like St. Gereon or St. Aposteln and other churches in the city, and we have the king's palace with a remarkable infrastructure from the treasure-room (as mentioned in the written sources), we have the market and we have the city fortification, it would be quite astonishing if between these elements there should be nothing, or just fields where the Franks grew their cabbage. But this raises other questions.

One question is how a city like this could be supplied with food in sufficient quantities, while the hinterland or the countryside was not in a good condition. This must have been done by means of some local, some medium-distance, and even some long-distance trade.

We are working now on the problem of when the early stockfish first appears, and this is quite early. We have lots of Scandinavian connections, and the early phases of Ribe are so similar that you could mix a box of finds from the Haymarket and a box of finds from the Ribe excavations and you could not tell the difference. Thus there are very early and very intensive Scandinavian connections but we do not know how these were organised and how they were affected by the local conflicts of the Lower Rhine. It must have been a very dangerous journey between Köln and Scandinavia.

In later times too we see that, in addition to a group of the typical Rhenish cattle having a shoulder-height of 1.10 to 1.20 metres, a group of large oxen existed 1.40 to 1.60 metres in height. The question is whether these were Danish oxen from the west coast of Jutland, which I mention later on, or where otherwise did they come from. We can state only that there is a large group which does not come from local livestock. This is not to be mixed up with some very distinctive Roman cattle which were also quite different from the smaller Germanic cattle. These are later. We find these types of Roman cattle down to the beginning and mid-fourth century. It is not there in the fifth century, as far as we know now, but our knowledge is still too limited. However, these other groups appear in the sixth and seventh centuries. Where they came from remains an open question.

I talked about the market and probable market-church which had been converted in the tenth century. Stiftskirche and Gross St. Martin then had a parish church to one side. I have tried to sketch the role of trade. It is complicated and completely different from the structure of the *emporium* of the Lower Rhine, Dorestad. It looks more as if, in late Roman times, the city's role as a market was much more important than its military one. In earlier times the fleet lay in Alteburg, a few kilometres south of Cologne, and even the position on the border, on the bank of the river, is not as good as that of other cities, for example Xanten which had a better position as a fortification on the river. Thus we think that the economy was dominant, not the military role of the city.

The Institutions

I have already mentioned that we have someone ruling continuously in Cologne, whether it is a king or later the bishop and then the archbishop; furthermore the Church is the most obviously continuous institution in the city. The cemeteries have not yet been analysed. I mentioned the publication of the large cemeteries not only of St. Gereon but also St. Severin, which have recently appeared and were edited by Bernd Paffgen, but the situation is so complicated, as I pointed out, that we cannot get a clear image from the enormous amount of material coming from these cemeteries. Also we have the same hinterland-problem because it is now a very large city and many parts are not accessible for archaeology. Furthermore, there is a lack of what we call in northern West Germany the *archäologische Landesaufnahme*, a complete record of all sites. Although we know the area, we do not know what find-spots are there. This work has to be done in the next ten years. We have a list of some *uillae rusticae* but how many there were we don't know. Some places may be identified only as a group of tiles and not as a *uilla rustica*. The hinterland-problem is there even for the earlier phases: we do not know what happened there economically. If you see in the early phases that a Germanic group, coming from soils which are very infertile, moved to a very fertile place but lived in a city, the question arises what they did in their surroundings. We do not know yet.

Potential for Future Research

The sources are limited because one third of the complete city has been archaeologically destroyed, another third is very severely affected by building, and only one third remains more or less untouched. As a result we cannot solve all the problems. The most important part of the waterfront was machined away in the 1980s without any observation; therefore, we cannot solve the problem of the nature of the harbour or the ships' landing place. Only a small residue of the waterfront is left for archaeological research and this will not be accessible for the next few years. So we have to leave a lot of questions open which we would like to solve.

In considering the relationships between the Rhineland cities, we see that the Roman *ciuitas* boundaries are reflected in the later borders of the dioceses, demonstrating strong continuity. This is in tune with the fact that in the recent excavations we saw no heavy destruction layers in the dark-age period; we see them very well, however, in the late ninth century.

I have again stressed the find material. Because in the past excavations have not been carried out in natural layers, the finds have mostly been unstratified. Large groups of pottery have been identified as Roman which are quite obviously not Roman because they appear naturally in later contexts. What this indicates is that the ceramics factories were still at work and produced pottery which still looked very much like the old forms made under the Empire, but is not Roman. Who controlled these factories? This pottery stands in sharp contrast with the grave-material. The grave-material contains only different forms of Knickwandtopf and hand-made ceramics, which would then be regarded as more Germanic while the wheel-thrown material is not considered so; but we have both groups. The household material is more traditionally Roman, while the grave material is more traditionally Germanic. Of course, hand-made types also appear in between these masses of wheel-thrown material and we have as well Knickwandtopf types made on the quickly rotating potting disk. Thus we have a lot of traditional forms, and also have forms of glazed pottery which seem not to have been exported from Cologne. We have a site very close to the production place of this ware where we found late Merovingian pottery with a glazed run over the fractures; this was produced in Cologne but we do not know for what purpose and we have found none in the graves.

Luxury production is paralleled in glass, for example. The metal finds seem to indicate probably copper and decorated things, and weapons too as later sources indicate that the Haymarket was one of the major trading places for weapons and other things—but much, much later.

So there were structural changes in Carolingian times and later which were more severe than at the beginning of the Middle Ages. Some structures can be traced back continuously. In the Haymarket we see how the market-place developed. All the organic material has been preserved, and in the coming years, if our project is put into effect, we will be able to excavate 8,000 sq.m. with 50,000 cubic metres of archaeology, which is a sheer horror, but I think we must do this. This site is several times larger than Dorestad and half of Hedeby, Haithabu, in size.

I want to conclude by returning to the position of the city. The Roman border-city was in fact not a border-city. Later on, when it arises as a very prominent and rich medieval city, the richest, and most populous city, perhaps, in all of northern, central and eastern Europe, its wealth—found in the tenth, eleventh and twelfth centuries—must have come from somewhere. Roots can in fact be traced back to earlier times. We have recently discovered stone built merchants' houses, secular stone structures from the late ninth century, when all the rest of Europe was building in wood; here, still, Roman houses of the most massive structure were in use, and only afterwards demolished.

We are not able to solve all of the problems only with archaeology; multi-disciplinary approaches will be able to answer some of these questions and it will take the work of more than a lifetime to solve even half of all this. What I have been able to give here are preliminary sketches of what we think could be the new image of a city with a continuous development as a city and not as a partially deserted settlement-place. I am conscious that lots of questions are open and new questions arise because of this, and I think we now have more questions open than we can solve on the basis of the few excavations of the last two years. We are convinced that in the long run only multi-disciplinary work will be able to solve these questions.

References

Borger, H.
  1979   Die *Abbilder des Himmels in Köln, Kölner Kirchenbauten als Quelle zur Siedlungsgeschichte des Mittelalters,* Band 1. Köln: Greven-Verlag.
Doppelfeld, O.
  1958   *Römische und fränkische Zeit. Ausgewählte Quellen zur Kölner Stadtgeschichte,* I. Köln: J. P. Bachem-Verlag.
  1960   Das fränkische Frauengrab unter dem Chor des Kölner Domes. *Germania* 38: 89- 113.
  1964   Das fränkische Knabengrab unter dem Chor des Kölner Domes. *Germania* 42: 156- 188.
  1970   *Das Fortleben der Stadt Köln vom 5. - 8. Jahrhundert.* (Early Medieval Studies 1, Antikvariskt Arkiv 38). Stockholm: Kungl. Vitterhets Historie och Antikvitets Akademien.
  1975a   Kölner Wirtschaft von den Anfängen bis zur Karolingerzeit. In *Zwei Jahrtausende Kölner Wirtschaft,* Band 1. Köln: Rheinisch-Westfalisches Wirtschaftsarchiv.
  1975b   Köln von der Spätantike bis zur Karolingerzeit. In *Vor-und Frühformen der europäischen Stadt im Mittelalter.* Göttingen: Vandenhoeck & Ruprecht.
Päffgen, B.
  1992   *Die Ausgraben in St. Severin zu Köln,* 3 Bde. Mainz am Rhein: Verlag Philipp von Zabern.
Steuer, H.
  1980   Die Franken in Köln. In *Aus der Kölner Stadtgeschichte.* Köln: Greven-Verlag.
Süssenbach, U.
  1981   Die Stadtmauer des römischen Köln. In *Aus der Kölner Stadtgeschichte.* Köln: Greven-Verlag.

Discussion

AXBOE: It is interesting that in Cologne you can demonstrate a continuity of town life from Roman times through the Migration period, which it has not been possible to establish in England.

SCHÜTTE: This relates to what has been called the continuity of ruins. They say all these people saw these ruins, and some of this could be used, and so they went there again and started up again. But we can't prove this by archaeology. There would have to be, for example, layers which show that there has been a ruin which was cleaned up again and re-used as a house, but we don't have this. We have now excavated more than 45 sites inside the city in the last two years and in none of these do we see this continuity of ruins, we see buildings either intact or, later on, demolished and given up. We don't see them abandoned and then dismantled for re-use in walls. This we can't demonstrate.

AXBOE: What is the date of the stockfish you mentioned?

SCHÜTTE: I don't have the dendro-dates yet, I have to say, but I think it should be the end or the second half of the sixth century, as far as we can tell from the potters. The stockfish is always the winter food and we have it in enormous amounts in the later layers, but the earliest examples seem to appear at this date. The layer contains datable wood but I do not yet have the dates. It is roughly that time.

GREEN: Could I make three points? You started by talking or mentioning the Ubians. Now these are a bone of contention in language studies and I would like to ask you where archaeologists, if we can generalise about them, stand as regards placing the Ubians between *Germani*, Celts, whether romanised or not, or, a third possibility—I do not know whether it has percolated through archaeological studies—in Hans Kuhn's Nordwest Block?

SCHÜTTE: It is very complicated: what material should we indentify as Ubian? Of course we have a lot of material from the first half of the first century, but as for the ethnicity of who they belonged to or where they came from, it does not give a lot of information. We have to leave such questions open at the moment. Maybe we will have some site complexes which will allow us to identify them as Ubian eventually, but the question is: "What is Ubian?".

GREEN: You are in no better position than philologists.

SCHÜTTE: The term 'Ubian wares' means a type of pottery which most would attribute as Roman ceramic, because it is wheel-thrown and even the forms are non-Gerrnanic. It is just not of classical Roman form, but it is very closely related to Roman ceramics. So what does this mean: are these people working for the Romans? Are these Germanic potters imitating Roman forms? Who produced this ceramic and for whom? We really have to confess we don't know, but the term exists and we know which group we name with this. But I wouldn't use this evidence because the pottery does not say anything about ethnicity.

GREEN: Could I put briefly my two other points? You mentioned, and that is fascinating, the parallels between the Cologne and the Ribe excavations, saying that it was almost impossible to distinguish one from the other. What date are these finds?

SCHÜTTE: Some of the earliest phases are eighth-century finds, but I am referring especially to slightly later finds of the following two centuries. The latest comparable points are the twelfth century for the stonewares imported from the Rhineland to Ribe, and some earlier ceramics are very very comparable. For example there are glass mosaic stones which were used in Ribe as raw material for bead-production in early Carolingian times. These glass mosaic stones have no traces of mortar on them, so the question is: "Where did they come from?". They appear in the same amount, in the same qualities, in the same contexts, in Cologne's Haymarket as in the excavations in Ribe. So you could put a box of them from Ribe here and one from Cologne there, and you couldn't tell which is which. These are the same colours, so it must be the same, or it is very, very closely, related material. The pottery is just the same.

GREEN: My last point is not a question, but just a supplementary point. You mentioned the difference between the west bank and the east bank, and the right side and the wrong side. There is a striking parallel to that, of course, in Basel, between Gross-Basel, on the left of the Rhine, and Klein-Basel beyond. That attitude is still continued today as it is in Cologne.

SCHÜTTE: And I think in Mainz as well. The Mainz-Kastell, which is highly comparable to Deutz, has the same structure. I think even today it is still a sort of border line, and the city remains as a border city. So, Cologne politicians, if they have money to give out, always prefer the left side of the Rhine, which means the western part. You can see it even in archaeology: if you look at the archives of our unit, you will see that although the eastern part is as big as the western part, the majority of reports comes from the western part. The east is too far away, and if I ask my colleagues who wants to have an excavation on the other side of the Rhine, nobody really wants to have one.

RICHARDS: Where is your Haymarket site in relation to the river?

SCHÜTTE: It is located very close to the river, but it is separated from the river by a quarter of small streets which, according to the theory, were originally part of this market but then formed the better-built part. For example, the wine trade required cellars, as early as possible, and we have found that and are doing a cadastre of cellars. We are mapping them all. We have found cellars going back to the tenth century, by the side of the river. This had the advantage that wine did not have to be transported over a distance; it could be stored in a cool cellar by the open space which was then west of it: that means behind a row of houses which divides the river from the actual market. This is a long square which spreads south of the ramp of Constantine's bridge. We have a reference to a *mercatus faeni* that is very late, twelfth-century. The open market was in the south but was full of small buildings.

From Roman times onwards it was a bazaar-like area full of small roads, small huts, small buildings of light construction. Beside this group were buildings of more massive construction, for example containing the cellars for the wine trade. We do not know what the earliest cellars would be like. We do not know where the Roman wine trade stored its wine. Maybe in the *horrea*, if they are *horrea*, but even this is doubtful now. Underneath these *horrea* is a large first-century Roman area encircled by walls and with a large basin. This has been thought to be a *natatio*, possibly for sport, but we doubt this because in this basin there are small compartments with wooden partitions. So, it could be that this was a fish tank, which would then imply market purposes for this whole structure too. And these *horrea* might not have served as *horrea* because this was an untypical form of building, which later housed the church; it could perhaps be a market basilica where the more valuable or more complicated goods were sold while the open space served the ordinary goods.

The cathedral in Ribe was later built of Rhenish tufa stones from the Eifel. So the complete church was exported from the Rhineland to Ribe. Even the architectural patterns were exported, later. The sculpture in Ribe cathedral is quite comparable to St. Aposteln in Cologne. The source need not be Cologne exclusively but it is certainly the Rhineland.

RICHARDS: Is the Haymarket outside the Roman walled town?

SCHÜTTE: This is a problem too, because before the Roman walls we have what they called the harbour island. This is a small island in the river, but the channel between this island and the river bank was filled up in the second century so that it was accessible as early as the second century. So there was a large space in front of the Roman city towards the river and the question is: "When was it fortified?". The earliest records go back to the tenth century. Around 945, the first stone wall is mentioned. But we think that if there was a church, a large market and the royal palace just behind the wall, this cannot have been without any protection. There was probably a palisade or a moat/bank fortification. We do not know, but we think that this area, the so-called Rhein Vorstadt, was fortified much earlier; however, we do not have any archaeological evidence for this at the moment.

RICHARDS: Does it *have* to be fortified? Is there evidence?

SCHÜTTE: It would be easily accessible to enemies on land. The waterfront need not have been fortified, but these two small sections from the Roman wall to the bank should have been protected somehow.

RICHARDS: My other question concerning your Roman buildings that were in use is in two parts.

Where were they, inside the walled town or outside? What was happening within them? I was not clear whether there were other buildings going up inside them or whether it was, actually, the Roman buildings themselves that were being used? And if so what was their use?

SCHÜTTE: We find them not only inside the Roman walls but outside as well in the *suburbia*, which were quite large. The fortifications of 1106 encircle exactly the shape of the Roman *suburbia*, i.e. the three additions, that means Oversburg, Niederich and St. Aposteln, encircled Roman *suburbia*. And even in there we find buildings. First we find new buildings inside Roman building complexes; we find Roman building complexes used, cared for and maintained for a long time; and we find places where the Roman buildings were replaced by early buildings of uncertain date at the moment because we do not have an exact chronology: that has to be built up by a stratigraphic analysis. So, we have all kinds of re use, continued use, and replacement.

RICHARDS: What is the nature of the occupation? Are there industrial activities there?

SCHÜTTE: No. Some use is official. We did not find anything which shows, for example, craftsmanship or manufacture being installed inside a Roman building or *atrium* houses used as workshops. They are still used for purposes of living or representation. We do not have so many, and sometimes we have only small segments of them, so we are not certain about their function. But these are found even at quite a distance from the inner city. They thought at first maybe only the western part was abandoned, but this is not true: we have building complexes in use even there. We do not know how many people lived in this settlement or city and we do not know what purposes these old buildings served. They must have undergone a change of function, but how things then looked we do not know. Why do they paint a Roman floor, a very simple Roman floor, covered with powdered brick material? This was then decorated with a red paint like we find in excavations in the Pfalz in the native period. The floor decoration is very similar to later medieval floor decoration, but it is applied to Roman floors. The hypocaust underneath this was out of use but it was re-decorated. So, we are not certain about the real function they served.

BALZARETTI: There are a couple of points. The first one covers what you said last, that you had a lot of houses in the late ninth century which I think you said were made of stone. You could certainly compare that with the Roman material, when there was a lot right at the same period, a lot of stone in fairly substantial amounts.

SCHÜTTE: This building I referred to is divided into four rooms and probably had two stories.

BALZARETTI: Are these buildings made of newly cut stone, or was it re-used?

SCHÜTTE: No, this was freshly imported tufa stone. They did not use any material from the ruins for this. They used the ruin material for building cellars and foundations, but the visible parts are very often built of new tufa stones.

BALZARETTI: The other point I want to discuss is the seventh century. You mentioned it occasionally; have you got much material?

SCHÜTTE: Reasonable quantities, but not much.

BALZARETTI: That is very unusual for town excavations.

SCHÜTTE: Yes, so it seems. In the excavations mentioned this material appears in a little less than say 50 percent. We are very astonished because we can compare our finds with the studies done on the Mayen kilns. The early Mayen material (near Koblenz), is very hard fired pottery. It appears at this date, and in large quantities there. And Mark Redknap who made studies of these kilns suggested quite an early dating for certain types, and this is absolutely in line with the Cologne development we have now found. It is interesting that it is not represented everywhere and that it is not as strong as the earlier or the later material, but I have to say that the amount of hand-made pottery is always quite low, and those parts that we know were the rich quarters; later on, for example, they have no early hand-made cooking pots and only small quantities of early Kugeltopf ware. This could indicate that they made an extensive use of metal vessels. As for the rest of the pottery, they preferred, if possible, hard-fired, oxidised, or decorated, or painted, or glazed ceramic, when available; they objected to low-fired, hand-made, dark grey ceramic. Some of the villages outside are full of these hand-made grey ceramics; they do not have a lot of oxidised, white, buff, pink, or whatever ceramics. It seems that the urban group preferred different types. Later on these types give way and were transformed to the decorated Hunneschans and Pingsdorf wares or whatever other decorated or painted oxidised wares were available. This fashion goes on for the next three centuries.

WOOD: One observation and question: I think this is incredibly exciting because one of the things that comes out of the literary material of the sixth century is how Roman Austrasia is. If you work through the poems of Venantius Fortunatus, it is the Austrasian court which is the really Roman court. It is the court of Sigibert I and Brunhilde. And it looks as if for the first time you are getting from archaeology something which echoes that Roman continuity. And, even more significant than the Venantius Fortunatus material, which you can just shrug off as an Italian poet being ingratiating, is the legislation of Childebert II, which is by far the most Roman legislation of a barbarian king during the sixth century; it is incredibly sophisticated, and was issued at Andernach, Maastricht and Cologne. So you have a very nice background to that.

The other point I would make alongside that, though I would be just a little worried by what you mean by the rise of episcopal power, is that you referred on a number of occasions to bishops taking over from kings. Clearly this takes place before about 700 with the episcopal republics; I would say it might be as late as the 680s. What strikes me is that royal power emerging in Gaul does not collapse until the 670s or 680s. It really is considerably strong until that moment. I would not use coinage as evidence of decline in royal power. I think the coming of episcopal coinage marks declining taxation and perhaps a rise in its significance for alms giving. It does not actually tell you whether kings were more or less important. And I think the only really good survey of episcopal power in any one Merovingian city is Jean Durliat's survey of Cahors (1975), which I think is by far the most significant piece on any Merovingian city.

SCHÜTTE: Of course you are right, it is a very complicated situation. For examples in the ninth century a *provisor mercatorum* is mentioned in Cologne. Only in Paris is another *provisor* mentioned for the market. This obviously cannot be a structure enforced by the bishop, but it is probably a remnant of royal power. He was probably the royal market official. This shows that there was a complicated relationship and that royal power may be more dominant there for a longer time than we might have thought. Attention gets caught by the written sources which are much more frequent in the episcopal and in the Church environment than in the royal context.

The background of the kings now becomes clearer if we excavate. We have a lot of these written records about what they did and how they did it. If you look at the foundation of the monastery of Plektrudis we see that when she builds the first buildings in St. Maria in Kapitol, she did not build inside a ruin. As far as we can see from archaeology it was another intact building. You know the source telling of missionaries who come to Cologne and say: "We saw a temple full of ex-votos". These were Roman ex-votos and early Christian ex-votos; and they burnt it down. Was this placed in an old temple, or was that a separate building for pagan religion? We have no indication of where this took place. But it shows that this was a community with points of religious service in the sense that it served a city of major settlement. We have to think of the earlier tradition of the *Ara Ubiorum*, the main sanctuary of Lower Germany, which vanished completely. It is still not located, but even in Christian times there should be traditions from this leading to surviving pagan forms.

DUMVILLE: Could you say something about the late-Roman epigraphic evidence from Cologne?

SCHÜTTE: There is a vigorous discussion now, because there has been quite recent work about inscriptions which more or less denies that there are any fifth-century inscriptions from Cologne. This conclusion is rejected by the majority of scholars. But the similarity of those inscriptions with earlier ones is the same problem as with the ceramics. They are not dated or given names; so you cannot identify a person as belonging to this or that group. We do not have names on grave-stones, and we do not have grave-inscriptions. It is very difficult to date the stones and to find a context for them. It could be the same problem on another level. Of course, there are lots of inscriptions, and the problem is dating them or placing them in context. Some were excavated very early and therefore lack contexts. And recent excavations did not reveal much either. This is a problem to be solved. There are later inscriptions there, but it is complicated. Even the architectural remains have not been reviewed. There are hundred architectural fragments of later date with Flechtband ornaments: these are 'braided' ornaments which do not belong to graves, but come out of profane or religious contexts. This is an enormous body of material which has been broadly ignored, because it could not exist. But there are dozens of very high quality pieces which will be reviewed by Dorothea Hochkirchen in the next two years. I think that this will also bring some more information about the rank of architecture in churches and in profane buildings.

DUMVILLE: What kind of thing is being recorded in inscriptions?

SCHÜTTE: These are mostly grave inscriptions. Most of what has been collected has been edited: but there are lots of fragments not yet reviewed. This is where most problems are because the state of preservation is not very good; since Cologne has no natural resources of stone, every stone was valuable and we have re-uses up to five times. In particular grave stones and inscriptions are very good material for re-use. It means that they are not in their original contexts and sometimes heavily damaged, because the re-users cut off parts. We can tell now that limestone inscriptions were preferred for later re-use, but originally came from Roman material. In later times limestone was not imported to Cologne, but the inhabitants used sandstone and other materials, basalt for example. We see that the waste-water canals of the eleventh and twelfth centuries are mostly built out of Roman street-basalts; so always one side is polished. That means that a large part of the Roman streets must have been accessible. The medieval inhabitants did not do any excavation for this. These canals required large amounts of basalt, tons of this material. You can walk on the Appia antica street-pavement, the old street-pavement: it looks much like these basalts. These are an indicator of the date by which the inhabitants had given up part of the street. We excavated one large site which was the medieval street; its other side was a Roman street, and we found all the negative of street basalts taken out. Then it was filled up and used as garden-land. And the medieval street was positioned 20 metres to the side of this. In the same dated layers we found the basalts back in those waste-water canals. So, they took out these basalts in the second half of the eleventh and first half of the twelfth century. Volcanic materials are used: tufa stone, basalt, and trachyte.

AUSENDA: Is there any trace in the fourth and fifth centuries of trade with Byzantium?

SCHÜTTE: Perhaps, but probably not of direct trade. I mentioned the silks found in the shrines, which could have come from Italy. At an earlier period they might have come from there. We do not have any sources to state direct contact with Byzantium up the Danube. It is possible, but at the moment we cannot tell. Later contacts with the Mediterranean are quite frequent, we have lots of oil-amphorae from the Iberian peninsula, much later imports, and we have Italian early majolica. In other words, western Mediterranean material is much more represented than eastern, as far as we can identify sources. Probably in other church-treasuries Byzantine imports might exist, but they might have come in much later periods.

References in the discussion

Durliat, J.
  1975   Les attributions civiles des évêques mérovingiens: l'exemple de Didier, évêque de Cahors(630-655). *Annales du Midi* 91:237-254.

THE IDEA OF GOVERNMENT IN SUB-ROMAN BRITAIN

DAVID N. DUMVILLE

Girton College, Cambridge CB3 OJG

The period of transition from Roman control in Britain to the barbarisation of the whole former Imperial diocese can be measured in its chronological dimension by a variety of very different criteria. Within that era, nevertheless, the writer known to us as Gildas is in every way central. His principal surviving work, *De excidio Britanniae*, 'The Ruin of Britain', provides at once surveys of the history of Britain since the fourth century and of the rulers of western Britain in his own day which have constituted prime fare for often disgruntled historically minded modern readers who have subjected it to use and criticism since it was printed in the mid-sixteenth century (Josselin 1567; Vergil 1525). More recently, students of late Latin language and literature have given considerable attention to the work, with the result that we now have a much clearer sense of the author's intellectual formation and of his literary intentions.[1] In so far as this has tied Gildas more closely to the larger world of Latin letters, there has been a tendency to attempt to measure his date by reference to the appearance of comparable linguistic, stylistic, and conceptual tendencies elsewhere in the Latin world.

There is a balance of gain or loss in these scholarly developments: while Gildas has been drawn—or pushed—into the orbit of late Latin literature and the culture which that presupposes, his work has not benefited from scrutiny by those concerned with the larger issues attending the transformation of the Roman world. Indeed, it is fair to say that, despite the publication of Professor François Kerlouégan's massive study of the linguistic and literary characteristics of Gildas's *magnum opus* (Kerlouégan 1987), Gildas remains an author largely unknown to Continental scholars. Standard works of the last generation on the cultural aspects of the barbarian invasions (Courcelle 1948/1964), on education in the sub-Roman period (Riché 1962/1976), on kingship and government (Reydellet 1981; cf. Wood 1987), and on patriotism and citizenship (Paschoud 1967)—all by Francophone scholars—have been written in apparent ignorance of Gildas. Although his work was edited by Theodor Mommsen for the *Monumenta Germaniae Historica* (Mommsen 1891-8, III,1-110), German scholarship has taken no interest in him in recent times.[2] And the great Latin and medieval-studies industry of modern Italy has so far given birth to only one very basic edition (Cazzaniga 1961) and a handful of studies, although the tempo does appear to be quickening (Braidotti 1982 and 1986/7; Muraglia 1987 and 1992; cf. Bertini 1984 and Santoro 1991).

Yet Gildas was a witness to and an eloquent commentator upon the process of barbarisation of his sub-Roman world. He is not unique in that or in the concerns which he addresses,

---

[1] For bibliography to 1983, see Lapidge & Dumville 1984; see further Lapidge 1984; Orlandi 1984; Sims-Williams 1984; Sutherland 1984; Wright 1984a, 1984b, 1985, 1991.

[2] For a recent and very inadequate notice, see Brunholzl 1975:160-2, 530-1; marginally better in the French edition 1990:159-60, 276-7.

AFTER EMPIRE:
TOWARDS AN ETHNOLOGY OF EUROPES'S BARBARIANS

but he is unique in location; and, for his date, he stands almost alone in his cultural context. Where Gildas is unique, his primary importance is for British cultural history; but where he can be integrated successfully within a larger framework of ideas and historical developments, he provides a capital resource for the student of the end of the Roman world.

British-Government: an Historical Framework for its Origins

In Britain, the process which was to lead to the island's departure from the Empire may be seen beginning at the end of the third century. Reaction to Continental barbarian threats to Britain's security within the Empire provided ostensible grounds for a cycle of rebellions against and withdrawal from central Imperial authority followed by eventual restoration of control from Rome (Salway 1981 for a standard account); in the interstices of this process might lie a significant period of self-government (Collingwood *et al.* 1937:288). When, in the years from 406 to 411, a profusion of local emperors and pretenders to a greater role once again sundered Britain (and briefly, parts of Gaul and Iberia) from central control, the expectation of all parties was (no doubt) that in due course normality would be restored. That this did not happen—unless an old theory of a limited Roman military reconquest until *ca* 425 be revived (Bury 1920; Collingwood 1922; Collingwood *et al.* 1937:291-301; Foord 1925; Schmidt 1931; cf. Salway 1981:437)—may, with the benefit of hindsight, be seen as a logical outcome of almost 150 years of periodic rebellion. It was probably not until the 440s that the Romano-Britons realised there to be little likelihood of Britain's resumption of a place which would allow its survival as an integrated part of the Empire. Even the history of that immediately—but (to contemporaries) not necessarily obviously—sub-Roman generation must have been complex in terms of attitudes and political history. But as what had been Roman Britain slipped further and further from an Empire which was itself in terminal decline, the natives would have had repeatedly to reassess for themselves the nature of the relationship between government and society. Gildas stood, as he himself recognised, at a critical moment in the development of British political thought (cf. Brooks 1983/4).

In various divisions of study of sub-Roman Britain, scholars have taken advantage of our ignorance of how continuity was maintained or how discontinuities occurred; the argument from silence has not merely been the preserve of the novelist or the popular historian. We have been assured of the continuity or discontinuity of government, of its taxation-system, its legal system, and its schools (e.g. Hanson 1968 and comment by Dumville 1993:13, 88, 114). What did rebellion and its aftermath mean for Britain in the first half of the fifth century, in terms of both intended results and unforeseen consequences? To what extent can we generalise from the snippets of information which have reached us?

By Gildas's time kingly government seems to have been a widespread phenomenon in Britain: Gildas dilates, as is well known to students of Welsh history in particular, upon the evils of many of those who held office at that time: *"Reges habet Britannia, sed tyrannos; iudices habet, sed impios...."* (II. 27, 1). He also stressed the dire consequences for British society of civil wars, to which he attributed the ghost-cities of his day (I. 26, 2): we might ask to what extent these wars coincided with the more general development of royal government. How did such phenomena develop?

In the last years of Roman Britain, as indeed for much of its history, the non-Pictish part of the island was divided into three zones—that independent of Roman rule, that under military government, and a region organised with Roman-style civilian government (cf. Salway 1981). The rulers of independent Britain were subjected variously to degrees of pressure from the Roman military government of the second zone just named (Salway 1965; cf. Crawford 1949, Hogg 1951, Richmond 1958). Their hostility towards the Roman diocese (as no doubt to one another) in principle may be assumed, even if only because of the economic inducements; but their ability to express that hostility was no doubt often restrained by Roman defensive strength or aggressiveness (to say nothing of the possible use of bribery with money and honours). When an Imperial defensive system could no longer be seen in place (cf. Dark 1992a on possible successor-arrangements), no doubt the consequent inducement to raid and conquer territory within the diocese was irresistible.

The problem of understanding the significance of this results from uncertainty about the second theme. The military or upland zone of Roman Britain has had its extent re-evaluated, albeit controversially, in the last generation (Simpson 1964): the suspicion has been voiced that significant quantities of the southwestern peninsula, of mid-Wales, and of the Pennine region had not had effective Roman government since at least the third century. If there was not Roman rule, we must suppose that native governance survived or resumed in those areas. In other words, an alternative model of British rule may have been exemplified much closer to the civilian zone than was once thought; given the circumstances of the fifth century, such native governance could have offered the romanised *ciuitates* a military threat as much as a model for change by imitation.

The city-states which provided the basis for Roman government in southern Britain faced a variety of threats as the fifth century opened: the reduction in military security occasioned by the events of the century's first decade; internal unrest (of a much disputed nature: cf. Thompson 1982 and 1984); religious conflict; possible threats from other British political units; barbarian invasion from east and west; and, hanging over all this, uncertainty about the nature of the practical relationship with the Empire. We may imagine that such a formidable combination of stresses would have led also to considerable economic difficulties, giving rise to a vicious cycle of developing problems. It is necessary for us to consider, in the almost total absence of evidence, how government in the Romano-British civilian zone changed in the course of the fifth and sixth centuries.[3]

In order to survive, each *ciuitas* would have had to acquire a military capability, and no doubt rather hurriedly so. Decisions would have had to be taken about whether to form alliances with neighbouring *ciuitates* or go it alone. Alliances, once formed, might have come to seem threatening to others. Whereas in Roman times trade would have moved freely across the country, now it would have been subject to the restrictions arising from the attaching of a greater importance to frontiers. The economic implications of an uneven distribution of natural and manufacturing resources may in these circumstances have provoked conflict.[4] In due course we see frontiers being fortified, or at least vigorously demarcated, by the construction of substantial earthworks. Mobilisation of considerable resources of labour would have been necessary for such tasks.[5] Similarly, once powers had

---

[3]   The only extended discussion of this period to have been published in recent times is that of Salway 1981:413-501, already outdated when it appeared; cf. now Dark 1994 and Esmonde Cleary 1989.

[4]   For some discussion of economics and politics in sub-Roman Britain, see Dark 1994 and 1995; on the role of trade see Fulford 1989 and Thomas 1990.

[5]   For specific examples, see Lethbridge 1957; Myres 1964; Wade-Martins 1974 and 1975:146, 149-50; Rutherford Davis 1982:40-50; a general study is needed.

been acquired to raise armed forces, those in control of such resources may have chosen to use them for internal political ends.

On the death of the usurping British emperor Constantine III on the Continent in 411, the British administration—if it still survived—would have been in the same position as on various previous such occasions, most recently on the death of Magnus Maximus in 388. Presumably we should envisage the continuing existence of an overall military command, not to mention more local ones, as well as the political authorities in the several *ciuitates*. Whether faction would determine that these various authorities got out of step with one another, with a consequent breakdown of relationships, is unknown. What Gildas tells us, looking back from a century's remove, is that civil wars and famine began in the first half of the fifth century (I.19, 3-4), preliminary to a British appeal to Aetius (Agitius) in 446 x 454 for help against barbarian invaders (Picts and Gaels, according to Gildas: see I.19, 1 and I.20, 1).

We have one piece of evidence to suport the idea of civil war, perhaps but by no means certainly involving fighting between *ciuitates*. This is provided by what Zosimus has to say about an anti-Roman revolt in 409 which spread to Armorica and where it was not suppressed until 417. The implication of the story is that the political basis of Romano-British society was overturned wholesale (discussed by Thompson 1977, 1982, 1984). It is difficult to credit that this revolution was as widespread as is implied, or that its results were necessarily stable for any lenght of time thereafter. But here is an implication that the British situation on the death of Constantine III in 411 was not entirely like that which had obtained in 388.

The one other piece of direct, if oblique, written evidence which remains to us is provided by Constantius's 'Life of St Germanus of Auxerre' (Borius 1965). The relevant episode was examined in considerable—perhaps too much—detail by E. A. Thompson who was inclined to suppose that the revolutionaries of 409 still controlled part or all of southern England in the late 420s and 430s (Thompson 1984). This is not a conclusion which emerges inexorably from the text. But in so far as I can deduce anything from what Constantius has to say about Britain, my impression is that he gives the reader no reason to think that anything other than a single authority was responsible for the area—reaching as far north as St Albans (Hertfordshire) on the boundary of the Roman *ciuitates* of the *Trinouantes* and the *Catuuellauni*—in which he travelled.

Was this the context in which flourished the *superbus tyrannus* of whom Gildas wrote? Again, we face numerous problems of interpretation, not least if we wish to join the evidence of various sources. There are, I think, too many imponderables for us to be able to reach any convincing conclusions. What a strict, or narrow, reading of Gildas requires me to suppose is that Gildas thought him to have lived in the late fifth century and to have had authority in at least what is now northeastern England (Dumville 1984:70-3, 83). This is not what subsequent accounts admitted, associating him instead with a mid-fifth century context and the settlement of Anglo-Saxons in Kent. As is well known, a southern Gaulish chronicler, more or less contemporaneous with events, placed in the early or mid-440s the reduction of the *Britanniae*, the provinces of Britain, to Saxon power {'Chronicle of AD 452' (Mommsen 1891-8, I.660, § 126) }.[6] Much ink has been spilt over what that statement means, but it would not be especially controversial to say that some part of southern or southeastern England which was best known in Gaul was overrun by (or even granted to)

---

[6]   On the work as a whole, cf. Muhlberger 1990:136-92.

Saxons at that time. We are left to wonder about the implications of such a development for the government of the remainder of what had been Roman Britain.

Sooner or later, the various parts of the former diocese which remained in British control would have begun to be separated from one another by intervening territory conquered by Germanic invaders. If fissiparous internal forces had not already separated *ciuitates* from one another, whether individually or in groups, the process of Anglo-Saxon (and perhaps, in the west, Irish) conquest would have effected some divisions of such a sort.

At least from the time of the appearance of the Saxons as significant threats to British control of their own land, a premium would have been placed on the value of military leadership. We have no reason to think that fifth-century Britons were so devoted to civilian constitutional government that all power could not fall into the hands of such leaders (whether by seizure or gift) in the desperate circumstances of foreign invasion. Seen from Gildas's day, the historical process appears to have been one of a shift to kingly rule. Whether a first-generation *dux* could become a king, or his heir became such by virtue of the transmission of authority across a generation, or persons possessing or claiming links to previous Roman emperors (whether universally or sectionally recognised) now became eligible for kingship, is of course unknown. That some kings named by Gildas as his contemporaries were at least third-generation royalty implies a period in or by which the development might have occurred. And indeed, as we follow his narrative, he appears to point to the generation after the mid-fifth century as decisive in this respect (I.21, and see Dumville 1984:68-70, 77, 83).

Fortunately, we have one other piece of evidence which gives some colour to these ideas. *Circa* 470, we learn from Sidonius Apollinaris (*Epistolae*, 3, 9), a British fleet led by a king called Riothamus turned up on the River Loire in circumstances of some political and military complexity. The event is also noted by the mid-sixth-century Italian historian of the Goths, Jordanes (*Getica*, §§ 237-8), whose source for this episode is unknown. According to Jordanes, the army of which Riothamus disposed was an incredible 12,000 men; even a figure of 1,200 would have constituted a remarkably large force. Nevertheless, here is a British king with an army and a fleet who was militarily active in Gaul. It would be hard to suppose that he came (or could be summoned) from anywhere in Britain except the south.

It has long been a suggestion that the context of Riothamus's availability thus is provided by British migration to western Gaul which led eventually to the creation of Brittany (see Fahy 1964/5 for a summary). This may indeed be so, but for our immediate purpose that presents no especial difficulty; for we must suppose, even if direct connection with the emigration is illusory, that Riothamus's situation tells us something of the nature of government in southern Britain, although the attendant circumstances there would be grimmer on one interpretation than on the other.

We must be careful not to generalise, however. If kings had emerged as rulers of some parts of southern Britain by *ca* 470, it does not mean that they had done so everywhere. But consideration of the possible circumstances across the area of the Roman diocese as a whole may suggest that the trend in that direction would have been widespread. At an earlier stage in this argument, I noted that British (viz, non-Pictish) areas not subject to Roman control *ca* 400 would have been under kingly rule and that these would have provided a model for imitation or a source of military threat (or both) to adjoining regions which had been part of the Roman diocese. In the upland regions of Wales and the North which had known only military government during the Roman period, the possibility of military command—whether over a broader or a narrower area—developing into hereditary rulership with assertion of royal title might be considered great. It was, after all, the Imperial army in Britain which had a history of raising its commanders by acclamation to the status of emperors. We may remember that Gildas's *superbus tyrannus* who devised the plan which was *excidium patriae* seems to have had authority over an area considerable enough that some part of it could be granted to the Saxons. This man was, for Gildas, "an arrogant usurper of legitimate authority" (I.23, 1). If he ruled in the Midlands or the North, he would be a candidate for the kind of rulership just deduced from the Roman-period circumstances. And, if it were the case that civilian-zone *ciuitates* were bordered to the north and west by rulers—kings—of such a sort, one can imagine that warfare, conquest, or requests for help against barbarians or other British warlords, could have allowed the extension of such rulership southwards and eastwards.

What might we make of how the populations of the *ciuitates* would have reacted to these hypothesised changes in their society? In this matter one can offer only arguments advanced tangentially. One can try to fill the gap in the development of political thought between the end of the fourth century and what Gildas has to say. One can appeal to the analogy of sub Roman situations in other regions of the former empire. And one may try to tease something out of Constantius's accounts of St Germanus's visit to Britain. Perhaps the most immediately useful course of action is to look to Gaul.

Increasingly, it seems, Imperial authority was collapsing in Gaul after the deaths of Aetius and Valentinian III. From 455 to 470 this process continued relentlessly (cf. Drinkwater *et al.* 1992:285-7). In the north it was marked particularly by the *regnum Romanorum of Aegidius* and Syagrius (461-486), centring on Soissons (cf. James 1988), and in the west by the apparent consolidation and extension of Visigothic power under Euric (466-484). Much can be carried over from the Gallic situation and applied to British history as a series of models which may help to explain how events developed in Britain. But first there is the question of direct linkage. One is bound to wonder how the fifth-century Britons regarded their own political and social history as it unfolded. When (if at all) did they come to realise that the Roman world known to them or their ancestors was finished and that they had to make themselves masters of their own fate—in 409, 410, 411, during the Saxon conquests of the 440s, or following the failure of the appeal to *Agitius ter consul*, presumably *ca* 450? Or was it when they saw what was happening in Gaul in the years after 455? And to what extent might Aegidius's *regnum Romanorum* have provided a model for imitation?—in as much as a British unit north of the Thames, perhaps based on the *ciuitates* of the *Trinouantes* and *Catuuelllauni* (and possibly including London), has been thought to have survived against the Anglo-Saxon tide even into the sixth century (cf. Rutherford Davis 1982), we may have at least a British parallel to the 'kingdom of Soissons' if not a polity inspired by it.

One aspect of the 'kingdom of Soissons' which has recently received attention is the terminology of royalty applied to its two rulers. It has been argued that, in so far as they were *reges*, imperial status was being claimed for or by them (Fanning 1992; on terminology, cf. Fanning 1991). We are reminded of the usurping emperors of Gaul and Britain in former times. This suggests one way in which matters might have developed among the Britons in the fifth century. Gildas's *superbus tyrannus* may represent a type: the classic application of *tyrannus* was of course to one who usurped Imperial status and authority in the Roman world. The *parentes* of Ambrosius Aurelianus who had "worn the purple" might have been emperors in Britain. And we may take up an old chestnut again in this context. The sixth century inscription at Castelldwyran in Dyfed (Nash-Williams 1950:107-8, no. 138, and plate III; Dark 1987, 1992b, 1992c; cf. Sims-Williams 1990:226) has attracted much derision for its description of Uoteporix, whom it memorialises, as *protector* (*protictor*, indeed): as a technical term, that was applied to the commander of the Emperor's praetorian guard (cf. Jones 1964: *passim*—index at III.439; Campbell 1982:21; Jackson 1953:175; Salway 1981:351, 488). What level of barbarity and vanity allowed it to be given to a sixth-century ruler in southwestern Wales? In the context of romanising empire (or empires) in Britain, however, would such a style be so far-fetched? Might not this Dimetian king have occupied a place of honour (with its accompanying title) at the right hand of a *rex Romanorum* in Britain? There could be much in the sixth- and seventh-century political history of Britain explicable in terms of an imperial tradition of rulership (cf. John 1966: 1-63).

Gildas on the Theory and Practice of Government in Sub-Roman Britain

In Gildas's *De excidio Britanniae* we meet an account of a region which had been a constituent part of the Roman empire until the first decade of the fifth century. It is doubtful whether those in Britain who were elevated to the purple by their troops intended that by their actions they would withdraw the diocese of Britain from the Roman world— only in 409 do we have any cause to suspect the presence of a political force favouring revolutionary, secessionist action. While we have every reason to think that the policies of such *tyranni* were dictated in part by the needs and fears of the local ruling classes, both landed and military, there is no evidence to suggest that such motives had even brought these groups of *potentes* to question their own place within the framework provided by the Empire at large. It has been colourfully observed that, in any century of the Roman era, even to contemplate the act of writing a separate history of one region of the Empire would have been tantamount to treason (Thompson 1979, 1984). Yet Gildas offers us no sense that in considering *Britannia insula* as a definable unit he is thinking radical thoughts: only in his intimation that, in his account of British history, he was not using sources written in Britain (I.4, 4) does he allow us to consider that Roman attitudes might long have continued to inhibit local literary activity on political and historical subjects.

Nevertheless, for Gildas *Britannia insula* is a concept which has geographical and political meaning (Wright 1984a), even though he could hardly have been familiar with all of the island and though political authority in his day was clearly fragmented. While he might at times speak of a narrower *regio*, never adequately defined, *patria and ciues* (and *nostri*) seem usually in their very lack of further precision to refer to Britain and the Britons (from whom the Picts are certainly to be distinguished). In his confident and unhesitating use of the medium of the Latin language, as in his terminology of citizenship and patriotism, Gildas relied on a Roman past. It is indeed remarkable that he could write thus, and perhaps yet more so that he addressed with assurance an audience—both secular and ecclesiastical— which he expected to be able to understand his trenchant political message. Have we here a literary equivalent of what archaeology has allowed us to glimpse at post-Roman Wroxeter (Shropshire), where some of the physical manifestations of Roman civilisation were recreated in new circumstances with adaptation of materials to new tasks but with old ideologies presupposed (Barker 1990)? Gildas had preserved his Roman inheritance and in his language and style he proclaimed it loudly, too loudly perhaps.

What is different is the central role of Britain in his historical and political thought. Although Gildas's cultural inheritance is, in its linguistic and literary manifestations, wholly Roman, nevertheless his discussion of the history of Britain and the Britons in relation to the Roman empire reveals both nationalism and some ambivalence towards the Romans. Given the overall message of his *magnum opus*, Gildas clearly felt a necessity to denigrate the Britons' moral character and consequent behaviour throughout history: the Britons have always been rebellious in spirit (1.5, 2), cowardly in war and faithless in peace—this "became a mocking proverb far and wide" (I.6, 2); Britain is a "*patria* which has always longed to hear some novelty and which has never taken firm hold of anything" (I.12, 3). Such an attitude could lay it so low that the country would even prove receptive when "the Arian...treason vomited its foreign poison upon us" (I.12, 3)—but at least that heresy was *transmarina*, not native: it is interesting that Gildas wrote nothing here about Pelagianism, although he has been caught quoting a Pelagian author by an ambiguous formula, "as one of us (*quidam nostrum*) well says" (II.38, 2 in Winterbottom 1978:153). Gildas was nevertheless deeply attached to his *patria*: he described its natural beauty and fecundity (I.2); he desired its rulers and citizens to save themselves and their country (I.1, 1); and he celebrated the fact that when the Britons had had determined and moral leadership "our people regained their strength" (I.25, 3).

That observation is not without irony, however, whether Gildas intended it or not. The leader in question, Ambrosius Aurelianus, we find described as a *uir modestus* (a statement of rank rather than personality) whose parents had "undoubtedly worn the purple", and who was "perhaps the last of a Roman *gens*" (I.25, 3) to survive the British upheavals of the preceding era of invasions and civil wars. Good leadership could raise the Britons above their naturally vicious level, but that leadership was Roman. Indeed, Rome had "brought the laws of obedience to the island" in the first place (I.5, 2). The conquerors eventually intended that "the island should be rated not as *Britannia* but as *Romania*" and all its precious metals "were to be stamped with the image of Caesar" (I.7). The image of the Roman army with its standards had a mixed meaning for Gildas, however: in the account of St Alban's martyrdom the *stigmata* are "displayed...to the most horrid effect...in the presence of wicked men" (I.11, 1), but when the Romans are portrayed as giving aid to the Britons against external foes the *stigmata* represent a "great and splendid army" (I.18, 1).

The island which had become part of *Romania*[7] nevertheless was "fertile of *tyranni*" (I.4, 3) and it produced such "a savage forest" of them that it "was still Roman in name, but not by law and custom" (I.13, 1). This was, for Gildas, how Britain left the Roman empire. It sent one of its usurpers, "Maximus to Gaul with a great retinue of hangers-on and even the Imperial insignia, which he was never fit to bear"; what is more, "he had no legal claim to the title" (I.13, 1). He had a "kingdom of wickedness (*facinoroso regno*)" which by attacking Gaul, Spain, and even Italy he turned into a "wicked empire (*iniquissimi imperii*)"; during his short and daring career he disposed of two legitimate emperors (*Duos imperatores legitimos*) and thus "cast down the crowned heads of the *regnum* of the whole world" (I.13, 2).

When the inhabitants of the now independent Britain faced military difficulties, however, they turned back to Rome for help. The Romans are now described as "our worthy allies (*auxiliares egregii*)" (I.17, 3). But they could not provide help for ever. They left, "meaning never to return" and "went back home" (I.18-19, 1). A final British appeal ad *Agitium romanae potestatis uirum* produced no response (I.20, 1). Rome then fades from Gildas's picture. The Romans had said that they would not return: they did not. Gildas offered us

---

[7]   On this usage see Zeller 1929, lacking reference to Gildas.

no hint of what he thought happened next in Roman history; but for his purpose it did not matter. The Romans had been led by emperors (I.4, 4), "kings from abroad (*transmarinis regibus*)" (I.4, 1), who had become "kings having...rule of the world" (*reges Romanorum... orbis imperium obtinuissent*) (I.5, 1). They placed governors in Britain (I.6, 1). The powers of the Roman senate were known to Gildas (I.6, 2) as was the institution's militant paganism (I.8). But in the end the British perfidiousness as manifested by their usurping rulers separated *Britannia* from *Romania*. With some disingenuousness Gildas remarked, "I shall be silent on the long-past years (*uetustos annos*) of dreadful usurpers (*immanium tyrannorum*)" (I.4, 3): but he could not avoid or resist dealing with Magnus Maximus who, for him, closed Romano-British history. Here is the origin of subsequent Brittonic political theory which yet relies on a very different interpretation of Maximus's standing (Dumville 1977:179-83; cf. Matthews 1982/3). The Romans had been by~turns magnificent, terrible, and friendly, but, for Britain, "the time of the Roman emperors" (I.4, 4) had been an era with a clear beginning and end. And for a century before Gildas's day they had been completely out of the picture.

A new political model was needed to give definition to Britain's modern history but which would yet allow a sense of continuity with the past, Roman and pre-Roman (I.4). That was provided by consideration of biblical history. The Britons could be seen as "the Lord's latter-day Israel" constantly to be tested as to whether they loved Him or not (I.26, 1). Just as the Old-Testament Israelites often failed to heed God, His commandments, and His prophets, the Britons were also found wanting in their fecklessness. They paid the same penalties: when the Saxons devastated the island in a major raid, "so it was that in this assault, comparable with that of the Assyrians of old on Judea, there was fulfilled according to history (*secundum historiam*) for us also what the prophet said in his lament" (I.24, 2). Gildas stood in the tradition of those prophets, desperately calling his *ciues* to timely repentance lest ruin overtake their country and themselves. Two centuries later, Bede was in no doubt as to the import of Gildas's message: the Britons had committed "unspeakable crimes which Gildas their own historian describes in doleful words" (*Historia ecclesiastica gentis Anglorum*, I.22).

Gildas's Moral Perspective

For Gildas, then, the Roman era—though one of foreign domination—had largely positive characteristics. It was in that period too that Christianity had first come to Britain and, although it had been received tepidly by the natives (I.8-9), nevertheless the sword of persecution created martyrs whose witness and whose subsequent cults produced an era of Christian enthusiasm which lasted until heresy was imported (I.10-12). Among the positive attributes of Roman rule—law, civilisation, Christianity (Thomas 1981), effective defence—could also be numbered language: when Gildas deliberately mistranslated the name of a British king into Latin, he referred to that as *romana lingua* (II.32, 1; also Muller 1923:11; Paris 1872). Gildas recognised in Britain's Roman inheritance much of what he most valued. But he had the task of commending those values to fellow-countrymen who lived in a world beyond Rome: the Bible, its exempla, and its precepts would be his guide, even if his writing was structured in language and style redolent of the secular tastes of late Antiquity (cf. Lapidge 1984). For a significant élite at least, Latin cannot have seemed a foreign language in the fifth and sixth centuries in Britain (cf. Jackson 1953:118-9 on the epigraphic evidence), and we have only to remember the massive impact of Latin on the British vernacular dialects to reassure ourselves of the large place which it must have occupied in British life (cf. Jackson 1953:76). What is more, one may recall here the increasing tendency among some scholars of early medieval Welsh history and archaeology to think that the romanising period of the Britons' history continued well into the seventh century at least (cf. Dark 1994).

Gildas's central problem was that among the Britons a culture had developed which he found immoral. The public manifestation of that culture comprised corruption and oppression. In the government of Church and State alike, interdependent as they were, rulers were rebelling against the needs of their own people. Bede began the historian's practice of accepting Gildas's assessment at face-value. On the other hand, nineteenth-century rebellion against Gildas's 'uncouth' invective has led to the view that he was a fundamentalist whose obsessive perception of his own era was so warped as to vitiate his usefulness to the student of sub-Roman Britain (Miller 1975).

To understand Gildas's analysis, to attempt to see what problems he addressed and what different views were taken by contemporaries, and to comprehend as far as possible the political forces and institutional structures which shaped those views and within whose frameworks they were expressed, are primary tasks for the historian. Gildas's prescription or message may then be evaluated and his use of the information available to him estimated. All these, of course, make no small task, for *De excidio Britanniae* is a complex and in many ways difficult work whose British cultural context is often deeply obscure in as much as controlling testimony is not easy to obtain.

What Gildas lamented was "a general loss of good" (I.1, 1). His position is summed up (III.90, 3) by his quotation from Ezekiel (XXII.24-6): "The princes (*principes*) in the midst of the land are as roaring lions ravening for plunder, devouring souls in their power and receiving bribes, and your widows are multiplied in your midst. And its priests have despised my law and polluted my holy places: they made no distinction between holy and profane, no divisions between clean and unclean; they veiled their eyes from my sabbaths and caused pollution in their midst". That there is direct linkage between these kingly and priestly failings is made very clear by one of Gildas's apostrophes to the clergy (III.75, 3): "Which of you under the shock of the tyrants (*in concussione tyrannorum*) kept rigidly to the rule given by the words of the apostle..., 'One must obey God rather than men'?"

Usurpation is a theme which unites Gildas's perceptions of the secular and ecclesiastical worlds. In the sphere of politics the *principes* or *reges* are *tyranni*, "unjust usurpers". In the Church we find usurpation of holy orders (III.66, 6): "Many, rather than being drawn into the priesthood, rush into it or spend almost any price on attaining it.... They have grabbed merely the name of priest (*rapto tantum sacerdotali nomine*), not the priestly way of life". Likewise, the rise of tyrants in fourth-century Britain showed that "the island was still Roman in name, but not by law and custom" (I.13, 1). Again, there is linkage between these two usurpations to be pointed out (III.67, 2): "But the error which they are most prone to...is that they buy priesthoods..., not from the apostles or their successors but from the tyrants and their father the Devil". A moral can be pointed up (III.67, 3): "For if these impudent men had suggested the same bargain...,to any holy priest or pious king, they would have got the same reply as Simon Magus...". Gildas went on to suppose that the problem could be traced back at least to the generation of the grandfathers of those who now purchased and assumed tainted orders (III.67, 4).

Gildas's criteria of legitimacy in respect of political office require investigation. A theme recurrent in his treatment of the *tyranni* he nonetheless stated most clearly in relation to wicked clergy: he noted the hostility of pastors to their flocks and their lack of care for them (III.95, 1-3). He put this most succinctly and bitingly in his aphorism that "kings were anointed in God's name but as being crueller than the rest" (I.21, 4). Evil behaviour in office and an unacceptable method of advancement to that position are the marks of usurpation which Gildas's writings offer us. At the larger political level Gildas's views are less clearly stated. On the face of it, since *tyranni* led to the overthrow of Roman rule in Britain, political legitimacy was in the hands of the Romans. As Gildas had observed, Rome "brought the laws of obedience to the island" (I.5, 2); his concern for his own day was that the apostolic dictum, "One must obey God rather than men" (Acts V.29), be upheld regardless of the *tyranni* (III.75, 3). In so far, then, as the Roman empire, though intrusive in Britain, represented on the whole a force for good, those who rebelled against it were to be deplored. That empire constituted a *"regnum* of the whole world" (I.13, 2). In as much as Gildas's narrative never hints at the Empire's termination or dissolution, he may have taken the view that it still represented an ultimate political authority. Nevertheless, he had to come to terms with the British realities of his day. Here, moral criteria would have to be applied, as tempered by at least one fundamental rule of life: one must not deny "honour to those placed in higher authority, for that is their due (granted, of course, that there is no harm to the faith)" (I.4, 1). Biblical values—and above all, Old-testament exempla—would provide the measure of acceptability of the behaviour of secular rulers and the necessary authority (and models) for their correction. Yet *"Reges habet Britannia sed tyrannos"* (II.27, 1). If all present authority was illegitimate, it was because of the origins of its power in rebellion against Rome and because of the current unjust exercise of its authority. That the position was not wholly irretrievable in Gildas's sight is made clear by his comments on Ambrosius Aurelianus (discussed above) and on the lapsed penitent, King Maglocunus (II.34), whom God had placed "higher than almost all the *duces* of *Britannia"* (II.33, 2).

If rulers could, by their moral qualities and their actions, steer the British people away from the course of vice which would lead them to destruction, what exactly must they do? Did Gildas, in other words, provide a mirror of rulership? The answer must be that he proceeded by negative example. As he himself said in the opening words of *De excidio Britanniae,* "In this letter I shall deplore...with mournful complaint...rather than denounce (*In hac epistola quicquid deflendo potius quam declamando...lacrimosis querelis defleam"* (I.1, 1). Jeremiah is indeed prominent in his work. Gildas held up to his readers a long series of images and biblical prophetic utterances which were intended to turn them—in fear of God—from committing or condoning evil. No doubt he would have offered detailed instructions on the practice of good if he had thought that the positive message would have proved effective. All the indications are, however, that he felt shock-therapy to be the only hope of arresting moral collapse, for "a great multitude has been lost, as people daily rush headlong to hell" (I.26, 3): "What will the Lord do with this great black blot on our generation? It has heinous and appalling sins in common with all the wicked ones of the world; but, over and above that, it has as though inborn in it a load of ignorance and folly which cannot be erased or avoided" (I.1, 13).

Gildas's Message through the Exempla

We must make allowance, therefore, for the negative character of Gildas's exempla. In these terms we may see the opening section (II.27) of his denunciation of British kings as a reflection of what Gildas thought proper to kingship and particularly to Christian kingship. He proceeded by stating a series of antitheses. The tone and form are set by the opening two pairs: "*Reges habet Britannia, sed tyrannos; iudices[8] habet, sed impios*". The functions seen as definitive of the just and false exercise of power follow.

1.   *saepe praedantes et concutientes, sed innocentes;*
     uindicantes et patrocinantes, sed reos et latrones.
     The role of the just ruler is to plunder and terrorise the enemies of the people (and, if it is a just people, therefore of God), thus defending and protecting *patria* and *ciues*, whether from external foes or the wicked within. In Gildas's perception of his Britain, right order stood on its head: the guilty are protected, while the innocent are persecuted. Gildas returns to this specific manifestation of moral decay in a subsequent antithesis.

2.   *quamplurimas coniuges habentes, sed scortas et adulterantes.*
     In his discussion of the behaviour of specific kings (II.27-36) Gildas cited no examples of kings maintaining more than one wife at the same time. However, he commented repeatedly on the kings' roving eyes and their successive unions, often illegitimate in his eyes because of the attendant circumstances: the unions may be achieved after murder or by rape or by what Gildas defined as incest.[9] The women are therefore whores and adulteresses or both. The just king would be chaste.

3.   *crebro iurantes, sed periurantes;*
     uouentes, sed continuo propemodum mentientes.
     The kings' language was blasphemous, no doubt, and their behaviour political in the worst sense. But the main complaint here seems to be against kings' formal swearing of oaths, only to perjure themselves as soon as was convenient. The just king would not take the Lord's name in vain.

4.   *belligerantes, sed ciuilia et iniusta bella agentes.*
     This is a subspecification of (1) above. The kings are vigorous in war, but they fight the wrong enemies: their wars are unjust and directed against other Britons. The just king would be fighting the enemies of the Church (cf. III.92, 3)—and no doubt particularly the barbarians as enemies of the Britons.

5.   *per patriam quidem fures magnopere insectantes,*
     sed eos qui secum ad mensam sedent non solum amantes sed et munerantes.
     "They chase thieves energetically all over the country": Gildas even managed to make this police-function of government sound like a failing! But his point is, as

---

[8]   On the meaning of *iudex* here, see Schaffner 1984.

[9]   Gildas does not seem to present us with evidence of institutionalised concubinage, although his words do not rule it out.

ever, in the contrast. The kings manifest hypocrisy. Their boon-companions are thieves: in the culture of corruption which, in Gildas's vision, oppresses Britain, the leading men were institutionalised plunderers of the people.

6.   *eleemosynas largiter dantes,*
   sed e regione immensum montem scelerum exaggerantes.
   "They distribute alms profusely": Gildas here anticipated his apostrophe of King Maglocunus (II.33, l): *largior in dando, profusior in peccato.* Almsgiving is a theme to which Gildas recurred on a number of occasions in this work: he found it distasteful because of the characters of those who gave and of those churchmen who as middlemen might receive the alms. (He took the same view of fundamental disobedience in another context: II.38, 3.) Nevertheless it is clear that the giving of alms, no doubt often in a publicly spectacular way, was a feature of the Christian society of Gildas's day.

7.   *in sede arbitraturi sedentes,*
   sed raro recti iudicii regulam quaerentes.
   A royal function in that society was to act as judge; but in Gildas's view the kings had no idea of or concern for the principles on which just judgement might be given.

8.   *innoxios humilesque despicientes,*
   sanguinarios superbos parricidas—commanipulares et adulteros, Dei inimicos, si sors ut dicitur tulerit, qui cum ipso nomine certatim delendi erant ad sidera prout possunt efferentes.
   This observation flows naturally from what has preceded. In as much as the kings were unjust judges (7) and rewarded the evil (1, 5), it was to be expected that their view of their fellow-citizens would be based on contempt for the meek and the powerless. Meanwhile, as Gildas had already remarked, the kings' companions—this time characterised by their military rather than by their social role—were figures of desperate immorality, enemies of God.

9.   *uinctos plures in carceribus habentes,*
   quos dolo sui potius quam merito proterunt catenis onerantes.
   The kings keep prisons, no doubt in view of their roles as pursuers of thieves (5) and givers of judgement (7). But their prisoners "are more often loaded with chafing chains because of intrigue than because they deserve punishment". Political prisoners are the principal occupants of royal jails, according to Gildas, this being in accordance with the culture of immorality in public life, the evil means by which the *potentes* succeed to office, maintain their position, and service their desires.

10.   *inter altaria iurando demorantes*
   et haec eadem acsi lutulenta paulo post saxa despicientes.
   This complaint is a variant on (3) above, but cast in a form which emphasises the contempt which the *tyranni* have for religion and its formal manifestations on earth. It leads indirectly to specific criticism of the first king named, *Damnoniae* [*sic*] *tyrannicus...Constantinus* (II.28, 1).

In sum, then, we may see kings as expected by Gildas to terrorise and punish the external and internal enemies of God and the people, to maintain prisons where criminals are kept, to give just judgement in court, to respect the Church and to give alms with pure heart, to respect and protect the weak and the humble members of society, to live a chaste life with one wife only, and to honour any promise given or vow made. Their companions, whether in peace or war, would be men of good character.

We do not know whether Gildas had an exemplary—or at any rate acceptable—contemporary king in mind. Certainly his language gives no hint of that possibility. We do not know what he thought of those British kings he did not denounce (or even mention). But even Gildas's hostile language cannot conceal that some proper functions of government were being exercised: thieves were being pursued, some criminals were being clapped in irons. A culture of almsgiving had been established. And there is no hint that British society admitted any religion other than Christianity.

Gildas's account of the specific iniquities of five named kings indicates a catalogue of failings comparable with the excesses found in Roman and early medieval political life. What is new, by comparison with the ancient world, is the exclusive role of the Church as the sole representative of religion (cf. II.38, 5) and the possibility, as in the case of Maglocunus (II.33-36), that a king might take monastic vows (presumably abdicating, but then reneging on his vows). We are led to suppose ancient, rather than early medieval, levels of literacy in Gildas's society, or at least among the British élite. But we see Gildas as a mediator of biblical (that is, Old-Testament) ideas of kingship into the Insular Celtic world: dynasties will fail because of royal evil (II.40, 1); God will seize kingship from the hands of morally rebellious and recalcitrant kings (II.38, 3); the king is a conduit of evil to his people (II.35, 6), for "if a ruler listens to unjust words, all his subjects are wicked" (Proverbs XXIX.12) and "a just king sustains his kingdom" (Proverbs XXIX.4). We hear of parasites and panegyrics (II.34, 6; 35, 3; 43, 1). Overkingship (II.33, 2), dynastic infighting and assassination (II.28, 1-2; 34, 1), and local warfare involving plundering (II.30, 1; 34, 1) are already features of the British political process.

While Gildas's approach to depraved rulership can certainly be paralleled in succeeding centuries, one is nonetheless struck by points of comparison with radical political and ascetic movements of the late Roman world. In quoting I Kings XI.Il, "I shall rend and tear your kingdom and give it to your slave", Gildas reminds us of the revolutionary politics culminating in the rebellions of the first half of the fifth century, both in Britain and in Gaul. There is much in the fiery and radical Pelagian tracts, *De uirginitate* and *De uita christiana*[10] which runs parallel to Gildas's exposition, as John Morris pointed out (Morris 1965 and 1966:148; cf. Salway 1981:441-2), as well as at least one specific quotation from *De uirginitate* (*De excidio*, II.38, 2, from *De uirginitate*, §6). It is a question whether Gildas, as an adherent of a monastic movement or party within the British Church(es), and as one well read in late antique monastic literature (Wright 1991), was heir thus to a tradition of political radicalism which derived from those militant ascetic trends of the late fourth and firth centuries which spawned heresy at least as much as they produced Church-Fathers.[11]

In Gildas's eyes, the behaviour of the contemporary British *tyranni* could be summed up in a few words: gross immorality, and in particular manifest and oppressive injustice and corruption, not to mention the enthusiastic pursuit of fornication. Isaiah I.23-24 was quoted by Gildas (II.43, 2) and may be taken as a convenient summary of the failings of the

---

[10] In the absence of a convenient edition of the Pelagian corpus, see the translation by Rees 1991.

[11] On controversy in fifth-century Gaul, see Mathisen 1989.

administrations of the *tyranni*: "Your princes are disloyal, they are thieves' accomplices. They all love bribes, pursue profit. They let the orphan's case go unheard, and the widow cannot plead before them".[12] Variations on the theme recur. "Woe to you...who give judgement for the wicked in return for bribes, and deprive the just man of his justice" (II.43, 4, from Isaiah V.22-25). "For there are found among my people wicked men laying traps...to take men.... So they have grown great and rich, fat and gross;...they have not pleaded the orphan's case, or judged the cause of the poor" (II.48, 3, from Jeremiah V.26-29). There is much more to the same effect. In positive mode, we read (II.50, 6, from Jeremiah XXII.3-5), "Make judgements and pronounce justice; free the man who is oppressed by force from the hand of his accuser; bring no sorrow to the stranger, the orphan and the widow. Cause no unjust oppression. Shed no innocent blood".

The *tyranni*, then, were well named. Whether in general or in particular, they represented usurped power: and usurped power would almost inevitably be exercised as tyranny. For Gildas, and perhaps for his society, the twin pillars which supported a framework of normal life were provided by secular government on the one hand and the Church on the other. The moral inadequacy of the one he found reflected in that of the other. Indeed, the rising tide of his invective swells from an account (Book I) of the sins of the British people, as reflected in the military disasters and foreign oppression which they had suffered, through a denunciation of the unfit contemporary holders of royal power (Book II), to a torrent of vilification of the secular Church (Book III) which was eloquent in its historic mission to "shine as a beacon" of goodness providing a proper example for its flock.

Gildas's Scourge of the Clergy

In Gildas's eyes the churchmen of his day divided into three groups: the evil, who were guilty of simony and a range of other offences which displayed them as indissolubly wedded to the "slime" of wordly life; those who were not themselves evil but who, in their failure to speak out against the wickedness of contemporary society and to suffer for their witness to truth, were also ultimately damned; and "the very few (*paucissimos*) good shepherds" whose protection he commended to God as he closed his work (III,110, 3).

Gildas's most benign statement on the exercise of authority in his Britain seems to occur in his preface (I. 1, 14): "Britain has her rulers, she has her bishops (*Habet Britannia rectores, habet speculatores*).... Yes, she has them...: if not more than she needs, at least not fewer. But they are bowed under the pressure of their great burdens and have no time to take breath". This may not be as mild a comment as at first appears, for Gildas gives little indication elsewhere in his work of a willingness to accept the weight of their official responsibilities as justifications for the failings of the clergy.

We may begin with the very few. Gildas had been "spurred on [to write and publish] by my own thoughts and the devout prayers of my brethren (*fratrum*); his exposition is "well intentioned towards every noble soldier of Christ (*quibusque egregiis Christi tironibus*), though burdensome and insupportable for foolish rebels (*apostatis*)" (I.1, 16). The "very few" would seem to include monks and Christian laypeople, as well as members of the secular clergy. "A great multitude has been lost [to God]...; and the rest are counted

---

12   Cf. the further quotations from Isaiah LIX which comprise *De excidio*, II.46.

so small a number that, as they lie in her lap, holy mother Church does not see them, although they are the only true sons whom she has left" (I.26, 3). Among the priesthood, the situation is desperate: "I have to speak...not of those who are in lawful possession of the apostolic seat and know well how to grant spiritual food in due season to their fellow servants—supposing that there are many such at the present day—but of the unskilled shepherd..." (III.92, 2). "Who then among the priests of today, plunged as they are in the blindness of ignorance, could shine like the light of the clearest lamp...with the glow of knowledge and good works? Who is there who is looked upon as a safe and obvious common refuge for all the sons of the Church...?" (III.93, 2).

Gildas acknowledged the existence of clerics not damned by their own evil behaviour. "But it may be said: not all bishops and priests as categorised above are bad, for they are not all stained with the disgrace of schism, pride, and uncleanness. I agree entirely. Although we know them to be chaste and good, I shall make a brief reply" (III.69, 1). The burden of Gildas's response to his own questions is that these worthy ecclesiastics do not compare with the biblical figures (III.69-73) or the saints (III.74-75) who clearly stood out against the evils of their time and suffered for it. He quoted an Old-testament prophet, speaking of God's words, to sum it up for him (III.91, 1 and 3): "And I looked among them for a man of upright behaviour who would stand up to me altogether at the crisis of the land, lest in the end I should destroy it" (Ezechiel XXII.30-31). "If you tell the wicked man of his ways in good time, so that he can turn from his way, but he fails to turn, he will die for his wickedness: but you will have got away with your life" (Ezechiel XXXIII.8-9). Gildas, apparently a deacon[13] (II.65, 1), must, after ten years' hesitation (I. 1, 2), step forward from this group to fulfill this role, to save his own soul, and to attempt to save the souls of his fellow-countrymen .

The great mass of the clergy are, however, sunk in depravity: "*Sacerdotes habet Britannia, sed insipientes, quamplurimos ministros, sed impudentes; clericos, sed raptores subdolos...*" (III.66, 1). His complaint parallels in form that against the *tyranni* (II.27) but is twice as long (III.66, 1-5).

1.   *pastores, ut dicuntur,*
     sed occisioni animarum lupos paratos.
     This sums up the inverted condition of current ecclesiastical morality; clergy are wolves in sheep's clothing. Gildas dilated elsewhere (III.95, 1-3) on the hostility of pastors to their flocks, and on their lack of care for their charges.

2.   *quippe non commoda plebi prouidentes,*
     sed proprii plenitudinem uentris quaerentes.
     The clergy are simply looking after themselves (and are no doubt guilty of gluttony also).

3.   *ecclesiae domus habentes,*
     sed turpis lucri gratia eas adeuntes.
     Their reason for attending their own churches is to make money, presumably by receiving for themselves the offerings of the faithful (and perhaps by turning their office to other profit).

---

13   I concur with Chadwick 1954, in spite of subsequent objections to his interpretation.

4.   *populos docentes,*
        sed praebendo pessima exempla, uitia malosque mores.
        Their bad character and immoral behaviour gives their flocks an evil example. Gildas
        observed elsewhere (II.40, 4), "For today also it is certain that there are some teachers
        (*doctores*) filled with a spirit of perversity, affirming evil pleasures in preference to the
        truth". It is an interesting question whether he had in mind anything more specific
        than the practice of evil living which he was denouncing as a bad example. He alluded
        elsewhere too to false prophets (III.81, 4) but also to learned fools, quoting II Timothy
        III.8 with reference to Jamnes and Mambres (cf. Dumville 1973:331-2): St Paul,
        remarked Gildas, "mentions something which we see spreading in our time, 'Always
        learning and never coming to knowledge of the truth...'".

5.   *raro sacrificantes et nunquam puro corde inter altaria stantes.*
        The implication seems to be that the clergy do not care to carry out their formal
        liturgical duties.

6.   *plebem ob peccata non corripientes,*
        nimirum eam agentes.
        This picks up two earlier complaints: not only do the clergy not perform their
        teaching and pastoral functions, but they share in the vices of lay society.

7.   *praecepta Christi spernentes,*
        et suas libidines uotis omnibus implere curantes.
        As Gildas wrote elsewhere (III.96, 1), "listen to the words of the Lord addressing
        the apostles and multitudes—words which, as I hear, even you are not ashamed to
        use often in public". In other words, hypocrisy is a prominent clerical vice. "What
        harsh fate is rushing upon these men who...shun, as though it were a savage snake,
        the reading of the word of God when it is in the slightest degree brought to their
        attention?" ((III.98, 3). Cf. (15) below).

8.   *sedem Petri apostoli inmundis pedibus usurpantes,*
        sed merito cupiditatis in Iudae traditoris pestilentem cathedram decidentes.
        They buy themselves into priestly office (Gildas was to discuss simony at length in
        the next section of his text: III.66, 6 - 67, 6), and they then betray Christ for the sake
        of money.

9.   *ueritatem pro inimico odientes,*
        et mendaciis acsi carissimis fratribus fauentes.
        Right order stood on its head (cf. (7)).

10.   *iustos inopes immanes quasi angues toruis uultibus conspicantes,*
        et sceleratos diuites absque ullo uerecundiae respectu
        sicut caelestes angelos uenerantes.
        These are, in effect, the charges which were also directed against the *tyranni*, that
        they were respecters of persons; but how much more shocking was it to Gildas that
        the clergy behaved thus!

11. *egenis eleemosynam esse dandam summis e labiis praedicantes,*
     sed ipsi uel obolum non dantes.
     The alms may be for the poor, but it seems as though they were mediated (often or
     always?) through the clergy. Gildas had observed that the wicked were forbidden to
     offer sacrifices or gifts to God, but continued "although we [ecclesiastics,
     presumably] in our greed receive things which are an abomination to God, and, to
     our own undoing, refuse to have them distributed to the needy and indigent" (II.42,
     3). In other words, alms given by the laity were appropriated by the clergy rather
     than spent for or given to the poor.

12. *nefanda populi scelera tacentes,*
     et suas iniurias quasi Christo irrogatas amplificantes.
     The clergy's silence about public evil, no doubt particularly involving the *tyranni*, is
     a major complaint throughout the work; but here their hypocrisy is also pointed up.
     One is probably to understand that the clergy were jealous of their privileges and
     noisy in defence of them.

13. *religiosam forte matrem seu sorores domo pellentes,*
     et externas ueluti secretiori ministerio familiares indecenter leuigantes
     uel potius (ut uera dicam licet inepta non tam mihi quam talia agentibus) humiliantes.
     Hypocrisy and lechery.

14. *ecclesiasticos post haec gradus propensius quam regna caelorum ambientes,*
     et tyrannico ritu acceptos defendentes
     nec tamen legitimis moribus illustrantes.
     The evil clergy are adept at seeking ecclesiastical preferment rather than heaven,
     and—a cruel shot—they take and hold such office like *tyranni*, usurping and
     exercising authority wickedly.

15. *ad praecepta sanctorum (si aliquando dumtaxat audierint,*
     quae ab illis saepissime audienda erant) oscitantes et stupidos,
     et ad ludicra et ineptas saecularum hominum fabulas
     (acsi iter uitae quae mortis pandunt) strenuos et intentos.
     (Cf. (7) above}. The interest in *ludicra et fabulae* is particularly wordly and
     inappropriate for clergy, and it was scandalous to Gildas that they ignored the
     precepts of the saints, as of Christ.

16. *pinguedinis gratia taurorum more raucos,*
     et ad illicita infeliciter promptos.
     Their shape indicates that they are given to vitious excess, and this is confirmed by
     their enthusiasm for forbidden fruits.

17. *uultus arroganter in altum habentes,*
     et sensos conscientia remordente ad ima uel tartarum demersos.
     Pride is a besetting sin of theirs, and yet what they are proud of is a mind intent
     upon hell.

18. *uno sane perdito denario maestos,*
    et ad unum inquisitum laetos.
    They behave like misers.

19. *in apostolicis sanctionibus ob inscientiam uel peccatorum pondus*
    ora etiam scientium obturantes—hebetes ac mutos,
    et in flexibus mundialium negotiorum mendacibus doctissimos.
    They fail to communicate the precepts of the apostles, because of ignorance and sin, yet they are very active and skilled in matters of business and politics. What is most interesting about this passage is the clear implication that they are silencing those who, like Gildas, would take a more robust Christian attitude.

20. *quorum de scelerata conuersatione multos sacerdotio irruentes*
    potius uel illud paene omni pecunia redimentes quam tractos.
    This is the opening of an extended treatment of simony. Gildas portrayed priestly and episcopal office as desirable for the corrupt because it opened the door to privilege, wealth, power, and immunity. They purchase these offices from the *tyranni* (III.67, 2) and the practice has become hereditary, therefore institutionalised (III.67, 4). If their fellows (*commessoribus*) in their diocese (*parochiam*) for any reason prevent them from buying such office, they go abroad to find ordination at whatever cost and return home in triumph (III.67, 5-6).

It seems to be no accident that Gildas ended his catalogue of ecclesiastical vices with one which is both a corruption *ab initio* of evil clerics' office-holding and also ties them to the *tyranni* whom, as a class, he had already excoriated, sometimes in very similar terms. His central question (III.75, 3) to clerics may be repeated: "Which of you under the shock of the tyrants kept rigidly to the rule given by the words of the apostle?".

Gildas can summarise his message effectively (III.68): flee from the priests, people! His words addressed to the *tyranni* (II.50, 1) seem applicable here too: "The few who have found the narrow path and left the broad path behind are prevented by God from pouring forth prayers on your behalf as you persevere in evil and so grievously provoke Him" (cf. II.49, 4). What Christ said "to the apostles about evil bishops (*antistitibus*), 'Let them be: they are blind leading the blind...both will fall into a pit'" (III.95, 4, quoting Matthew XV.14), is to be applied here.

De excidio Britanniae closes with Gildas's taking his ecclesiastical audience for Book III through the *ordo* for the consecration of clergy, drawing matter from it to illustrate his theme. His point is that British priests contradict in their behaviour everything said and vowed on that occasion: it is a brilliant, if cruel and damning, climactic conclusion to the whole invective. One imagines that Gildas hoped that this would finally effect what he had sought earlier (III.95, 4): "But which of you would not be wounded in the secret recesses of his heart by the testimony which follows?"

Gildas in the Perspective of his Age

From Gildas's perception of the Church of his day we may conclude that it was, and had for some while been, anchored securely in British society. There was an at least superficially pious laity which was accustomed to almsgiving. The Church's hierarchical structure provided a route to advancement in society, around which fact numerous moral problems clustered. Many of its members, notably including Gildas himself, were very well educated. A close relationship seems to have existed between Church and State. The moral failings of secular rulers might go unchallenged by ecclesiastical leaders: on Gildas's testimony at least, there was no Martin or Ambrose to hand, and if there was a Columbanus it was Gildas himself. There was a monastic or ascetic party in the Church, which Gildas, referring to it rather obliquely, calls very small—in overall influence perhaps rather than necessarily in absolute numbers. But we know that it was the next two generations which saw the Insular explosion of monastic enthusiasm.

In the course of his denunciation of the *tyranni*, Gildas observed (II.38, 5) that "these wicked men...should be proud of themselves for abstaining from conspicuous sacrifice to the gods of the heathen". His immediate point is that they were nonetheless guilty of idolatry in as much as that is defined as "to be recalcitrant towards God". However, the observation about kings' abstention from heathen sacrifice can be taken in two different ways. Either these nominally Christian rulers—and King Maglocunus was, it seems, very much more visibly interested in the practice of his religion than were the other targets of Gildas's wrath—should take no comfort from being baptised and (on the evidence of Gildas's denunciation of the clergy) presumably communicating members of the Church in an ostensibly Christian society; or the kings should claim as a special merit for themselves in the eyes of other Christians that they were not themselves pagans (as, by implication, others in society as well were). Whatever the correct interpretation may be, Gildas leaves us with no sense that inherited paganism (as opposed to the heathenism of the barbarian Saxons) was a threat to the Church or British society.

A comparable problem attends Gildas's endorsement of a predecessor's observation (III.92, 3): "One of us (*quidam nostrorum*) is right to say, 'We greatly desire that the enemies of the Church (*hostes ecclesiae*) be our enemies also, with no kind of alliance (*foedere*), and that [her] friends and protectors be not only our allies (*foederati*) but our fathers and masters (*patres ac domini*) too'". In recent years (since Winterbottom 1978:154; cf. Dumville 1984:81-2) this has been taken as meaning that "we should have no pagan anti-Christian *foederati*, but that our proper allies should be Christian rulers who are defenders of the faith". John Morris, whose words these are (in Winterbottom 1978), added that, "The context is unclear, but seems to rebuke the bishops who favour [a policy of involvement with] anti–Christian *foederati*". This is of course a possible interpretation but the passage can be taken in other ways. First, we should note that it is a quotation and the original context of the remark is at present unknown. Secondly, although we see here language which could be referring to formal alliance and allies it is not clear that its use was exclusively (and still in Gildas's day) technical.[14] Finally, and most importantly, we must note the context in which Gildas deployed this quotation. With the aid of the gospels he is addressing "irregular priests (*inordinatis sacerdotibus*)" (III.92, 2). These are priests who are not "in lawful possession of the apostolic seat" and "who abandon their sheep and pasture them on folly". Such a priest is "no lawful shepherd or even middling (*mediocrem*) Christian". The quotation then follows; in these circumstances its *hostes ecclesiae* would seem to be for Gildas the wicked clergy. It is with such people that there can be no *foedus*. "We" (the party of God, as it

---

[14]   For discussion of the terminology, see Chrysos 1991.

were) desire to have as our rulers only good priests, "supposing that there are many such at the present day" (as Gildas had said a few lines before). It is quite possible, one may add, that Gildas was putting the cited opinion into a wholly new context, but equally likely that he was quoting from a controversialist tract originating in an ascetic faction (as in the case of his quotation from the Pelagian *De uirginitate* in II.38).

In Gildas's account of his own day, the barbarians remain a largely unspoken threat. Unless the sentence just examined does in fact refer to them—in which case we should have to suppose that the policy initiated in the previous century by the *superbus tyrannus* had found either its modern equivalent or its latter-day advocates—the barbarians are confined to the historical narrative which occupies Book I of *De excidio Britanniae*. Their presence in the island ensures that by the *lugubri diuortio* mentioned in I.10 important *loca martyrum* are inaccessible to many Britons. Otherwise their presence on his account is historical, but in such a way that their availability to do God's work of punishing the Britons in their faithlessness to the Almighty is menacingly implied (cf. Hanning 1966). But this is never, I think, made explicit in the *De excidio*.

The barbarians who had been the great threat to the Britons of the last two or three generations (counting also Gildas's own) were "the ferocious Saxons (whose name is not to be spoken!), hated by man and God", "a people whom they feared worse than death even in their absence" (I.23, 1-2). But, apart from some hostile epithets—they are 'wolves', 'lion cubs', 'dogs', 'villains'—the Saxons receive little abuse from Gildas: "an enemy much more savage than the first" (I.2), they are terrible rather than vile. In this the "easterners" (I.24, 1) contrast markedly with "the peoples of the north" (I.23, 1). These make their appearance in I.14: the Britons were "trodden under foot for the first time by two exceedingly savage overseas nations, the Gaels (*Scotti*) from the north-west and the Picts from the north". They were "like greedy wolves, rabid with extreme hunger" (I.16), "wild barbarian beasts" (I.18), "the foul hordes (*tetri...greges*) of Gaels and Picts, like dark throngs of worms who wriggle out of narrow fissures in the rock when the sun is high and the weather grows warm", "they were readier to cover their villanous faces with hair than their private parts and neighbouring regions with clothes" (I.19, 1), and included "impudent Irish pirates" (I.21, 1). Clearly, Gildas had no liking for any of these barbarians—they were, by definition, uncouth and savage: but the language of contempt, of racial hatred, seems applied to "the peoples of the north" while the terror which the Saxons inspired may have given rise to a colder language. For whatever reason, the Gaels and Picts seem not to be part of Gildas's contemporary picture: perhaps they were rhetorically displaced by the more terrible Saxons from any useful role in Gildas's narrative; perhaps they were indeed no longer a major threat to the Britons.

There is then, a paradox in Gildas's relationship to the barbarians, indeed perhaps more than one.[15] As I have argued elsewhere (Dumville 1984:82-3), Gildas seems to have had information about each of the three barbarian peoples which would suggest either first hand knowledge of each or a seeking out of information about them. Unless Gildas, in spite of the general thrust of his argument, was in fact as complacently confident as he alleged his countrymen to have been about their strength vis-à-vis the barbarians, he was surprisingly restrained in not making direct references to them in Books II and III as future instruments of God's wrath. Would there have been a risk of such assertion being considered treasonable?

---

[15] For two important discussions of late Roman attitudes to barbarians, see Brezzi 1961 and Ladner 1976.

The Britons' post-Roman problems had been, in Gildas's eyes, repelling the northern barbarians (Gaels and Picts) and controlling their own moral feebleness. The two problems were of course connected. In so far as slaughter on the "northerners", causing a significant retreat by these barbarian peoples (I.20, 2-3). But when eventually they seemed to be about to return in force, the Britons "convened a council (*initur namque consilium*) to decide the best and soundest way to counter the brutal and repeated invasions and plunderings" (I.22, 3). "Then all the members of the council (*omnes consiliarii*), together with the proud tyrant (*una cum superbo tyranno*) were struck blind" (I.23, 1); what was decided was *excidium patriae*, to hire the Saxons "to beat back the peoples of the north". Using biblical language (Isaiah XIX.Il), Gildas characterised the situation as *stulti principes...dantes...consilium insipiens*, "idiotic princes giving stupid advice" (II.23, 2). Very various, and more or less grandiose, contextual interpretations have been provided for this episode (cf. Dumville 1984, 70-1); but it is easy to take it in terms of overkingship or the exercise of widespread authority (as in the biblical text the princes of Zoan give foolish advice to Pharaoh), with matters of supreme defence of the *patria* being the concern of more than one group of Britons; this interpretation, though by no means assured, coheres with questions about the defence of the north which have recently been asked on the basis of accumulating archaeological evidence (Dark 1992a). Gildas does not seem to have found the concept of British cooperation incredible, only the result.[16] Otherwise, as we have seen, his concern was with the predisposition of British rulers to attack one another rather than barbarian enemies.

Where defence failed in face of barbarian assaults, Gildas's narrative shows us a variety of results: *ciuitates* (apparently in the sense of towns or cities, rather than city-states) abandoned, massacres, civil disorders caused by food-shortages (I.l9, 3-4), famine, surrender, and guerrilla-resistance (I.20, 2-3). Or, on a subsequent occasion, all the *coloniae* were destroyed and the inhabitants killed (I.24, 3-4); some Britons surrendered into slavery, "others made for lands beyond the sea" (1.25, 1 - 26, 1)). Nevertheless, the *ciuitates* (towns and cities, as in I. l 9, 3) remained abandoned and civil war resumed (I.26, 2). The result of the whole process was loss of territory, genocide, and thoroughgoing transformation of the British polity.

The fractured polity which emerged was that of Gildas's latter-day *tyranni*, heirs in usurpation to the likes of Magnus Maximus but having rule only over local areas, whether tribally (*Demetae, Dumnónii*) or regionally defined. Dynasties seem to have emerged, within which a great deal of in-fighting was prone to occur. Gildas gave a variety of examples in his denunciations of the five western kings in II.27-36. He also mentioned the grandchildren of the British leader Ambrosius Aurelianus (I.25, 3) in such a way as to suggest that they might have been comparable with the *tyranni* excoriated in Book II. In effect, then, the medieval polity of the British West had already emerged by Gildas's day, and perhaps two generations before; in the case of kingdoms occupying territory not held by the Romans for some considerable time and even then within the military zone (Dyfed, for example), the political arrangements may have been of some long-standing. From Gildas's descriptions, it seems as though the internal political dynamic of dynasty and segmentation (familiar to us from our knowledge of the Middle Ages) had already emerged, indeed was in effect universal in western Britain. It is also plain that the *comitatus*, the war-band, and its ethic were a result, and a constant cause, of the continual warfare which had become a prominent

---

[16]   Isaiah, quoted here by Gildas, foresees Egypt's servitude to Assyria.

feature in the political life of British society. We have to remember that, alongside Gildas, British society of this period also encompassed the poets who celebrated the warrior aristocracy of the West and North: if Aneirin and Taliesin were historical figures, they were probably younger contemporaries of Gildas; the poetry associated with their names suggests that their patrons' enemies were Anglo-Saxons and other Britons rather than Gaels and Picts, testimony very much in line with what we read in *De excidio Britanniae*. The parasites of the *tyranni* denounced as they both were by Gildas, celebrated their patron's martial deeds. their aristocratic values, and their Christianity, and were very conscious of family. Dynasty and family were becoming the principal determinants of British politics: no reader of either Gildas or British heroic poetry will be surprised by such an assessment.

The Empire and the state had receded from British political consciousness. *Patria* (in the shape of Britain) and *ciues* (the Cymry <*combrogi*, 'fellow-countrymen', Britons) were still prominent and were forces which might occasionally encourage cooperative action. However, the stresses which the British polity had endured since its formal emergence at the beginning of the fifth century had broken it in practice into smaller and often competing units. While the Church might have been in some measure a force for unity, the close association (alleged by Gildas and not at all unbelievable) between *tyranni* and bishops must have tended to particularise religious institutions as well. There too, if Gildas is to be credited, family and heredity were often determinants. But the Church at least had ideological divisions which we see in vigorous action as Gildas's *magnum opus* unfolds before us. There is little evidence in Gildas's account that the established Church had come to grips with the reality of the Germanic barbarian settlers. On the face of it, the Picts had been contained, and there is some evidence that British Christianity had penetrated their territory in the sub-Roman period[17] (Ashmore 1978-80; Thomas 1968). The Gaelic settlers in Britain appear to have been absorbed, even in Dyfed and *Dumnonia* where settlement seems to have been heaviest; Irish raiding and further settlement may also have ceased by Gildas's day, although his testimony gives us little warrant for saying so and omits to mention the process of Christian conversion of Ireland which was proceeding in his day (Dumville 1993). The extent to which the Germanic settlers in Britain had been affected by the natives' Christianity remains quite unknown as yet. A substantial amount of British territory had been seized and settled by the English in the second half of the fifth century and it is not impossible that they enjoyed treaty-relationships with British *tyranni*. It was on the bodies of sub-Roman successor-states, presumably not unlike that in which Gildas lived and those others which he knew, that Germanic power in Britain was established. We are still a long way from understanding the extent to which the culture and institutions of the Britons affected those non-Britons who settled in their territory.

Acknowledgements——I am greatly indebted to Giorgio Ausenda for his invitation to participate in what proved to be an exceptionally stimulating and very enjoyable colloquium, and for all the energy and enthusiasm which he has devoted to the project from inception to publication. To my fellow participants, including Giorgio Ausenda, I am obliged for a variety of helpful observations and references, as well as for the general good humour and range of knowledge which they brought to bear on issues of common interest. And I am very grateful to Nicholas Perkins (Pembroke College, Cambridge), a fellow-enthusiast for Gildas, for reading and commenting on a draft of this paper.

---

[17] On a site of particular interest see Rutherford *et al.* 1974/5 and Cowie 1977/8.

References

Textual sources:

Bede

> *Historia ecclesiastica gentis Anglorum*: see Colgrave *et al.* 1969.
> *Chronicle of AD 452*: see Mommsen 1891-8.

Constantius

> *Life of St Germanus of Auxerre*: see Borius 1965.

Gildas

> *De excidio Britanniae*: see Cazzaniga 1961; Josselin 1567; Vergil 1525; Williams 1899-1901; Winterbottom 1978.

Jordanes

> *Getica*: see Giunta *et al.* 1991.

Pelagian tracts

> *De uirginitate, De uita christiana*: see Rees 1991.

Sidonius Apollinaris

> *Epistolae*: see Anderson 1936/65.

Zosimus

> *Historia nova*: see Paschoud 1971-89.

Bibliography:

Ashmore, P. J.
  1978-80   Low cairns, long cists and symbol stones. *Proceedings of the Soclety of Antiquaries of Scotland* 110: 346-355.

Barker, P.
  1990   *From Roman Viroconium to Medieval Wroxeter. Recent Work on the Site of the Roman City of'Wroxeter*. Worcester: West Mercian Archaeological Consultants.

Bertini, F.
  1984   La storiografia in Britannia prima e dopo Beda. In *Angli e Sassoni al di qua e al di là del mare*. Settimane di studio del Centro italiano di studi sull'alto medioevo, XXXII. Pp. 281-303. Spoleto: C.I.S.A.M.

Borius, R. (ed. & transl.)
  1965   *Constance de Lyon: Vie de saint Germain d'Auxerre*. Paris: Les Éditions du cerf.

Braidotti, C.
  1982   A proposito del termine *conquestus* tramandato nell'opera gildaica. *Quaderni catanesi* 4: 451 -456.
  1986/7   Gildas fra Roma e i barbari. *Romanobarbarica* 9: 25-45.

Brezzi, P.
  1961   Romani e barbari nel giudizio degli scrittori cristiani dei secoli IV-VI. In *Il passaggio dall'antichità al medioevo in Occidente*. Settimane di studio del Centro italiano di studi sull'alto medioevo, IX. Pp. 565-593 631-645. Spoleto: C.I.S.A.M.

Brooks, D. A.
  1983/4   Gildas's *De excidio*. Its revolutionary meaning and purpose. *Studia Celtica* 18/19: 1-10.

Brunhölzl, F.
  1975   *Geschichte der lateinischen Literatur des Mittelalters*. Munich: Wilhelm Fink.
  1990   *Histoire de la littérature latine du moyen age*, I. Turnhout: Brepols.

Bury, J. B.
  1920   The Notitia Dignitatum. *Journal of Roman Studies* 10: 131- 154.

Campbell, J. (ed.)
  1982   *The Anglo-Saxons*. Oxford: Phaidon.

Cazzaniga, I. (ed.)
  1961   *Le prime fonti letterarie dei popoli d'Inghilterra: Gildas e la Historia Brittonum.*
              Milano: La Goliardica.
Chadwick, O.
  1954   Gildas and the monastic order. *Journal of Theological Studies*, N. S. 5: 78-80.
Chrysos, E.
  1991   Die Römerherrschaft in Britannien und ihr Ende. *Bonner Jahrbücher* 191: 247-276.
Colgrave, B., & R. A. B. Mynors (eds. & transl.)
  1969   *Bede's Ecclesiastical History of the English.* Oxford: Clarendon Press.
Collingwood, R. G.
  1922   The Roman evacuation of Britain. *Journal of Roman Studies* 12: 74-98.
Collingwood, R. G., & J. N. L. Myres
  1937   *Roman Britain and the English Settlements.* Oxford: Clarendon Press.
Courcelle, P
  1948/64   *Histoire littéraire des grandes invasions germaniques.* Paris: Études augustiniennes.
Cowie, T.
  1977/8   Excavations at the Catstane, Midlothian, 1977. *Proceedings of the Society of
              Antiquaries of Scotland* 109: 166-201.
Crawford, O. G. S.
  1949   *Topography of Roman Scotland North of the Antonine Wall.* Cambridge: Cambridge
              University Press
Dark, K. R.
  1987   Towards a post-numerate taxonomy. *Nicolay: Arkeologisk Tidskrift* 47: 41-49.
  1992a   A sub-Roman re-defence of Hadrian's Wall? *Britannia* 23: 111-120.
  1992b   Epigraphic, art-historical, and historical approaches to the chronology of Class I
              inscribed stones. In *The Early Church of Wales and the West.* Nancy Edwards &
              A. Lane (eds.), pp. 51-61. Oxford: Oxbow.
  1992c   *The Inscribed Stones of Dyfed.* Llandysul: Gomer.
  1994   *Civitas to Kingdom: British Political Continuity 300-800.* London: Leicester
              University Press.
  1995   *External Contacts and the Economy of Late Roman and Post-Roman Britain.*
              Woodbridge: The Boydell Press.
Drinkwater, J., & H. Elton (eds.)
  1992   *Fifth-century Gaul: A Crisis of Identity?* Cambridge: Cambridge University Press.
Dumville, D. N.
  1973   Biblical apocrypha and the early Irish: a preliminary investigation. *Proceedings of
              the Royal Irish Academy* 73 (C): 299-338.
  1977   Sub-Roman Britain: history and legend. *History*, N. S. 62: 173-194. [Reprinted in
              the same author's *Histories and Pseudo-histories of the Insular Middle Ages.*
              Aldershot: Variorum 1990].
  1984   The chronology of *De excidio Britanniae*, Book I. In *Gildas: New Approaches.*
              M. Lapidge & D. N. Dumville (eds.), pp. 61-84. Woodbridge: The Boydell Press.
              [Reprinted in the same author's *Britons and Anglo-Saxons in the Early Middle Ages.*
              Aldershot: Variorum].
Dumville, D. N., L. Abrams, T. M. Charles-Edwards, A. Correa, K. R. Dark, K. L. Maund,
& A. P. McD. Orchard
  1993   *Saint Patrick, A.D. 493-1993.* Woodbridge: The Boydell Press.
Esmonde Cleary, A. S.
  1989   *The Ending of Roman Britain.* London: Batsford.
Fahy, D.
  1964/5   When did Britons become Bretons? A note on the foundation of Brittany. *Welsh
              History Review* 2: 111 - 124.

Fanning, S.
    1992   Emperors and empires in fifth-century Gaul. In *Fifth-century Gaul: A Crisis of Identity*. J. Drinkwater & H. Elton (eds.), pp. 288-297. Cambridge: Cambridge Univ. Press.
Foord, E.
    1925   *The Last Age of Roman Britain*. London: Harrap.
Fulford, M. G.
    1989   Byzantium and Britain: a Mediterranean perspective on post-Roman Mediterranean imports in western Britain and Ireland. *Medieval Archaeology* 33: 1-6.
Giunta, F., & A. Grillone (eds.)
    1991   *Iordanis de origine actibusque Getarum*. Roma: Istituto storico italiano per il Medio Evo, Palazzo Borromini.
Hanning, R. W.
    1966   The *Vision of History in Early Britain from Gildas to Geoffrey of Monmouth*. New York: Columbia University Press.
Hanson, R. P. C.
    1968   *Saint Patrick, His Origins and Career*. Oxford: Clarendon.
Hogg, A. H. A.
    1951   The Votadini. In *Aspects of Archaeology in Britain and Beyond, Essays presented to O. G. S. Crawford*. W. F. Grimes (ed.), pp. 200-220. London: H. W. Edwards.
Jackson, K.
    1953   *Language and History in Early Britain*. Edinburgh: Edinburgh University Press.
James, E.
    1988   Childéric, Syagrius et la disparition du royaume de Soissons. *Revue archéologique de Picardie* 3-4: 9- 12.
John, E.
    1966   *Orbis Britanniae and Other Studies*. Leicester: Leicester University Press.
Jones, A. H. M.
    1964   *The Later Roman Empire, 284-602: A Social, Economic, and Administrative Survey*. Oxford: Blackwell.
Josselin, J.
    1567   *Gildae, cui cognomentum est sapientis, de excidio et conquestu Britanniae*. London: John Day; reissued 1568.
Kerlouégan, F.
    1987   *Le De excidio Britanniae de Gildas: Les destinées de la culture latine dans l'île de Bretagne au VI siècle*. Paris: Publications de la Sorbonne.
Ladner, G. B.
    1976   On Roman attitudes toward barbarians in late Antiquity. *Viator* 7: 1-26.
Lapidge, M.
    1984   Gildas's education and the Latin culture of sub-Roman Britain. In *Gildas: New Approaches*. M. Lapidge & D. N. Dumville (eds.), pp. 27-50. Woodbridge: The Boydell Press.
Lapidge, M., & D. N. Dumville (eds.)
    1984   *Gildas: New Approaches*. Woodbridge: The Boydell Press.
Lethbridge, T. C.
    1957   The riddle of the dykes. *Proceedings of the Cambridge Antiquarian Society* 51: 1 -5.
Mathisen, R. W.
    1989   *Ecclesiastical Factionalism and Religious Controversy in Fifth-century Gaul*. Washington, DC: Catholic University of America Press.
Matthews, J. F.
    1982/3   Macsen, Maximus and Constantine. *Welsh History Review* 11: 431-448. [Repr. in the same author's *Political Life and Culture in Late Roman Society*. London: Variorum].

Miller, M.
1975   Bede's use of Gildas. *English Historical Review* 90: 241-261.
Mommsen, T. (ed.)
1892-8   *Chronica minora saec. IV, V, VI, VII. Monumenta Germaniae Historica. Auctores antiquissimi,* 9, 11, 13. Berlin: Weidmann.
Morris, J.
1965   Pelagian literature. *Journal of Theological Studies,* N. S. 16: 26-60.
1966   Dark Age dates. In *Britain and Rome. Essays presented to Eric Birley on his Sixtieth Birthday.* M. G. Jarrett & B. Dobson (eds.), pp. 145-185. Kendal: privately printed.
Muhlberger, S.
1990   *The Fifth-century Chroniclers. Prosper, Hydatius and the Gallic Chronicles of 452.* Leeds: Francis Cairns.
Muller, H. F.
1923   On the use of the expression *lingua romana* from the first to the ninth century. *Zeitschrift für romanische Philologie* 43: 9-19.
Muraglia, M
1987   *Gilda "profeta" e il "praesens Israel".* Studi sul De excidio et conquestu Britanniae. Palermo: Università degli Studi.
1992   I valori guida proposti da Gilda nel *De excidio et conquestu Britanniae. Schede medievali* 22/23: 19-42.
Myres, J. N. L.
1964   Wansdyke and the origin of Wessex. In *Essays in British History Presented to Sir Keith Feilin.* H. R. Trevor-Roper (ed.), pp. 1-27. London: Macmillan.
Nash-Williams, V. E.
1950 '   *The Early Christian Monuments of Wales.* Cardiff: University of Wales Press.
Orlandi, G.
1984   *Clausulae* in Gildas's *De excidio Britanniae.* In *Gildas: New Approaches.* M. Lapidge & D. Dumville (eds.), pp. 129-149. Woodbridge: The Boydell Press.
Paris, G.
1872   Romani, Romania, lingua romana, romanicum. *Romania* 1: 1-22.
Paschoud, F.
1967   *Roma Aeterna. Études sur le patriotisme romain dans l'Occident latin à l'époque des grandes invasions.* Roma: Institut suisse de Rome.
1971/89   *Zosime. Histoire nouvelle.* Paris: Les belles lettres.
Rees, B. R. (trans.)
1991   *The Letters of Pelagius and His Followers.* Woodbridge: The Boydell Press.
Reydellet, M.
1981   *La royauté dans la littérature latine de Sidoine Apollinaire à Isidore de Séville.* Rome: École française de Rome.
Riché, P.
1976   *Education and Culture in the Barbarian West from the Sixth through the Eighth Century.* Columbia, SC: University of South Carolina Press.
Richmond, L. A.
1958   *Roman and Native in North Britain.* Edimburgh: Nelson.
Rutherford, A., & G. Ritchie
1975   The Catstane. *Proceedings of the Society of Antiquaries of Scotland* 105 (19724): 183-188.
Rutherford Davis, K.
1982   *Britons and Saxons. The Chiltern Region 400-700.* Chichester: Phillimore.
Salway, P.
1965   *The Frontier People of Roman Britain.* Cambridge: Cambridge University Press.
1981   *Roman Britain.* Oxford: Clarendon.

Santoro, V.
  1991   Sul concetto di *Britannia* tra antichità e medioevo. *Romanobarbarica* 11: 321-334.
Schaffner, P.
  1984   Britain's *iudices*. In *Gildas: New Approaches*. M. Lapidge & D. N. Dumville (eds.),
              pp. 151 - 155. Woodbridge: The Boydell Press.
Schmidt, L.
  1931   Das Ende des Römerherrschaft in Britannien. *Historisches Jahrbuch* 51: 213-215.
Simpson, G.
  1964   *Britons and the Roman Army: A Study of Wales and the Southern Pennines in the 1st-
              3rd Centuries*. London: Gregg.
Sims-Williams, P.
  1984   Gildas and vernacular poetry. In *Gildas: New Approaches*. M. Lapidge & D. N.
              Dumville (eds.), pp. 169-192. Woodbridge: The Boydell Press.
Sutherland, A. C.
  1984   The imagery of Gildas's *De excidio Britanniae*. In *Gildas: New Approaches*.
              M. Lapidge & D. N. Dumville (eds.), pp. 157-168. Woodbridge: The Boydell Press.
Thomas, A. C.
  1968   The evidence from North Britain. In *Christianity in Britain, 300-700*. M. W. Barley
              & R. P. C. Hanson (eds.), pp. 93-121. Leicester: Leicester University Press.
  1981   *Christianity in Roman Britain to AD 500*. London: Batsford.
  1990   'Gallici nautae de Galliarum provinciis' - a sixth/seventh century trade with Gaul
              reconsidered. *Medieval Archaeology* 34: 1-26.
Thompson, E. A.
  1977   Britain, A.D. 406-410. *Britannia* 8: 303-318.
  1979   Gildas and the history of Britain. *Britannia* 10: 203-226.
  1982   *Romans and Barharians. The Decline of the Western Empire*. Madison, WI:
              University of Wisconsin Press.
  1984   *Saint Germanus of Auxerre and the End of Roman Britain*. Woodbridge The Boydell
              Press.
Vergil, P. (ed.)
  1525   *Opus nouum Gildas brittannus monachus....* Antwerpen.
Wade-Martins, P.
  1974   The linear earthworks of west Norfolk. *Norfolk Archaeology* 36 (1974-7): 23-38.
Williams, H. (ed. & trans.)
  1899-1901   *Gildas*. London: Honourable Society of Cymmrodorion.
Winterbottom, M. (ed. & trans.)
  1978   *Gildas: The Ruin of Britain and Other Works*. Chichester: Phillimore.
Wood, I. N.
  1987   Review of Reydellet 1981. *Speculum* 62: 984-985.
Wright, N.
  1984a   Gildas's geographical perspective: some problems. In *Gildas: New Approaches*.
              M. Lapidge & D. N. Dumville (eds.), pp. 85-105. Woodbridge: The Boydell Press.
  1984b   Gildas's prose style and its origins. In *Gildas: New Approaches*. M. Lapidge &
              D. N. Dumville (eds.), pp. 107-128. Woodbridge: The Boydell Press.
  1985   Did Gildas read Orosius? *Cambridge Medieval Celtic Studies* 9: 31 -42.
  1991   Gildas's reading: a survey. *Sacris Erudiri* 32: 121-162.
Zeiller, J.
  1929   L'apparition du mot *Romania* chez les écrivains latins. *Revue des études latines*
              7: 194-198.

Discussion

WOOD: I think that where the work of Evangelos Chrysos (1991) is useful from your point of view is on the fifth century. Where people who work on Continental material have not drawn comparisons between the Continent and Britain is for the sixth century. Perhaps that is partly because the Germanic kingdoms of the period are so different from anything presented in the *De excidio*. If I might just follow on from the point about Chrysos, I think you do underestimate the amount of work done, the number of comparisons between Gildas and the Continental sources made by people working on the fifth century. Strictly speaking you are right to say he is largely unknown to Continental scholars, when you mean scholars who are living on the Continent—but that is partly because it is very, very difficult to find a Continental scholar since Pierre Courcelle (1964) who has written anything about the political history of the fifth century on the Continent: it has not been an industry.

DUMVILLE: As opposed to political theory.

WOOD: As opposed to political theory. And, therefore, you have not got people picking up the questions of whether there are parallel developments on the Continent. Of course, in terms of anglophone scholarship there is much more. There are, for example, one or two useful points in Steven Muhlberger's book (1990) on the fifth-century Gallic chronicles. He has noticed some very interesting parallels with Gildas, but it is only a few pages in his book. Edward Thompson (1982) has drawn some quite striking parallels between Hydatius on Spain and the evidence from Britain.

DUMVILLE: Yes, but I must say that I find it problematic to use fifth-century Spain for comparative purposes, not because the situation was not similar—it may have been very similar—but because it seems to me exceptionally difficult to get a handle on what was happening in its political history at that period.

WOOD: Well, it is the same for Spain as for Britain, and I think that Muhlberger's book helps quite a lot, I should like to pursue that a little bit more. It seems to me that with regard to some of the parallels with the Continent there are one or two points which may be picked up. You talk about Gildas and Magnus Maximus and say, "Here is the origin of subsequent Brittonic political theory". One of the things which Muhlberger has done— devastatingly well, I think—in his book on the fifth-century chronicles is to point out that the 'Chronicle of 452' does exactly the same. And the interesting thing is, if you accept my published argument, that the 'Chronicle of 452' may have been written by Faustus of Riez, it may, therefore, be in some sense a British text. Muhlberger is also interesting on the question of how the chroniclers picked up biblical history. Again, the fifth century moralists are already doing something which Gildas is going to do. Whether one is to conclude that there is a direct influence or not, I have a couple of Continental parallels. You say, "What is new by comparison with the ancient record is the exclusive role of the Church...". That is precisely the sort of area in which the Gallic councils are already significant in the fifth century; it is something which is developing within the ecclesiastical tradition. And then you go on to say, "The possibility is...that the king might take monastic vows"; of course there is a king who has just taken monastic vows on the Continent, Sigismund who takes his in 521.

DUMVILLE: Yes, thank you. That is all extremely helpful: the fifth-century 'anticipations' of Gildas's thinking are of great interest and importance and will need careful assessment. This leads me to wonder further about Cassian.

WOOD: The influence of Cassian's thought on Gildas, to which you have drawn attention, is interesting because Cassian was a teacher of Faustus of Riez.

DUMVILLE: You are putting Faustus at the centre of a very interesting stage!

WOOD: Moving on, I always see red with people who tell me that Riothamus has something to do with the creation of Brittany. He went to Orléans and then to Lyon; how he created Brittany I just do not see.

DUMVILLE: In seeing red you are missing the point, which is a very simple one. It seems to me that there are two possibilities which I have laid out quite clearly. Riothamus's presence on the Continent has been taken as occurring in the context of British migration thither. In other words, his availability in Gaul, as I think I put it here, can be seen in that context, if you think that context appropriate to the period *ca* 470. The position is not that he himself was leading a force which ultimately ended up in Brittany, which (it is perfectly clear) he did not, as you say. The other possibility is that he was in Gaul in a political context which has nothing to do with migration: this ought to be thought about. I should not want to stick my neck out in either direction at present. I do not think I need to, and do not think I have done here.

WOOD: Another point on page [182] where you followed Steven Fanning on Aegidius as *rex Romanorum*: I think that that is extremely difficult. Fanning has only a late sixth century source relating to a mid-fifth century figure, and there is nothing in the works of Sidonius or anybody else to say that Aegidius was regarded as *rex Romanorum* in his own day. One of the things which always strikes me is that one tends to put the parents of Ambrosius Aurelianus in a different category from the *tyranni*. It seems to me they must have been usurpers just as every other ruler was. I want to signal they are not entitled to assume that they were different.

DUMVILLE: Can I just come back on the last point? The *parentes* of Ambrosius Aurelianus had worn the purple, and might have been emperors in Britain. By definition, therefore, they would be *tyranni*. I shall gladly take that point: thanks very much; it is extremely helpful.

GREEN: I am uncertain what you mean by speaking of the "process of barbarisation of the sub-Roman world". Do you mean it was "now barbarian"? Or that his world, because it was sub-Roman, had "always been barbarian"?

DUMVILLE: I am thinking in terms of the features which elsewhere in the sub Roman world one would describe as developing from a barbarian element, but which, in Gildas's chunk of Britain, have to be explained by native developments and therefore, for example, the emergence of royal *duces* with warrior-bands, the *comitatus*-question. I am using 'barbarisation' in the general sense, not in the sense of incoming '*barbari*'.

GREEN: You talk about a *dux* becoming a king. How early within your British context are vernacular terms for a *dux* and a king attested and can those earliest attested terms be traced back and applied to the period of Gildas?

DUMVILLE: The difficulty is that you get into a very large problem about kingship terminology which has not been entirely satisfactorily sorted out yet, either in terms of the historical development of the words used in Brittonic or in terms of how one relates that to modern English usage. What I could not offer you from the pre-twelfth-century period is a word which would convey the sense of *dux* in anything other than its most general sense of leader. What we have, instead, is a variety of kingship-terminology attested from the mid sixth century (if you are prepared to accept the heroic poetry attributed to the sixth century as having a basis in that era), contemporary with Gildas, otherwise the first contemporary sources are going to be in the ninth century. The position has been vastly improved in the last few months by the appearance of Thomas Charles-Edwards's book (1993a) on Irish and Welsh kinship, all 700 pages of it, in which much which bears on this particular matter has been discussed; but he has not in that book pursued the terminology at all levels of political authority. One of the most suggestive pieces of work, though combining earlier and later Celtic evidence, is his paper, 'Native political organisation in Roman Britain', in the memorial volume for Manfred Mayrhofer, *Antiquitates indogermanicae* (1974).

GREEN: There is a parallel to which I should like to draw your attention. You spoke about the sense of sub-Roman continuity with the Roman and pre-Roman periods, and then you go on to the Old Testament. I should like to draw your attention to Otfrid von Weissenburg's version of the New Testament, written in the 860s: in his prologue he set aside the eastern Franks, for whom he was writing, from the western Franks. He argued that they were the equivalent of the Romans and the Greeks and, indeed, traced their origin back to Alexander, on top of that he discussed the three holy languages but mentioned by name only Greek and Latin, not Hebrew. Instead, he insinuated the Frankish tongue. It might be dubious to argue there on the basis of negative evidence that he was excluding Hebrew, save for the fact in that same passage he described the wealth and prosperity of the east Frankish kingdom in terms taken from the Old Testament for the description of the Promised Land, thus making much more explicit his argument that the Franks had taken over from the Jews as the chosen people. I mention this simply as a parallel which may or may not be useful to you.

DUMVILLE: Thank you very much.

GREEN: You have spoken about the massive impact of Latin on the British vernacular dialects. Can you tell us what are the main lexical categories in which Latin makes its massive impact on the British vernaculars?

DUMVILLE: No, because I would be listing just about everything. There are several pages in Kenneth Jackson's (1953) *Language and History of Early Britain* where the categorisation is effected, and the place to which I referred is his summary. One can argue about some of the ways in which he has categorised words, and Patrick Sims-Williams had a certain amount of fun in 1984 doing just that. There was a significant impact on morphology as well.

GREEN: You make it sound as far, far greater than in any Germanic dialect.

DUMVILLE: There are those Celtic philologists who like to say, only half in jest, that Neo-Brittonic is in effect a Romance language.

GREEN: What are the British vernacular terms for the *comitatus*? Are such terms attested and, if so, when?

DUMVILLE: The principal term is Welsh *teulu*, which is from British Celtic **tegoslougos* 'house host'. That is the word which runs right through the tradition of Welsh heroic poetry from its sixth-century origins to the demise of the tradition of writing panegyrics for war leaders in the late thirteenth century. Alongside it you get the use simply of the word *llu*, 'host'. Because of our uncertainty as to the nature of British military organisation in the sub-Roman period, it is not clear whether this implies a distinction from *teulu*.

GREEN: You mean 'host' in the sense of an 'army'?

DUMVILLE: Yes. Now I dare mention Riothamus again. If you can come back usefully to the questions of size of the force of which he might have disposed, we might be onto something interesting. But there is no direct information, of which I am aware which would tell us anything about the size of British armies or, more directly, about what may stand behind the military activities of the royal leader's personal military retinue, whether we are dealing with a relatively small raiding band, or group of shock-troops, or whether we have the possibility, as we certainly do at a later date, in Welsh history at any rate, of the raising of a larger army on a different basis.

GREEN: A last question. You say that Germanic settlers in England were not affected by native Christianity. Is there no linguistic evidence at all for that?

DUMVILLE: There can be an archaeological argument for it, but the linguistic evidence which has been adduced over the last 30 years amounts to just one thing, the appearance within English place-names, of the Primitive Welsh element *egles*, from Latin *ecclesia*, which has survived in an untidy and very small distribution in eastern England, somewhat more favourably between the Severn and the Ribble, and then a fair collection up the eastern coast of Scotland, which raises other issues about the relationships between the Britons and the Picts. The problem is that which emerges from all attempts to interpret Brittonic elements within what are ultimately English place-names. These are not vast and numerous, but they are there, more or less, all over England. As to how you interpret the survival of a Celtic element in a variety of situations, the classic example is *penn*, 'hill'. Do these *egles*-names imply in each case the existence and the continuation of an identifiable Christian site with perhaps a Christian community attached to it, or can they also be read as pieces of information acquired at certain points, which do not necessarily imply continuity? Scholars hit upon these items of evidence and then rush to a conclusion, because they are rarities, and because some scholars are interested in demonstrating a degree of continuity which often does not seem to be justified.

HINES: The place-name 'Eccles' is the only item which I would have put forward. It does not provide definite evidence for significant influence upon the English, only for some sort of contact between them and late Roman Christianity in the area which was to become the heartland of early Anglo-Saxon England.

DUMVILLE: If I remember right, there are about 25 of these over length and breadth of what in the Anglo-Saxon period was England, and then a number more farther north.

GREEN: Thank you.

WOOD: Can I pick up the *comitatus* question? I should have thought that the best contrast with Riothamus is Ecdicius of Clermont. Ecdicius is a little bit like Falstaff, in the sense that in the first description of his defeat of the Visigoths he is said to have eighteen men, and that goes down to ten men when he next appears. But it is quite clear that in this case we see a late Roman military official who had his own *comitatus*.

DUMVILLE: The word is not used by Gildas at all, as far as I know.

WOOD: It would be worth checking Sidonius's references to Ecdicius. What is clear is that Ecdicius's *comitatus* was very small. What is equally clear is that Riothamus's force was very large. You do not have to believe Jordanes, but the fact that Riothamus's troops, when billeted in *Lugdunensis*, were causing absolute mayhem with the locals suggests that this is something much more like an army. Law-suits arose because the Britons were seizing slaves belonging to Gallo-Roman aristocrats. The very fact that Ecdicius, and Aegidius farther north, could organise themselves into beating barbarians when they wanted, suggests that, if they could not defeat Riothamus, his was a very sizeable troop.

DUMVILLE: The question then is: was it all deployed from Britain? To that there is no answer. But certainly there was a fleet.

AUSENDA: It seems that you two would coincide if Gildas had written at the end of the fifth century or the beginning of the sixth.

DUNVILLE: It depends what you mean by coincide [laughter].

WOOD: There is complication in that particular question, because I date Gildas slightly earlier than does David, and I am unrepentant in doing it—although I should push him back only twenty years. I think that the interesting thing is that the picture provided by Gildas seems to show what might have happened in Gaul if the barbarians had not seized control of the Roman power-structures and made them work. One point which strikes me more and more is that Merovingian *Francia* is more Roman in 600 than it had been in 500, that the barbarians in general made Roman government work from the mid-sixth century onward. It was in the wars of the fifth century that everything went to pot. Potentially if Ecdicius and Aegidius and their like had gone on doing what they were doing, probably Gaul would have ended up with exactly what we see in Gildas's Britain.

DUMVILLE: I agree in principle, but I see one extra element which complicates the picture. It would be fine if Gildas had been writing about any lowland British political unit. The trouble is that he appears to be describing directly, in respect to his own time rather than in his peculiar historical survey, either areas which may have managed to keep their native political organisation throughout the Roman period and others which were sufficiently close to them to have that model available. What I suppose to have happened farther to the east was that you had processes of creation of the institutions of government out of the government of the *ciuitates* or out of the possibilities of the behaviour of local strongmen, people using their clients, rather the way you talk about Ecdicius. But of course, all that is lost to us, and we are dealing with a stage further on: this is one of the reasons why it is so difficult to compare Gildas with the Continental fifth century, because we need a British fifth century as well. We have essentially to hypothesise what was happening in the British fifth century. There is a long-standing question amongst students of Welsh literature and early medieval British culture in general as to why it was that Britons saw poets of the sub Roman North, Aneirin and Taliesin, as the founders of British poetry. It strikes me that these poets were performing in areas where the native tradition of rulership had in some cases the possibility, in some cases the certain fact, of continuity through the Roman period. Whatever would have emerged in the sub-Roman South-east, or in East Anglia, for example, would have been based much more on a romanising tradition than these Northern poets were. So the lost British fifth century is in part a key to what Gildas.was seeing and talking about, but in part the key to it is native, and in the long term Celtic. To what extent could that have been the case in Gaul where there would not have been a model of native, of Gaulish, rulership available?

WOOD: I am not so very certain about that. You are right if you are talking about Marseilles or somewhere like that; but Clermont, for example, has no Roman history to speak of before the fifth century, and it is every bit as much highland zone as northern England, in fact very much higher than any major English settlement.

DUMVILLE: But the facts of physical geography are not what I am talking about. We have two kinds of evidence for Britain which have indicated that native political structures, from top to bottom of the pre-Roman scale, could have continued: one is from those areas never under Roman rule, in the case of the *Uotadini*, for example, where it is generally thought that this was a client state-arrangement throughout the Roman period; then we have the areas in which there appears to have been Roman withdrawal, argued purely on archaeological evidence, in the third century, perhaps even in the late second, from the highland regions of the north and west, and where the possibility therefore exists of an interrupted continuity of British political institutions. Could any such case be made for a 'highland' area of Gaul, or would it be unimaginable?

WOOD: I do not think it is unimaginable, no. You cannot get it on the political terms because we know very little about the internal political arrangements of any Gallic *ciuitas*. But you could get at it from another point of view. There are some very, very strange late saints' lives concerning the mountainous zone above Clermont, which suggest a very archaic pattern of control of transhumance, which links with religion. And quite clearly this Celtic religion was simply being christianised. Equally, alongside Clermont I should like to put Galicia. It is unfortunate we have only Hydatius' view of Galicia because Hydatius was like Gildas: he had Roman-style patriotism. But it is quite clear that he does not represent the normal viewpoint.

DUMVILLE: What worries me in that argument is making the leap from cultural continuity, however broadly defined, to continuity of political authority at an uppermost level which I, looking from the outside, find it difficult to imagine that the Imperial government would have been content with. But this may be much too simplistic a view of Imperial government.

WOOD: I think the modern understanding of Imperial government is moving the way in which you are reading the situation in Britain. I am thinking of the work of Peter Garnsey in particular.

HINES: Can I just try and open up your dialogue a little? First of all taking up the point which you two have just been discussing, I think that, when one talks of continuity of native rulership within Britain, one should not give the impression that this is continuity without change. There is bound to be development over time, as indeed we see in the archaeological record. By the fifth century, with the re-occupation of hill-fort sites, there are physical manifestations of power-structures changing quite markedly. Where you talk about rulers in independent Britain, you say: "...their hostility toward the Roman diocese...in principle may be assumed". I should not consider the assumption unrealistic, but it might be rather too simple, especially since you mentioned the probable client-status of the *Uotadini*. The ability of client groups to be hostile towards the Roman state when it suited them, and equally their ability to be friendly when it suited them, could be usefully pointed out. Is there any good evidence, rather than pure probability, of any other group than the *Uotadini* having this sort of relationship with Roman Britain?

DUMVILLE: Where it has been argued, but not proved, is for the *Dumnonii* the ancestors of the people of the kingdom of Dumbarton/Strathclyde. The argument for the *Uotadini* has sometimes been put in terrns of evidence from Brittonic documentation and it seems to me that that argument simply will not stand. The argument which I accepted, instead, is essentially based on continuity at Traprain Law and the conspicuous consumption of Roman material on that site and the other principal sites in Uotadinian territory. I suspect this pattern of interpretation may have gone a little too far in writing about Britain. Indeed, it is being carried to new lengths: it has been hypothesised by Gordon Maxwell (1975) in recent times that the *Uotadini* were even encouraged to expand into southern Picts' land by the Romans, in other words that their friendly status introduced a military-client relationship which encouraged forward movement. I certainly take your qualification, however.

HINES: I was interested to see that you referred to writers like Claudian and Salvian as sources to go to to find parallels to Gildas's attitudes towards rulership. Are there any other clear definite sources for political theory?

DUMVILLE: It is not, I think, that one goes back to Claudian and to Salvian—two more different authors it would be difficult to imagine, deliberately singling them out. But ideas emerge from these particular writers which can find points of comparison or contrast in what Gildas is saying. The generic difference between Claudian the panegyrist, and then Salvian or Gildas who, in terms of the nature of their writing, can be compared much more easily, is very great. And I imagine that Claudian, had he been around in the sixth century, might have been denounced by Gildas as a parasite! In terms of relationship to barbarian government, what I should like to put my finger on is whether there is any developing sense in political thought, as expressed in a literary way, of what might have underpinned the activities of local aristocrats who, given suitable circumstances, might have taken supreme political power into their own hands in the regions. That is for me where the real difficulty lies, because that would be the necessary and the most interesting immediate point of comparison with Gildas. Instead, one is working on a much, much larger context, where it is difficult to see what is precisely relevant, and yet everything in a changing situation is in some ways directly relevant.

WOOD: This leads to a point I have been wanting to raise. The panegyrics are obviously an excellent source for looking at what the Empire wanted to say. Strictly speaking, one might remark that the only piece of political thought available is in Book 19 of the *De ciuitate Dei*, where Augustine demolished Varro; this is one of the crucial texts because it helped to spawn what you might call his anti-political thought. Otherwise, it seems to me that the real piece of political thought is not Salvian's *De gubernatione Dei*, but his *Epistola ad Timotheum*. I have never understood why E. A. Thompson did not treat it at length. That is the 'Marxist' work par excellence: it denies inheritance; it is the most remarkable document.

DUMVILLE: This would also be true of the political content of Pelagian literature and in some measure of the Priscillianist tracts.

WOOD: Sure, sure, except, in the latter case, there is the problem how much is Priscillian's own. You raised also the question of non-Imperial political thought, and that ties up with your question of patriotism. Sidonius is absolutely clear on the patriotism of the *Aedui*. He had a particular patriotism in respect of Autun, his mother's city, distinct from his attitude to Lyon, his father's city. There is already patriotism in fifth-century writers.

DUMVILLE: Surely, and this again can be taken in terms of the *ciuitas-patria* identification. I have not homed in on that, and obviously I should have done, because there is a point in this recurrence to what one can look at as pre-Roman forms of identity and organisation. But what I looked for in vain is identification beyond that, to whether the Roman provinces have created some form of identity.

WOOD: No, but of course the Roman provinces of Gaul were repeatedly redivided and reorganised in the century after 284. They effectively double in number. Accordingly it is not very surprising that we do not meet that sort of identification.

DUMVILLE: They were altered thus also in Britain. What do you make of that repeated assertion of Edward Thompson's (1979), that before the fifth century to contemplate writing a history of a province or a diocese of the Empire would have been in effect treasonable, that it was neither the one form of traditional identification nor the other? It would in some sense be racially based and non-Roman and therefore, as he said, treasonable. It is a striking statement. I am not sure how to handle it.

WOOD: I think that it is very arresting, but it might need modifying. In certain areas, geography might have made such writing possible. I could imagine a fourth-century history of Spain.

DUMVILLE: One of the reasons of posing this question about identification with a larger unit is not simply wanting to find a parallel to what Gildas seems to have been doing or reflecting. For Gaul Caesar provided the necessary material to help us. What he wrote about Chartres as the navel of Gaul, and our ability to parallel that in other Celtic areas and Celtic cultures, does suggest that Gaul could be perceived by natives as a unit by its native inhabitants.

WOOD: That is true. See Ausonius's work, for example. You can write an epic poem on the cities of Gaul. You just do not happen to put 'history' in it.

AUSENDA: I was not clear about what you said concerning Gildas's view of the difference between the Britons' fear of Gaels and Picts on the one hand and of the Saxons on the other. You observed that the real threats from overseas were Gaels and Picts, but then you stated that Saxon barbarians remained an unspoken threat. Were the Britons more afraid of the Saxons or of the Picts and Gaels?

DUMVILLE: For Gildas, the barbarians are the Gaels, (*Scotti*), the Picts and *Saxones*. They are all clearly barbarians for him. They come into two separable categories in Gildas's thinking. The language used of the Picts and Gaels is of a different quality from that which he employed about the Saxons. I do not know exactly what that reflects. Perhaps there was a long-standing British contempt for their native neighbours, the Picts (to the north) and the Gaels (initially to the west, but also later to the north) while the Saxons represent a new threat, at least to the western Britons, and come with a long (one or two-century) sequel of stories about them; they may have inspired more terror than contempt. I am trying to speculate from the two ways in which Gildas wrote of the two groups. For his own day one gets no sense that the *Scotti* and the *Picti* are an immediate threat, whereas one certainly does have hovering in the background all the time the threat posed by the *Saxones*.

AUSENDA: The Saxons may have been menacing, but the Britons made treaties with them against the Gaels and Picts.

DUMVILLE: They may have made treaties with them. We have two types of evidence. There is what Gildas himself has to say about the *superbus tyrannus* who devised a plan which was *excidium patriae*, to settle Saxon federates on Brittonic territory as a counterbalance to what he calls the northern people, in other words the Picts and Gaels. Then from the seventh century we have specific evidence for political linkage in specific military alliances betwen Britons and English, in the complicated religious situation where some of the English were Christian and some not, and the Britons were. From the eighth century, in the context of a generally Christian Insular polity, we have evidence for strategic alliances across the whole length of Britain between different political groups, regardless of what their racial background is. Given that long history, if we take on board what Gildas wrote about that *superbus tyrannus* it is possible that in his day such linkages were being made. But we cannot demonstrate the point. It was that undoubtedly which provoked John Morris (Winterbottom 1978:154, footnote) into his argument he made about *foedus* in the third book of the *De excidio* in a context which may not apply to that situation at all.

AUSENDA: It looks as if the Saxons, being settled within Britain, were despised for their crude customs, but, just as the Roman government had already done with other Germanic barbarians, were used for defence against outside groups, such as Gaels and Picts, who, because they lived farther away from the Britons, were feared as a continuing threat. There is a parallel for this in the attitude which Dalmatian and Istrian Italians had, and Triestini still have, to Slavs who live in the countryside surrounding their cities: they might be fearful of their numbers and proximity, but they despise them for their uncouth mores.

DUMVILLE: The Picts may have been far away but they seem to have developed a maritime capability, at least in this period, and the Gaels were not far away. The Irish Sea was open to this kind of activity. There were Irish settlers on the British mainland. But, what Gildas never stated in the *De excidio* is that there was British missionary activity in Ireland in his day. One presumes that colleagues of his were involved in that. And that may have some bearing on what in his writing can be read as a diminution of the threat from the West.

TURTON: On the question of relationship, what one can gather about the attitude of Britons to their various neighbours is fascinating. The picture which I get is that the Britons felt morally superior to the Gaels and Picts but perhaps they did not to the Saxons. They despised the Gaels and Picts, but feared and hated the Saxons. In other words, the Gaels and Picts were a military threat, but not a political one, but the Saxons were a political threat also; the Britons saw them as potentially taking them over. That would tie in, perhaps, with Bede's comments that they so hated the Saxons that they were not motivated to convert them: it looks a little peculiar that they should instead wish to convert those whom they despised, unless one sees missionary activity as closely associated with political occupation or colonialism. If Gildas was reflecting a general view, and perhaps he was not, the different attitudes could be explained as fear of the political takeover versus the exasperation with a long-standing nuisance.

DUMVILLE: Yes, this makes a lot of sense in a variety of ways. The central problem, on which you have put your finger, is the extent to which Gildas is typical or whether his political axe(s) to grind, both in the ecclesiastical and in the secular context, so coloured his views that we have to allow the possibility that his ideas are untypical. There is another element to this and it is one which has to be well known to students of Celtic languages, but which I have never seen stated anywhere—that in the fifth century, British and Irish must have been mutually intelligible; in the sixth century they may have been; and in the seventh century, it is absolutely inconceivable that they were. The changes were so great that the languages became mutually unintelligible.

GREEN: Changes on both sides?

DUMVILLE: Yes, drastic changes on both sides. The beginnings of British missionary work in Ireland, which are complicated and lacking a well understood background, must have started on the basis of mutual intelligibility and of similarities in the social structure, and so on. That provides a context of contact—and to some extent mutual identification— which can also be seen on the British mainland in areas where Gaels are settling. It is one of the oddities of scholarship that nobody has ever addressed in a direct way the colonial situation in western Britain where there were Irish settlements and where we have clearest archaeological and linguistic evidence for those settlements. But these were assimilated fairly rapidly and became British even in areas where we are tolerably certain that there was Irish political dominance. I assume that the linguistic and social similarities had a great deal to do with that. There is always lurking behind that a problem of numbers which looms large in such discussion as there is about what happened to Britons in the area seized by Anglo-Saxons.

TURTON: Is there any evidence about the motivations of this missionary activity? I do not mean the individuals involved, but some kind of larger pattern. How did it fit in with the political reality?

DUMVILLE: This unfortunately has to come from separate angles because of the circumstances. There is a general background which has just received a shot in the arm from a paper published this year by Thomas Charles-Edwards (1993b), which has to do with the willingness of the papacy and of the Church at large and, in the fifth century context, of Imperial political leadership to contemplate missionary work. And the first bishop whom we know of in Ireland, Palladius, was sent from the Continent. But of the Britons whom we know as having been involved in missionary work in Ireland, though more in the sixth and seventh centuries than in the fifth, St Patrick is the most prominent. And in his case we are talking, because of the nature of the source-material, exclusively about his personal motivations, his personal mission. Scholars have made passing speculations about whether it was ever thought that if Christianity was carried to neighbouring peoples they would calm down and stop their attacks on neighbouring Christian peoples.

TURTON: Christianity would take them over in some sense?

DUMVILLE: Yes. But this has never been more than a passing speculation, because it is very difficult to see how to demonstrate the possibility.

GREEN: And that position would not hold for the Germanic settlers if the Britons refused to proselytise among them.

TURTON: The Saxons were not so much despised, but hated and feared because they were seen as potentially the politically dominant group.

DUMVILLE: Or, in Gildasian or Salvianic terms, if the Saxons were perceived as having a moral superiority. That is hardly likely to have been the position of the mass of the Britons, but, for some faction among them, such as that represented by Gildas, it is not an unimaginable attitude.

TURTON: I can think of examples from the ethnographic record, when the members of one group hate another, they may have a certain respect for it; being afraid of that second group's violence, they fear its members as their equals and possibly their superiors, recognising the ability of that group to take over. On the other hand, different groups may be feared because they can cause havoc, but they may be regarded by the first as almost sub-human and therefore despised—the sort of epithets would be used to describe them which Gildas used against the Gaels and Picts.

DUMVILLE: The Britons would have had every possible reason to fear the Anglo-Saxons.

HINES: A possible afterword which could be added to this is that the Saxons had their own attitude to Britons. Some Old English words, not least *walh* (which gives Modern English 'Welsh'), shows a very clear contempt and a sense of the very low status of those who were regarded as Welsh. If that were general at the right time, I should imagine that any British mission to the Saxons would have had little chance of success for that reason at that moment.

DUMVILLE: The glee with which Bede descended upon Gildas's testimony to justify the English takeover of much of Britain is very clear evidence that Gildas's message was used, later at least, in that kind of way. In terms of mission-fear a parallel might be with what was happening in England in the later ninth century when Vikings were making themselves manifest. There is a moment at which ecclesiastical organisation at its uppermost level started disappearing under the impact of Scandinavian invasion and settlement. There may have been a period of ten, fifteen, even twenty years (870 x 890) in which the English ecclesiastical establishment was mentally, perhaps morally, paralysed. And then a process got under way, which we cannot see at all but by which the Scandinavian settlers began to be converted to Christianity. What we do have is a wonderful letter from Pope Formosus, who wrote to the English episcopate, "Having heard that the abominable rites of the pagans have sprouted again in your territories and that you kept silent 'like dogs unable to bark', we have considered striking you from the body of the Church of God with the sword of separation". If we are talking about terror, and I should argue we have every reason to consider fifth-and sixth-century relations between British and Anglo-Saxons in such terms then we have good reasons for the picture which Bede's testimony offers.

GREEN: I fully take the point about the derogatory implications of the word 'Welsh', but I should not like to take the further step of supposing that for that reason Anglo-Saxons would not have been prepared to receive Christianity from the Britons, because I am struck by the initial process of conversion of the Goths—they were converted by prisoners of war and slaves.

WOOD: I just wonder whether there is not some sort of metaphorical bind in which people like Gildas could be caught. Gildas might have thought about evangelising. He was pious enough to become a missionary. But he also decries the Saxons as the scourge of God. Many ecclesiastics at a later date took the same view about the Vikings. How can one think about evangelising the scourge of God? This might be a parallel to the point which you are making. I do not know whether in that period anybody would have dared to evangelise the scourge of God.

DUMVILLE: That is wonderful! [Laughter].

References in the discussion

Textual sources:

Augustin
        De ciuitate Dei: see Mc Cracken *et al.* 1957/72.
Ausonius:
        see Evelyn White 1919/21.
Bede
        Historia ecclesiastica gentis Anglorum: see references at end of paper.
Caesar
        De bello gallico: see Edwards 1917.
Claudian:
        see Platnauer 1922.
Formosus
        Letter of Pope Formosus to the bishops of England: see Birch (ed.) 1885/93; Whitelock 1979 (trans.).
Hydatius
        Chronicon: see references at end of paper.
Otfrid von Weissenburg:
        see Erdmann 1962.
Salvian
        De gubernatione Dei and Epistola ad Timotheum: see Dekkers *et al.* 1961.
Sidonius Apollinaris
        Epistolae: see Anderson 1936/65.

Bibliography:

Anderson, W. E. (ed. & trans.)
  1936/65   *Sidonius: Poems and Letters.* Cambridge, MA: Harvard University Press.
Birch, W. de G. (ed.)
  1885/93   *Cartularium saxonicum*, (II. 214-216 (no. 573)). London: Whiting.

Charles-Edwards, T. M.
   1974   Native political organization in Roman Britain and the origin of MW *brenhin*.
               In *Antiquitates indogermanicae*. M. Mayrhofer, W. Meid, B. Shlerath & R. Schmitt
               (eds.), pp. 35-45. Innsbruck: Institut für Sprachwissenschaft der Universität
               Innsbruck.
   1993a   *Early Irish and Welsh Kinship*. Oxford: Clarendon Press.
   1993b   Palladius, Prosper, and Leo the Great: mission and primatial authority. In *Saint
               Patrick, A.D. 493-1993*. D. N. Dumville *et al.* (eds.), pp. 1-12. Woodbridge: The
               Boydell Press.
Chrysos, E.
   1991   See references at end of paper.
Courcelle, P.
   1964   See references at end of paper.
Dekkers, E., & E. Gaar
   1961   *Clavis Patrum latinorum*, (p. 112 (nos. 485-487)). Steenbrugge: Abbatia Sancti Petri.
Edwards, H. J. (ed. & trans.)
   1917   *Caesar: The Gallic War*. Cambridge, MA: Harvard University Press.
Erdmann, O. (ed.)
   1962   *Otfrids Evangelienbuch*. Tübingen: Niemeyer.
Evelyn White, H. G. (ed. & trans.)
   1919/21   *Ausonius*. Cambridge, MA: Harvard University Press.
Fanning, S.
   1992   See references at end of paper.
Garnsey, P., & R. Saller
   1987   *The Roman Empire*. London: Duckworth.
Jackson, K.
   1953   See references at end of paper.
McCracken, G. E., *et al.* (eds. & trans.)
   1957/72   *Saint Augustine, The City of God Against the Pagans*. Cambridge, MA: Harvard
               University Press.
Maxwell, G. S.
   1975   Casus belli: native pressure and Roman policy. *Scottish Archaeological Forum* 7: 31 -49.
Muhlberger, S.
   1990   See references at end of paper.
Platnauer, M. (ed. & trans.)
   1922   *Claudian*. Cambridge, MA: Harvard University Press.
Sims-Williams, P.
   1984   See references at end of paper.
Thompson, E. A.
   1979   See references at end of paper.
   1982   See references at end of paper.
Whitelock, D. (trans.)
   1979   *English Historical Documents c. 500-1042*, {pp.890-892 (no.227)}. London: Eyre
               Methuen.
Wood, I. N.
   1992   Continuity or calamity: the constraints of literary models. In *Fifth-century Gaul: A
               Crisis of Identity?* J. Drinkwater & H. Elton (eds.), pp. 9-18. Cambridge: Cambridge
               University Press.

DANISH KINGS AND DENDROCHRONOLOGY: ARCHAEOLOGICAL INSIGHTS INTO THE EARLY HISTORY OF THE DANISH STATE

MORTEN AXBOE

The National Museum, Frederikholms Kanal 12, DK-1220 Copenhagen K

In recent years, a lively debate has been waged amongst Scandinavian archaeologists on the subject of the processes that led, down through the Scandinavian Iron Age and the Viking Period, to the formation of the states that we find around the beginning of the historical period. This is a topic that can be approached from many perspectives, and the purpose of this paper is to present some of them: the historical sources, which initially provide only fleeting glimpses; scientific datings of major archaeological structures, which in recent years have supplemented our knowledge in an important way; and the insight archaeology can provide into general social development through the Iron Age. Looked at together, these seem to reflect a development from smaller to larger polities, although they cannot show when a unified Danish realm first appeared, or what particular events led to this outcome.

Historical Sources

In the third book of his 'Histories', Gregory of Tours reports that:

> The Danes sent a fleet under their King Chlochilaich and invaded Gaul from the sea. They came ashore, laid waste one of the regions ruled by Theuderic and captured some of the inhabitants. They loaded their ships with what they had stolen and the men they had seized, and then they set sail for home. Their King remained on the shore, waiting until the boats should have gained the open sea, when he planned to go on board. When Theuderic heard that his land had been invaded by foreigners, he sent his son Theudebert with a powerful army and all the necessary equipment. The Danish King was killed, the enemy fleet was beaten in a naval battle and all the booty was brought back on shore once more (Gregory of Tours III:3. Trans. Thorpe 1974:163 ff.).

This episode took place within the second or third decade of the sixth century.[1] We do not know where the Danes referred to came from or how large an area their king ruled, nor indeed what sort of power he could exercise there. But the attack was clearly sufficiently serious for the Austrasian king to have to send his son as the leader of a 'powerful' army, and the victory was noteworthy enough to be remembered a few generations later when Gregory wrote his Histories. It may also be worth noting that Gregory explicitly uses the term *rex* for the defeated Danish king. He was careful not to use this of the lords of peoples who were more or less subordinate to the Franks such as the Frisians, the Thuringians or the *Alamanni* (Hedeager 1992b:40). The battle was remembered outside the Frankish realm too, for Chlochilaich seems to be the same as the Geatish king Hygelac who appears in Beowulf (sections XVIII, XXXIII, XXXV and XL. Trans. Gordon 1970).

---

[1] Thanks to Ian Wood for clarification on the dating of the attack (p. 247).

AFTER EMPIRE:
TOWARDS AN ETHNOLOGY OF EUROPES'S BARBARIANS

There are further sixth century historical sources that mention the Danes as a powerful force. Procopius relates how the *Heruli* from the Continent had to pass the territory of the *Danoi* on their way to and from Ultima Thule (the Scandinavian peninsula); Jordanes tells of how the Danes, who derived from the Swedes, had driven the *Heruli* out of their original homelands; Venantius Fortunatus mentions victories over Danes and Saxons in his panegyrics on Frankish princes (Hoffmann 1992:159 ff.; Wood 1983). But we must undoubtedly be cautious in interpreting these reports: we can hardly impose either later medieval or Roman concepts of 'peoples' or 'kings' onto situations outside the Roman Empire in the late Roman period or the Migration period. By way of example we can point to the Goths, who in the fourth and fifth centuries included groups from many different peoples, and in relation to whom even contemporary Romans had trouble interpreting the Gothic terms *reiks* and *kindins*; the Goths in fact also used the title of *thiudans*, which could be used of the Emperor but which seems in practice to reflect no reality in Gothic society at the time (Nasman 1988; Wolfram 1988:67 ff., 94, 114 ff.).[2] In the two centuries that followed, we find only scattered references to the Danes and their kings in contemporary sources. We know, however, that the missionary Willibrord visited a King Ongendus, who ruled over 'the wild tribes of the Danes', at some time within the period 690-714. Again, concrete information is scanty, but we can at least infer that the meeting took place somewhere on the west coast of Jutland (Alcuin, *De vita S. Willibrordi*, Ch. 9. Trans. Skovgaard-Petersen 1981:27 ff.). Only at the end of the eighth century and in particular in the first half of the ninth century do the annals of the Frankish kingdom provide fuller information on Danish kings, who emerge as opponents of Charlemagne and his successors worthy of respect. We are given the names of a number of kings, including Godfred (mentioned between 804-810), and get the impression of a kingdom that includes Skåne and the area around the Oslofjord (*Annales Regni Francorum, s.a.* 811 and 813 in Albrectsen 1976).

The Danish kingdom apparently ran to the same extent at the end of the ninth century, according to the Norwegian Ohthere/Ottar's and the Anglo-Saxon Wulfstan's reports to Alfred the Great (Lund *et al.* 1983). Here, Ottar says that he had Denmark on the port side all the five days it took him to sail from *Sciringesheal* in southern Norway to Hedeby, and Wulfstan informs us that Langeland, Lolland, Falster and Skåne belonged to Denmark while Blekinge belonged to the Swedes and Bornholm had its own king. This is when the term 'Denmark' is first used. Later in the tenth century, it appears again on the two royal runestones at Jelling, and from the eleventh century onwards the extent of the Danish kingdom is for the most part well known.

We also get a glimpse of a powerful Danish kingdom in 934, when Henry the Fowler defeated Chnuba/Gnuba, a king of the Danes, made him tributary and forced him to accept baptism. Contemporary sources refer to this as a major victory; amongst others, the Langobard Liutprand wrote that 'this victory over the formerly indomitable people, the Danes, perhaps made Henry most famous' (Andersen 1977:46).

Both the Jelling stones and the earlier sources give indefinite information. One can argue over whether the Danes in the sixth century ruled all of later Denmark or only parts of it. Equally uncertain is the extent of 'Denmark' in the Viking period. Was northern Jutland part of Denmark in Ottar's account, and what significance is to be attributed to the references to North-Danes and South-Danes in Alfred the Great's translation of Orosius (Müller-Boysen

---

[2] For Wolfram's interpretation of *reiks* and *kindins*, which I quoted in the version presented at the conference, see Dennis Green's remarks in the discussion (p. 239).

1992)? Was the area around Hedeby a separate kingdom in the first half of the tenth century, perhaps under a Swedish ruling family, namely Gnuba and his successors who are known from Hedeby runestones (most recently Lund 1991; Moltke 1985a)? Or can the scattered kings' names be collected into 'dynasties', which superseded one another as rulers of a unified Danish state (Andersen 1987)?

Scientifically Dated Structures

For a long time, it has been the preserve of historical sources to be able to date events or structures in calendar years. But with the development of dendrochronology, archaeology too can contribute absolute datings which on occasion can be just as precise and as informative as 'normal' historical data (Fig. 9.1). If we begin on the threshold of the historical period, the more northerly of the two royal barrows at Jelling seems to have been built around 959. If the northern mound was built by Harold Bluetooth as a memorial for his father Gorm, he must then have been in power by this date. The southern mound is later, and most probably was completed around 970 (Andersen 1988:18). Harold must also have been responsible for the extension of the Danevirke earthwork-system right across South Jutland between the Schlei fjord and the marshy areas to the west (Fig. 9.2). Here, the oldest phase of the

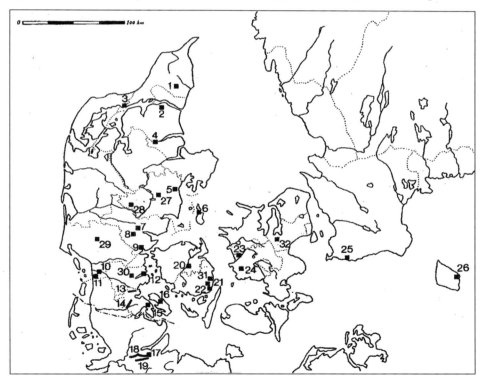

Fig.9.1 - Map of sites mentioned in the text.
1: Stentinget; 2: Bejsebakken; 3: Aggersborg; 4: Fyrkat; 5: Århus; 6: Kanhave canal; 7: Jelling; 8: Ravning bridge; 9: Gudsø Cove; 10: Ribe; 11: Dankirke; 12: 'Æ lej' 8 'Queen Margrethe's Bridge'; 13: 'Æ vold'; 14: Olgerdiget; 15: Nydam; 16: Hjortspring; 17: Hedeby; 18: Danevirke; 19: Kovirke; 20: Nonnebakken; 21: Gudme; 22: Lundeborg; 23: Trelleborg (Sjælland); 24: Neble; 25: Trelleborg (Skåne); 26: Sorte Muld; 27: Illerup; 28: Hedegård; 29: Hodde; 30: Ejsbøl; 31: Langå; 32: Lejre.

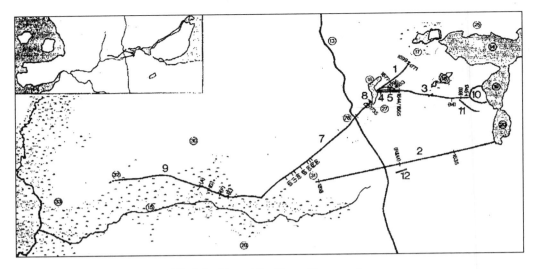

Fig.9.2 - Map of the Danevirke complex.
1: North Rampart; 2: Kovirke; 3: Rampart connecting Main Rampart & Hedeby; 4: Double Rampart;
7: Main Rampart; 10: Hedeby (Andersen *et al.* 1976).

Double Rampart, the western part of the rampart linking the Danevirke itself and Hedeby, is dated to 968 (Andersen 1992; Andersen *et al.* 1976:77, 90 ff.). The semicircular rampart around Hedeby seems to be older, but still belongs to the tenth century, like the ramparts around Århus and Ribe (Andersen *et al.* 1971:264; Jankuhn 1986:67 ff.; Jensen 1991a).

In the years before his death, around 987, Harold must also have been the originator of the building of the ring-forts of the Trelleborg type, of which Trelleborg itself, on Sjælland, contains timber from 980/81, and Fyrkat is apparently of the same period, dated to 978 or later (Bonde *et al.* 1982; K. Christensen *et al.* 1991; Christiansen 1982; Nielsen 1990:143 ff.). From the ring-fort at Nonnebakken a piece of timber out of the moat has been dated, but unfortunately can only be identified as having been cut after 967; it is, all the same, perfectly possible for Nonnebakken to be precisely contemporary with the two forts mentioned (AUD 1988:244; Jensen *et al.* 1988-89). As yet, there are no comparable datings from Aggersborg or the newly-found ring-fort at Trelleborg in Skåne.

Harold Bluetooth must also have been the builder of the 5 m. broad and more than 700 m. long wooden bridge across the Vejle river valley at Ravning, which has been dated to 979±1 (Ramskou 1980). Altogether, these are building works that served to create a stable structure in the kingdom, whatever Harold meant exactly by having written on the large Jelling stone that he 'won all Denmark for himself'. They also have to be viewed in light of the conflicts with the German Emperor in 974 and 983.

It is less easy to identify structures that can be associated with the historically-known Danish kings of the ninth century. We can, however, consider the settlement north of the brook at Hedeby which is dendrochronologically dated to 811 (Jankuhn 1986:87). The Frankish chronicles state that in 808 King Godfred destroyed the trading site of Reric, which was tributary to him, and brought the merchants to the port of Sliesthorp. He also decided to build a rampart "from the eastern bay, which they call Ostarsalt, to the western sea, all along the north bank of the Ejder". The Danevirke itself has not produced datings from this period, but one can point to the radiocarbon dating of the Kovirke which could be consistent with construction sometime in the eighth or ninth century but hardly later (Tauber in Andersen *et al.* 1976:86). Unlike the Danevirke, the Kovirke was built in a straight line in a single phase, which would seem to be most appropriate for Godfred's demonstrative act.

We find a new group of dendrochronologically-dated major structures in the first half of the eighth century—thus in the period around Willibrord's meeting with King Ongendus. Most striking is the Danevirke system again, where we have datings to 737 from both the Main Rampart and the North Rampart. There are many phases in the development of the Danevirke, and the recurrent military rebuilding of the structure has often more or less destroyed earlier phases, which can make the interpretation of archaeological sections very difficult.

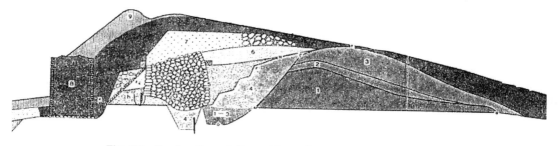

Fig. 9.3 - Section through Danevirke main rampart, from the north-east.
1, 2, 3, 4: Oldest phases, with ditch 1-3 & 4; 5: Boulder wall; 8: Brick wall (Kramer 1984).

One of the most striking elements in the structure is a wall of boulder stones, 3 m. high and more than 3.5 km. long, laid in clay (Fig. 9.3). This is a technique that immediately looks like a mistake in the wet Danish climate: one is reminded of the wall of sun-dried brick from the sixth century BC at Heuneburg in south-western Germany, which seems to be inspired from a drier, Mediterranean area. But the boulder wall in the Danevirke seems to have had a protective timber façade and strong internal supporting beams. Its dating has been a problem: the wall has been readily ascribed to the eleventh or twelfth century when churches began to be built in brick and ashlar. But dendrochronological analyses of the internal beams in the wall seem now to date it to the years around 737 and thus contemporary with other parts of the Main Rampart {Kramer 1984 (*contra* Andersen 1985); Axboe 1988; Andersen 1992 (with a new view of the dating)}. A substantial navigation barrier in the Schlei east of the Danevirke, which has to be viewed in the strategic context of the rampart system, now too seems to belong to the beginning of the eighth century according to provisional newspaper reports (Jydske Vestkysten 1993).

In historical times, the Danevirke played a central role in the defence of the Danish kingdom. The system of fortifications is nearly 14 km. long, and closes the 'Schleswig pass' between the Schlei fjord, which cuts in from the east, and the marshy areas around the rivers that flow into the North Sea. As noted, the system was strongly developed under Harold Bluetooth, and we know that there was a battle here in 974 in the course of the struggles between Harold and the German Emperor Otto II. Under Valdemar the Great in the twelfth century, the Danevirke was reinforced with a 3.7 km. long brick wall, 2 m. thick and about 7 m. high (Fig. 9.3). This was a defensive work on a European scale, and a strong symbol of Denmark's independence from the German Empire; the wall is consequently mentioned both by contemporary historians and on the lead plate that was deposited in the king's grave. The military significance of the area was emphasised by the fact that the

Danevirke was fortified again during the wars in Schleswig in the middle of the nineteenth century, and German tank pits were constructed there during the Second World War. The corridor past Schleswig was the entrance to Jutland, and any Danish state-formation of any significance had to have control over this area. The defensive works are also of a size that must mean that the successive powers that built them had control over substantial areas, in order to be able to undertake the construction itself, to ensure the necessary forces for maintenance and guarding, and on occasion to be able to call up the necessary defenders.

Although the debate concerning the foundation of the Danevirke and the dating of the boulder wall cannot yet be regarded as concluded, it is clear that substantial building activities took place around the year 737. And if the dating of the boulder wall proves secure, it is intriguing that there are several phases of ramparts that are stratigraphically even older. In that case, the oldest parts of Danevirke could belong back in the Migration Period or even the late Roman Iron Age.

A little older than the dating of the boulder wall conjectured above is the 11 m. wide and nearly 1 km. long Kanhave Canal on Samsø from 726. This runs right across the narrowest part of the island and made it possible to sail out to the west from the protected Stavns fjord on the east coast of the island. It is a construction that cannot have had any sensible local purpose but which has to be understood as an element in some large-scale naval control over the inner Kattegat (Olsen 1988). We cannot tell, however, whether the power behind the digging of the canal was based on Sjælland or in Jutland or indeed had control of both shores.

Earlier still is the foundation of the planned market site at Ribe, which was parcelled out within the period 704-710 (Bencard *et al.* 1990; Christensen 1990; Jensen 1991a). As in the case of Danevirke and the Kanhave Canal, this is an enterprise that must presuppose some governing power with lordship over at least a good part of what was later to be Denmark and with an international political outlook (cf. Wood 1983:18 ff.).

In the eighth-century layers at Ribe, more than 160 silver coins have now been found, mostly *sceattas* of the Wodan/monster type. Already the first scores of coins led D. M. Metcalf to suggest that the type was actually struck in Ribe, which also ought to presuppose royal control. The idea is disputed but not absolutely rejected, and in the meantime the number of *sceattas* from Ribe has doubled (Bencard *et al.* 1990:147 with further refs.). Otherwise the earliest known Scandinavian coins are the so-called Hedeby coins that were struck from around 825, quite likely indeed in Hedeby, which King Godfred had left his mark on a few years earlier. Two of Godfred's successors provided Anskar with land for churches both in Hedeby and in Ribe in the middle of the ninth century—another sign of the connection of the two towns to the royal power (Rimbert, *Vita Anskarii*, Chs. 21 & 28; Jankuhn 1986:139; Skovgaard-Petersen 1981).

Ribe was developed in the course of the Viking period into a properly fortified town. In the summer of 1993, according to newspaper reports, what appears to be a ring fort about 100 m. in diameter has also been found. The dating is still uncertain; it seems only to be later than about 800 and earlier than *ca* 1100 (Stig Jensen, pers. comm.).

As we go further back in time the datable structures seem to have more local significance. One phase of the navigation barrier 'Æ lej' ('The Gate') in southern Jutland is dendrochronologically dated to the year 403 (AUD 1988:233; 1989:194, 289). It is a pole barrier about 600 m. long cutting across the Haderslev fjord. Another barrier in the same fjord, 'Queen Margrethe's Bridge', was built around 370, extended around 397-98 and repaired in 418-19 (AUD 1991:260, 262). We are now back in the period of the great bog weapon-deposits, and the most recent datings show that the deposition of the Nydam boat may have taken place at about the same time. The building of the boat can be approximately dated by dendrochronology to 310-20, and a period of use should, of course, be added to this (AUD 1990:231; Bonde 1990; Bonde *et al.* 1991).

Even older are the ramparts Olgerdiget and 'Æ vold' ('The Rampart') in southern Jutland. Both are much smaller structures than the Danevirke. Olgerdiget can be traced over a stretch of some 12 km., alternating with marshy areas (Neumann 1982). The structure runs NE-SW and consists of a palisade of oak poles on the north-western side which was renewed several times. Some metres behind this runs a flat-bottomed ditch, behind which in turn is a low bank. 'Æ vold' is situated 15-20 km. north of Olgerdiget and was constructed to the same pattern (Wulff Andersen 1990), with a palisade to the north, a 4 to 5 m. wide and up to 1.5 m. deep ditch and a bank of similar dimensions (Fig. 9.4). With certain reservations both 'Æ vold' and the latest phase of Olgerdiget can be dendrochronologically dated to the year 278/9, while the earliest phase of Olgerdiget is dated to the year 219 (Ethelberg 1990:93). It is not so easy to interpret these two ramparts. They immediately look too weak to withstand an attack, and their location in the landscape is not entirely convincing strategically. One would imagine that the hypothetical defenders would stand on the bank, with the ditch and the palisade between themselves and the attackers who then would have come from the north. But in several places 'Æ vold' runs along the northern edge of bog

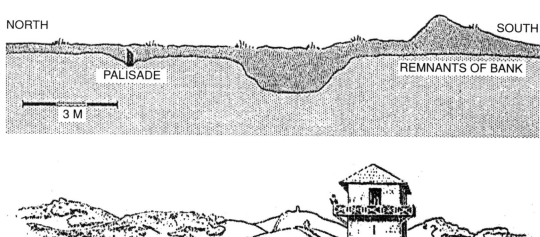

Fig.9. 4 - Above: Section of *Æ* vold'. Below: Reconstruction of the *Limes*.

tracts so that the defenders would not have had any place behind them to fall back into if the enemy crossed the bank, and also the attackers would have the advantage of the higher ground in front of the structure. Perhaps the ramparts are just as much a marking of a group's territory; in any case there seem to be differences between the archaeological material north and south of Olgerdiget (Neumann 1982) while a similar difference cannot be demonstrated in relation to "Æ vold'. It is also reasonable to believe that the structures were inspired by the Roman *limes*, which also had the palisade-ditch-bank structure, and which also functioned just as much as a formal and economic border marker as as an effective military barrier.

Whatever their purpose was, both the raising and maintenance of these Jutlandic ramparts and their possible defence represents an effort that has to have been based upon participation from a substantial area. And these are not unique: we know many more or less well-preserved stretches of rampart in Denmark which are often situated across old routeways and which at times can also be interpreted as territorial boundaries (Schou Jørgensen 1988). But as yet it is only Olgerdiget and 'Æ vold' that can be dated.

As has been noted above we do not know when the oldest rampart at Danevirke was built, but as the smaller ramparts like 'Æ vold' and Olgerdiget were not renewed after the third century it would seem that they became redundant quite quickly while the Danevirke was repeatedly reinforced. I would take this as a sign that the smaller territories, each comprising only of a part of Jutland, were superseded by a larger realm, be it of Jutland alone or of the whole of Denmark.

Evidence of the organisation of larger areas also comes in an exceptional way from the bog deposits, where troops of several hundred men on either side must have been involved. The finds include part of the equipment of whole armies: swords, lances and throwing spears, bows and arrows, shields and in some cases mailcoats (but almost no helmets), horses and harness, and also personal property like clothes, brooches, knives, combs, fire steel, and Roman coins. They are interpreted as sacrifices to the gods after a victory, when the equipment of the enemies which had fled or been killed was destroyed and deposited in the bog, a custom which is recorded in classical sources.

How large the troops that were involved actually were can be difficult to say, because the recent investigations at Illerup (most recently Ilkjær 1990) and Nydam (Bonde *et al.* 1991) show that there may have been repeated large deposits in the same bog, and that weapons from the same deposit may be distributed over large areas of the bog, on occasion with a degree of sorting into 'artefact categories'. The Ejsbøl-North deposit, from period C2 (250/260-310/320) contained weapons from a troop of about 200 men (Ørsnes 1988:25). But as early as period C 1b (210/220-250/260) Illerup A, an assemblage of more than 10.000 objects, contains equipment from a significantly larger troop, out of which at least 350-400 men did not carry their weapons away from the battle; we also have to bear in mind that only about 40% of the find-yielding area of the bog has been excavated.

According to recent analyses of the bog-deposit finds, they seem to be evidence of repeated attacks over an extended period which, it would seem, the local forces were repeatedly able to repulse. At Illerup and at Thorsbjerg it can actually be shown that the combs, respectively the brooches, are of types that are foreign to the area. Both for the attackers and the defenders this must be evidence of organisation over rather large areas (Ilkjær 1990:333-9; Ilkjær 1991), just like the navigation barriers of the same period point in the same direction.

The 'classic' great bog finds of southern Scandinavia belong to the (late) Roman period and the Migration period. There is, however, one important exception: the equally classic find from Hjortspring in southern Jutland with, *inter alia*, a boat. This clearly belongs to the pre-Roman Iron Age and has now been radiocarbon-dated to the fourth century BC (AUD 1987:240). The weaponry here represents a troop of at least 60 men (Kaul 1988). Remarkably, a stake barrier in Gudsø Cove by Kolding a little further north in Jutland has proved to be almost as old. Apart from a Viking period phase, there are stakes dated to the later part of the pre-Roman Iron Age (AUD 1988:219, 225).

It should not be any surprise that the dated structures noted here become larger and larger as the Iron Age progresses, from the Hjortspring find, which need not have involved forces from areas much larger than a couple of present-day parishes, to the large ring-forts of the Viking period. As with the written sources, it is only glimpses of history that these provide, and although several of them imply a collective contribution from 'considerable areas' we have no way of attempting a more accurate geographical delineation of their background. Looked at as a whole, however, they show growing organisation in the later Danish territory.

Some Examples of Roman Influence in Southern Scandinavia[3]

The great Danish bog finds have yielded the largest collections of Roman sword-blades known. This should not be taken as sign of any Roman attacks; for one thing the minor personal belongings of the attackers, for instance their combs, are of Scandinavian manufacture. But the arms are just one aspect of a wide range of Roman influence on Germanic society, both in areas of *Germania libera* adjacent to the Empire and in more distant Scandinavia. After all, the Romans and the Germanic peoples were neighbours for something like 500 years.

Archaeologists usually concentrate on the concrete, material influences that are found in the artefactual record. These are influences which appear early, as early as the first century AD, both in utilitarian, daily items such as dress accessories and pottery—items which a good proportion of the population must have used—and in highly precious imported goods such as glass and bronze vessels.

However, less tangible influences can also be traced through the find material: changes in agricultural methods, textiles (Bender Jørgensen 1986), games, road construction, weight systems (Fonnesbech-Sandberg 1987), and in the social structure as a whole. What we have here is very wide-ranging and long-term cultural influence going far beyond the copying of imported artefacts by local craftsmen and which must also have had its impact in a field which is difficult to investigate archaeologically: the conceptual and cognitive world of the Scandinavians.

Both the material and the spiritual imports may have become possible in a variety of circumstances, among which may have been service in the Roman army (Axboe *et al.* 1992; Rausing 1987). However that may be, repeated and intensive personal connections would seem necessary to explain many of the influences, which cannot be understood just as imports of actual objects, but which seem to reveal a knowledge of the ideas which the Romans attached to them. One instance of this is the finding of the scale of a pine-cone (*Pinus pinea*) and a bladdernut seed (*Staphylea pinnata*) in an early Roman Iron Age

---

[3] This section was added after the conférence.

(Period B2) grave at Blidegn on Fyn (Mackeprang 1936). The stone pine has its range in the Mediterranean lands, the bladdernut in Central Europe from the Balkans through Bohemia and southern Germany to the south of France. The seeds of the pine were eaten in the Mediterranean countries, and to the Romans the pine cone was also a symbol of immortality. As such, it appears on Roman grave monuments.

The great quantities of Roman weaponry in the Danish bog deposits could of course have been imported or appropriated as plunder. The same applies to two second- or third-century Roman decorations, *phalerae*, which were found in the Thorsbjerg bog, but it is striking that Germanic animal figures have been added to these (Werner 1941). These thus kept an active function after they had left the Roman empire. The Thorsbjerg find also includes, amongst many other things, a Roman helmet and several pieces of garments which Lise Bender Jørgensen has suggested come from the dress of a Roman auxiliary (Bender Jørgensen 1986:146-55; Wild & Bender Jørgensen 1988). To judge by the Gerrnanic artefacts found in this deposit, the brooches in particular, the defeated attackers came from north-western Germany (Ilkjær *et al.* 1982).

In the first or second century AD the Germanic peoples invented their own script, the runes (Moltke 1985b:64). We may discuss whether the runes were first meant for magic or also for more everyday purposes, and also which alphabet was their immediate source of inspiration. In any event the inventors of the runes must have had a thorough knowledge of writing and of its possible functions, and both these and a sufficient number of other people must have felt a need to transplant literacy to their homelands. The prerequisites for this could virtually only have been found in the Roman empire. We even have examples of Scandinavian weapons 'signed' in runes in much the same way as Roman weapon-smiths signed their products (Stoklund 1986).

The late Roman-period Broskov road at Præstø, with its large stones, finely fitted together, looks like a local version of the carefully constructed Roman road systems (Schou Jørgensen 1988:101 ff.). And the construction of roads and public amenities were indeed amongst the tasks that the legionaries were occupied with in peacetime.

Finally, it is remarkable that in certain rich graves both in Scandinavia and elsewhere in *Germania libera* we can find the adoption of the classical idea of placing the Charon's fee in the mouth or the hand of the deceased. Remarkably enough, Roman coins were hardly ever used in Scandinavia for this purpose; they were replaced by 'local currency' in the form of small pieces of gold or silver. In southern Gotland, indeed, special coin-like bracteates were struck for this purpose. In undisturbed inhumation graves these have even been found by the jaw of the deceased. One of the cremations with similar 'coins' stands out by being encircled by carefully dressed stones with stonemason's marks (Lamm *et al.* 1989). Both this feature (which is not entirely unique to Gotland), and the sudden flowering of high-quality dressed-stone monuments on this island, have been taken as the products of Roman influence (Nylén *et al.* 1981:10, 18).

Major Trends in Iron-age Social Development, Archaeologically Indicated

A tendency towards a growing organisation of the area which ended up as the medieval kingdom of Denmark can be seen through the study of the archaeological finds from the Iron Age. Here it is not precise datings or imposing single structures that come into play, but long-terrn tendencies in social development.

In a large-scale study, Lotte Hedeager has made a bold attempt to bring together the archaeological finds from the period *ca* 500 BC to 800 AD in order to discover the social developments that resulted in a unified Danish state (Hedeager 1992a). Here, she places great weight upon the active role that ideology plays in communal life as a means of legitimizing the political power of the dominant groups. This power could not be taken for granted: it continually had to be recreated and legitimized through rituals (Hedeager 1992a:27 ff.). We find the material traces of these rituals in the archaeological record, principally in graves and hoards. 'Prestige goods' play a special role here, both locally made items of bronze and precious metals and, particularly, imported Roman glass and bronze vessels. Élite status was demonstrated by access to such goods; abundant wealth was shown by depositing them in graves; and status was consolidated by giving these to others who thus came under an obligation to the giver, or by sacrificing them and thus demanding good fortune as a reciprocal gift from the gods.

In the earlier part of the pre-Roman Iron Age, the graves are furnished in a very uniform manner, and are mostly grouped together in large cemeteries. Towards the end of this period some graves begin to stand out, containing weapons or other marks of status, and this tendency becomes very strong in the early Roman period, when the richest graves include imported Roman goods as well as a rich selection of local products and are found in small, reserved cemeteries. This trend culminates in the late Roman period, when graves on Sjælland in particular sometimes contain rich grave goods such as imported glass and metal vessels, and when, in contrast to the previous period, gold neck- and arm-rings can occur in graves.

In the Migration period, there is, on the whole, a cessation of furnished burial; on the other hand we now have a large number of gold hoards in which arm- and neck-rings appear again, together with bracteates, brooches, hackgold etc. (Hedeager 1992a:70). An investigation of the hoards shows that particular types and combinations of types play an important role. One cannot, of course, ignore the possibility that valuables were buried for safe-keeping, but the special combinations and frequent deposition in bogs from which it would have been difficult to recover the valuables must mean that in many cases these represent ritual deposits, in other words sacrifices, and not private 'bank box' deposits for safe-keeping (Hedeager 1992a:75 ff.; Hines 1989).

The rich grave goods of the Roman Iron Age too are far more 'ritual' than 'private', which means that we are faced with a marked shift in ritual deposition from grave goods in the Roman period to hoards in the Migration period. Hedeager sees the funerary rituals of the Roman Iron Age as a stage in the establishment of a new social order with a politically and militarily active élite. Its status was heritable: very young men could be given rich burials with weapons and so on (Hedeager 1992a:159 ff.) and women's graves are just as rich as the men's. In the Migration period, the status of the élite was consolidated: one no longer needed to demonstrate a link with one's dead ancestors, but sacrificed primarily to the gods as the maintainers of the established world order. From the Vendel period which follows we have neither grave nor hoard deposits, perhaps because the social and political situation was relatively stable (Hedeager 1992a:80 ff.).

If we look at the geographical distribution of the grave finds, it might appear as if, as early as the early Roman period, the rich finds fall into a pattern which corresponds, in a rough way, to a situation in which each chieftain led his own district (approximately a modern Danish '*herred*'), perhaps with a few 'petty kings' who were able to gather support from a larger area over them. Hedeager reckons with "the earliest central power in the form of kingship in Denmark" at the transition from the early Roman period to the late (Hedeager 1992a:246-50). The chieftains had a retinue of warriors which can be traced, through weapon graves, back into the later pre-Roman Iron Age; a phenomenon which may have been reinforced by contact with the Roman Empire and through service in the Roman army (Hedeager 1992a:234, 246 ff.; cf. Axboe l991a; Axboe *et al.* 1992; Rausing 1987). Such a retinue, whose members were linked to the leader by ties of personal loyalty without regard to family ties, was of great importance to the élite's ability to break up the old clan-based society (Hedeager 1992a:243 ff., 248 ff.), and a professional warrior group with permanent leadership must be a prerequisite for the military expeditions that the bog finds reflect. And the maintenance of a retinue also practically requires some (primitive) form of taxation in the form of tribute, fines and the like (Hedeager 1992a:246 ff.).

At the transition from the early Roman period to the late there is a reorganisation of agriculture, from small villages with both larger and smaller farms and houses without stalls to fewer, larger villages with larger farmsteads only. At the same time, the old 'Celtic field' systems that had been inherited from the pre-Roman Iron Age were abandoned, apparently in favour of a system with an intensively cultivated infield surrounded by pastures and commons (Hedeager 1992a:219 ff.). Hedeager takes this reorganisation as an indication that there already existed a central (royal) power that was able to organise the redistribution of land and to solve the many disputes that would inevitably arise in connection with it (Hedeager 1992a:246 ff.), but this is not entirely convincing. It is difficult to conceive of so early a royal power being able to interfere so radically in vital aspects of the farmers' life; this must in any case presume a unity of interest with the leading farmers who apparently reaped the rewards of this reorganisation.

Altogether, however, Hedeager's studies point to the increasing stratification of society and to sacrificial practices associated with burials and religious cults that can be viewed in the context of a powerful élite that was establishing its status around the middle of the Roman Iron Age and later made sacrifice in order to maintain and legitimize this status.

A similar élite system, with the redistribution of imported status-bearing goods, also emerges from Ulla Lund Hansen's studies of Roman imports in Scandinavia. The Stevns area of Sjælland in particular exerted such powerful control over importation in period C lb (210/220-250/260) of the late Roman Iron Age that one could keep for oneself the unique objects and, on the whole, let only the mass-produced ones pass on. But this system was unstable: centres of importation shift from period to period (Lund Hansen 1987, 1988).

Finds from the Past Few Years

Hedeager's studies can also be supplemented by a number of more recent finds that again reveal increasing social differentiation down through the Iron Age. As early as the later part of the pre-Roman Iron Age we have examples of chieftains standing out from the common groups of finds. Long-familiar finds are the graves from Langa, eastern Fyn (Albrectsen 1954:29 ff.) and the chieftain's farmstead at Hodde in south-western Jutland which is distinguished from the rest of the village by its size, its especially strong fence and by a concentration of the finest pottery. The other farmsteads at Hodde, with their different sizes, indicate that the village contained several social layers (Hvass 1988). At Hedegard in Central Jutland one of the richest cemeteries in Denmark from the period around the birth of Christ is being excavated, with many weapons, gold and bronze jewellery, and various early Roman bronze vessels. The associated settlement is as yet known only from the results of minor trial excavations. It is unusually large, has a culture layer up to a metre thick, and was fenced by strong, closely spaced posts (Madsen 1992).

From the pre-Roman Iron Age we must also remember the navigation barrier from Gudsø Cove that has already been discussed.

Later in the Iron Age, a picture begins to emerge of a settlement structure containing a number of central places which stand out from the ordinary, rural settlements. This is, amongst other things, thanks to the large number of metal finds that have emerged in recent years as a result of the excellent co-operation between many Danish museums and local amateurs with metal-detectors (Axboe 1991b, Axboe 1993). The central places that currently appear most clearly are Stentinget in North Jutland (Nilsson 1990), Bejsebakken in Ålborg (Ørsnes 1976), the Gudme-Lundeborg complex in south-eastern Fyn (Kromann *et al.* 1991; Thrane 1992, 1993), Neble in south-western Sjælland (Bendixen *et al.* 1990) and Sorte Muld on Bornholm (Watt 1991, 1992).

Besides their wealth of metal finds, several of these central places seem also to have a special, complex layout, with several clusters of farmsteads together to form an unusually large settlement (Fig. 9.5) (Axboe 1991b, Axboe 1993; Jørgensen 1994). These clusters were contemporary; it is not the pattern known from Vorbasse and other rural settlements where the village intermittently moves *en bloc* from one site to another (Hvass 1988). There are, of course, differences amongst the rich and complex sites, but as a general rule the metal finds start gradually in the late Roman/Migration period and become really significant from the beginning of the Vendel period.

Gudme remains the most outstanding and the best known of these sites, with its many gold finds both in the Gudme area itself and in the surrounding district, with Denmark's largest Iron-age cemetery at Møllegårdsmarken, and with the associated coastal trading site by Lundeborg. Most recently, in the summer of 1993, an unusually large, late Roman period building has been found at Gudme. With a length of 47 m. and a width of more than 9 m. it is the largest known early Iron Age building in Denmark, and with roof-bearing posts 70 cm. in diameter it was exceptionally strongly built. Beside this are other buildings of a similarly extraordinary character which are still being excavated at the time of writing (Nielsen *et al.* 1993). That Gudme played not only an economic and political role but also had some cult function is indicated both by its name, *Gudheim* (the home of the gods), and by several neighbouring place-names (Hauck 1987).

Sorte Muld too must have fulfilled some cult function which is reflected in the more than 2,300 stamped gold-foil leaves (*guldgubber*) that have been found there. But the finds from Sorte Muld generally stand out from the other known settlement sites on Bornholm (Watt 1991).

We should also note the Dankirke settlement in south-western Jutland, although this is probably an individual chieftain's farmstead which stood above the average and not a whole settlement like the other central places. It is as yet unclear how Dankirke is related to the first real urban site at Ribe only about 7 km. away, but it is interesting that amongst the latest finds from Dankirke there are five Wodan/monster *sceattas* matching those already noted from Ribe (Jarl Hansen 1988-89, 1989; Jensen 1991b).

All of the central places are located a few kilometres inland, giving them a degree of protection against sudden attack from the sea. Correspondingly, it appears as if settlement on Fyn in the Migration and Vendel periods moves away from the coasts, in contrast to

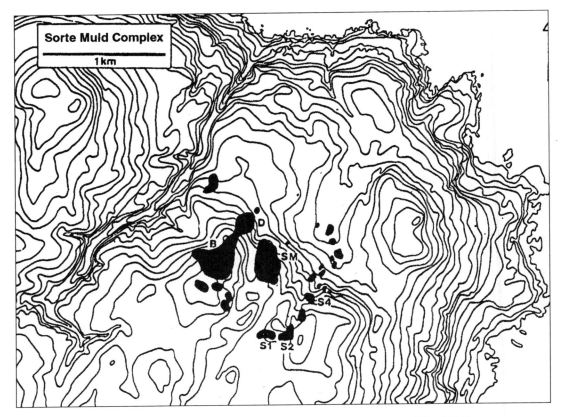

Fig.9.5 - General plan of the Sorte Muld settlement complex (Watt 1991).

both the Roman and the Viking periods, which could then be evidence of especially turbulent times (Christoffersen 1991). On the other hand, both the central places and the minor trading sites such as Lundeborg and a whole series of others that appear in the course of the later Iron Age (Axboe 1991b, Axboe 1993; Ulriksen 1990), imply powerful leaders, who could protect and guarantee trade.

From the Vendel period and the Viking period, there is an unusually large building complex under excavation at Old Lejre on Sjælland: in other words at the mythical seat of the Danish kings of legend (Christensen 1991). The structure includes a large timber building measuring 48.5 m. x 11.5 m. that was rebuilt several times; the available radiocarbon datings from the building fall into two clusters, in the seventh and ninth centuries AD. This is the largest building from Danish prehistory yet found, and is a prestige structure on a European scale, fully comparable with the *aula regia* buildings of Charlemagne's contemporary *Pfalz*-complexes (Axboe 1991b:30). There are also several smaller buildings, together, apparently, with a craft area, connected to the main complex. Contemporary with the earlier cluster of datings from the Lejre hall is the neighbouring grave mound 'Grydehøj', the primary cremation burial which contained remains of gold-braided cloth and which, according to radiocarbon datings, is most probably to be assigned to the seventh century AD (S . Wulff Andersen, pers. comm.).

Politics and Religion

I have already referred to the importance that Lotte Hedeager attaches to grave goods and votive deposits as 'public' and thus politically significant, religious activities in the Roman Iron Age and the Migration period.

Another characteristic feature of the turbulent and gold-rich Migration period is the gold bracteates. In archaeological terms, they are a short-lived phenomenon, perhaps limited to just a couple of generations (Lund Hansen 1992) and at any rate not much more than a century. All the same, they come to appear in quite large numbers and with a rich and varied iconography. They belonged to the leading stratum of society—this is evident by the precious material they were made of—and they were clearly the object of rather brief but thus all the more intensive interest for these groups.

According to Karl Hauck's studies over many years, it is essentially Woden who is shown on the bracteates although other divine figures can appear in the iconography too (Hauck 1978; Hauck 1993, with references; Hauck *et al.* 1985 ff.), and the bracteates undoubtedly had some religious function as amulets. But the situation is one of such a marked focus upon Woden, who is portrayed as the lord of the gods, both with the Roman Emperor's diadem and brooch and with Germanic symbols of lordship such as long, plaited hair (Figs. 9.6, 9.7), at the expense of the other gods, that one is tempted to look for a secular explanation.

Fig.9.6 - A- bracteate from Tjurko, Blekinge, showing a human bust with the Roman emperor's diadem and circular brooch. Diam 24.8 mm. (Hauck *et al.*, Vol.1, 1985, No. 183).

Fig. 9.7 - C - bracteate from Tranegilde Strand, Sijælland. Human head with stylised diadem and long, plaited hair, with bird's head at front, over animal. Diam. 25.5 mm. (Hauck *et al.*, Vol. 2, 1986, No. 355).

In the Scandinavian Migration period, religion and politics must have been inextricably intertwined, just as they were in the Roman empire and the Middle Ages. As I see, the bracteates may indeed illustrate political ideas, by the repeated use of symbols of lordship and their focus upon Woden. Both features fit well into the ideology of an élite that itself was striving for lordly power (Axboe 1991a; Axboe *et al.* 1992). The images on the bracteates can thus be seen as a projection of the political ideals of the élite into the religious sphere so that the promotion of a heavenly lord could serve to legitimize worldly princes' efforts to establish and maintain their power in Scandinavia.

Several Germanic royal families later claimed to have had a divine ancestor—as a rule, even Woden himself. This can well be regarded as an aspect of the legitimacy of the family and a sort of parallel to the 'king by the grace of God' of later times. According to Snorri Sturluson, King Skjold, the ancestor of the Danish Skjoldung kings, was the son of Woden, and Earl Hakon of Norway also traced his descent from a son of Woden. The Swedish kings of Uppsala, by contrast, descended from Yngvi/Freyr, one of the Vanir (*Ynglinga saga*, Chs. 5-10). The Ostrogothic Amal clan too claimed a divine or semi-divine ancestor, Gaut (Wolfram 1988:31, 110). In the case of England, Bede comments that many kings traced their descent from Woden (Bede, *Historia ecclesiastica gentis Anglorum*, I, 15. Trans. Sherley-Price 1972:156; cf. Loyn 1962:230).

In recent English research, Scandinavia—primatily Denmark—is seen as a pagan counterweight to the Christian Frankish realm that the Anglo-Saxon kingdoms in England could associate themselves with in order to mark their distance from Merovingian demands for overlordship (e.g. in Carver 1992; cf. Axboe n.d.). Lotte Hedeager has persuasively shown how Denmark and the Merovingian Empire can be seen as established power centres, both of which were surrounded by peripheral areas that to some degree would have been dependent on the centres and where less stable power relations made it necessary for the élite to mark its status (Hedeager 1992c). In this context, it would be interesting if Sam Newton (1992) is right to find Danish kings in Ælfwald of East Anglia's genealogy: it would be significant if these were important in legitimizing an Anglo-Saxon ruler just like Uoden/Woden and Caser/Caesar who begin the genealogy.

We do not have a concrete knowledge of the political geography of Scandinavia in the Roman Iron Age and the Migration period. We can see in the finds that an élite was marking its power, but we do not know whether the members of this élite should be called chieftains, petty kings, 'jarls', 'Sakralkönige' or kings, or how large the areas were that their influence extended over, although we can certainly sketch a number of 'kingdoms' (Ramqvist 1991). Nor do we know what power a 'king' could exercise, whether his role was military, religious, legislative or judicial, or to what extent he united several of these functions.

It cannot be unreasonable to believe that some form of state-formation took place earlier in the fertile and accessible area of southern Scandinavia than in Norway and Sweden. Personally, I am willing to believe that a major part of medieval Denmark was united under a single king in the early eighth century when Ribe, the Kanhave canal and the Danevirke testify to major activities within a short period. Perhaps the process took place even earlier: the lord of Gudme must have gone a good way down this road, and one must remember that Gregory of Tours refers to Chlochilaich by the respectful title of *rex*.

Both Lotte Hedeager (1992c) and other scholars (e.g. Andersen 1987) appear to take the great barrows at Lejre and Jelling as the starting points for new dynasties. It seems likely enough that a new ruling family would need to mark its power in this way, though on the other hand we know of both the Merovingian dynasty and the later medieval Danish kings that they did not use the same church for burial for any lengthy period but often chose new ones. Shifts of burial place therefore need not have been due to a change of ruling family. Like the Merovingians, all the Danish kings of the late Viking period and the Middle Ages came from one and the same family—with just one exception, Magnus the Good (1042 47), who was the son of the Norwegian king Olaf the Saint and already King of Norway. This involved, as a matter of fact, some fairly generous recognition of royal bastards and maternal connections, but no member of the *Hvide* or any other leading family attempted the throne at all, not even in the especially turbulent periods of the twelfth and fourteenth centuries when for certain periods the kingdom was divided or more or less dissolved. In the period from the 790s to the 860s too, when the Frankish chronicles tell us about fights between Danish kings, it appears largely to be brothers and cousins who struggled for power. As far as I can see, this indicates that despite a formal element of election to the kingship it was a single family, corresponding to the Merovingians, who held power, and such a prerogative would undoubtedly have had its basis not only in substantial landownership but also in religious legitimation.

The present Queen of Denmark, Margrethe II, can—via the illegitimate and female lines mentioned—trace her descent back to Gorm the Old, who was ruling around the year 950. We cannot know whether even Chlochilaich was of the same kindred, but we have to be prepared to accept long continuity in the development of society in spite of all the changes. Thus Margrethe II's right to the throne of Denmark may ultimately be based on the fact that Gorm—and before him Godfred and Chlochilaich?—were regarded in their time as descendants of Woden.

Acknowledgements—I wish to thank John Hines for translating this paper and all the participants for the ideas I obtained during the lively discussion which followed the presentation.

References

Albrectsen, E.
  1954   *Fynske jernaldergrave 1. Førromersk jernalder.* Copenhagen: Ejnar Munksgaard.
  1976   *Vikingerne i Franken.* Odense: Odense Universitetsforlag.
Andersen, H. H.
  1977   *Jyllands vold.* Århus: Wormianum.
  1985   Zum neuen Schnitt am Hauptwall des Danewerks. *Archäologisches Korrespondenzblatt* 15: 525-529.
  1987   Vorchristliche Königsgräber in Dänemark und ihre Hintergrunde - Versuch einer Synthese. *Germania* 65: 159-173.
  1992   Opus Danorum - Befestigungswalle im altdanischen Grenzland. *Archäologie in Deutschland* 3: 18-21.
Andersen, H. H., P. J. Crabb & H. J. Madsen
  1971   *Århus Søndervold, en byarkæologisk undersøgelse.* (Jysk Arkaeologisk Selskabs Skrifter IX). Århus: Århus Univ. Press.
Andersen, H. H., H. J. Madsen & O. Voss
  1976   *Danevirke.* (Jysk Arkæologisk Selskabs Skrifter XIII). Århus: Århus University Press.
Andersen, H.
  1988   Gåden om Gorm. *Skalk* 2: 18-28.
AUD
  1984 ff.   *Arkæologiske udgravninger i Danmark.*
Axboe, M.
  1988   Danerkonge og Danevirke. *Sønderjysk Månedsskrift* 2:35-44.

Axboe, M. (*cont.*)
1991a   Guld og guder i folkevandringstiden. Brakteaterne som kilde til politisk/religiøse forhold. In *Samfundsorganisation og regional variation. Indlæg fra et symposium på Sandhjerg Slot 11. -15. april 1989.* C. Fabech & J. Ringtved (eds.), pp. 1-16. Jysk Arkæologisk Selskabs Skrifter. Århus: Århus University Press.
1991b   Metal og Magt? Detektorfund fra jernalderbopladser/Precious Metals and Power? Detector Finds on Iron Age Settlements. In *Arkæologiske udgravninger i Danmark* 1991, pp. 18-32. Copenhagen: Det Arkæologiske Nævn.
1993   A Die for a Gold Bracteate. Postgården and other Danish settlements with unusual metal detector finds. In *Sources as Resources. Festschrift for Birgit Arrhenius.* (PACT, Journal of the European Study Group on Physical, Chemical and Mathematical Techniques Applied to Archaeology) 38: 379-394. Rixensart: Council of Europe.
1992-93. Review of Martin Carver (ed.): The Age of Sutton Hoo (1992). *Journal of Danish Archaeology* 11: 167-170.
Axboe M , & A. Kromann
1992   D N ODINN P F AUC? Germanic 'Imperial Portraits' on Scandinavian Gold Bracteates. In *Ancient Portraiture: Image and Message.* Acta Hyperborea, Danish Studies in Classical Archaeology, Vol. 4., pp. 271-305. Copenhagen: Museum Tusculanum Press.
Bencard, M., & L. Bender Jørgensen
1990   Excavation and Stratigraphy. In *Ribe Excavations 1970-76*, Vol. 4. Esbjerg: Sydjysk Universitetsforlag.
Bender Jørgensen, L.
1986   *Forhistoriske textiler i Skandinavien.* (Nordiske Fortidsminder, Ser. B 9). Copenhagen: Det kongelige Nordiske Oldskriftselskab.
Bendixen, K., F. Kaul, A. Kromann, E. Munksgaard & H. Nielsen
1990   En vikingetidsskat fra Neble, Sjælland. *Nationalmuseets Arbejdsmark* 1990: 208-223.
Bonde, N.
1990   Dendrochronologische Altersbestimmung des Schiffes von Nydam. *Offa* 47: 157-168.
Bonde, N., & K. Christensen
1982   Trelleborgs alder. *Dendrokronologisk datering. Aarbøger for Nordisk Oldkyndighed og Historie* 1982: 111-152.
Bonde, N., C. Christensen, F. Rieck & P. Vang Petersen
1991   Jernalderbåde og vabenofre - Nationalmuseets Nydamprojekt. *Nationalmuseets Arbejdsmark* 1991: 99-114.
Carver, M. O. H. (ed.)
1992   *The Age of Sutton Hoo.* Woodbridge: The Boydell Press.
Christensen, K.
1990   Wood-anatomical and dendrochronological Studies. In *Ribe Excavations 1970-76*, Vol. 4, pp. 169-181. Esbjerg: Århus University Press.
Christensen, K., & N. Bonde
1991   Dateringen af Trelleborg - en kommentar. *Aarbøger for Nordisk Oldkyndighed og Historie* 1991: 231- 236.
Christensen, T.
1991   Lejre Beyond Legend - The Archaeological Evidence. *Journal of Danish Archaeology* 10: 163-185.
Christiansen, T. E.
1982   Trelleborgs Alder. Arkæologisk Datering. *Aarbøger for Nordisk Oldkyndighed og Historie* 1982: 84-110.

Christoffersen, J.
1991 Iron Age finds in Funen (Fyn) - some archaeological problems of defining maritime sites. In *Aspects of Maritime Scandinavia*. O. Crumlin Pedersen (ed.), pp. 55-66. Roskilde: Vikingeskibshallen i Roskilde.

Ethelberg, P.
1990 To grave fra Højvang, Sønderjylland. Dendrodatering og absolut kronologi. *Kuml* 1990: 85-97.

Fonnesbech-Sandberg, E.
1987 Vægtsystemer i ældre germansk jernalder. *Aarbøger for Nordisk Oldkyndighed og Historie* 1987: 139-160.

Gordon, R. K.
1970 *Anglo-Saxon Poetry*. London: Everyman's Library.

Hauck, K.
1978 Brakteatenikonologie. In *Reallexikon der Germanischen Altertumskunde*, begründet von Johannes Hoops. 2. Auflage, Bd. 3, pp. 361-401. Berlin: Walter de Gruyter.
1987 Gudme in der Sicht der Brakteaten-Forschung. Zur Ikonologie der Goldbrakteaten XXXVI. *Frühmittelalterliche Studien* 21: 147-181.
1993 Das Aufkommen des erfolgreichsten Motivs der völkerwanderungszeitlichen Brakteaten. Zur Ikonologie der Goldbrakteaten XLVIII. In *Sources as Resources. Festschrift for Birgit Arrhenius*. (PACT, Journal of the European Study Group on Physical, Chemical and Mathematical Techniques Applied to Archaeology) 38: 403-434. Rixensart: Council of Europe.

Hauck, K., M. Axboe, K. Duwel & L. von Padberg
1985 ff. *Die Goldbrakteaten der Völkerwanderungszeit 1-3*. (Münstersche-Mittelalter Schriften 24,1-3). Munich: Wilhelm Fink Verlag.

Hedeager, L.
1992a *Iron Age Societies: From Tribe to State in Northern Europe, 500 BC to AD 700*. Oxford: Blackwell.
1992b Mellem oldtid og middelalder: Europa i folkevandringstiden. In *Carlsbergfondet, Frederiksborgmuseet, Ny Carlsbergfondet: Årsskrift 1992*, pp.39-45. Copenhagen: Rhodos.
1992c Kingdoms, Ethnicity and Material Culture: Denmark in a European Perspective. In *The Age of Sutton Hoo*. M. O. H. Carver (ed.), pp. 279-300. Woodbridge: The Boydell Press.

Hines, J.
1989 Ritual Hoarding in Migration-Period Scandinavia: A Review of Recent Interpretations. *Proceedings of the Prehistoric Society* 55: 193-205.

Hoffmann, E.
1992 Der heutige Stand der Erforschung der Geschichte Skandinaviens in der Völkerwanderungszeit im Rahmen der mittelalterlichen Geschichtsforschung. In *Der historische Horizont der Götterbild-Amulette aus der Übergangsepoche von der Spätantike zum Frühmittelalter*. K. Hauck (ed.), pp. 143-182. (Abhandlungen der Akademie der Wissenschaften in Göttingen). Göttingen: Vandenhoeck & Ruprecht.

Hvass, S.
1988 The status of the Iron Age settlement in Denmark. In *Archeologie en landschap*. M. Bierma, O. H. Harsema & W. Van Zeist (eds.), pp. 97-132. Groningen: Biologisch Archaeologisch Instituut.

Ilkjær, J.
1990 *Die Lanzen und Speere. Textband. Illerup Ådal 1*. {Jutland Archaeological Society Publications, 35 (1)}. Århus: Århus University Press.
1991 Mosefundene i perspektiv. In *Samfundsorganisation og regional variation. Indlæg fra et symposium på Sandbjerg Slot 11. -15. april 1989*. (Jysk Arkæologisk Selskabs Skrifter). C. Fabech & J. Ringtved (eds.), pp. 277-281. Århus: Århus University Press.

Ilkjær, J. & J. Lønstrup
   1982   Interpretation of the Great Votive Deposits of Iron Age Weapons. *Journal of Danish
               Archaeology* 1: 95-103.
Jankuhn, H.
   1986   *Haithabu. Ein Handelsplatz der Wikingerzeit* (8. Aufl.). Neumünster: Karl
               Wachholtz Verlag.
Jarl Hansen, H.
   1988-89   Dankirke. Jernalderboplads og rigdomscenter. *Kuml* 1988-89: 201-247.
   1989   Dankirke: Affluence in Late Iron Age Denmark. In *The Birth of Europe*.
               K. Randsborg (ed.), pp. 123-128. (Analecta Romana Instituti Danici, Supplementum
               16). Roma: L'Erma di Bretschneider.
Jensen, N. M., & J. Sørensen
   1988-89   Nonnebakkeanlægget i Odense. En ny brik til udforskningen. *Kuml* 1988-89:
               325-333.
Jensen, S.
   1991a   *The Vikings of Ribe*. Ribe: Den antikvariske Samling i Ribe.
   1991b   Dankirke-Ribe. Fra handelsgard til handelsplads. In *Høvdingesamfund og Kongemagt.
               Fra Stamme til Stat i Danmark 2*. P. Mortensen & B. M. Rasmussen (eds.), pp. 73-88.
               {Jysk Arkæologisk Selskabs Skrifter 21 (2)} Århus: Århus Univ. Press.
Jydske Vestkysten
   1993   Søfæstningsværk ved Dannevirke. (Naval defence near Danevirke). *Jydske
               Vestkysten* 28th January, 1993.
Jørgensen, L.
   1994   The Find Material from the Settlement of Gudme II - Composition and
               Interpretation. In *The Archaeology of Gudme and Lundeborg. Papers Presented at a
               Conference at Svendborg, October 1991*. P. O. Nielsen, K. Randsborg & H. Thrane
               (eds.), pp. 53-63. (Arkæologiske Studier 10). Copenhagen: Akademisk Vorlag.
Kaul, F.
   1988   *Da våbnene tav. Hjortspringfundet og dets baggrund*. Copenhagen: Arnold Busck.
Kramer, W.
   1984   Die Datierung der Feldsteinmauer des Danewerks. Vorbericht einer neuen
               Ausgrabung am Hauptwall. *Archäologisches Korrespondenzblatt* 14: 343-350.
Kromann, A., P. O. Nielsen, K. Randsborg, P. Vang Petersen & P. O. Thomsen
   1991   Gudme og Lundeborg, et fynsk rigdomscenter i jernalderen. *Nationalmuseets
               Arbejdsmark* 1991: 144-161.
Lamm, J. P., & M. Axboe
   1989   Neues zu Brakteaten und Anhängern in Schweden. *Frühmittelalterliche Studien*
               23: 453-477.
Loyn, H. R.
   1962   *Anglo-Saxon England and the Norman Conquest*. London: Longman.
Lund, N.
   1991   'Denemearc', 'tanmarkar but' and 'tanmaurk ala'. In *Peoples and Places in
               Northern Europe 500-1600. Essays in Honour of Peter Hayes Sawyer*. I. Wood & N.
               Lund (eds.), pp. 161-169. Woodbridge: The Boydell Press.
Lund, N., O. Crumlin-Pedersen, P. Sawyer & C. E. Fell
   1983   *Ottar og Wulfstan, to rejsebeskrivelse fra vikingetiden. Oversat og kommenteret af
               Niels Lund med bidrag af Ole Crumlin-Pedersen, Peter Sawyer og Christine E. Fell*.
               Roskilde: Vikingeskibshallen i Roskilde.
Lund Hansen, U.
   1987   *Römischer Import im Norden. Warenaustausch zwischen dem Römischen Reich und
               dem freien Germanien*. (Nordiske Fortidsminder, Ser. B, Vol. 10). Copenhagen: Det
               kongelige Nordiske Oldskriftselskab.
   1988   Handelszentren der römischen Kaiserzeit und Völkerwanderungszeit in Dänemark.
               In *Trade and Exchange in Prehistory. Studies in Honour of Berta Stjernquist*. (Acta
               Archaeologica Lundensia, Series in 8). 16: 155-166. Lund: Lunds Universitets
               Historiska Museum.

Lund Hansen, U. (*cont.*)
1992   Die Hortproblematik im Licht der neueren Diskussion zur Chronologie und zur Deutung der Goldschätze in der Völkerwanderungszeit. In *Der historische Horizont der Götterbild-Amulette aus der Übergangsepoche von der Spätantike zum Frühmittelalter*. K. Hauck (ed.), pp. 183-194. (Abhandlungen der Akademie der Wissenschaften in Göttingen). Göttingen: Vandenhoeck & Ruprecht.
Mackeprang, M. B.
1936   Om et Træskrin med Amuletter og undergørende Planter samt andet mærkeligt i en Grav fra Romersk Jernalder. *Fra Nationalmuseets Arbejdsmark* 1936:42-50.
Madsen, O.
1992   Midtjysk magt. *Skalk* 1992 (2): 3-8.
Moltke, E.
1985a   Det svenske Hedebyrige og Danmarks samling. *Aarbøger for Nordisk Oldkyndighed og Historie* 1985: 16- 28.
1985b   *Runes and their origin. Denmark and elsewhere*. Copenhagen: Nationalmuseet.
Müller-Boysen, C.
1992   "on thæt bæcbord Denamarc". Politische Geographie von Bord eines Wikingerschiffes betrachtet. In *Mare Balticum. Beiträge zur Geschichte des Ostseeraums in Mittelalter und Neuzeit. Festschrift zum 65.Geburtstag von Erich Hoffmann*. W. Paravicini (ed.), pp. 21-37. (Kieler Historische Studien 36). Sigmaringen: Jan Thorbecke Verlag.
Näsman, U.
1988   Analogislutning i nordisk jernalderarka ologi. In *Jernalderens stammesamfund. Fra Stamme til Stat i Danmark*, 1. (Jysk Arkæologisk Selskabs Skrifter XXII). P. Mortensen & B. M. Rasmussen (eds.), pp. 123-140. Århus: Århus University Press.
Neumann, H.
1982   *Olgerdiget - et bidrag til Danmarks tidligste historie*. (Skrifter fra Museumsrådet for Sønderjyllands Amt 1). Haderslev: Museumsrådet for Sønderjyllands Amt.
Newton, S.
1992   *Beowulf* and the East Anglian Royal Pedigree. In *The Age of Sutton Hoo*. M. O. H. Carver (ed.), pp. 65-74. Woodbridge: The Boydell Press.
Nielsen, L. C.
1990   Trelleborg. *Aarbøger for Nordisk Oldkyndighed og Historie* 1990: 105-178.
Nielsen, P. Ø., & P. 0. Sørensen
1993   Jernalderhal udgravet i Gudme. *Nyt fra Nationalmuseet* 59 (juni-august): 4-5.
Nilsson, T.
1990   Stentinget. En indlandsbebyggelse med handel og handværk fra yngre jernalder og vikingetid. En foreløbig meddelelse. *Kuml* 1990: 119-132.
Nylén, E., & J. P. Lamm
1981   *Bildsteine auf Gotland*. Neumunster: Karl Wachholtz Verlag.
Olsen, O.
1988   Royal Power in Viking Age Denmark. *Syvende tværfaglige Vikingesymposium*, pp.7-20. Århus: Hikuin.
Ramskou, T.
1980   Vikingetidsbroen over Vejle a-dal. *Nationalmuseets Arbejdsmark* 1980: 25-32.
Ramqvist, P. H.
1982   Über ökonomische und sozio-politische Beziehungen der Gesellschaften der nordischen Völkerwanderungszeit. *Frühmittelalterliche Studien* 25:45-72.
Rausing, G.
1987   Barbarian Mercenaries or Roman Citizens? *Fornvännen* 82: 126-131.
Schou Jørgensen, M.
1988   Vej, vejstrøg og vejspærring. Jernalderens landfærdsel. In *Jernalderens stammesamfund. Fra Stamme til Stat i Danmark 1*. P. Mortensen & B. M. Rasmussen (eds.), pp. 101-116. (Jysk Arkæologisk Selskabs Skrifter XXII). Århus: Århus University Press.

Sherley-Price, L.
    1972   *Bede. A History of the English Church and People.* Harmondsworth: Penguin
             Classics.
Skovgaard-Petersen, I.
    1981   The written sources. In *Ribe Excavations 1970-76*, Vol. 1. Esbjerg: Sydjysk
             Universitetsforlag .
Stoklund, M.
    1986   Neue Runenfunde in Illerup und Vimose. *Germania* 64: 75-89.
Thorpe, L.
    1974   *The History of the Franks.* Translated with an Introduction by Lewis Thorpe.
             Harmondsworth: Penguin Classics.
Thrane, H.
    1992   Das Reichtumszentrum Gudme in der Völkerwanderungszeit Funens. In *Der
             historische Horizont der Götterbild-Amulette aus der Übergangsepoche von der
             Spätantike zum Frühmittelalter.* (Abhandlungen der Akademie der Wissenschaften in
             Göttingen). K. Hauck (ed.), pp. 299-380. Göttingen: Vandenhoeck & Ruprecht.
    1993   *Guld, guder og godtfolk - et magtcentrum fra jernalderen ved Gudme og Lundeborg.*
             Copenhagen: Nationalmuseet.
Ulriksen, J.
    1990   Teorier og virkelighed i forbindelse med lokalisering af anløbspladser fra
             germanertid og vikingetid i Danmark. *Aarbøger for Nordisk Oldkyndighed og
             Historie* 1990: 69- 101.
Watt, M.
    1991   Sorte Muld. Høvdingesæde og kultcentrum fra Bornholms yngre jernalder. In
             Høvdingesamfund og Kongemagt. Fra Stamme til Stat i Danmark 2. P. Mortensen &
             B. M. Rasmussen (eds.), pp. 89-107. (Jysk Arkæologisk Selskabs Skrifter XXI: 2).
             Århus: Århus University Press.
    1992   Die Goldblechfiguren aus Sorte Muld. In *Der historische Horizont der Götterbild
             Amulette aus der Übergangsepoche von der Spätantike zum Frühmittelalter.*
             K. Hauck (ed.), pp. 195-227. (Abhandlungen der Akademie der Wissenschaften in
             Göttingen). Göttingen: Vandenhoeck & Ruprecht.
Werner, J.
    1941   *Die beiden Zierscheiben des Thorsberger Moorfundes.* (Römisch-Germanische
             Forschungen 16). Berlin: Walter de Gruyter.
Wild, J. P., & L. Bender Jørgensen
    1988   Clothes from the Roman Empire: Barbarians and Romans. In *Archaeological
             Textiles. Report from the 2nd NESAT symposium 1. 4. V. 1984.* (Arkæologiske
             Skrifter 2). Copenhagen: Arkæologisk Institut,Københavns Universitet.
Wolfram, H.
    1988   *History of the Goths.* Berkeley: University of California Press.
Wood, I. N.
    1983   *The Merovingian North Sea.* (Occasional Papers on Medieval Topics 1). Västerås:
             Viktoria Bokförlag.
Wulff Andersen, S.
    1990   "Æ vold" ved Øster Løgum. *Sønderjysk Månedsskrift* 1: 7- 15.
Ørsnes, M.
    1976   Bejsebakken. In *Reallexikon der Germanischen Altertumskunde*, begründet von J.
             Hoops, 2. Auflage, Bd. 2, pp. 173 ff. Berlin: Walter de Gruyter.
    1988   *Ejsbøl I. Waffenopferfunde des 4.-5. Jahrh. nach Chr.* (Nordiske Fortidsminder, Serie B,
             Bind 11). Copenhagen: Det kongelige Nordiske Oldskriftselskab.

Discussion

GREEN: In your precirculated paper you show dependence from Wolfram [p. 218] when you equate *reiks* with 'tribal chieftain' and *thiudans* with 'judge'. The trouble with Wolfram's equations is that his terms come from classical sources and Wulfila's Bible translation, and that he simply equates them without arguing the case. The equations are arbitrary and you are exposing yourself to attack from philologists needlessly.

AXBOE: That is of course outside my own field of study, and I am glad to know!

GREEN: My second point is a question. On page [225], you ascribe imports to "...a variety of circumstances among which may have been service in the Roman army". Is there evidence for mercenaries in the Roman army coming from Scandinavia?

AXBOE: None from the Roman side, alas; no inscriptions or things like that. But Roman influence in Scandinavia can be seen in many ways, although I have only mentioned a couple of them in my presentation: in the Migration period the Scandinavians used emperor's symbols in a correct way on the gold bracteates, and there are Roman weapons in the bog finds of the late Roman Iron Age.[4]

GREEN: How do you distinguish trade from returning mercenaries?

AXBOE: One cannot see whether Roman objects were imported or acquired by service. But the idea that quite a few Scandinavians may have known the Roman empire pretty well arises from the overall influence on society as such. Another example: roads over wet areas were nothing new in the Iron Age, and most of them were built from sticks, gravel and pebble, like in the previous periods. But a few, like the Broskov road, were built like Roman roads, with large stones carefully fitted together. I suppose the more 'primitive' roads actually served better, but there is a feeling of a sort of 'status symbol' about the Broskov type: "We will build a Roman road".

GREEN: Although I find it far-fetched: could the Scandinavian view of Valhalla (warriors fight every day against opponents entering from all directions) be a mythical recollection of Germanic warriors in the Colosseum, as has been suggested?

AXBOE: I find it far-fetched, too! Actually, Woden's warriors are fighting each other, but not in that hall with many doorways, which should be the image of the Colosseum. That hall is where they go back every evening to have a big feast.

AUSENDA: Migration for temporary work in towns hundreds of kilometres away is fairly common both among Hadendowa and Beni Amer pastoralists in eastern Sudan and northern Eritrea to obtain the wealth needed to procure wedding gifts and pay for wedding expenses.

WOOD: The length of service was twenty years, rather late to get married.

AXBOE: If they started service at 16-18, they would still be at an age where they could be married when they came back. The activities of the Roman veterans inside the Empire shows that they were to be reckoned with as active citizens. And the mean age at death for men found in Danish Iron Age graves is *ca* 39 years, meaning that once you had survived the dangerous years of childhood, you had something like a 50% chance of reaching an age of 39 or more (Sellevold *et al.* 1984:207 ff.).

HINES: Some scholars, in discussing the strategic significance of the Kanhave Canal, have indicated that it would be of benefit to a power based to the east of Samsø, not to the west; in other words, to a Danish rather that a Jutlandic power. Can you explain this?

---

[4] See the section "Some examples of Roman influences..." which was added to my paper after the symposium.

AXBOE: Well, a naval base on Samsø would be able to command the central Danish waters: The southern Kattegat and the entrance to the Belts. I'm not sure it makes much difference whether the power in control of Samsø would have come from Jutland or from Sjælland, or whether it might have controlled both areas: the purpose may have been to control the surrounding sea and the traffic going north-south.

WOOD: It might be a matter of the prevailing wind. That is what the argument must be based on.

HINES: I suppose so. I had not thought about it.

SCHUTTE: That might be.

HINES: What is the prevailing wind direction?

AXBOE: In Denmark it is from the west.

WOOD: So, if you are sailing from the east you would be tacking all the time. The canal would then save time.

HINES: Whichever way you go you have to go north and south to get around the island.

WOOD: I agree with you that that is what the argument is based on.

RICHARDS: Is it not also a question of which side would be suitable harborage?

AXBOE: The sheltered harborage is on the eastern side. From there you can go out west through the canal. But that would say nothing about the enemy or the ships to be controlled, or tolled, or whatever, where they would come from, and neither does it indicate from where the builders of the canal came. I wouldn't build an argument on the direction of the wind.

HINES: This is part of a much larger point that I wanted to make, which is to question the time-depth of the unity and continuity of the Danish kingdom. If here, in the 730s, we have a structure that is to the advantage of a Jutlandic power against a Danish power then we have a big division in the historical kingdom of Denmark.

AXBOE: Yes, but I am not sure you can use Kanhave as an argument in this connection.

HINES: Why not?

AXBOE: Well, I would take it to indicate that *somebody* had the outlook and the power to be interested in commanding the inner Danish waters. Similarly, at the same time somebody was building a rampart at Danevirke and founding Ribe as a market place. But we don't know whether the same power was behind or not. At least I would assume that Jutland would be one unity, and perhaps the whole of Denmark was. We don't know— I would not mind, but I cannot prove it.

DUMVILLE: That is a big assumption.

HINES: The point is that this is an exercise in joining the dots. In fact, your presentation of this case is the most sceptical discussion of this particular body of evidence and its interpretation that I have seen; it should be borne in mind that some scholars are much more eager to join up these dots and find the kingdom of Denmark drawn there. The general interpretation I prefer is that all of this evidence, going back through so many centuries, is good evidence that the condition for the unified kingdom of Denmark, or for substantial state-like political entities there, are in place and evolve and develop over many centuries. But that there is a continuity of kingship and, indeed, a royal family—even a continuity of kingdoms in terms of which particular areas individual royal families are controlling—this continuity, I believe, is not proven by the evidence. After all, now we have one date for the construction of the Kanhave Canal, but no dates for any maintenance works there. Is there more than a single dendro-date for the Kanhave Canal?

AXBOE: We have a date for the construction, but no evidence for maintenance, I think.

HINES: It could have soon gone out of use then.

AXBOE: Yes, even within a year or so; a good sandstorm would be enough. But as far as I remember the excavations have not been properly published, and I do not know whether there may have been any maintenance.[5] But perhaps we may compare to the similar situation with the bridge at Ravning, which is dated to 979 AD and thus must have been built by Harold Bluetooth. This is an enormous piece of work: more than 700 m. long and 5 m. broad. We have had engineers estimating how much it would carry, it was about five tons. It is constructed in one turn and it has taken whole woods of oak to build. And then, after all these efforts, there are no indications that any maintenance was done. Actually the next bridge on that site was built only at the end of the nineteenth century. Apparently there was no lasting need at all for a bridge there. If you want to go from northern Jutland to Germany, you would just follow the watersheds, which run north-south about 10 km. west of the bridge. That is where the old 'Oxen Road' runs, and the Ravning bridge hasn't offered the long-distance travellers a short cut of any significance. It was only of importance if you were to cross the river valley from some place nearby, and again, if there had been a lasting local need for that, the bridge would have been maintained and renewed. So it must have been some specific, short-term need, which caused the construction of the bridge. Jelling, which was one of the seats of Harold Bluetooth, is only a few kilometres north of Ravning and it may be the explanation that he wanted to be able to move out quickly to the south. As Jelling declined as a royal seat, the bridge fell into decay. The Kanhave Canal may be comparable: a structure, possibly with a military function, which was built in a specific historical situation, but which fell redundant as conditions changed.

RICHARDS: I have a few points. You talked about hoards as ritual deposits [p. 227], and you emphasised in your presentation that you thought that many of them had been votive offerings.

AXBOE: Of the gold hoards.

RICHARDS: Yes, particularly because they seemed to contain some fixed unit items, as if these were of special significance.

AXBOE: Yes, that is one reason. Another is that quite a few of the hoards had been deposited in bogs where it would be very difficult to get the things back again, so that it is unlikely that they were placed there for safe-keeping.

RICHARDS: I accept that those bog finds may be seen in that context, but on the same page you made reference to the importance of gift giving. I wondered whether it was not possible to see a lot of these hoards as being gifts which were being collected together. It would take quite a long time to gather the items you would want to present to someone as a prestige gift.

AXBOE: Would that be 'bank box' deposits for safe-keeping?

RICHARDS: Yes, I suppose there is the intention of recovering. And I do not think that conflicts with there being fixed items in there, because gift giving is likely to have been ritualised, in the sense that you have to give certain items.

AXBOE: Well, one of the fixed 'sets', which we may find, is two gold neck-rings, and I would think that would make a nice gift, but of course we do not know what was expected

---

[5] In November 1994 additional dendrochronological datings from the Kanhave Canal have been published. The building year 726 was confirmed, but one piece of timber seems to indicate that the canal was repaired in or around 750 AD (Bonde *et al.* 1993:299 ff.).

or what was necessary. I would see those hoards more like gifts for the gods, thus to establish a dependence: "I do something for you, you do something for me".

RICHARDS: Maybe there is a continuum between gifts to humans and gifts to gods.

AXBOE: Yes, I think you might see those offerings as a parallel to gifts given between humans, which also would aim at establishing a mutual dependence.

RICHARDS: On the same point I want to ask for a bit more information about the sites that you mention [p. 229], as being made through metal detector finds of recent years, at least the high status rural sites.... You said they dated from the Iron Age onwards, but that many were of the Vendel period. I am particularly interested in these because in England we have a group of Middle Saxon sites that are very rich rural sites which have been discovered by metal detector users. You described them as having a 'town plan'. I wonder what exactly you meant by 'town plan' and how late these sites were.

AXBOE: Well, I described some of them as having that sort of 'town plan' or settlement layout which you see in fig. 9.5. Because that is not a normal village. It is partly the size— it is much larger than usual rural settlements—but also the separate house clusters within the larger settlement. The Hodde village which I showed during the presentation is much more normal, just some farms lying together within a common fence. Variations of this more usual layout we find in Vorbasse and Nørre Snede and at quite a lot of other sites (see the village plans in Hvass 1988).

RICHARDS: You mean that streets were laid out?

AXBOE: No, no! I put 'town plan' in inverted commas, because it was the best two words I could find.

HINES: In fact I translated that. It was *byplan* in the original, or something like that. Unless you really do want to emphasise some analogy or links with the towns that develop in early medieval Europe it would be better to use a rather more long-winded but potentially less misleading phrase such as 'complex settlement plan'.

AXBOE: Yes, perhaps I should consult my translator.

HINES: Indeed, yes.

RICHARDS: So, the evidence that you have got from Ribe is not suggesting that they are like Ribe. You are not arguing that.

AXBOE: No, definitely not. On the other hand, they are not normal rural settlements. And not only because of their layout and their size but also because of the metal finds. We must conclude so because we have a control group of other settlements where checks and counterchecks have been made just as intensively with metal detectors without anything being found. One example is even Vorbasse, the classic village, where they have walked on 10,000s of square meters and found something like three objects. On the rich sites you may find several hundred objects.

RICHARDS: We have a similar problem in that the excavated settlements have very few metal finds, whilst metal detector users are finding other sites that are very rarely excavated but very rich. How late do your metal finds go from this category of sites?

AXBOE: That depends; into the Middle Ages or even later.

RICHARDS: So they definitely overlap with the Viking period?

AXBOE: Yes, Viking period finds are included and some later finds too. But, of course, that is different from site to site.

RICHARDS: Is Gudme the only one that is being excavated?

AXBOE: No, only Gudme is the one which is being most intensively examined of these sites. Of the others, Sorte Muld has been partly excavated, Stentinget in northern

Jutland is being excavated, while at Neble on Sjælland there have only been some small excavations. A site with many metal finds is Bejsebakken in the modern city of Ålborg where it is difficult to excavate, but actually some 'Grubenhäuser' have been found. But it is a difficult site also because other parts of the rich area have been excavated without any traces of settlement structures being found: they may have disappeared because of sandstorms which may have removed the culture layers through the centuries, leaving only the heavier objects. On the other hand there is also the possibility that they came from destroyed graves.

RICHARDS: My final point is the question of how far back can you trace a unified Denmark? If you see unified Denmark going back much further, isn't it going to become difficult to explain why Harold Bluetooth goes into his massive building program and is so concerned to legitimize his power?

AXBOE: Well, he had serious troubles with the German emperors Otto I and Otto II. Harold was one rebuilder of Danevirke and he had to fight there, but we know that he lost some of the battles with the Germans.

SCHÜTTE: What I find astonishing is that, contrary to all political conflicts between the Danish and the German kings, there is a strong stream of trade running to Denmark from late Merovingian or early Carolingian times on, which seems quite intensive. And even later you mention [p. 233] the exception, Magnus the Good son of Olaf the Saint. We have found the grave of Rudolf of Schleswig, the bishop sitting in Schleswig. He was a Cologne cleric and very closely related to Magnus the Good; he was especially involved in minting in Schleswig and we see that he was active in the triangle between Frisia, the Rhineland, Denmark, and Flanders, and his activities were less ecclesiastical than economical. And, if we see what he has in his grave, his embroideries are very highly comparable to the tenth century Birka finds; they are almost identical. This group of people related to noble families or maybe even to the kings, were promoters of trade. So, it is very interesting to see how goods do come into Scandinavia in spite of all political contrasts. Rudolf died in the same year as Magnus the Good and he was buried in Cologne. One can see that there must not necessarily be such a contradiction: even if they fought against each other there was also a lot of trade going on.

TURTON: You cannot have trade without some kind of understanding—without the existence of normative ties between people. And it seems that warfare, certainly in the ethnographic literature, and also particularly destructive and unpleasant warfare, takes place precisely where there is a set of ties and obligations between people on either side. This could suggest that the 'purpose' of war is to overcome these ties, to create and maintain separate political identities. In other words, war is not the result of there being separate political units already in existence. It's about creating them.

SCHÜTTE: As I mentioned the example of early Ribe and early market finds in Cologne, these mosaic-stones of glass, as raw material for bead production in Scandinavia, are almost identical.

TURTON: The impression I have been getting in the past couple of days is that there was an awful lot of movement of goods and people over very large distances. As an outsider to this discussion, I have the impression that the idea is that there was first a period when everybody stayed in their own places and then came a period of 'transition' when there was a lot of movement. But is it conceivable that there was ever a time when movement was not taking place? Should one not assume that movement was the norm?

WOOD: The exception is large scale movement across the Roman frontiers. There is a constant grouping and regrouping of people and movements of peoples to the north of that frontier. The reason why southern Scandinavia is involved is due to the breaking of the imperial frontier. This is just a new geographical area which becomes heavily permeated.

HINES: It is also appropriate to say that one of the reasons why the movement of people is enjoying some tentative emphasis at the moment is that the fashions of archaeological theory for the last 30 years have been totally against the old sort of notion that if, for instance, you got Beaker pottery in graves you must have had a 'Beaker folk' to bring it in. The emphasis on stable populations has been so intense that in investigating the development of material culture it has been impossible to assume that movement of substantial populations or even of individuals was a common state of affairs. Now, however the tide has turned, and at least within the first millennium AD, much of the evidence that researchers are finding is suggesting that considerable movement and long-distance contact was common and frequent. This is what would bring Danish soldiers—I would rather say southern Scandinavians—into the Roman empire. It does not seem an eccentric idea to entertain.

AXBOE: But those soldiers need only to be the younger sons of the better families or something like that. At least in Denmark we must also assume constant populations, or at least that important parts of the population stayed where they were. We have settlement and even village continuity through centuries.

GREEN: Another consideration, I think, is that we tend too much from our modern point of view to see trade and warfare as diametrically opposed to each other. Whereas in this whole period we are concerned with, I think we should see the two as changing, readjusting alternatives. It is not by chance, for example, that the Gothic migration, the Gothic contacts with the Baltic and Finnish coastline follow earlier Gothic trading routes to these areas. Just as the route they took from northern Poland down to the Ukraine and the Black Sea had been, long before the Goths, established as a trading route between the South and the North so that what Gothic migratory tribes or groups may have done, was to follow indications given to them by traders, hoping this was a route where happy hunting grounds could be found. We have to see these two possibilities more in conjunction, not as antitheses.

HINES: On this question of migration, I would not want to suggest that everybody moved as a matter of course; simply that some members of society did.

I was most impressed by the presentation of a section of the Danevirke, showing the substantial phases that are earlier than the ones that have been dated to the eighth century. You mentioned 'Olgerdiget' and 'Æ vold' being built at the end of the third century, but not renewed after that time. The Danevirke we know got a substantial facelift in the 730s, and we know there were phases that were earlier than that but we do not know how far back they go. What is most interesting for me about Danevirke and Olgerdiget/Æ vold is that they lie on the southern and northern boundaries respectively of what, from the third to fifth centuries, one can reasonably suspect was the territory of the Angles.

AXBOE: Yes, I think I would be more pleased than surprised if the oldest Danevirke should appear to be a rampart of a more modest size, dated to 287 or something like that.

HINES: What then is very interesting is that the differentiation between the Angles and the people to the north—their political, physical or symbolic separation from people further north who, for want of a better term, let us call them Jutes—disappears somewhere, according to this evidence, between 400 and 700 AD. This itself is a period for which we have historical traditions stating that the Angles migrated from just that area to Britain, and Bede in the

730s saying that their homelands "remained deserted to the present day". I suspect that an explanation of what Bede said is that, unlike in the case of the Saxon and Jutish homelands, he did not have any information that a group called the Angles still lived on the Continent. It would not suggest he really had reason to believe there was no one living there at all, or that he put a hyperbolic distortion into his history to make the migration story sound more credible; he may simply have had no source that could tell him there were still *antiqui Angli* living on the Continent and from this he inferred the total abandonment of the area.

AXBOE: Yes, but after all, to this day there is still a peninsula named Angeln.

HINES: Yes, the name has survived. But I do not know what the earliest record of that place-name is.

AXBOE: I hope it is not an antiquarian construct!

HINES: I worry about that every time I refer to it too.

GREEN: This brings up an intriguing and very contentious aspect of place-name studies in Germany and in England: if one can see these migrations, as we are more and more agreeing as we go along, not as migration of tribes but as migrations of groups which are becoming and unbecoming tribes and incorporating new groups as they go along, one has to imagine this really as an ethnic hodge-podge on the move, if I may put it that way. One has a nice parallel in that in Germany, far south of the original home of the Angles we have place-names with first element *Engel* or *Ingel* which are tied up with *Angli*, suggesting that some may have been swept up with another group, not with the 'English' group, and got carried farther south. Just as on the English side we have got Swabians who were dislodged from their own group and now find themselves in Swaffham or Swavesey. One has to imagine all this as a hodge-podge of tribal splinters being regrouped on the move.

TURTON: This is a very characteristic feature of African migration myths. One is told, "We collected (such and such a group) on the way". There is often a distinction between 'aristocratic' clans, which are seen, in the oral accounts, as having set out from a particular place, and those they 'collected' *en route*. Obviously, the historical reality is a process that took place over many many years. [Recess].

DUMVILLE: A starting point, since you raised the matter when you started your presentation, about a 'Bretwalda-system' is perhaps to come in from that angle.

Ian and I found ourselves in a discussion almost ten years ago with a German scholar who referred to the 'Bretwalda-Amt'. English historiography went through a long phase as far as Anglo-Saxon history was concerned, also as far as later medieval history was concerned, of working on the assumption of a natural, indeed almost an inevitable progression towards the modern British state, perceived as the English state. Indeed, I can still remember the examination-questions of 20 years ago which were always loaded with that assumption.

The early stages of that inevitable progression were seen in terms of what 'Bretwaldas' were doing. There is a group of problems here, and I shall not try to pursue all of them. First of all, I think that it is reasonably clear now that the word 'Bretwalda' itself is a ghost. The word which we have in the Anglo-Saxon Chronicle is *brytenwealda*, and it is not quite clear what the first element is. It may mean 'wide', giving to the compound a sense of 'wide ruler', or it may mean 'Britain'. So, in using that term one is in a difficulty.

There are various reasons, not the least that it is first attested in the late ninth century, for not using that word and instead to try to work out one's own terminology, more in sympathy with contemporary source material for the seventh and eighth centuries; then, with its aid, we can start to talk more clearly about the development of kingship and overkingship in Anglo-Saxon England.

What is now clear to me is that there is no necessary progression from smaller state organisation to larger state-organisation or from chiefdom to state. What is more, there is no unilinear and progressive movement in that direction in England. And, therefore, with the English historiographical experience in mind, I wonder whether you would be prepared to rethink your approach to the Danish evidence. For Denmark I take John's caution that others are arguing for early state-formation more radically. But I wonder whether you were doing or were trying to do for Denmark through the archaeology what English historians have tried to do for England through written sources, and whether there would be something to be said for deliberately adopting also another perspective, to see whether that could do any damage to the first approach. At various points in your written paper you gave an opening for the reader, I think, to consider that there were bursts of activity producing new forms of political organisation or structures of society, and then perhaps periods when something like that was not happening.

I wonder if an attempt to see whether one can find state-collapse as well as state-development periodically through this era might also be fruitful, in other words, not to look at things in terms of one single progressive development. And the risk, it seems to me, of the focus on the modern state is that you risk, if not now, then perhaps later, being accused of writing nationalist archaeology. Concerning Scotland in the same period, one sees now a very similar kind of approach, with a similar thought-pattern; it is interesting and it is provocative, but I wonder whether the starting point is not the modern world rather than the ancient world or the medieval world (e.g. Driscoll 1991). There is almost an implication, again very familiar to historians, that a progression towards a state is somehow a natural or, what is worse, a good thing.

AXBOE: We have the problem that when written history begins for Denmark we start up with a state, some sort of state, and we may ask the question "How did that come about?" Because it did come about.

DUMVILLE: It is an entirely fair question, but I wonder then if one does not need to be more circumspect in one's approach. It is a procedural thought which is worrying me. Two other things, one of which is related to that.

Interpretation of linear earthworks, of linear boundary-works. Is it necessarily the case, on comparative grounds, that the creation of a linear earthwork necessarily requires something which one might describe as a proto-state apparatus to create it? I think with anxiety of various linear works which might have belonged to the Dark-Age period in Britain and from which various conclusions have been drawn over a period of time. I do not necessarily want to overturn your approach to this, but it worries me that the interpretation may be loaded because one is looking for the origin of a state.

AXBOE: Well, of course, two or three men might build a linear earthwork provided they had time enough. But why should they? Naturally, we should not overemphasise the needs for providing for the building operation, but there must have been some sort of community purpose for such a project. By the way, in my argumentation I have only used the few earthworks which have been securely dated and not included the many undated ones— I know that one of the British earthworks seems to be pre-Roman, not Dark Age.

VOICES: More than one.

DUMVILLE: What I am groping around for is that I am not sure that everybody would agree, even in a group as small as this, on what a state was or what state-creation was.

While I hesitate to suggest 'state' for our hypothetical glossary, it does seem to me that, if one is arguing in those kinds of terms, it would be helpful to give a definition within your eventual paper.

AXBOE: I would almost say that I have carefully avoided trying that, because I do not want to tie up to any specific model.

DUMVILLE: How then do we judge the success or otherwise of your attempt? What do we measure against?

AXBOE: Well, I have tried to present some evidence which seemed to mean some line of greater organisation. But I am not a model builder. I do not have a square Marxist or other point of view. I do not always understand such models, and I prefer not to pretend that I do.

DUMVILLE: Do not built it, but give us some criterion by which to assess what you yourself are attempting.

Lastly, one simple technical point. Just listening as a non-archaeologist over the last few years to people using dendrochronological dating, I take the precise dating which is produced by this method to be based on the assumption that timber when felled was immediately pressed into service. Is this the working assumption?

AXBOE: Yes, what is dated is when this particular tree was cut down. We have cases where we can see that timber has been re-used, like parts of buildings being used as framing for a well and things like that. But in the large earthworks you have tree, after tree, after tree cut down and used for a palisade and no traces of re-working....

DUMVILLE: That was not quite what I was driving at. I know nothing about how timber is prepared for use in different circumstances. What I simply wondered is whether for some purpose or other one would fell trees and then store, or do something to the wood over a longish period before use.

SCHÜTTE: I do not think so, because oak wood is worked with the axe and it is only possible to work oak wood in the first three months after cutting it down, otherwise it hardens rapidly, and then you can use it for carvings. This is the one and only purpose for storing oak wood for a long time. But for building purposes the wood should be worked within the first three months, so you have the date plus three months. Normally the tree is cut in winter or in autumn. If it is cut earlier, which sometimes was necessary, you can see it from the development of the last ring.

DUMVILLE: Thank you very much. That is very clear.

WOOD: I have some minor points. When you cite Gregory of Tours [p. 217], refer to the *Histories,* not *History of the Franks*. On the date of Hygelac's raid, this can be any time in Theuderic I's reign (511-33). Gregory appears to place it sometime between 511 and 525, but we do not know that he knew the date.

You follow Staubach on the date of Clovis' conversion: but this could have taken place at any time up to 508. Also Staubach misrepresents the text of Avitus of Vienne, who praises Clovis as being acute enough to renounce what his ancestors believed in. Staubach takes a more extreme view (Staubach 1983:29 ff.).[6] On a point of Wolfram, the question of the Amal claim to divine ancestry. What the text says is that they claimed to be *ansis id est semidei*. You need to be careful about sacral kingship. All the descriptions supposedly relating to sacral kingship among the Goths concern magic or warrior status.

---

[6]   These points refer to the pre-circulated paper; they have been corrected in the printed version.

AXBOE: I am not sure the members of the royal families would necessarily consider themselves to be gods even if they claimed their remote forefathers to be divine. Compare that to the fact that several Greek heroes were *semidei* or had a divine father or mother.

WOOD: Hercules becomes a god when he dies.

AXBOE: I would see the divine ancestry as a parallel to the later kings' claim to have their power "by the grace of God".

GREEN: Then one would have to look at the question (but this is David's field) of Anglo-Saxon royal genealogies, because then one could ask: if an East Anglian king traces his descent back to Woden, does that make the East Anglian king himself divine? But what happens then if he also traces his descent back to Caesar? Does that make Caesar divine?

AXBOE: But Caesar *was* divine! [Laughter]. Well, I think it is a question of legitimacy.

GREEN: We are talking not about whether Caesar was divine in Roman eyes, but whether he was held to be divine in Anglo-Saxon eyes.

AXBOE: Yes, and whether in Anglo-Saxon eyes the descendants of a god needed to be divine themselves.

GREEN: That is the point which Ian has just made.

AXBOE: I think the descent 'Woden, Caesar', and so on, is similar to tracing one's people back to Troy, as the Romans did and others after them. Similarly, many years ago David Dumville wrote in *Early Medieval Kingship* that it was very important for British rulers to trace themselves back to Magnus Maximus, the last emperor in Britain (Dumville 1977:81).

DUMVILLE: Among the Britons.

AXBOE: The point was to establish that "we are the legitimate rulers". I understand the 'descent' from Woden and/or Caesar as a sort of a pagan parallel to "... by the grace of God".

HINES: To talk of 'Anglo-Saxon eyes' is to make an impossible generalisation. We need to distinguish at least pagan Anglo-Saxon eyes from Christian Anglo-Saxon eyes, to say nothing of Anglian eyes, Saxon eyes and so on. But I understand Morten's point that this is a way of claiming a legitimacy in the pagan world.

AXBOE: Yes, and for the Christians I would refer to David Dumville's observation that Bede had no problems when telling that many kings traced their pedigree back to Woden: Woden apparently expressed no more than a means of defining royalty (Dumville 1977:78 ff.).

DUMVILLE: That certainly is one view, yes.

AXBOE: That was your view in 1977....

DUMVILLE: It was a view accepted from somebody else (Miller 1975:254 n. 1) and I hope that the footnote shows this. But, yes, and I think that is a very defensible point of view, in fact, a minimalist point of view.

AXBOE: I think that showing, "I have the right royal status" can be demonstrated in many ways, and one of them would be descent from Woden, another descent from Caesar, or Saxnot, or some later emperor, or perhaps for Anglo-Saxons even Danish kings, as proposed by Sam Newton in the new book on Sutton Hoo (Newton 1992).

DUMVILLE: There is a whole book arguing that by Sam Newton (Newton 1993).

AXBOE: Yes, he is announcing that in the 1992 paper.

TURTON: Can I make a suggestion which may be totally heretical? I was struck when you said that the question "How did the state develop?" is an obvious one. I just wondered whether it actually is a good question to ask. In order to answer it you have to tell a story, you have to write a narrative, but it's an odd narrative because you know the end but not the beginning. So it's a story that must be told with a particular ending always in mind. The right question is "How can we explain that canal?" You need a hypothesis and there are presumably several available, such as the one you put forward. But you didn't consider the other possibilities because they didn't fit in with the story you were telling.

AXBOE: I have of course considered other uses of the canal. It has taken some amount of work to construct, and we must look for a purpose where it was worthwhile digging it. Local people would hardly dig it. Why should they?

TURTON: But, as I understand it, the digging of the canal was used, in your argument, to support a hypothesis rather than the other way round—it was used as evidence to support a larger hypothesis.

AXBOE: Yes, or I would say that it fits nicely in. But if I am to try to explain this canal, there might be two possibilities: one, as a communication line, to allow sailing across the island of Samsø; the other, as a defence line to avoid passing on foot between the northern and the southern part of the island. The latter explanation is hardly likely, considering the small size of the island of Samsø and especially the small northern part, being too small to defend itself but on the other hand much too large to be defended as a fort. Besides, there are no reports of any rampart on any side of the canal.

So we will have to stick to the hypothesis that it actually was a canal built for sailing. However, bearing in mind the large sheltered bay on the eastern side of the island, to local people, such as fishermen, it would have cost much less work to have an extra boat if they wished to go fishing from both shores, or even to drag their boats across the isthmus. Similarly, pirates would be better off with an extra ship. One could of course imagine some larger trading site at the bay, but would a spared sailing distance of something like 15-20 km. for the merchants of Jutland justify the construction of the canal? I think that's a much too modern thought. So we come up to some sort of military function and, I think, necessarily some large-scale function, with strategics reaching far beyond the island of Samsø.

RICHARDS: Can I find out what exactly you are trying to say with the archaeological evidence about the organisation of Danish society before the transition? I do not think you can dodge the question of a unified Danish state at that stage. These highly organised activities may be happening in a number of different areas, but it is wrong to join the dots and say they belong to a unified whole.

WOOD: Except that in the 730s you have this astonishing cluster of material, at exactly the same time in three different places. Do you not?

AXBOE: Well, within a generation or so.

WOOD: Yes, Ribe....

AXBOE: Starting with Ribe and then the Kanhave canal and Danevirke.

HINES: I believe this is a case where considering the history of recent research can help us. This has been quite a central topic in historical research for some 15 years. It was not driven by people looking for the origin of the Danish state; it was led by people wishing to understand social organisation in the prehistoric period who, as they investigated that, came to believe that in fact they had discovered the origins of the Danish state, at a much earlier date than was previously thought. That step having been taken, some scholars may well now be over-eagerly finding that all the dots can join up and so perhaps overstate the level of continuity. But this was not a case of a programme of research being carried out in which the desired answer was already known. The people who went into this area looking for social organisation certainly had their own preconceptions. No one is exempt from that.

There was a preconception of what social organisation would be like. But they did not set out to discover the origins of the Danish state and this, I believe, is one reason why so many scholars have felt uninhibited about pursuing the topic: many of them represent schools of thought where they really do consider themselves entirely free from any possible charge of nationalism.

TURTON: I was not thinking directly of nationalism but of all history as being, to some extent, driven by present interests, driven by a desire to legitimize, explain and justify the present. In the past, anthropologists took this to extreme lengths and tended to disregard all history treating it, in Malinowski's words, as 'mythical charters'. Clan histories, for example, were seen as 'charters' to explain the present territorial distribution of clans; they were not seen as connected with what actually happened in the past. But I presume all history, even written history, has something of that about it.

Deleuze and Guattari made the point that: "History is always written from a sedentary point of view and in the name of a unitary State apparatus...even when the topic is nomads" (1987:23). So it is always thought necessary to explain why people move around, not why they stay in the same place. Anthropology is also "written from a sedentary point of view". In fact, I cannot think of a single anthropologist who has tried to explain sedentism. Moving around is seen as a 'problem' but staying in one place is seen as 'natural'. But it only seems so to us. The people I worked with think the most 'natural' thing of all is to move around. There are so many practical problems of getting on with other people if you are stuck with them all the time. One of my colleagues in Manchester, Paul Baxter, wrote an article to explain the general absence of witchcraft amongst nomads and he gave it the title 'Absence makes the heart grow fonder' (Baxter 1972).

AUSENDA: Also for practical reasons, sanitation not the least.

TURTON: Oh yes, absolutely.

References in the discussion

Baxter, P.
  1972   Absence makes the heart grow fonder. In *The Allocation of Responsibility*.
              M. Gluckman (ed.), pp.163-192. Manchester: Manchester University Press.
Bonde, N., T. Bartholin, K. Christensen & O. H. Eriksen
  1993   Dendrochronological Dating at the National Museum of Denmark. *Arkæologiske*
              Udgravninger i Danmark 1993: 294-310.
Deleuze, H. G., & F. Guattari
  1987   *A Thousand Plateaus: Capitalism and Schizophrenia*. Minneapolis, MN: University
              of Minnesota Press.
Driscoll, S.
  1991   The Archaeology of State Formation in Scotland. In *Scottish Archaeology: New*
              Perceptions. W. S. Hanson & E. A. Slater (eds.), pp. 81-111. Aberdeen: Aberdeen
              University Press.
Dumville, D. N.
  1977   Kingship, Genealogies and Regnal Lists. In *Early Medieval Kingship*. P. H. Sawyer
              & I. N. Wood (eds.), pp.72-104. Leeds: The School of History, University of Leeds.
Hvass, S.
  1988   See references at end of paper.
Miller, M.
  1975   Bede's use of Gildas. *English Historical Review* 90: 241-261.

Newton, S.
1992   See references at end of paper.
Newton, S. (*cont*)
1993   *The Origins of Beowulf and the Pre-Viking Kingdom of East Anglia.* Cambridge: D. S. Brewer.
Sellevold, B. J., U. Lund Hansen & J. Balslev Jørgensen
1984   *Iron Age Man in Denmark. Prehistoric Man in Denmark*, Vol. III. (Nordiske Fortidsminder, Serie B, Bind 8). Copenhagen: Det kongelige Nordiske Oldskriftselskab.
Staubach, N.
1982   Germanisches Königtum und lateinische Literatur vom fünften bis zum siebten Jahrhundert. *Frühmittelalterliche Studien* 17: 1-54.

PAGAN RELIGIONS AND SUPERSTITIONS EAST OF THE RHINE FROM THE FIFTH TO THE NINTH CENTURY

IAN N. WOOD

School of History, University of Leeds, Leeds LS2 9JT

Paganism and Christianity

The religious history of the territories east of the Rhine during the early Middle Ages is usually characterised by the polarity of paganism and Christianity.[1] This polarity is problematic in more ways than one. Allegations of paganism are at times no more than identifications of alternative Christianities. This is relatively clear from the writings of Boniface and his disciples, who dismiss Christians associated with other political and religious circles as heretics and pagans (Wood 1994:309-10). More generally, to use the labels 'pagan' and 'Christian' is to risk locking oneself into the cultural constructs and value judgements of the early medieval missionaries.

There is, nevertheless, some justification for retaining such terminology. First, to talk of religion *tout court* would require a study of enornus length encompassing both Christianity and paganism. Such a study would, of course, be immensely valuable in breaking down cultural assumptions, but it could not be attempted in a few short pages. Second, and more important, the starting point for any study of religious beliefs east of the Rhine must be an understanding of what the Christians envisaged when using such terms as *paganus* and *superstitio*. Without our Christian documentation the subject would be one for prehistorical, as opposed to historical, research. For instance, we can only be certain that cremation was regarded by some as a pagan forn of burial because of Charlemagne's *Capitularia de partibus Saxoniae* (7). And cremation is almost alone in being a probable indicator that a burial is non-Christian: the orientation of the body and the presence of grave goods cannot be taken as diagnostic (Bullough 1983:190-1). As for the iconography of pagan religion, this has been explored in the context of the bracteates. Nevertheless the meaning of these gold medallions, manufactured in a relatively small area of northern Europe, and perhaps only for two generations, can be no more than speculation (Wallace-Hadrill 1983:17). Only the origins of the iconography, in late Roman coinage, are unquestionable.

The Literary Evidence

In so far as we have any certain knowledge of pagan cosmology in the early medieval period, it derives from a handful of written texts. Most extensive are Daniel of Winchester's

---

[1] This paper has been radically revised in the light of the comrnents made by all the other participants at the San Marino conference. In particular, I have tried to respond to the challenging, and helpful, criticisms of David Turton and Dennis Green.

AFTER EMPIRE:
TOWARDS AN ETHNOLOGY OF EUROPES'S BARBARIANS

© C.I.R.O.S.S.
San Marino (R.S.M.)

comments, which are of uncertain worth because he himself never worked among the pagans east of the Rhine (Boniface, *Ep.* 23). Shorter, but of more certain value, are such documents as baptismal formulae, condemning Donar, Wodan and Saxnot (Lange 1962:176), and the Merseburg charms, which invoke Wodan and Frija (Braune *et al.* 1958:86). Although we may wish to use earlier, Roman, or later, medieval, evidence to elucidate the beliefs of the pagan contemporaries of Charlemagne, to do so without caution is to assume that Germanic paganism scarcely changed over time. We may be right to think that the most significant Germanic gods of the Merovingian and early Carolingian age were Donar, Wodan and Frija, and to flesh out our knowledge of them by reference to Roman and Viking Age sources, but our most detailed eighth- and ninth-century evidence relates to the cult of the little known, and probably regional, god Fosite (Alcuin, *Vita Willibrordi* 10; Altfrid, *Vita Liudgeri* I, 22).

In considering pagan religion and superstition our written sources may alone bring the subject from prehistory into history, but these sources are themselves distinctly problematic. There are, for instance, many references to 'pagan' activity in ecclesiastical legislation and works of theology. All these references, of course, represent a Christian viewpoint. It is, moreover, well known that writers in ninth-century Germany often borrowed their descriptions from south Gallic and Spanish theologians of the sixth century (Boudriot 1928). As a result it is necessary to ask whether the information borrowed really did have a relevance to the regions east of the Rhine. Are the comments of such theologians as Burchard of Worms no more than literary borrowings (a question largely ignored by Flint 1991)? A similar problem is raised by the so-called *interpretatio romana* (e.g. Tacitus, *Germania* 9. Lund 1988:137, 226; Much 1967:171-2, 479-81). Do the references to the *spurcalia* and to Mercury and Jupiter (e.g. *Indiculus superstitionum* 3, 8, 20) reflect a tendency to see Germanic gods and rituals in Roman terms, or did Roman paganism influence its Germanic counterpart in the centuries before Constantine (Wallace-Hadrill 1983:18-9)?

Certainly there is a strong case for thinking that the presence of the Church itself created 'unorthodox' religions in its shadow. That something of this sort could happen is clear enough from what is arguably our best source for 'Germanic paganism', the *Indiculus superstitionum et paganiarum*. This is a short list of superstitious and pagan practices compiled either by Boniface, archbishop of Mainz, or by someone in his circle at the time of the *Concilium germanicum* of 743 (Dierkens 1985). Among the practices condemned are sacrileges committed in church (*Indiculus* 5), sacrifices performed in honour of saints (*Indiculus* 9), worship of saints performed in improper places (*Indiculus* 18), and the seeking of what belongs to St Mary (*Indiculus* 19). That these actions are spin-offs from Christianity is clear enough. Whether they were performed by pagans, or by Christians of dubious orthodoxy, is impossible to determine. It is certainly possible that some pagans incorporated Christian elements into their religious practices: the case, as we shall see, is particularly plausible for Anglo-Saxon England. At the same time it is certain that some Christians incorporated pagan elements into their religious practices. The Merseburg charms were undoubtedly copied by clerics or monks. And in Boniface's letters we even meet Christian priests performing pagan sacrifice (*Epistolae* 80). In all this, however, it is important to remember that Boniface and his followers were rigorists, and that their categorisations may have been stricter than most. The evidence of our most important canonical sources thus presents huge problems of interpretation.

The interpretation of narrative sources is as difficult as that of theology and canon law. Once again there can be a problem of literary borrowing. For instance the account of the shrine of Fosite in Altfrid's *Life of Liudger* (I, 22) is undoubtedly related to that in Alcuin's *Life of Willibrord* (10). In this case the borrowing does not pose a serious evidential problem because both texts refer to a single place. More difficult to cope with is the possibility of outright invention. This problem is perhaps most acute in a rather later source, relating to Scandinavian paganism. Adam of Bremen's twelfth-century description of the temple at Uppsala, with its three great statues and its human and animal sacrifices hanging from trees, is among the most cited descriptions of an early medieval cult site (*Gesta hammaburgensis ecclesiae pontificum* IV, 26-27). Since Adam was unquestionably presenting a misleading account of the christianisation of Sweden for reasons of Church politics (Sawyer 1987:88), it is difficult to know the extent to which his description of Uppsala is determined by his personal agenda (see also the structuralist analysis in Alkemade 1991:283-4). Only excavation can come anywhere near to resolving this dilemma. Adam's biases are well enough known to prompt the researcher to caution. Other authors, whose intentions are not so easily detected, also require intense scrutiny (Wood 1987a; Wood n.d.).

Paganism: Organisation and Practice

In short, the sources from which we must reconstruct non-Christian religion east of the Rhine, legal, hagiographical, or indeed epistular, present very considerable problems. If, however, we do not concentrate on the details of cosmology or belief, but rather on what is known of the organisation and practice of religion within society before official conversion to Christianity, it may be possible to remain on relatively firm ground. Nevertheless, even such basic elements of paganism as temples, idols and priesthoods present problems of interpretation. These elements, and others including sacrifice and divination, require discussion, each in turn, before any more general observations can be made on the nature of public religion, and indeed on that of private superstition.

Temples

Temples are mentioned in the Continental record of the eighth and ninth centuries, but they seem not to have been common (Helm 1953:171), and for the most part they seem to have been fairly insignificant structures. The *Indiculus superstitionum* (4) talks of small temple buildings (*de casulis, id est fanis*), and in his first Saxon capitulary Charlemagne envisages shrines for idols (*vana idolorum*) (*Capitulare de partibus Saxoniae* 1; compare Eigil, *Vita Sturmi* 22). Alcuin, in his *Life of Willibrord* (14) talks of an idol kept within a villa on Walcheren, which may imply that some temples were no more than sections of ordinary houses. Yet he also mentions temples (*fana*) in his description (*Vita Willibrordi* 10) of an island, probably Helgoland, dedicated to the god Fosite (compare Altfrid, *Vita Liudgeri* I, 19). Altfrid later refers to the same temples (*Vita Liudgeri* I, 22). In addition he talks of Liudger being sent to destroy other temples and idols among the Frisians (*fana deorum et varias culturas idolorum in gente Fresonum*) (*Vita Liudgeri* I, 16). So too, Willehad destroyed temples (*fana*) in the region of Drenthe (*Vita Willehadi* 4). Another temple is described in the *Annales regni Francorum* (*s.a.* 772) in the account of Charlemagne's destruction of the Irminsul during his Saxon campaign of 772. Here the king is said to have destroyed a temple and taken its gold and silver. A second account, however, talks only of an idol (*idolum*), and even ignores the existence of a temple (*Annales qui dicuntur Einhardi, s.a.* 772).

None of these accounts give us any clue as to the nature of these temples, to their size or their form. They could all be shrines of inconsiderable dimensions. Nor has archaeology exposed any unquestionable major temple-building in the territories to the west of the Slav lands, where sizeable temples are unquestionably to be found. Before concluding that large temple-structures were not a feature of Germanic paganism, however, it is necesary to consider the Anglo-Saxon evidence. Sixth- and seventh-century England was certainly not devoid of pagan temples, though archaeology has so-far produced no sites which can be so identified without question (Hope-Taylor 1977:262-4). Even the identification of a temple at Yeavering is open to doubt (despite Hope-Taylor 1977:97-102). In the absence of archaeological finds, place-names provide the only evidence for numbers of temple sites (Gelling 1978:154-61; Mayr-Harting 1991:24). On the nature of the temples the written sources are a little more informative. The most graphic evidence for Anglo-Saxon temples comes from Northumbria where, after a debate on Christianity, the high priest Coifi mounted a stallion and rode to the place where the idols (*idola*) were kept, and threw a spear into the temple (*fanum*) (Bede, *Historia ecclesiastica* II, 13). Yet, comparatively extensive as this description is, it proves no more than the existence of a sacred enclosure, with a shrine, of uncertain size, for idols. Bede also describes another temple-building (*fanum*) which had an altar for Christian sacrifice and an *arula* for offerings to demons (Bede, *Historia ecclesiastica* II, 16). This description of a temple with a Christian and pagan altar, however, is part of a hostile account of King Redwald, and it would be unwise to build a great deal on it. Even if it is accurate, Bede may be describing a church with a pagan altar, rather than a temple with a Christian one. Redwald was, after all, already a Christian. This is a building from an age of transition, rather than an example of a classic pagan temple.

Indeed, the Germanic paganism of the British Isles may have differed considerably from its Continental origins because it was implanted in a once-Roman province whose Roman temples and Christian churches still stood, and where Christian communities may have survived (Gelling 1978:96-9). Thus, when Gregory the Great, writing as a result of information supplied by Augustine, advised that well-built shrines (*fana*) be sprinkled with holy water to convert them to Christian usage (Bede, *Historia ecclesiastica* I, 30), he might have been responding to a situation unique in the Germanic world. We should only extrapolate from the evidence of Anglo-Saxon England with caution. Even so, there is nothing in the literary sources relating to the *Germani* in England or on the Continent to suggest that substantial temple-buildings were an aspect of Germanic paganism.

In fact we should not be surprised at the poverty of information for temple-sites in the Germanic world. Talking of the first century AD Tacitus (*Germania* 9) even seems to deny that the *Germani* had temples. It was places rather than buildings that were sacred. A similar impression may be gained from later evidence too (for sixth-century evidence, Cameron 1968:109). In Alcuin's description, though not in that of Altfrid, the temples of Fosite, take second place after the island itself and, more especially, its spring (*Vita Willibrordi* 10; cf. Altfrid, *Vita Liudgeri* I, 22). Alcuin also talks of a herd of sacred cattle. In other words it is not just the temple itself, but the whole island which seems to have been of religious significance. The account of the destruction of the Irminsul in the *Annales qui dicuntur Einhardi* (*s.a.* 772) may suggest that there were springs associated with that site too. Springs, like groves, are listed in the *Indiculus superstitionum* (6, 11). They are also condemned in Charlemagne's *Capitulare de partibus Saxoniae* (21; cf. Eigil, *Vita Sturmi* 22), and they were associated with pagan practices by Gregory III in a letter to the people of Germany (Boniface, *Ep.* 43).

Idols

Some natural objects must effectively have been idols. At Gaismar we hear of an oak of extraordinary size, 'which in the former terminology of the pagans is called the oak of Jupiter' (Willibald, *Vita Bonifatii* 6). In Willibald's *Life of Boniface*, at least, this is a cult-object of very considerable importance. There is, in addition, clear evidence for idolatry in our sources. This is amply attested in the canonical legislation of the Christians. Idols are also common in the narrative sources. On Walcheren there was an idol (*idolum*), which Willibrord destroyed (Alcuin, *Vita Willibrordi* 14). Like Willibrord, Liudger destroyed idols in Frisia (Altfrid, *Vita Liudgeri* I, 16). Later the pagan Saxons invaded and forced the Frisians to sacrifice to idols as they had once done (Altfrid, *Vita Liudgeri* I, 21). Most significant of all seems to have been the Irminsul, destroyed by Charlemagne in 772 (*Annales regni Francorum; Annales qui dicuntur Einhardi*). Unfortunately we can only guess at the nature of the idol which was culted there. Nor are we any better off in envisaging the shape of any of the other idols referred to in our sources, though crude, and not so crude, wooden objects, which may have had cultic significance, are known from Denmark and elsewhere (e.g. Dixon 1976:81; Roesdahl 1980:148). Idols, in fact, present us with as much of a problem as do temples (Helm 1953:184-6). Further, although idols and idolatry feature regularly in the correspondence of Boniface, it is not always possible to be sure whether the reference is based on anything more than an assumption, drawn from the Old Testament, that pagans were idolaters (Boniface, *Ep.* 17, 19, 21, 23, 25, 63, 64).

Priests and guardians

Clearly there were cult-sites and objects, whatever the problems they present. There were also religious functionaries, though they too pose problems. Alcuin talks of a guardian (*custos*) of the idol on Walcheren, but he makes no mention of a priest (*Vita Willibrordi* 14). At the shrine of Fosite, however, he does not even refer to a guardian: Willibrord's sacrilege is witnessed simply by pagans (*pagani*), who report the event to the king (*Vita Willibrordi* 10). A shrine with temples, a sacred spring and a herd of cattle is unlikely to have been without attendants. Nevertheless, the absence of comments on priests in the narrative and hagiographical record is striking. It is especially so in that there were good Old Testament models for describing the confrontation between a holy man and a pagan priest, most notably in the story of Elijah and the prophets of Baal. This story was, actually, picked up in the context of Swedish paganism by the ninth-century hagiographer, and bishop of Bremen, Rimbert, in his account of his predecessor, Anskar, although tellingly even Rimbert makes no mention of priests (*Vita Anskarii* 19; Wood 1987a:39).

In fact there is only one tale from the early Middle Ages which provides a detailed reference to a Germanic priest, and that is the story of Coifi told by Bede, in the conversion of the Northumbrian king, Edwin (*Historia ecclesiastica* II, 13). While there is nothing to support Bede's account of Coifi, it has to be said that there is much in what he has to say which commands attention. In particular, his statement that "a priest of their holy rites was forbidden to bear arms or to ride anything other than a mare" conjures up a very plausible world of taboos, which Coifi, by borrowing arms and a stallion from the king, deliberately broke before desecrating the temple. Yet, however plausible Bede's description of Coifi might be, it would be extremely rash to take the Northumbrian high-priest as a model for an understanding of religious authority on the Continent.

The absence of pagan priests on the Continent in the early medieval narrative evidence contrasts with the account provided by Tacitus (*Germania* 10), in which a state priest is responsible for the casting of lots. It is also apparently at odds with the evidence of linguistics. There are, for instance, known words for priests in most of the early Germanic languages: thus *blostreis* (*guthblostreis*) and *gudja* in Gothic, and *gothi* in Old Norse (Helm 1953:186 90).[2] Admittedly the Gothic words are attested in Christian (Biblical) contexts. Nevertheless it is clear that *gothi*, which is philologically related to *gudja*, had pagan connotations, and it is likely that *blostreis*, with its implication of blood-sacrifice did so too. This apparent discrepancy between language and narrative can perhaps best be accounted for by an investigation not of a priesthood but of the performance of priestly rites. In other words, were priestly functions performed by individuals whom we would not normally regard as being priests, as seems to have been the case in Viking Age Iceland, where the *gothi* were essentially aristocratic landowners who were responsible for the performance of cult on their own farms (Olsen 1966)?

Unfortunately our linguistic and narrative evidence does not coincide exactly, although in the case of the fourth-century Goths it does appear that it was the aristocracy, here called *megistanes*, who controlled cult (Heather *et al.* 1991:112-13 with n. 22). It is, nevertheless worth exploring the evidence for Frisia and for Saxony, which can reasonably be seen as following different traditions of religious organisation. In Frisia, although we hear of nothing more elevated than a *custos* on Walcheren (Alcuin, *Vita Willibrordi* 14), Radbod, as king, seems to have acted as religious leader. According to Alcuin it was he who was expected to take action after the Christian desecration of the shrine of Fosite (Alcuin, *Vita Willibrordi* 11). In a rather less reliable text, the Vita *Vulframni* (6-8), he is the recognised authority in cases of children condemned to be sacrificed to the gods. In so far as anyone is seen to have a religious function in Frisia it is the king.

In eighth-century Saxony, they had no king. Instead each *pagus* had a 'satrap'. Once a year all the satraps gathered at Marklo, together with twelve nobles and as many free and half-free men from each *pagus* (*Vita Lebuini antiqua* 4). At Marklo all prayed to the gods together, *iuxta ritum*, asking for protection for the country and that the outcome of the meeting might be worthwhile and pleasing (*Vita Lebuini antiqua* 6). Here, appropriately for the oligarchic structure of Saxony, no one seems to have taken the lead in religious affairs. The apparent absence of any priestly figure at Marklo may find an echo in the fact that there is no known word for a 'pagan priest' in the Old Saxon language, and in the use of the term *biscop* to describe Caiaphas in the *Heliand* (line 4146), an Old Saxon version of the New Testament—although here, of course, the word may have been chosen for other, poetic, considerations. Whatever the solution, it seems that, while in the kingdom of Frisia the king carried out a priestly function, in Saxony the satraps and the representatives of the *pagi*, acting effectively as the elders of the people, performed religious acts in concert. In neither place, however, does there seem to have been an institutional priesthood. England, and the priest Coifi, offer a clear contrast—perhaps strengthening the case for seeing Anglo-Saxon paganism as influenced by the religious structures of Roman Britain.

---

[2]   I leave aside *êwart* in Old High German and *æweweard* in Old English because, while *êwart* is used to describe pagan priests of the Roman period, the cognate *æweweard* is used only in the context of the Jewish (Biblical) priesthood, for which, semantically, it is entirely appropriate. Both words may, therefore, have originated in a Christian context. I am indebted to Joyce Hill for discussing this problem with me.

On the other hand, while there is no evidence for a priesthood on the Continent, in free Germany, as in England, all the evidence suggests that priestly functions were carried out, and that they were carried out exclusively by males.

Festivals and sacrifice

Turning from shrines and priests, it is possible to make some observations on pagan festivals and ritual acts. The Anglo-Saxon names of the months give some indication of a religious timetable. In particular April was *Eosturmonath*, the month of the goddess Eostre, whose name gives us Easter (Bede, *De temporum ratione*; Mayr-Harting 1991:22). From the *Indiculus superstitionum* (3, 8, 20) we learn of a feast in February, and feasts dedicated to Mercury and Jupiter (perhaps Wodan and Donar). Probably to be associated with these feasts were drinking bouts. Jonas of Bobbio, in both his *Life of Vedast* (7) and also his *Life of Columbanus* (I, 27), records miracles involving the destruction of sacriligeous containers of beer. At Bregenz, for instance, Columbanus came across a group of men drinking beer in honour of Wodan or Mercury, from a large container, a *cupa*, which could hold twenty *modia*. The saint blew on the cup and destroyed it. There were also special fires (*Indiculus superstitionum* 15; Boniface, *Ep.* 56), as well as sacrificial meals (Boniface, *Ep.* 26; *Capitulare de partibus Saxoniae* 21), and meals for the dead (*Indiculus superstitionum* 2; Boniface, *Ep.* 44, 56, 80; cf. Salin 1959:35-9; Bullough 1983:188). Among the fourth-century Visigoths the eating of sacrificial meat became a test of paganism (Heather *et al.* 1991:113, 115). The question of eating sacrificial meat appears subsequently, in Boniface's letters (*Ep.* 26). There was clearly a problem about the continuance of this practice among the Christians.

Boniface talks on several occasions about the matter of sacrifice (*Ep.* 23, 25, 26, 43, 80). Worse still, Christian priests are said to have sacrificed bulls and goats to pagan deities (*Ep.* 80). According to the sixth-century Byzantine historian Agathias, the Alamans were notable for sacrificing "horses and cattle and countless other things by beheading them" (Cameron 1968:109). This is perhaps one of the contexts in which the Christian taboos on the eating of horse meat should be understood (Boniface, *Ep.* 28, 87; on horses see also Tacitus, *Germania* 10). The question of sacrifice may be illuminated by Alcuin's account of the sacred herd on the island of Fosite (*Vita Willibrordi* 10). Here it is also possible to compare a narrative source with a legal one. The *Pactus legis salicae* legislates against the theft of sacrificial cattle (*Pactus legis salicae* 2, 16). The *Pactus* was issued during the reign of Clovis, almost certainly before his baptism (Wood 1994:108-13). It is, therefore, unique in being a Germanic law-code issued by a non-Christian king, and as a result it is of particular value over the question of livestock assigned to pagan shrines. But it was not just animals that were sacrificed. Procopius records the Frankish sacrifice of Gothic women and children after the capture of Pavia (*Wars* VI: 25, 9). His account may be inaccurate, since the Franks were officially Christian at the time. Possibly a wartime atrocity has been transformed into a religious act; possibly there were pagans, not necessarily Frankish, in the Frankish army. Certainly human sacrifice is attested east of the Rhine in the eighth century (Helm 1953:199-201). Writing to Boniface, Gregory III condemned the fact that some Christians sold their slaves to pagans to be sacrificed (*Ep.* 28). The *Capitulare de partibus Saxoniae* (9) also talks of sacrificing humans and offering them to demons.

The fullest accounts of human sacrifice and more generally of ritual deaths are to be found in the evidence relating to Frisia. The anonymous *Life of Wulfram of Sens* has several references to human sacrifice: it talks of a boy condemned to being sacrificed to the gods after he had been ear-marked by lot (6), of two other boys also condemned (7), of two more boys condemned to ritual drowning, along with countless others condemned to execution on the gallows, in nets and by drowning (8). There is much in the *Life of Wulfram* which is open to question. Indeed the whole text is a ninth-century forgery of very dubious worth (Wood 1991:13-4). It would certainly be rash to make much of its account of a golden palace offered to King Radbod by the devil (10), though even that may be an echo of pagan cosmology. Nevertheless there is enough in other sources to suggest that ritual drowning was known in Frisia. Thus, information on drowning in ritual, although not necessarily sacrificial, contexts, comes from Altfrid's *Life of Liudger* (I, 6-7). When the saint's mother, Liafburg, was born, her pagan grandmother ordered her execution, because she wanted only male grandchildren. The baby was therefore taken, and thrown into a pool. A neighbour, however, retrieved the child and fed it with honey; once the child had tasted food, it was illegal to kill it.

The casting of lots and divination

Equally significant in the account of Frisian paganism given by the *Vita Vulframni* is the role of lot-casting. This is certainly attested in more reliable sources. Alcuin's *Life of Willibrord*, a work with which the *Life of Wulfram* is closely associated (Wood 1991:13), associates the casting of lots with the death penalty meted out for the violation of religious taboos. After Willibrord and his companions had desecrated the sanctuary of Fosite they were taken to Radbod who sought to determine their fate by casting lots for three days (*Vita Willibrordi* 11). Here again Radbod seems to have been fulfilling a priestly role, since in Tacitus's day (*Germania* 10) the casting of public lots among the *Germani* was apparently the responsibility of priests. In the case of Willibrord's trial the result was the execution of one of the party (Wood 1987b:356). The *Lives* of Willibrord and Wulfram seem to set executions in a religious context. Both texts also imply a relationship between lot-casting and execution. Even under the Carolingians lots continued to play a role in indication of guilt in Frisia. The *Lex Frisionum* (14) reveals a christianised use of them in identifying culprits in obscure cases of murder.

The casting of lots relates more generally to the world of divination. As such it was a procedure which had its Judaic, Roman and Christian counterparts, however much the more rigorous clergy might condemn it. The *sortes biblicae*, the random opening of the Bible to predict the future, for instance, were apparently acceptable to Gregory of Tours (*Libri historiarum decem* IV:16, V:14), although their orthodoxy was distinctly dubious (Flint 1991:217-26). Lot-casting, in short, was not confined to pagans, nor was it necessarily a religious act.

Divination of various kinds is mentioned in the *Indiculus superstitionum*: there are titles relating to the observation of birds, horses and of cattle dung (13; for birds and horses cf.Tacitus, *Germania* 10), observation of fire (17), to diviners and prophets (14). The latter are linguistically attested in Old High German by the word *wizzago*. Much of this was also covered by Carloman's legislation (*Concilium germanicum* 5; Boniface, *Ep.* 56; Dierkens 1985). Some of it was also the subject of Charlemagne's Saxon legislation (*Capitulare de partibus Saxoniae* 23). Information about such matters reached the papacy from Boniface, since Pope Gregory III dealt with soothsaying, auguries and sorcery in a letter addressed to the people of Germany (Boniface, *Ep.* 43). So too there was concern about amulets and other phylacteries (*Indiculus superstitionum* 10; Boniface, *Ep.* 56, 78).

Religion and Superstition

With divination, amulets and phylacteries we come to the problem of the distinction between pagan religion and superstition (Helm 1953:117-66). To the author of the *Indiculus superstitionum* there was no real distinction: *paganiae* and *superstitiones* could be lumped together. This is, of course, a proper ecclesiastical stance, even if the condemnation of sacrifices to saints (*Indiculus superstitionum* 9) and their worship in improper places (*Indiculus superstitionum* 18) as 'pagan' may seem extreme. The *Indiculus* simply lists what was not acceptable to a group of zealots. For the modern historian, however, the identification of borders between acceptable superstition, unacceptable superstition and paganism presents genuine problems of classification. The observation of the flight of birds could be linked to the rhythms of rural life; indications of the changing seasons for Christians and pagans alike. The use of amulets might be pagan, but might not. Willehad, when he was destroying a temple in Drenthe, was saved from a pagan's sword by the relics he had around his neck (*Vita Willehadi* 4). In what sense was the relic not an amulet? Moreover there was nothing to confine the use of auguries and amulets to the east of the Rhine. Boniface in a somewhat tetchy exchange of letters with Pope Zacharias (*Ep.* 50, 51) condemned the observation of auguries and the use of phylacteries in Rome itself. Pagans and Christians alike had to make their peace with an environment which they did not understand, and their solutions were not so very dissimilar. Indeed pagans would even exploit what they must have regarded as Christian magic when necessary. In the ninth century pagans from Birka became Christian in Dorestad to gain protection on the return voyage (Rimbert, *Vita Anskarii* 27). Moreover, the problem posed by distinctions is not only a Christian one. The Germanic pagans, like their Roman counterparts, recognised a distinction between a proper and an improper relationship with the supernatural. Thus the *Pactus legis salicae* protected sacrificial cattle (2, 16), but condemned sorcery and witchcraft (64). To judge by the existence of the Gothic word *haljarunae* the pagan Goths too had a concept of witchcraft. Charlemagne attributed to the pagan Saxons the belief that male or female witches could eat other people (*Capitulare de partibus Saxoniae* 6). He also condemned them for killing witches, roasting them and eating them. Whether or not this was a common problem, Charlemagne's condemnation does not indicate that all Saxons approved of witchcraft. Nor did such concepts end with conversion. The Christian Franks considered the problem of witches eating men right into the Carolingian period (*Pactus legis salicae 64*, 3; *Lex salica* 37; Flint 1991:64, 124, 297). Faced with these problems of distinctions it may be most useful to re-categorise non-Christian rites and actions east of the Rhine along a spectrum ranging from community to individual-religion, effectively from public to private.

Public and Private

This categorisation undoubtedly raises problems of its own. It still fails to make a distinction between acceptable and unacceptable magical practices. It also creates its own grey areas, particularly with regard to family activity. Nevertheless, setting the evidence for non Christian beliefs to the east of the Rhine against this spectrum is a useful exercise, not least because it helps to clarify certain aspects of the history of christianisation.

Essentially the distinction between public and private is that between formal pagan practice and individual superstition. Thus temples, idols and religious zones fall entirely into the realm of the public. Although there may have been some private sacrifice, the executions recorded for Frisia were certainly public. So too, while some auguries might have been cast privately, there was unquestionably a tradition of public divination. Tacitus states that priests were responsible for the casting of public lots in the first century though he linked auguries as much with Roman as with Germanic religion (*Germania* 10). The casting of lots in the presence of Radbod suggests that they could still be public in the eighth century (Alcuin, *Vita Willibrordi* 11). Auguries and lots fall across the divide between public and private. More exclusively private would be amulets, and the practice of witchcraft. In contrast with the evidence for public religious activity, where the evidence refers only to male activity, it is clear that women as well as men could be witches.

Geography and politics

Our evidence for witchcraft, and for private superstition, suggests a relative uniformity in the Germanic world. The assumed relationship between witchcraft and cannibalism, for instance seems to be a constant and it is a relationship not only confined to the early Middle Ages or Europe (e.g. Brain 1970:173-4). The same uniformity is not to be found in the evidence for public religion. In certain simple respects divergence was inevitable. Frisian paganism seems to have been associated not just with water, but specifically with tidal water. Boys are left to drown as the tide rises (*Vita Vulframni* 8). Although the *Life of Wulfram* is suspect, the importance of water is also clear from the attempt to drown Liafburg described by Altfrid in the *Life of Liudger* (I, 6). Such practices are only conceivable in a coastal society. Public paganism seems to have been regional in other ways as well. Fosite seems to have been associated exclusively with Helgoland. Wodan, Donar and Saxnot may have been rather less confined geographically, but it may be possible to use Anglo-Saxon genealogies to infer that different *gentes* associated themselves with different gods (Dumville 1977:77-8). More certainly their relative importance appears to have been varied chronologically (Helm 1953:251-6).

Geography was not the only factor influencing public paganism. Political structures seem to have been equally significant. At least from the later seventh-century Frisia was a kingdom, ruled by a king. From the evidence of Alcuin's *Life of Willibrord* the king seems to have had a religious function. It was Radbod who had to adjudicate in a case of sacrilege, even if only to the extent that he presided over the casting of lots (Alcuin, *Vita Willibrordi* 11). This somewhat limited role seems also to be attested in the, admittedly dubious, evidence of the *Life of Wulfram*, where Radbod was explicitly unable to overturn the ruling of the lots (*Vita Vulframni* 6, 8).

In contrast to Frisia, eighth-century Saxony is portrayed in our sources as an oligarchy in social and political terms. Bede's comment on the absence of kings and the presence instead of satraps (*Historia ecclesiastica* V, 10) was taken over by the *Vita antiqua* of Lebuin (4), but then dramatically amplified in the hagiographer's account of the meeting of the Saxon satraps at Marklo (6). The meeting, according to the hagiographer, was prefaced by prayers to the gods for the protection of the fatherland. These prayers were offered up not by a priest, but by the satraps in unison (*in unum conglobati*). Saxon religion of the eighth century, therefore, seems to have been organised in a manner appropriate to the social and political structure of the region. Moreover, it was not just the satraps who were intent on preserving the status quo. When the Hewalds attempted to convert a Saxon satrap, the local villagers killed them, according to Bede, because they were alarmed about the extent of cultural change that his conversion would entail (Bede, *Historia ecclesiastica* V, 10; Wood 1987b:352). Whether the emergence of Widukind as a warleader opposed to Charlemagne undermined the oligarchy, and whether Widukind's undoubted use of paganism in opposition to the Franks altered the nature of Saxon religion prior to christianisation, are unprovable possibilities, which should at least be borne in mind. Certainly, to judge by Charlemagne's legislation, Widukind made paganism central to his stand against the Franks (*Capitulare de partibus Saxoniae; Capitulare saxonicum*). Moreover the *Annales regni Francorum* (*s.a.* 778) and the Frisian evidence (Altfrid, *Vita Liudgeri* I, 21) suggest that, under Widukind, Saxon paganism became an aggressive religion. There is no hint of this in the previous generation, at least as described by *Vita Lebuini antiqua*. As the political structure of Saxony had changed, under threat from the Franks, so had its religion. Widukind's career might profitably be compared with the careers of more recent prophets, such as the Mahdi, who emerged in response to the spread of colonial power although, in the case of Widukind, his final baptism (*Annales regni Francorum, s.a.* 785; *Annales qui dicuntur Einhardi, s.a.* 785) rather undermines the image of him as a prophetic leader.

Public religion in pagan *Germania* was not a constant. It was influenced by geography, politics and no doubt by other factors. In Britain the paganism of the Anglo-Saxons may have drawn on religious features, Christian and pagan, already present in the country. Since public religion was so closely associated with political structures it is not surprising that the formal elements of Germanic paganism collapsed in the context of Frankish expansion. The public rituals that we find in the *Indiculus superstitionum* are not surprisingly, for the most part, unorthodox Christian (or syncretist) festivals though of course there may have been other, more obviously pagan, rites which survived, but were not recorded (cf. Sharpe 1979; McCone 1986). Private superstitions, on the other hand, that is the use of auguries and amulets and the supposed practice of witchcraft, were not tied to political structures. Consequently they seem to have survived well into the Christian period.

The family

The categories of public and private thus help elucidate our understanding of pagan weakness and survival. With this in mind, it is worth returning to the family. Placed midway between public and private, and consequently hard to categorise, it was, nevertheless, of immense religious importance. This can be seen in the story of Radbod's near conversion, in which he already had one foot in the font when he discovered that the majority of his ancestors, being pagan, would remain in hell, since baptism alone ensured the entry of an individual into heaven (*Vita Vulframni* 9). The anecdote is unlikely to record an actual event. Nevertheless it does point to the importance of religion in the self-definition of a group and of a family. The same point is apparent in the letter addressed by Avitus of Vienne to Clovis, after the king had been baptised as a catholic. As the bishop remarked:

> Many in this matter are inclined to set out the custom of the race and the ritual of family observation, if they are moved (either by the exhortation of bishops or of any companions) to a con sideration of belief for that health which should be sought; thus (harmfully prefering shame to safety, while preserving a futile reverence for their ancestors in guarding unbelief), they confess that they do not know what they should choose (Avitus of Vienne, *Ep.* 46).

Family and tradition were, therefore, important factors in opting to remain pagan. To change religion ought to mean disassociation from ancestors. Significantly, although the Christian Franks did preserve some traditions about the pagan past of their ruling dynasty (Fredegar III, 9), they seem to have forgotten fairly quickly the whereabouts of the tomb of Clovis's pagan father, Childeric (Wood 1994:44). An alternative was to christianise one's ancestors, as happened at Jelling in the tenth century (Roesdahl 1982:171-6). Here we also encroach on the whole issue of the shift from pagan to Christian cemetery, and indeed to burial in church. In this context, Charlemagne's legislation against the Saxons being buried near their pagan burial mounds rather than in Christian cemeteries (*Capitulare de partibus Saxoniae* 22) can be seen as using the relationship between family, religion and burial to strike at the heart of Saxon social and religious structures. But while formal religion was changed by force, it is fairly clear that individual superstitions were not: they, like the family itself, could provide continuity in a world of considerable religious and political upheaval.

To say that religion in an early medieval context must have been integral to the whole fabric of society, from the family upwards, is to utter an unprovable truism. Yet it is an observation which has very considerable implications for an understanding of paganism east of the Rhine immediately prior to the christianisation of the region, since there were no uniform social or political structures. The peoples of Bavaria, Hesse and Thuringia had long been part of the Christian Merovingian world, however variable the intensity of Frankish control might have been. They were ruled over by *duces* who were, in origin at least, Merovingian appointees (Wood 1994:161-2). The religion of the area was also largely Christian, despite Boniface's outbursts on idolatry and superstition (Wood 1994:307-10) Saxony and Frisia were somewhat different from these other, christianised regions. Here, differences in political and social structures were as important as differences in belief when it came to the organisation of any public religious cult.

Conclusion

The evidence, therefore, points not to a single paganism, but to paganisms. And the differentiation is not just a matter of the regional dominance of one or other god of the Germanic pantheon, or of the significance of a local god, like Fosite. It is also a matter of differentiation determined by geographical factors and by contrasting social and political structures. The geographical factors provided a varied, but stable, bedrock on which different religious practices were built. The social and political structures, by contrast, changed over time. The Anglo-Saxon kingdoms were new creations of the sixth century: Frisia may only have become a kingdom in the seventh century: Widukind's wars against Charlemagne may have brought change to the oligarchic state which Saxony had been. Political variables of this sort may explain why so much of what Tacitus had to say about German religion in the first century AD (*Germania* 9-10) is not echoed by the evidence relating to the seventh and eighth centuries. They suggest that paganism was in a constant state of development, and that it was not the same in any two places. The period of christianisation—which was also a period of acute political change—was merely the last phase in the development of Germanic paganism. And while Christianity destroyed the public religion of the peoples east of the Rhine, it was nowhere near so successful in dealing with superstitions which were not tied to social and political structures. The superstitions of individuals were associated more with private than with public beliefs and practices. They were, moreover, not confined to the Germans, nor to the pagans. Not surprisingly they remained a significant factor after the worship of the gods had ended.

References

Textual sources:

Adam of Bremen
          Gesta Hammaburgensis ecclesiae pontificum: see Trillmich 1978.
Alcuin
          Vita Willibrordi: see Reischmann 1989.
Altfrid
          Vita Liudgeri: see Diekamp 1881.
Annales qui dicuntur Einhardi: see Kurze 1895.
Annales regni Francorum: see Kurze 1895.
Avitus of Vienne:
          Aviti Viennensis Opera: see Peiper 1883.
Bede
          Historia ecclesiastica gentis Anglorum: see Plummer 1986.
          De temporum ratione: see Jones 1943.
Boniface
          Epistolae: see Tangl 1916.
Capitulare de partibus Saxoniae: see Boretius 1883.
Capitulare Saxonicum: see Boretius 1883.
Concilium Germanicum: see Werminghoff 1906.
Eigil
          Vita Sturmi: see Pertz 1829.
Fredegar:
          see Krusch 1888.
Gregory of Tours
          Libri historiarum decem: see Krusch *et al.* 1951.
Heliand: see Behaghel 1984.
Indiculus superstitionum: see Dierkens 1985.
Jonas
          Vita Columbani and *Vita Vedastis*: see Krusch 1905.
Lex Frisionum: see Richthofen 1863.
Lex Salica: see Eckhardt 1969.
Liber constitutionum: see Salis 1892.
Pactus legis Salicae: see Eckhardt 1962.
Procopius
          Wars: see Dewing 1914/28.
Rimbert
          Vita Anskarii: see Trillmich 1978.
Tacitus
          Germania: see Lund 1988, or Much 1967.
Vita Lebuini antiqua: see Krusch & Levison 1910.
Vita Vulframni: see Krusch & Levison 1910.
Vita Willehadi: see Poncelet 1910.
Willibald
          Vita Bonifatii: see Levison 1905.

Bibliography:

Alkemade, M.
    1991   A history of Vendel Period archaeology: Observations on the relationship between written sources and archaeological interpretations. In *Images of the past. Studies on ancient societies in northwestern Europe*. N. Roymans & F. Theuws (eds.), pp. 267-297. Amsterdam: Albert Egges van Giffen Instituut.
Behaghel, O. (ed.)
    1984   *Heliand und Genesis*. Tübingen: Max Niemeyer.

Boretius, A. (ed.)
    1883   *Capitularia regum Francorum,* 1. *Monumenta Germaniae Historica.* Hanover:
                Hahn.
Boudriot, W.
    1928   *Die altgermanische Religion.* Bonn: Röhrscheid.
Brain, R.
    1970   Child witches. In *Witchcraft Confessions and Accusations.* (ASA Monographs, 9).
                M. Douglas (ed.), pp. 161-179. London: Tavistock Publications.
Braune, W., & K. Helm
    1958   *Althochdeutsches Lesebuch.* Tübingen: Max Niemeyer.
Bullough, D. A.
    1983   Burial, Community and Belief in the Early Medieval West. In *Ideal and Reality in
                Frankish and Anglo-Saxon Society.* P. Wormald (ed.), pp. 177-201. Oxford: Basil
                Blackwell.
Cameron, A.
    1968   Agathias on the early Merovingians. *Annali della Scuola normale superiore di Pisa*
                37: 95-140.
Dewing, H. B. (ed.)
    1914/28   *Procopius, History of the Wars.* (The Loeb Classical Library). Cambridge, MA:
                Harvard University Press.
Diekamp, W. (ed.).
    1881   *Die Vitae sancti Liudgeri.* Münster: Theissing'schen Buchhandlung.
Dierkens, A.
    1985   Superstitions, christianisme et paganisme à la fin de l'époque mérovingienne. In *Magie,
                sorcellerie, parapsychologie.* H. Hasquin (ed.), pp. 9-26. Brussels: Université de Bruxelles.
Dixon, P.
    1976   *Barbarian Europe.* London: Phaidon.
Dumville, D. N.
    1977   Kingship, Genealogies and Regnal Lists. In *Early Medieval Kingship.* P. H. Sawyer
                & I. N. Wood (eds.), pp. 72-104. Leeds: School of History.
Eckhardt, K. A. (ed.)
    1962   *Pactus legis Salicae. Monumenta Germaniae Historica, Leges nationum
                Germanicarum,* 4, 1. Hanover: Hahn.
    1969   *Lex Salica Monumenta Germaniae Historica, Leges nationum Germanicarum,* 4, 2.
                Hanover: Hahn.
Flint, V. I. J.
    1991   *The Rise of Magic in Early Medieval Europe.* Oxford: Oxford University Press.
Gelling, M.
    1978   *Signposts to the Past.* London: Dent.
Helm, K.
    1953   *Altgermanische Religionsgeschichte,* 2. *Die nachromische Zeit* 2. *Die Westgermanen.*
                Heidelberg: Carl Winter.
Hope-Taylor, P.
    1977   *Yeavering.* London: Her Majesty's Stationery Office.
Jones, C. W. (ed.)
    1943   *Baedae opera de temporibus.* Cambridge, MA: Medieval Academy of America.
Krusch, B. (ed.)
    1888   *Fredegarii et aliorum Chronica. Vitae sanctorum. Monumenta Germaniae Historica,
                Scriptores rerum Merovingicarum ,* 2. Hanover: Hahn.
    1905   *Ionae Vitae sanctorum Columbani, Vedastis, Iohannis. Monumenta Germaniae
                Historica. Scriptores rerum Germanicarum in usum scholarum..* Hanover: Hahn.
Krusch, B., & W. Levison (eds.)
    1910   *Passiones vitaeque sanctorum aevi Merovingici.* (III) *Monumenta Germaniae
                Historica. Scriptores rerum Merovingicarum ,* 5. Hanover: Hahn.
    1951   *Libri historiarum X.Monumenta Germaniae Historica, Scriptores rerum
                Merovingicarum* 1, Teil 1. Hanover: Hahn.

Kurze, F. (ed.)
1895   *Annales regni Francorum inde ab a. 741 usque ad a. 829, qui dicuntur Annales Laurissenses maiores et Einhardi.. Monumenta Germaniae Historica. Scriptores rerum Germanicarum in usum scholarum separatim editi.* [6.] Hanover: Hahn.
Lange, W.
1962   *Texte zur Bekehrungsgeschichte.* Tübingen: Max Niemeyer.
Levison, W. (ed.)
1905   *Vitae sancti Bonifatii archiepiscopi Moguntini. Monumenta Germaniae Historica, Scriptores rerum Germanicarum in usum scholarum separatim editi.* [57.] Hanover: Hahn.
Lund, A. A.
1988   *Publii Cornelii Taciti, Germania.* Heidelberg: Carl Winter.
McCone, K.
1986   Werewolves, Cyclopes, Díberga, and Fíanna: Juvenile Delinquency in Early Ireland. *Cambridge Medieval Celtic Studies* 12: 1-22.
Mayr-Harting, H. M. E.
1991   *The Coming of Christianity to Anglo-Saxon England*, 3rd ed. London: Batsford.
Much, R.
1967   *Die Germania des Tacitus*, 3rd ed. Heidelberg: Carl Winter.
Olsen, O.
1966   Hørg, hov og kirke. *Aarbøger for nordisk Oldkyndighed og Historie* 1965.
Peiper, R. (ed.).
1883   *Alcimi Ecdicii Aviti Viennensis episcopi Opera quae supersunt. Monumenta Germaniae Historica. Auctores Antiquissimi* 6, 2. Berlin: Weidmann.
Pertz, G. H. (ed.)
1829   [*Scriptores rerum Sangallensium. Annales, chronica et historiae aevi Carolini.*] *Monumenta Germaniae Historica. Scriptores* (in Folio), 2. Hanover: Hahn.
Plummer, C. (ed.)
1986   *Venerabilis Baedae opera historica.* Oxford: Oxford University Press.
Poncelet, A. (ed.)
1910   *Acta Sanctorum.* November, iii. Brussels: *Apud socios hollandianos.*
Reischmann, H.-J (ed.).
1989   *Willibrord Apostel der Friesen.* Darmstadt: Wissenschaftliche Buchgesellschaft.
Richthofen, K. von (ed.)
1863   *Lex Frisionum. Monumenta Germaniae Historica. Leges* (in Folio), 3. Hannover: Hahn.
Roesdahl, E.
1980   The Scandinavians at home. In *The Northern World.* D. M. Wilson (ed.), pp. 129-158. London: Thames & Hudson.
1982   *Viking Age Denmark.* London: British Museum Publications.
Salin, E.
1959   *La civilisation mérovingienne*, 4. Paris: Picaud.
Salis, L. R. von (ed.)
1892   *Leges Burgundionum. Monumenta Germaniae Historica. Leges nationum Germanicarum*, 2, 1. Hanover: Hahn.
Sawyer, B.
1987   Scandinavian conversion histories. In *The Christianisation of Scandinavia.* B. Sawyer, P. Sawyer & I. N. Wood (eds.), pp. 88-110. Alingsås: Viktoriabokforlag.
Sharpe, R.
1979   Hiberno-Latin *laicus*, Irish *láech* and the Devil's Men. *Ériu* 30: 75-92.
Tangl, M. (ed.)
1916   *Die Briefe des heiligen Bonifatius und Lullus. Monumenta Gemaniae Historica. Epistolae Selectae*, 1. Berlin: Weidmann.
Trillmich, W. (ed.)
1978   *Quellen des 9. und 11. Jahrhunderts zur Geschichte der hamburgischen Kirche und des Reiches.* Darmstadt: Wissenschaftliche Buchgesellschaft.
Wallace-Hadrill, J. M.
1983   *The Frankish Church.* Oxford: Oxford University Press.
Werminghoff, A. (ed.)
1896   *Concilia aevi Karolini [742-842]. Monumenta Germaniae Historica. Concilia*, 2. Hanover, Hahn.

Wood, I. N.
  1987a   Christians and pagans in ninth-century Scandinavia. In *The Christianisation of
            Scandinavia*. B. Sawyer, P. Sawyer & 1. N. Wood (eds.), pp. 36-67. Alingsås:
            Viktoriabokförlag.
  1987b   Pagans and Holy Men, 600-800. In *Irland und die Christenheit*. P. NíChatáin &
            M. Richter (eds.), pp. 347-361. Stuttgart: Klett-Cotta.
  1991   Saint-Wandrille and its Hagiography. In *Church and Chronicle in the Middle Ages*.
            I. N. Wood & G. A. Loud (eds.), pp. 1-14. London: Hambledon.
  1994   *The Merovingian Kingdoms*, 450-751. London: Longman.
  1994   Missionary hagiography in the eighth and ninth centuries. In *Ethnogenese und
            Ueberlieferung*. K. Brunner & B. Merta (eds.), pp. 189-199. Vienna: Oldenbourg.

Discussion

AUSENDA: I have three remarks.You note [page 257]: "The absence of comments on priests in the narrative and bibliographical record is striking". I would like to comment that the absence of a priesthood may only mean the absence of a category of full time priests. In simple societies elders are known to carry out the part time function of priests.

You write [page 263]: "...the emergence of Widukind as warleader opposed to Charlemagne undermined the oligarchy, and whether Widukind's undoubted use of paganism in opposition to the Franks altered the nature of Saxon religion...". This suggests a prophetic movement led by Widukind, such as many known from all over the world which arose in response to foreign pressure when kinship links alone were insufficient to produce a unified group capable of the necessary reaction.

You noted [in preliminary draft]: "Political variables of the sort may explain why so much of what Tacitus had to say about German religion in the first century AD is not echoed by the evidence relating to the seventh and eighth century", and just below you contrasted the variability of "German religion" with the fact that: "Superstition, however, was not tied to social and political structures...remained a significant factor after the worship of the gods had ended". I fully agree with you and I would like to add that it is quite likely that religion, tied to the 'state' structure changed in parallel with the changes that structure underwent, while superstition, related to individual behaviour, was more constant in time.

SCHÜTTE: There is no real evidence for temples. They might consist of boards encircling a sacred area or a wooden building with a roof.

GREEN: You refer [in preliminary draft] to the tendency to see Germanic gods in Roman terms. It would assist your argument if you could bring into play two complementary features: *interpretatio romana* and *interpretatio germana*. Germanic gods were given the nearest name of Roman gods and viceversa.

You say [in preliminary draft] that Woden, Thor and Frey are the dominant deities. Woden and Thor I can accept (although in the south-Germanic context we should say Donar, not Thor). Frey, however, is a north-Germanic deity with no certain counterpart in the south. If you were to add Frija (a goddess, cf. 'Friday') I should be in full agreement. There is also a god Tiu.

You say [page 256] that a report concerning King Redwald is possibly unreliable, because the account is biased. Could this not be an example of a mixed, syncretist cult for which there is a number of other cases (cf. W. Baetke 1937)? It would be dangerous to dismiss this account with such an isolated explanation, ignoring these further parallels.

On the same page, concerning the letter of Gregory the Great to Mellitus. I use that evidence as an extralinguistic parallel to what can be established about the nature of Christian vocabulary of Old English as opposed to the Christian vocabulary of Gothic, in that Old English Christian vocabulary is much readier to make use of formerly pagan terms and baptise them to Christian use than is the case with Gothic which avoids pagan terminology like the plague, whenever it can. In other words, if I may compare the pagan temple, to which Gregory makes reference, to the pagan word, you undermine the significance of that pagan temple by inserting a Christian cult, just as you undermine the significance of a pagan word by inserting a Christian meaning.

You wrote [in preliminary draft, modified on page 257]: "...what is also perhaps significant is the comparative silence on organised priesthood". I accept that statement subject to your condition, "organised" priesthood. But I would then draw attention to the fact that we do have across *Germania* a number of terms for pagan priest, so that something corresponding to that existed within *Germania*, otherwise it is difficult to account for this terminology. It is not just isolated cases, but cases where there are links between one dialect and another, not strong, but they are there. For example, in Gothic we have a word for the pagan priest, *gudhja*, and that corresponds to old Norse *gothi*, so there is a link; in Old High German we have *êwart*, literally someone who guards the divine law, with a parallel in Old English. One has to take account of this terminology in assessing whether there was such a thing as a priesthood in pagan *Germania*.

WOOD: Obviously there are people who perform priestly functions, like the king in Frisia, and presumably some sort of priestly function is involved when the satraps all meet in Marklo.

GREEN: Yes, but more than that: I think there are priests who perform a priestly function, otherwise there would be no point in designating, in making use of these terms to designate the priest. One would otherwise expect a term for the king or satrap performing that function. If instead, reference is made to these priests, then one must assume not an organised priesthood, but a priesthood.

WOOD: I am just wondering whether that has to be true.

GREEN: Across *Germania*.

WOOD: But also diachronically?

GREEN: That we cannot prove because the evidence does not reach that far.

WOOD: The other thing which goes through my mind is with, say, *êwart* or some other word, would the Latin translation be something to do with a priest, or would it be *custos*? Quite clearly we have *custodes*.

GREEN: I cannot answer that off hand.

WOOD: There are quite clearly guardians.

GREEN: Certainly in Old High German, these are glossary terms, but I cannot recall what the Latin is. In Old High German *êwart* denotes a pagan priest, as well as a Jewish or Christian one. I agree, *Germania* shows no traces of an organised priesthood, and the links between one Germanic dialect and another are tenuous, but they do exist.

You expose yourself needlessly when you say [in preliminary draft; modified on page 258] that the author of the *Heliand* had to resort to the word for bishop when he had no word other than *biscop* to describe Caiaphas. I think you go too far here. First you are arguing a negative (saying there was no term he could use), because we do not know these terms did not exist. Secondly, you suggest the presence of linguistic compulsion at work on the author of the Heliand. I agree, but it is not necessarily the linguistic compulsion which you have in mind. The *Heliand* is composed in alliterative long lines, where most leading terms have clustered around them a string of variations, but also each long line has three alliterations. The word *biscop* is there because it has to alliterate with a word beginning with b. That is the linguistic compulsion. Yours may also be present, but we have no proof that the word did not exist in Old Saxon. The most I would be prepared to do to come to meet you, in this respect, is to draw your attention to the fact, which I am sure has not escaped you, that the terminology for the Germanic pagan priest, which I have listed, covers Gothic, Old Norse, Old High German, and Old English, but not Old Saxon. So, there is an opening for you, but do not expose yourself to the danger of saying what you do say.

DUMVILLE: I feel like an innocent foreigner in a souq. What is the difficulty in making the simple assumption that the word you would use for 'high priest' is the word for 'bishop'? Is it not a natural equation? If you have to say in Christian language "what is a high priest?" would you not say "bishop"?

WOOD: The problem is that Caiaphas is the villain.

GREEN: You refer to Procopius [in preliminary draft; modified on page 259]: "... his account may be misleading since the Franks were Christian at that time". I go back to the points I made about mixed beliefs and syncretism. In view of this, the fact that the Franks were Christian does not invalidate this account.

WOOD: There has been a long historical debate about that, because it is also possible that Procopius has listed the wrong people. It may not be the Franks at all, but may be Frankish pagan allies. This was the passage that you referred to when you said Theudebert made a sacrifice. In fact there is a huge literature on this.

GREEN: Would it not be safer for you to hint at that in a footnote?

You refer to diviners and prophets [page 260]. An interesting sidelight is thrown on prophesying as an aspect of pagan religion by the Old High German word for prophet, *wizzago*. What happens with that word is significant: as a result of Christian censorship it changes its spelling and pronunciation slightly so as to render it innocuous. It becomes *wissago*, a 'wise speaker', a 'Weissager'. Even that is felt to be too dangerously close to what it had been: in late Old High German we abandon even that attempt and fall back on a safe loanword from Latin *propheta*.

WOOD: What does that do other than back up the fact that there are diviners and prophets?

GREEN: Had there not been this practice in Germanic pagan antiquity there would have been no reason why in the ecclesiastical vocabulary of Old High German it should have been necessary to shift away from this dangerous implication of using a word of a Christian prophet which was originally used of a pagan prophet.

WOOD: Yes, the *Indiculus* makes it quite clear that there were pagan prophets.

GREEN: Yes, but I am drawing a parallel which helps your case. It is not meant to contrast your case. What I wanted to do is add to it. In same paragraph [page 261]: "amulets and phylacteries". There are two or three Old High German glosses that gloss the word 'phylacteries' by *rûnstaba*, 'rune staves', that might be useful to you, pointing then to a rich runic magic.

HINES: There are some sharks with very large mouths as soon as you mention the word 'runes'.

GREEN: There are two points which I added as you spoke your introductory remarks.

You made reference to Christian priests carrying out magical practices. I would only support that and point out that it was Christian priests who wrote down the Old High German charms we have. It is inconceivable that anybody else wrote them down, especially since we know that many of the charms were used for a pseudo-medical purpose, and that priests were interested and culted that practice.

Lastly, you spoke about Christianity affecting late paganism. A lot of work has been done by W. Baetke (1937) again on that aspect of North Germanic paganism, so much so that it is dangerous to claim as Germanic paganism anything from Scandinavia which comes from the late period, but it is all under the suspicion of being, if not direct Christian influence, at least an adaptation to the danger Christianity represents to paganism. I think it is much clearer in Scandinavia than it is elsewhere, and to draw attention to that, I think would help.

RICHARDS: I only have five points [laughter].

Despite the fact that you were rightly very cautious about the interpretation of individual instances, you seem to make some confident statements.

Having dismissed, quite rightly, I think, the Yeavering building as a certain temple [page 258], you say [in preliminary draft; modified on page 256]: "Anglo-Saxon England was certainly not devoid of pagan temples" and that it "...is perhaps better served than the rest of the Germanic world". I wonder whether the places you refer to actually need structures, buildings as such? We certainly have not found any structures, and if one follows what we know about Celtic religion as an open-air religion, are these places not better understood as clearings in forests?

WOOD: One has to assume that Gregory the Great has some information when he orders the sprinkling of water in shrines.

RICHARDS: You do not think he is making assumptions on the basis of his knowledge that those things normally happen in buildings?

DUMVILLE: Does a shrine have to be a building?

GREEN: Exactly. We also have linguistic evidence for open air ritual rather than ritual inside a building.

WOOD: So you think there may have been no standing temples at all.

RICHARDS: I would have expected to find a few more.

WOOD: I agree, I was being cautious in terms of assuming there were some.

HINES: I would strongly support Julian here, and was going to make a very similar point. I would argue that all one can confidently say is that there were sacred sites and that somehow these sites were constructed or they were somehow conceptually marked as enclosures. Details of the vocabulary used, such as the Latin word *fanum* or Old English *leah*, are consistent with this. However, John Blair (1993) in a paper read at this summer's International Society of Anglo-Saxonists, put a case that a certain set of structures that can be attributed to the early Anglo-Saxon period may be pagan cult sites. These are square enclosures, in some cases with a round barrow inside them, which he argued could be derived from the *cella* structures of late-Roman temples. I can't say that I was convinced; I thought I could make at least as good a case for one of the sites he identified being an early Christian cemetery.

WOOD: What do you make of Bede's account of Coifi?

HINES: He says Coifi throws the spear into a *fanum*: which could well mean he hurls a spear into a sacred enclosure.

DUMVILLE: I think that one desecrated a church in Ireland by throwing a weapon across the boundary, but not into any building. It is very clear, there is a sense of boundary.

HINES: We know that Scandinavian paganism lasted much longer than Anglo-Saxon, but all the way through to the Viking period you still cannot find any real temple buildings.

WOOD: Though it is possible that one was discovered last summer at Uppsala.

GREEN: Really?

HINES: Well, one then.

RICHARDS: I think there may be a similar problem with the existence of idols and objects. You mention "idols" [page 259], and then further down on the same page at the last paragraph you then say [in preliminary draft; modified on page 257]: "… there were cult sites and objects". I did not see that that conclusion followed from the evidence.

WOOD: Well quite clearly there are idols in the texts, although we have no idea what they looked like.

RICHARDS: The point that you make, that Christians are expecting there to be idols may apply to all these literary references, because these are Old Testament references to pagan idols and, therefore, they assume that there should be cult objects.

WOOD: I take a fairly literary stance on most of those sources, but you would have to take a more literary stance than I do to say there wasn't anything at Walcheren. There is said to be a *custos*. Whether he looked after a tree-branch or a statue I have no idea. We do not have the faintest idea of what these things looked like, but I think there must have been objects.

I am worried about sacrifice, but I think that it is fairly clear from the *Indiculus* that sacrifice did take place in a religious context. It is also fairly clear that there were sacrifices which may not have been religious: some of them may have been simply judicial. This is why I put sacrifice in an area which falls off into being grey. You would have to reckon that the canons were very misled to assume that they were absolutely wrong, but some sacrifices are not necessarily religious.

At the same time we are told that Christian priests sacrificed bulls and goats to pagan deities, but you may say that Boniface was mistaken.

RICHARDS: That is the danger of looking at things through biased eyes.

WOOD: There is a methodological problem here. In writing about missionaries obviously one concentrates on their actions and the texts they create. Once one tries to probe further into the religious context of missionary activity the questions of the acceptability and meaning of evidence become much more problematic. I accept your sense of caution. I would agree, for instance, that my paper did not make enough of the way in which sacrifice, like feasting, falls off into a grey area which may not be religious. Sacrifice in Frisia, for instance, can be part of the legal process.

DUMVILLE: Christian sacrifice, Christian human sacrifice. There is one theme thread which runs through Irish hagiography, the idea of sacrificing a person when founding a monastery. It would be interesting to know whether there is archaeological evidence for this.

RICHARDS: My next point concerns the survival of native paganism in Britain through the Roman period. You say [in preliminary draft]: "…in Britain Anglo-Saxon paganism was an implant into a Roman province". That is certainly true but I think pagan beliefs may have survived through the Roman period and may have found the Anglo-Saxons a sympathetic audience.

WOOD: The problem is that the best evidence for that type of survival of Roman paganism comes in the Romano-British West, which is the last place reached by the Anglo-Saxons.

RICHARDS: I do not know whether you are familiar with Eleanor Scott's (1990) work on infant sacrifice during the Roman period.

You also say it is probably difficult to argue much for Anglo-Saxon burial, which I quite agree with. I think you perhaps do neglect evidence from settlement sites that hints towards pagan beliefs or curious things which would otherwise be difficult to explain. Things such as deposits of skulls near buildings still require some sort of explanation. I think this is related to paganism.

Final point. At the end of your presentation you said that the popularity of water cults in Frisia was in some ways determined by their concern with flooding. Water cults were very widespread of course.

WOOD: Yes, but the performance of such religious rites in Frisia is specific to places with a tidal margin because they depend on the tide rising: Frisian sacrifice depended upon pinning people down below the high water mark.

TURTON: On prophets I fully agree with Giorgio—about the way these figures emerge in response to outside threats and incursions.

WOOD: But is this largely to do with the anthropology of the Islamic world?

TURTON: No, not at all. There's a book coming out soon from Oxford University Press, by Douglas Johnson, an historian, on nineteenth-century prophets amongst the Nuer of southern Sudan. And then there are the Melanesian 'Cargo cults' mentioned by Giorgio. The leaders of these cults were religious figures, but they also had a political role. In fact prophets emerged again recently in the Sudan as a result of the civil war there. One contemporary Nuer prophet has mobilised thousands of people.

HINES: They are also found in northern Germany and Denmark in the seventeenth century.

SCHÜTTE: Yes, also the sixteenth.

TURTON: Anthropologists have used the term to refer to individuals who have emerged in response to outside incursions to unite a larger number of people than was possible under the traditional political system.

WOOD: It is a very striking way of reading Widukind.

TURTON: You asked about terminology from an anthropological point of view. The term 'paganism' seems pretty well established in your literature to refer to 'unorganised' religion, but this would be a worrying term for anthropologists. Christian missionaries in Africa use the term 'animism' to refer to indigenous religion—one is asked "Are the Mursi animists?". But this is just a blanket term for any religion which is not Christian. Similarly, it would be better not to use the term 'pagan'—not to talk about Saxon paganism but Saxon religion. But I suppose that would create a problem because some Saxon religion is Christian.

WOOD: Yes.

TURTON: But it nevertheless seems to me to create a problem where there should not be one since there are, exactly as you argue, as many 'paganisms' as there are 'pagan' groups. In other words, we have a number of identifiable groups of people with their own religious beliefs and practices. Christianity has created 'paganism', not in the sense that it influenced these religious beliefs and practices, which it presumably did, but in a categorical or conceptual sense.

I don't like the term 'organised religion' either, because I find it difficult to imagine the opposite—an 'unorganised' religion. Could you say 'formal'?

WOOD: 'Formal' is very difficult because the actions of somebody simply casting lots could be formal.

TURTON: So can we just talk about 'religion'?

WOOD: You have to keep the distinction between religion and superstition.

TURTON: You have to make a distinction for practical purposes between what we have come to call religious beliefs and practices and say, magic, sorcery, witchraft, but I wouldn't be happy with an absolute distinction, a kind of 'natural' dichotomy. Durkheim's distinction is very useful because it depends on the idea that magic is carried on at the individual level while religion has to do with moral authority; and the only possible source of moral authority for Durkheim is the community.

By 'organised' religion you seemed to have in mind such things as priesthood, temples—something structured, visible that could be clearly recognised and separated off from the rest of society. That creates a problem for me because, for the people I know in Africa, it wouldn't make sense to ask "What is your religion?" or even "Are you religious?". I don't even know a word for 'religion' in Mursi. To be a Mursi, or a Nuer or whatever, is to have a certain culture, language, set of beliefs, some of which we, as outside observers, will want to call 'religion'. This doesn't mean we can't talk about 'Nuer religion', or 'Mursi religion'; it's just that when we do we are not talking about a discrete institutional sphere, with an 'organised' priesthood and places of worship, but simply one aspect of community life.

Another point concerns sacrifice. I think the interesting question is not whether sacrifice is necessarily a religious act but rather: "What is sacrifice?". What is going on when an ox is smeared with blood and slaughtered, as among the Nuer and Mursi? The sacrificial object seems to act as a kind of intermediary between the community and some order beyond the community. I think sacrifice is by definition a religious act, so the question is, which acts involving killing—of a human being or animal—come into the category we should call sacrifice?

In a book called *Sacrifice in Africa* Luc de Heusch (1985) says that Christian theology has in fact defined our notion of sacrifice for us. And Evans-Pritchard (1956), a Catholic convert, has been accused by some of virtually turning the Nuer into Roman Catholics in his book *Nuer Religion*.

Your definition of a priest seems to be a member of a 'priesthood'—an 'organised', presumably hierarchical, structure of roles and positions. I'm not surprised to hear what Dennis [Green] had to say about there being words for 'priest' in 'pagan', pre-Roman....

GREEN: 'Pre-contact' I think I would say.

TURTON: I would see a priest as essentially a mediator between the community and some external power. Such people don't *have* to be appointed. All the members of a certain clan—e.g. the Cohens of Israel—may be *potential* priests. They may exercise a certain amount of secular influence, which may lead an outside observer—a colonial administrator for example—to think of them as 'chiefs'. When Evans-Pritchard (1940) was writing *The Nuer*, which is essentially a political account, he described someone he called the 'leopard skin chief'. When he wrote his book on Nuer religion, several years later, this figure had become the 'leopard skin priest'.

WOOD: I can see the point you make from the anthropological point of view. But I am worried about using a word like 'priesthood' or 'priest' in a context relating to missionary activity, where the norm is going to be that people assume that your priesthood looks a little bit like your Christian priesthood. In a sense I would want a word that is less loaded.

TURTON: I would argue the opposite, that it's the Christian priesthood that looks like the 'pagan' priesthood. If the essential role of the priest is to be a go-between through whom the community can be in touch with an order beyond itself, then priesthood is much, much older than Christianity.

WOOD: I accept that. Obviously, if one comes to the contrast between pre-Christian priesthoods and Christian priesthoods there is no problem there. On the other hand, since the Christian priesthood of the sixth and seventh centuries is so highly organised, using a word like 'priesthood' in the context of Germanic religions makes them sound more organised.

TURTON: I take your point.

AUSENDA: I understand what Ian is saying...he wants to stay away from the word 'priest', he wants to suggest a word that will let the reader understand that these people are not priests in our sense.

WOOD: Essentially a lot of new definitions are required.

SCHÜTTE: You want to get away from Christian centrism.

TURTON: But you shouldn't capitulate to the reader's biases.

WOOD: Yes, but you have to make the reader understand the danger of just using the words 'priest' and 'priesthood'.

GREEN: There is another detail. I was fascinated about what you had to say about the role of the priest as the intermediary or the go-between, and that certainly can be seen as the function of the Germanic priests. The trouble is, however, that can also be seen as a function of the Germanic king. I am not smuggling in divine kingship by the back door, hut....

TURTON: Why is there a problem?

GREEN: Because you are then extending the role of a priest to a king, and I....

TURTON: Perhaps the two roles are very close, if not the same.

WOOD: In Frisia they clearly overlap.

GREEN: In certain parts of *Germania* for a certain period of time they can overlap, but in certain parts they cannot, as for example, in those parts where there is no king, as in Saxony.

TURTON: But what do you mean when you say there is no king? It depends on what you mean by 'king', doesn't it?

DUMVILLE: There is another whole horror there. Historians in the last generation have been trying to clean up their usage in modern language in relation to kingship, to get rid of King with a capital K. It is important to listen to medieval writers' usage, not to impose current notions of what 'a real king' is.

GREEN: And then there is another hornet's nest, namely the rise of Germanic kingship.

TURTON: What about Frazer's 'Divine King'? I'm just trying to think of cases where the roles of priest and king were....

GREEN: . . .coterminous.

TURTON: Exactly.

GREEN: I accept that certainly as a possibility, but you cannot assume that by any means and in any case, and certainly not in the whole of *Germania*.

AXBOE: What were the powers and functions of the king?

AUSENDA: The Roman *rex* in antiquity had religious functions.

TURTON: The Mursi priest, or *komoru*, has got kingly aspects to his role, in the sense that he symbolises the community. They say he must never leave the community—his presence within the community guarantees its success and survival.

GREEN: That certainly rings bells as regards certain aspects of the Germanic king. Alive or dead, he must remain in his community, for him to act efficiently still as an intermediary.

AUSENDA: I would like to recall that in the Muslim religion there is no 'organised priesthood'. Anyone can lead the prayer and preach, provided he is passably read in the Quran. It used to be the elders who carried out these functions: the word for religious performer is *sheikh*, which means 'elder'. Among certain Muslim populations there are several 'religious' clans, whose members teach the Quran, i.e. some reading and writing; they also preach, and treat illness by praying and exorcising the *jinn*, the malignant spirits.

GREEN: May I remind you of the etymology of 'priest', *presbyteros*, 'elder'.

HINES: Can I jump to a couple of points?

I feel strongly, Ian [Wood], that a positive definition of 'religion' is wanted. You seemed to me to be concentrating your efforts on removing things from a religious category rather than saying precisely what it was that would make something religious. Now David [Turton] has given a very clear statement of this kind by citing Durkheim. But I find Durkheim's atheistic definition of religion almost impossible to use. It seems utterly impracticable when you are faced with very definitely theistic religions such as we have with Christianity and Germanic paganism. It utterly collapsed the distinction between the social and the religious, which is undesirable and unrealistic even if we accept that these two areas of activity will merge inseparably with one another along a certain line. And I think, indeed, the difficulty came out when David [Turton] talked about sacrifice, and invoked there an order beyond the social: the notion of another world, another realm of a different order. It is very very hard, perhaps impossible, to get away from this.

TURTON: Durkheim would simply say that that order which people think of as being outside and beyond society is, in fact, society itself. He's not saying you *cannot* have gods in religion.

HINES: I quite agree with that. But I would argue that when I had to write about Anglo-Saxon paganism, I concluded that I had to find some way of distinguishing the specifically religious within the general cultural activities or to abandon religion altogether as a meaningful category, and that this factor seemed to be an effective and justifiable criterion.

TURTON: What about Buddhism?

HINES: Well, I was not talking about Buddhism. I was discussing religion in north-western Europe in a particular period.

This question of defining religion in order to identify activities as religious or not came to a head for me where you said that the casting of lots was definitely religious in some cases.

You also said, with some reservation, that there is practically nothing one could confidently identify as pagan in the archaeological record from Anglo-Saxon England. I would go further and assert that there is absolutely nothing that falls into this category. The best candidate we have for a pagan religious feature is the possible temple at Yeavering. At one point you stick your neck out and suggest that "cremation is almost certain to be an indication of paganism". This is only paganism in the sense that cremation is a practice that early Christianity would not willingly tolerate, although it had to for a while. To suggest that the cremation rite in itself is an expression of pagan belief or ritual begs many questions. How would you cope then with the fact that in the pre-Christian period you have such a variety of burial rites, not least both cremation and inhumation? You seem to be creating an unnecessary problem. Of course, religion tends to get involved with funerary rituals. But by identifying cremation as a glimpse of Anglo-Saxon paganism you have actually said no more than that if one wants to find religion one will probably find it in funerary ritual.

WOOD: Perhaps I should have given the sentence a footnote: it is Charlemagne who says cremation is pagan.

HINES: Christianity came into England with a very clear idea of how burial should be carried out, and this instantly created a category of non-Christian burials, even if pre-Christian burial practice was not especially religious in pagan terms.

TURTON: Can I ask you a question about the word 'pagan'? Perhaps the reason it is so common among historians and archaeologists is that the people you are talking about are not here to answer back. Would you be happy to call contemporary non-Christians pagans?

DUMVILLE: Yes. Half jocularly, of course.

SCHÜTTE: It depends on where you are. In catholic Cologne they use the term pagan as the real characterisation of non-Christian groups. In protestant areas I think it is not used in this strict sense, in a more humourous one probably: "I am an old pagan". I think in some areas it is still used as a real expression to characterise non-Christians. The Catholic church uses it.

GREEN: Would you use it?

SCHÜTTE: No. I would not use the word 'primitive' either because it is derogatory.

DUMVILLE: Why is it derogatory?

SCHÜTTE: It has negative connotations. In Muslim countries it is applied to non-believers or pagans.

TURTON: Why shouldn't we stop using it of past populations?

AUSENDA: The same as primitive people sometimes are called 'non-literate', could one call pagans 'non-Christians'?

HINES: I cannot imagine any circumstances in which I would want to create a single general category of this kind. I would certainly want to distinguish between Muslims, Jews, etc. and those who simply hold no recognisably religious beliefs nor observe any religious ritual.

TURTON: So a pagan is a religious person who is non-Christian?

HINES: This is how I would use the term. Is 'pagan' only a difficult term if we cannot distinguish between a positive religion which is not Christianity and a mere lack of religion? Religion is all around us.

WOOD: Part of the problem is that when I, as an historian who works largely on written texts, as opposed to archaeologists or other types of specialists, talk about paganism I am identifying those whom my sources call *pagani*. To throw out the word *paganus* altogether is perverse.

TURTON: It depends what you want to do. If you want to understand the nature of religion among these people, the very first thing you might have to do is throw out the word 'pagan'. Just as, if you want to understand the nature of religion in Africa, you have to get rid of the word 'animist' because it simply blocks the way forward.

HINES: But isn't that because 'animism' in Africa has a specific meaning, denoting a particular character? It must have done so to begin with.

TURTON: I think the difficulty is that even Christianity is 'animistic'—that is, it's a religion which attributes some kind of non-material quality to material things.

HINES: I am not claiming that it is a good term. What I am arguing is that you cannot necessarily equate the problem of using 'animist' with the problem of using 'pagan'.

AUSENDA: The word 'pagan' has the same vague connotation, because *paganus* originally meant somebody living in a village and, therefore, considered less sophisticated and having a religion fraught with superstition. I think David [Turton] is perfectly right: if Ian wants to establish a separation and try to understand, he should take an anthropological stance there, and maybe by a footnote explain what he means.

WOOD: Can I just respond very briefly in terms of how I might try to recast my material? To do so let me just take the problem of dividing paganism and superstition. It seems to me that any pattern one sets up is unsatisfactory. You raised the question of lot-casting, pagan or superstitious? Well, in certain cases it has unquestionably to do with religion; in some cases it may not. If you define religion in relation to deity, the fact remains that some superstitions attacked by Boniface may relate to deities. To cope with this problem of classification I think I would want a modified Durkheimian position. The problem with a straight division into religion as community activity and superstition as private activity is that the family gets right in the middle: is it community or is it individual? Much of what is normally classified as superstition is actually family activity.

The solution, as I think about it, seems to be to set up a spectrum, to put Durkheim's definitions at either end of that spectrum, and then to place material along it.

TURTON: Perhaps the distinction could be between the public sphere, or community, and the domestic sphere, or family.

HINES: One of the problems that I tried to solve by means of some definition of religion is that precisely the same act can be religious or non-religious in different contexts. Manuring the soil can be just a practical art that helps the crops to grow, or it can be feeding or propitiating a goddess, Mother Earth, purely according to the attitude of the person who is doing it. How, under a Durkheimian approach, does one deal with this sort of contrast? Isn't it really an anti-religious definition, marginalising the divine and privileging the social?

TURTON: Durkheim's thesis was that religion is just about one of the most fundamental aspects of human society. He was an atheist, but he was saying that the function of religion is absolutely crucial. It does not mean to say that in all societies you get it played out in relation to gods.

HINES: The particular term 'god' needn't be a serious difficulty. Gods represent a spiritual otherworld, which is usually imagined as populated in some way—perhaps, I suppose, as a mirror-image of our world. A long time ago, Andrew Lang (1898:51-2, discussed in Sharper 1975:43-71)) indicated that the alternative to gods as a constant of religion is a "vague sense of numinism" in the human—perhaps indeed the social—mind, and that neither of these concepts can be satisfactorily explained in terms of social function.[3]

TURTON: I don't see a problem. Durkheim wanted to explain this belief in a world beyond society. For him it was just a projection of the moral authority which the group exerts over the individual. On your question about how Durkheim would deal with the difference between manuring the soil and feeding the Earth Goddess, again I don't see a problem. I think he would say that, even if it is seen by the individual in question as feeding the Earth goddess, it should not be counted as religion unless it is connected in some way with the community actually coming together. If it is just an individual act he would want to put it into the category of magic.

AUSENDA: I would like to remind you that we should leave promptly at six, because our *custos* wants to go to the community bingo game.

VOICE: That would be a church [laughter].

---

[3] Lang's phrase was in fact "an unanalysable *sensus numinis*", and his argument was specifically directed (*inter alia*) at demonstrating the inadequacy of "materialist" explanations of these phenomena.

References in the discussion

Baetke, W.
   1937   *Die Religion der Germanen in Quellenzeugnissen.* Frankfurt: Diesterweg.
Blair, J.
   1993   'Squaring the circle: Is it possible to identify Anglo-Saxon pagan shrines?' Paper
             presented to the 6th Meeting of the International Society of Anglo-Saxonists, Wadam
             College, University of Oxford, 1st - 7th August 1993. A revised version of the paper
             is expected to be published in *Anglo-Saxon Studies in Archaeology and History* 8
             (1995).
Evans-Pritchard, E. E.
   1940   *The Nuer: A description of the modes of livelihood and political institutions of a
             nilotic people.* Oxford: Clarendon Press.
   1956   *Nuer Religion.* Oxford: Clarendon Press.
Heusch, L. de
   1985   *Sacrifice in Africa.* Manchester: Manchester University Press.
Johnson, D.
   1994   *Nuer Prophets.* Oxford: Oxford University Press.
Lang, A.
   1898   *The Making of Religion.* London: Longman, Green & Co.
Scott, E.
   1990   A critical review of the interpretation of infant burials in Roman Britain, with
             particular reference to villas. *Journal of Theoretical Archaeology* 1: 30-46.
Sharper, E. J.
   1975   *Comparative Religion: A History.* London: Duckworth.

CONCLUDING DISCUSSION

AXBOE: Being the first to speak of course gives me the chance to say the obvious things and to leave it to the rest of you to be more ingenious. This symposium was meant to be interdisciplinary, and I think it has been so—and it has been a good meeting, too. I think Giorgio [Ausenda] has played a good hand in bringing us together—some of you I knew as names, but only one in person, and some I must admit I didn't even know existed [laughter]. But now I know you! It seems to me that as a group we have functioned well, everybody discussing everybody else's papers, and such personal contacts across the limits of our fields may be very useful in our future work.

To me it has been a challenge having to present my material to people from other disciplines, not knowing what they would know about beforehand and thus having to present things so that they could be understood anyway. And it has been a rewarding challenge to read the pre-circulated papers, having to try to understand them and consider "What can we learn from that?". I think David Turton made a point saying that the results and models of anthropology cannot just be taken over by archaeology and applied to past societies, but that anthropology in confronting us with other societies can make us aware of our own preconceived ideas and to be conscious of them in our research.

Contact with philologists may be of more direct use to archaeologists, not only to teach them humility, but because their methods and results are more readily applicable to the period we have considered here, and can add extra dimensions to the picture drawn by archaeology. It has been interesting to get a glimpse of the Germanic world through the philologist's eyes. And I think, Dennis [Green], that when the book you are working on appears, you should do some serious marketing among archaeologists to make us aware of the additions you can offer to our source material. You can start by sending me a copy [laughter], so that I can review it in some appropriate journal.

At too many symposia we just meet the usual colleagues and discuss more or less the same things again and again. Here I have met, well, I might call you 'the unusual-people'; strangers in the definition that strangers are friends you just haven't met yet. My point is that there is a danger to Giorgio's plans for future symposia on more restricted themes like The *Ethnography of the...*'. If I was to propose some participants for a symposium on the ethnography of the Danes, it would be Lotte, Ulla, Ulf, and Stig, and so on; the usual people, and we would fairly well know beforehand what each other was working on and what would be said. We might get the latest news from Ribe, but we do get that every year. So to avoid 'inbreeding' you should take care to maintain interdisciplinarity.

DUMVILLE: Then, of course, that is where pre-circulation is very useful, because you can in that way involve people who are not immediate specialists, if they have enough reading matter to inform them well in advance.

AXBOE: Yes, but the first point is to think of which subjects would be of interest and to find the actual people to be invited. For a symposium on the Danes, place-names would be one possibility but, again, as I have already been to one or two symposia with some of those people, the 'shock effect' will be much less.

DUMVILLE: But if there were place-name specialists in French, rather than in Dutch or German, the shock-effect for both parties would be much greater!

AFTER EMPIRE:
TOWARDS AN ETHNOLOGY OF EUROPES'S BARBARIANS

© C.I.R.O.S.S.
San Marino (R.S.M.)

AXBOE: Yes, very much greater. Well, that was about what I had thought to say.

AUSENDA: Any critiques? Critiques are just as useful.

AXBOE: Less discussion about paganism [laughter].

AUSENDA: [To start the discussion on new approaches he suggested a project to build a data bank for ancient European populations similar to what the Human Relations Area Files have done for contemporary ones].

AXBOE: There is a problem in connecting Germanic tribal names with specific archaeological finds. In some cases it may even be a nuisance to know, for example, that the Langobards were in an area at some time. How are we to decide exactly which types of pots or brooches belonged to them and not to other tribes? And were differences of 'tribe' necessarily linked to differences in material culture? We know that there were Danes in southern Scandinavia in the Migration period, but not exactly where, nor whether there were also Jutes or other tribes as well.

SCHÜTTE: On Germanic tribes in Scandinavia there was a thirty-year discussion on who was who and identifying which were which....

AUSENDA: I am not saying it is a brilliant idea, I am just saying it is an idea. If you have other ideas please bring them up, because it seems to me that the future of this type of approach depends on ideas, organisation and cooperation.

WOOD: I can see what you are trying to get at. I am not certain that the way you suggest is necessarily the best way of doing it. It does seem to me that making things readily comparable is a very good way forward: one always needs to be reminded of what the tribe next door is doing. Now, whether you can actually do this by listing the material in any clearly categorised form, or whether the best thing to do is to make certain that you regularly have somebody who knows about the Anglo-Saxons sitting next to somebody who knows about the Danes, sitting next to somebody who knows about the Franks, maybe that is the crucial thing; but I think you are absolutely right in saying that only by building in that sort of regular contact, is there going to be rapid development. I think that is absolutely right.

GREEN: And I would stress the superior advantage of the second of the two methods, because it is so much more elastic. One can move about much more quickly from one field to another sitting around like this, a relatively small group around the table, rather than doing it any other way.

SCHÜTTE: I think it is more open minded to have all these, really sometimes contrasting, subjects, as for example the discussions about terminology or centrisms, Danish or other ethnocentrisms. I think it is a real advance to be more open minded. If you look at archaeology, some discussions have been boiling in their own sauce for some thirty years, and there is no real progress. Like this catalogue of graves, where nothing really comes out—excepting the St. Severin publication—this is for me something that I do not appreciate. It is much more interesting to look at the question: do wine barrels really arrive in northern Poland, or does only the word arrive? This implies that archaeologists go ahead and look for the wine barrels, not just symbols. I imagine this is useful. I think it gives new ideas, and new approaches can be developed out of this, and I think that your remark that there is a large demand for some new sources, especially in archaeology, is very interesting because, I think, this will not be so in linguistics or written sources; there will not be a big enlargement in the sources, but in archaeology there will—and not in graves, I think, but in settlements, urban or rural settlements. I think many of the questions you raised in your paper, Giorgio, might not be solved but could be illuminated if further archaeological research takes place in areas where it has not taken place yet. So, I think, if I look at northern Germany, there are endless urn fields, endless grave fields, and some rural settlements, but the question of urban settlements has not been treated really seriously. Maybe this is the same for northern Italy, though not for England, I think, maybe because it has a more developed urban archaeology in general. But a lot of new sources will appear, and these could imply a lot of new things. Ravenna, yesterday, was really a point I want to refer to. What was in between all these mosaics and churches would be a marvellous point to establish. It should not be that such an important place consists only of some architecture, some historical sources and these mosaics, with everything in between except the *cathedra* of the bishop left more or less alone. I am sure that it will reveal a lot of new things if you go to these places and look at what is going on there. It must be possible for archaeology to say if there was an urban settlement or there was none.

AXBOE: In Ravenna it seems one would have to make recourse to underwater archaeology.

SCHÜTTE: Organic material would be preserved. And in other cities of northern Italy as well, as well as in some parts of Germany, Mainz or other important places, where this has not been done yet.

AUSENDA: Do you have any critiques?

SCHÜTTE: Yes, it is good that these worlds met, but some are quite hermetic, I think, in some way. It is good for the others to know what linguistics does, but sometimes it is a world in itself with its own terminology as archaeology is. I think it was very good to have people who are already working interdisciplinarily or multidisciplinarily. I think no one at this table is only working in his own field, everybody does already work interdisciplinarily, but sometimes it is a little hermetic and some problems seem to me rather closed up.

AUSENDA: Could you give an example?

SCHÜTTE: I think there is no discussion about terminology for 'paganism' because the question is not put. Of course it is the common term used and it is not questioned. I think linguists have never officially asked archaeologists to prove whether something is a trade word or not. There is a trade word 'so and so' running along the Danube: is it one, or is it a fiction? This is the question I have.

Archaeology is hermetic as well. I think it is a very good idea to squeeze grave fields for some information to come out. But it is limited as you could see from the discussion between you two. There may be a tradition whether this represents religion. It may be possible to get some information out of it, from the statistics which can be very striking. Morten says: "I do not like the whole approach". I think one should try it, whatever comes out, because the other has been tried for several years now. Obviously there is hidden information. I think we should try to read this and to understand the meaning of this language, or whatever it is. I wonder what consequences this will have. Will the term 'paganism' vanish in publications? I doubt that it will vanish [laughter]. Will all these centrisms vanish as well? I doubt this because if the Danish government finances all the archaeology, it would want to see some results concerning Denmark. I agree that 'objectivity', whatever that may mean in historical sciences, "has been bought at the price of social irrelevance" as you said. Is it really relevant? I think this is the opposite of what Giorgio intended. His sentence was: "Better understand the nascent stage...and the attitudes that are at the base of present-day Europe", which means to support an understanding of present-day Europe. This leads to the question: "What is it all for? What do we want to know for this period?" And sometimes during the meeting I was not really sure about what we wanted to know for the whole period. Some people were asking what were the structures like. Of course there was a lot in common, I think, because some researchers have worked for twenty, thirty, even forty years, then they became a world in themselves and they are not so open to other researches on the same subject. I think it is a very complicated field, for example, cooperation between archaeologists and historians. Maybe it is because of my English, but I did not always understand, for example, the distinction between historical sources and archaeological sources; I think archaeological sources are historical as well, but one type are written and the others are not. Yet there is always a distinction between these two. So, what are the consequences; will there be more intensive cooperation between archaeologists and historians? What does it mean then? Do we force historians to come to the excavation and say: "Look, what is this?" or the other way around.

WOOD: We could do that.

SCHÜTTE: Yes, we ought to do this in this group, but I look at the average German archaeologist and he is not present; he might be present in this group but he is not present in the general case. Of course, it is a necessity.

DUMVILLE: There is difficulty in enforcing understanding between historians, say, and archaeologists. You can drag a non-archaeologist along to a site, and you can point out a number of things but understanding is not necessarily increased if the methods of archaeological excavation and research are not grasped. This is not scholarship, it is tourism, intellectual tourism.

SCHÜTTE: I think you have to find a language in common and explain what you want to know about in your approach to the whole thing. It is not that you have to make somebody look at something. This is really tourism. The question is find a language in common to make it better, what do we want from this side, this and the other way around. So, for future approaches the question is, "Can a group like this initiate, maybe not projects directly, but a preliminary stage of projects for the future?"

What are the demands? Is there a list of demands? What do we want to know? Do we ask Italian archaeologists to go out in the outskirts of Milan and dig [laughter]? If you will look at your temples, there was a discussion of "are there any temples, or are there none?" This can be solved somehow. Maybe it is hidden information, but we have then to look for what could be meant by a simple fence. Even your Mursi ritual leaves some traces in the soil. So, if it is buried early enough, you will find these enclosures: some small postholes from the branches or whatever, and the fire burning there and whatever.

How do we interpret structures? Probably the question is what structures are we looking for? There could be some list of future demands of what we want to know and how to use the old material. The catalogues provide us with useful information, but, are we using it the right way, or is it not the right way we apply our knowledge about these grave fields? What do we really want to know from this?

AXBOE: If I might add, the 'paganism' debate after Ian's lecture knocked me down for the moment. You asked for temples, but what sort of 'temples' are we to look for? I mentioned the weapon sacrifices in the bogs. During these events, those bogs were sites where religious activities took place; but the same bogs were also used for mundane activities like peat-digging. And similarly we suppose that religious activities took place in the settlements—one indication of this would be the small gold foils, *guldgubber*, found in large numbers at Sorte Muld, and also represented in Gudme, Lundeborg, Stentiget and other 'central places'. Perhaps we are wrong to look for specialised temples.

WOOD: Certainly. With regard to the point I was making, we have clear evidence of sacred zones in the texts. We also have *fana*. The problem is what is a *fanum*? You may be right: a bog is presumably included within a sacred zone rather than within a *fanum*.

AXBOE: We have also been talking of trade routes—it is much discussed in archaeology what sort of 'trade' we should consider for this period. Was it mercantile, long-distance, so to speak 'modern' trade, or was it bartering, gift-exchange or 'administered trade'? How did Roman goods come to Scandinavia? Did the Romans sail directly all the way around Jutland to eastern Sjælland, from where the objects apparently were redistributed, or what happened?

SCHÜTTE:-I think the important thing is to consider the whole of Europe, leaving the borders of your own country. Sometimes it seemed to me a little Anglo-centric. If you are talking about east of the Rhine, Britain is, as far as I know, not east of the Rhine. Sometimes it switched just to Anglo-Saxon England.

WOOD: Yes, that is certainly because the two descriptions of temples happen to be in Anglo-Saxon texts relating to England.

SCHÜTTE: But if you see, for example, that northern Italy and some parts of Germany are highly comparable, future work has to take place on a European scale. France does not exist, it is a black hole in the discussion. It should be done more across the borders, especially now that eastern Europe is more accessible.

AXBOE: Or we became accessible to them—we could go there all the time, but it is only now that they too can travel.

SCHÜTTE: But you know it is more the other way around. The colonisation process runs more to the east than the other way.

HINES: I fully agree that this should be done, but it is very difficult to be confident that it is a particularly practical proposition. My impression is that, for instance, one of the reasons why France is a 'black hole' as far as many outside archaeologists are concerned is simply the excavation policies that there have been there. One of the main reasons for my visit to Poland in April this year was to assess the scope for comparative research work. It was possible to see that potential comparability is there, but also that it would take perhaps ten years of different excavation and research priorities to achieve that potential in respect of the topic I was concerned with. Now, while I could present my ideas and hope to interest scholars there in them, neither I nor any other individual or group have a right to expect people in other countries to be interested in these questions just because I am. They have their own traditions which define topics that they are most interested in. It will be a long time, I think, before one can write a substantial comparative ethnography of the Germanic and Slavonic peoples of the early Middle Ages. What, however, we can do is to bring people together, to begin talking about comparative work, in purely hypothetical terms to start with—and points of contact and common ground will certainly emerge. Actual, comprehensive, comparative work is still a long way off, but, if we believe that in the future this will be an important and useful enterprise, we have to start talking about it now.

SCHÜTTE: I did not mean that next year this and that site should be excavated, but, if a way of influencing that was found, maybe during the next fifteen or twenty years things could be initiated. Of course the history of every individual country is very influential in this. You see that Italian archaeology discovered urban structures late. And the same is true in Germany. In the East they have their traditions of research, and it will take ages to influence them and to bring everything to the same level, especially France. It isn't only a language problem, it is also a historical problem of how research was done and what importance was put on it. Look at East Germany, where Slav archaeology was favoured very much in the last years. Not everything, but lots of things were put aside; and still continuity did not 'switch on' after the opening of the old border. It will take some twenty years to influence them.

HINES: And, of course, influence will run in both directions. One of the most encouraging things I found in eastern Europe was to see how close philology and archaeology still habitually are. Many professional archaeologists seem to have a basic grasp—even training— in Indo-European problems and think in terms of language history alongside archaeological history.

GREEN: Are you talking mainly of Poland or other countries too?

HINES: I am still talking of Poland, although I also know of Russian, Ukrainian and other archaeologists in the former Soviet Union who approach their work in this way. So I have inferred it to be likely that this will be found in other places too.

AUSENDA: From what you say it seems to me that there should be some effort devoted to this aim. In other words, scholars should be made aware of the idea that greater cooperation, a more developed interdisciplinary approach and more attention to that period could give a considerable impulse to the understanding of what happened during those times. One of the problems in Italy is that the early Middle Ages are considered less important than the Roman period. Some pressure should be brought to bear on both academics and responsible government structures. Don't you think so?

WOOD: Yes, I was already trying to fight that war. I would have thought the most likely Italian to be involved was Federico Marazzi.

BALZARETTI: He is a historian of the eighth, ninth, and tenth century, of the Papacy as well.

WOOD: Well, moving back actually.

BALZARETTI: But he is very open. He does a lot of archaeology.

WOOD: He does a lot of archaeology with Richard Hodges.

RICHARDS: There can be no doubt that this meeting has been invaluable in demonstrating that an interdisciplinary approach is essential for synthesis in the early medieval period. But at the same time I think it has highlighted the problems of working on this period, especially because of the nature of the sources, and because they are not always informing us about the same thing. As you said, the history of the period inevitably has to be primarily a political history, whereas the archaeology, as always, relates much more to social and economic issues. I also do some work on the later medieval period, and I think that an interdisciplinary work is far more natural there.

AUSENDA: At which level of communication is interdisciplinary work more understandable?

RICHARDS: In the later medieval period. I think that in England in post-conquest archaeology you get a greater degree of historical sources to rely on.

DUMVILLE: ...documentary sources, as opposed to literary sources.

RICHARDS: Yes.

BALZARETTI: Medieval historians of the earlier period tend to keep saying their sources are very very diffficult to use, which tends perhaps to put off 'outsiders' from daring to study it.

WOOD: Yes, I think I would like to make another point. If you go back to the 1920s, the only history that was being written about this period was social. Now there are historians who say: "Hang on, we need to look at the political framework before we can deal with the social". But, if you throw specific questions at them and say: "How do you go about telling us about this sort of issue?", there is no reason why we cannot try to answer.... Now the answer can be very, very methodological, saying: "Well, this particular text belongs to this particular date, and it has all these sorts of problems". In a sense we are doing no more than what the archaeologists are saying: "Look, this pot belongs to this particular date". But if you fire direct questions at us and do not mind us airing all the dirty washing on the way, we can do something about it.

RICHARDS: I think this raises the question of the level at which the disciplines should be integrated. Should they be integrated at the level of research questions, or should they be given more leeway at the research stage and then only the conclusions pulled together?

SCHÜTTE: But I think both are practised because they normally work separately from each other, and it is a very rare occasion for them to meet. Of course, it would take 200 years to get enough information—we shall never have enough information from any of the subjects. But there is always the present stage. It is rare enough that people and ideas meet.

DUMVILLE: The logical solution to what Sven [Schütte] and Julian [Richards] are worrying about would be to define and create a project with a range of specialists—no doubt including a range of people who, themselves, work in more than one discipline—and have each of these people doing his own individual work, but also have a standing conference so that at short intervals people are arguing with one another and airing the interim results and so on all the way through. Of course, there are many ways of defining what interdisciplinarity is, and of organising interdisciplinary work. The standing conference would simply be one way of approaching that.

SCHÜTTE: I think that standing conferences are a marvellous idea and would be the most fruitful thing.

VOICE: They are very expensive.

SCHÜTTE: A standing conference, a common conference of totally different groups working on the same point.

AUSENDA: Do you mean periodic meetings?

DUMVILLE: Yes, a standing group of people meeting periodically to address developing problems.

HINES: There are actually two issues involved here. One is the problem of providing a forum for interdisciplinary exchanges; another is the problem of achieving truly interdisciplinarily generated projects. I think particularly of a 'Medieval Town' project that there has been in Denmark. This was very interdisciplinary in its constitution. The results have been quite impressive in certain cases and one can see that co-operation has worked out quite well here. Yet one can also feel that the initial idea of a 'Medieval Town' project was itself fairly predictable; it is not the sort of project of which you would say, "Oh gosh, no one would ever have thought of that if there had not been a meeting of minds from different corners". This sort of work may very well have to start with something predictable like that.

DUMVILLE: It is an area of work rather than an issue; interdisciplinary work will be at its most effective if from the beginning it involves formulating questions.

VOICES: Yes.

AXBOE: And it is a question of defining a subject which would appeal to a research council.

HINES: Of course, yes. Yes, it has to be 'safe' for a research council to back it.

AXBOE: Yes.

RICHARDS: I think one of the key issues that has come out of this meeting is actually the problem of defining a suitable study area. What I mean is the identity of the people, of the group of people to be studied, and what has come out explicitly on a number of occasions is that historically named people are not necessarily coterminous with the groups that archaeologists observe and also do not necessarily coincide with language groups, so that, in fact, each of our separate disciplines could draw lines, or try to draw lines on a map showing the extent of the people under study, but they would not necessarily coincide; although we might think we were talking about the same people, we would be using the term, say, Anglo-Saxons, but what historians are talking about when they discuss Anglo Saxons does not necessarily coincide with what archaeologists would be talking about. This goes back, in archaeology, to Gordon Childe's discussion of what an archaeological culture was, and he used to define that as a basic building block in archaeology. It seems safest to define it solely in archaeological terms as a group of people who are living with the same cultural norms, having the same type of culture. So, my feeling is that none of those units, either the linguistic group or the historical group has any greater reality than any of the other groups. One cannot say that the name Anglo-Saxons, for instance, would have any greater reality than what I map as a group of people who have an Anglo-Saxon burial rite. But they are probably not the same people. What I call people with Anglo Saxon burials would probably include Romano-British.

WOOD: As you formulate it there, it seems to me that the excitement comes in the next question, which is that, once you have made that observation, the historians, at least, can go off and try and ask why the group is defined in that particular way on paper. There is the question of why a particular myth is created.

RICHARDS: Yes, it could be that in some periods of history those three circles on the map would move closer together and in other periods they would move further apart. In the Migration period we were saying that often these groups are defined by the very act of migration and I think that is probably true that groups crystallise out at this moment of stress and change. It might be that at those moments they come together, and then that at other moments they came apart.

GREEN: Groups are defined at the moment of migration. Ethnogenesis is a process predicated on tribal fission and fusion. One should stress chronological variability.

WOOD: Take the followers of Odoacer. They seized Italy in 476, and they were destroyed in 493. If Odoacer had lived, people would have defined his followers as a single tribe. It is useful to see a group interrupted in the process of being established.

RICHARDS: The most interesting comparisons are between groups rather than within groups.

TURTON: I would like to begin by referring to something Giorgio said a little while ago about the Human Relations Area Files (HRAF). Speaking on behalf of my own tribe (of British social anthropologists), I have to express some scepticism. The HRAF has not been used much in Britain on the grounds that you don't get very far in comparative work simply by defining, classifying and comparing institutions taken from vastly different cultural contexts. What we need is what I called in my paper, following Whitehead, 'imaginative generalisation' or, to put it more bluntly, guesswork—based, of course, on observation. Whitehead contrasted 'imaginative generalisation' with 'rigid empiricism', the essential characteristics of which is that it depends *entirely* on observation. We observe, as he put it, 'by the method of difference', which means (I'm quoting from memory here and may not have got it quite right) that 'sometimes we see an elephant and sometimes we don't.

The result is that an elephant, when present, is noticed'. It would not be noticed if it were always there.

Now, if you are looking for what things have in common—the equivalent of Whitehead's 'metaphysical first priciples'—then you are not going to be able to *observe* them because, as he again put it, they 'never fail of exemplification'. So you would have to resort to imagination, guesswork. Radcliffe-Brown would now be castigated for thinking that interesting generalisations would somehow emerge automatically by piling up ever more meticulous descriptions of particular cases.

DUMVILLE: A pejorative word for that at my end of the business is 'antiquarianism'.

TURTON: I shall approach the task of appraising our meeting egocentrically—that is to say by asking 'What did I get out of it?' Before I came to San Marino I was pretty doubtful as to what I could contribute—what light the study of age organisation in present-day Mursiland could shed on the early Middle Ages. I was probably right to be doubtful. I also had great difficulty trying to imagine what I would gain from the meeting—apart from the intrinsic interest of the topic. So what do I think now?

The first point I want to make is that, while it is only relatively recently that anthropologists have started to take history seriously, the kind of history they've been particularly drawn to has been, for obvious reasons, oral history. In the field of African studies, the analysis of oral history by trained historians has had a lot to contribute to anthropological understanding and a great deal of mutual respect has been built up between these 'new' historians and anthropologists. One reason for this is probably that they both rely heavily on the ethnographic method—fieldwork. For all I know there may still be some reluctance on the part of 'traditional' historians to accept oral history, as was the case of A. J. P. Taylor who was quoted as saying: "In this matter I am an almost total sceptic.... Old men drooling about their youth—No" (Thompson 1978:62). But oral historians might have a useful part to play as a kind of bridge between anthropology and the kind of history which is based on the study of written texts.

Secondly, it's become clear to me during our discussions that there is an overall similarity between the events we've been concerned with in early Medieval Europe and the events in the non-European world which formed the backdrop of modern anthropology: the confrontation between hegemonic political power on the one hand and emerging centres of resistance on the other. Anthropologists working in Africa during the colonial period, for example, were studying a situation which was characterised—even if they chose not to focus on this—by the decline and fall of European imperialism. Missionary activity, as a mechanism of cultural domination, is another common factor. So what I hadn't realised was that there was this similarity between the political context which historians of early Medieval Europe are directly concerned with and that within which anthropologists have carried out their studies—and, unlike historians, been part of. Anthropology, after all, is one of the means by which the West has 'objectified' the non-European world. In the light of this it's not surprising to discover that many of the topics we've been discussing closely resemble topics anthropologists have also given a lot of thought to: the processes by which political identities are created, the 'freezing' of ethnic identities through colonial administration, the relationship between religious and secular power, and so on.

Thirdly, it has become clear to me that historians, as much as anthropologists, are faced with the problem of how to achieve a culturally neutral position. In fact, of course, this is a dilemma, not a problem, since it can only be grappled with, not solved. It must have been the impossibility of achieving cultural neutrality that Evans-Pritchard had in mind when he said, as reported by Rodney Needham (1975), that "There is only one method in social anthropology, the comparative method, and that's impossible". This is a dilemma for both anthropologists and historians but there is one important difference: the populations we anthropologists are dealing with are our contemporaries: they can, and increasingly do, answer back. This means that, in their attempts to achieve cultural neutrality, anthropologists are brought face to face with certain ethical problems which historians can conveniently ignore, simply because the people they are writing about are dead. But this doesn't mean that historians would not benefit from considering what would be the consequences if the subjects of *their* investigations could also answer back.

Fourthly, we seem to have all been in agreement that, while anthropology does not provide a window on the past which can be used to fill in the gaps in the historical and archaeological record, it can nevertheless help in stimulating new approaches to, and understanding of, historical and archaeological data. The papers by Giorgio Ausenda and Ross Balzaretti were cases in point. Another way of putting this is to say that anthropology can help the historian and archaeologist to become aware of, and adopt a critical stance towards, his or her cultural biases—the idea, for example, that barter is a simple, crude, or 'primitive' form of exchange. It can make us think about our basic cultural assumptions.

It is simply that our basic assumptions are the cultural equivalents of Whitehead's elephants: because they are always present we don't see them. And another thing about basic assumptions is that they don't live in their own little boxes—they are all tied in together so that to question one of them is to question the whole set, the whole system. Anthropologists, of course, react in the same way when radically new ideas come along—there is a great deal of resistance.

That's why I found our argument about 'paganism' so interesting. I'm not going to go through the argument again, you'll be pleased to know, but I'm totally unrepentant about raising it, for two reasons. Firstly, it's my job, as an anthropologist, to question cultural assumptions and I'm sure that all anthropologists would agree that the validity of 'paganism', as a category of historical understanding, is at best dubious. Secondly, what I find most interesting about this is the difficulty you—the historians that is—seem to have in accepting this. Why is there so much resistance to this particular anthropological contribution when other things anthropologists have to say—about, for example, the complexity of barter as a system of exchange—are readily taken up and used by historians? The answer may be that to question the use of the category 'paganism' is to question a whole way of 'doing' history. Could it be that what this argument reveals is the preoccupation of historians with elucidating and interpreting literary texts, as an end in itself and at the expense of understanding what was actually going on at the time? Could it be that the texts—and their authors—have become the real, that is direct, focus of historical study, rather than the behaviour they purport to record?

One final point. If, with the benefit of hindsight, I were now to sit down and write a paper for the meeting we have just had, I would not write about the Mursi age organisation but about Mursi migration. Having listened to you all talking about the 'Age of Migrations', I'm convinced that this is the area where I would have most to learn, in my own research, from historians and archaeologists and where anthropologists could have a lot to contribute to your work. Most of what I have written on the Mursi in the last five years has been concerned, in one way or another, with the connection between population movements and the creation of new political identities. One highly relevant contribution to this topic, which historians of the 'Age of Migrations' might also find useful, is a book by a German anthropologist, Gunther Schlee (1989), called *Identities on the Move*. It's about what he calls 'inter-ethnic clan identities' in northern Kenya. He points out that clan-identities are much older than, and cut across, ethnic or tribal (if you prefer to say political) boundaries. Political identities emerge and fall away over time, but clan identities are more long-term. I think this is an area—in contrast to that of 'paganism'—where we would find immediate and mutual benefit in comparing findings, methods and approaches.

GREEN: Can I make two points? The first concerns the historical dimension, and I think you put your finger on what certainly was my reservation when I came here and knew that you would talk about the anthropology of your area in Africa. Not that I was questioning the relevance of an area totally outside Europe, obviously not. That could have been helpful, and in fact it was helpful, but what I wondered about was how far anthropology, as a discipline concerned with the state of tribal society at any one given point in time could contribute to our essentially historical problem. And I remember the relief and delight with which I heard you, on the very first day, say that an anthropologist could not conduct his discipline without being aware of the relevance of the historical background to the present position which he was consulting. So, that is one point on the historical side. The other point on that same issue is one that you brought up this morning, namely oral history. Now oral history, in the sense in which it is understood and in the sense in which I believe you understood it, obviously cannot contribute to our study of this past historical period, but I think it is essential to see orality and history in terms of historiography over any period of time based on oral as opposed to written sources, and that is highly relevant to our concern. It is not the same type of connection between orality and history as concerns you, but it might provide a common basis. I am interested in that too, because I have just finished, as I said before, a book on orality and literacy in which history plays a considerable part. So that I am here, as it were, wearing two hats, an oral one as well as a migrationary one.

If I may make under the historical dimension one small suggestion, Giorgio [Ausenda], for any general editorial comments you make—I am speaking *pro domo*, but then we are all speaking *pro domo*, and I do not think there is any reason to apologise for being what you call egocentric: only by being egocentric can we contribute to a common discussion and exchange of views—it is this: when referring to the nature of the evidence we are concerned with, I from my point of view have no objection to using the word linguistic, linguistic terminology, linguistic evidence, and so on and so forth. I do think it is dangerous, though, if when referring to the discipline of the people concerned with this we were to use the word linguistics or linguists, because these terms have been appropriated by modern linguistics and, as such, they operate in a non-historical dimension, precisely the dimension I feared you might be operating in before you pronounced the magic words on the first day. I know there are reasons to doubt the alternative I am going to put forward, but to refer to the discipline as philology and to people operating in this field as philologists certainly imposes a historical dimension which is germane to the rest of our concerns, whereas to talk about linguists and linguistics, I think, could create precisely the wrong impression.

And my second point: the term 'paganism', which we hotly debated at dinner again last night, I would like to say that whilst we remain as unrepentant as you, let me assure you that I do not think we will use the word 'paganism' in our context without carefully thinking about it before we put pen to paper. I promise no more [laughter].

WOOD: I want to make a number of points about paganism. First of all I accept the anthropologist's stance, totally and utterly, but I think, that the term is a shorthand, dependent on theological sources. You can quite rightly throw bricks at us and say we ought to change our categories, standpoint and so on. Some of us are trying to chip away at the problem slowly. It may be that one needs a sort of radical revolution, rather than chipping away. You might argue a Kuhnian type of revolution. I think that, simply in terms of current expression, to say something like 'non-Christian' religion, instead of 'paganism', gets us into an awful problem of expression—talking about the influence of Christianity on a 'non Christian' religion. This is a nasty mess. I think what I would want to say is that in an ideal world what would happen is that the new categorisation that you are proposing would actually begin by saying something about Christianity and paganism at the same time. If you just substitute 'non-Christian religion' you are being equally Christo-centric, whereas what is actually needed is somebody to sit down and not just deal with non-Christian religion east of the Rhine, but to deal with religion east of the Rhine, or with religion *tout court*, shall we say, in the Frankish world, or wherever, where you subject paganism and Christianity to exactly the same sort of questions. The implication, though, is that one would have to write a six-volume work. I see the absolute logic about that; it seems to me not to be possible to begin in that way. I accept your standpoint absolutely in logical terms. I just do not know whether it is feasible to make that leap very quickly.

AXBOE: I do not think anybody would speak of neolithic 'paganism', he would speak of neolithic religion.

RICHARDS: What you say is quite right on the basis of one of the main arguments you put forward originally that you should abide by what your sources used. I think it does come back to the fact of using the categories used by the various sources.

WOOD: Yes, but one has to understand the sources.

DUMVILLE: Yes, but there are problems with the ways in which different historians would define 'understanding'. For example, what I am interested in, more than many historians, is the process of the transmission of knowledge. Often I am interested in investigating a source with that in mind, rather than in asking questions about what it is telling us about even political organisation, let alone social.

TURTON: You are defining your objective differently.

DUMVILLE: On oral history, it occurs to me that one oral historian who is definitely not an anthropologist, but has been much involved in disseminating anthropologists' ideas, is David Henige whose books on the chronology of oral tradition and oral history are considerable contributions. Another scholar whose works have been widely read and, in some places, have been very influential, perhaps more influential simply because of where they have been published, is Jan Vansina. Indeed, I think that the two of them may have been colleagues at the University of Wisconsin (Madison), so that, in fact, better writing about historical method and the study of oral culture which has obviously been relevant to medievalists has in fact come from one centre. Henige's work in particular is well written, easy to take on board stylistically, while at the same time being of a high intellectual calibre.

GREEN: Can you give the name and reference again?

DUMVILLE: David P. Henige, *The Chronology of Oral Tradition*, Oxford U.P., 1974, and there has been more than one subsequent book by him. He is an African historian. His journal, *History of Africa*, used to carry a magnificent comparative bibliography.

GREEN: What do anthropologists think of Vansina's work?

TURTON: It's taken seriously. He's probably one oral historian that all anthropologists will have heard of, even if they haven't read him. Another thing that's happened in anthropology—apart, that is, from the new respect which is accorded to oral tradition—is that there has been an upsurge of interest in the activity of speaking itself—the so-called 'ethnography' of speaking.

AUSENDA: Is there some doubt about philology being the study of the origins of texts, whilst the historical study of languages is called 'glottology'?

GREEN: No, philology can be said to embrace both language and literature, but I would say that now the tendency is towards using philology more restrictedly in the sense of the study of language, but the study of language essentially in its historical dimensions, which is not true of linguistics.

DUMVILLE: Is that true if you are speaking German as well?

GREEN: No.

DUMVILLE: Historically there is a divide between anglophone and other European cognate words.

GREEN: I put that forward without that restriction or that afterthought, because, after all, our proceedings are in English.

AUSENDA: So, we should change our 'linguistics' to 'philology' if we are talking about the diachronic aspect.

GREEN: 'Linguists' and 'linguistics', I think, raise false assumptions, and the terms would be in conflict with our concern.

TURTON: You would not approve of 'historical linguistics'?

GREEN: No. It is better than 'linguistics' by itself, but then you run up against the problem, how do you refer to the people who engage in that?

TURTON: 'Historical linguists'.

GREEN: Yes, but then you have a clumsy adjective lying in wait.

HINES: I have come to use this working definition: just as modern linguistics is a general linguistics, attempting to account for language as a complete phenomenon and not particularly interested in peculiarities of specific languages, historical linguistics, as I understand it, attempts to establish general theories of how languages change diachronically, while philology is properly concerned with the history of specific languages or language groups. So, you have a philologist of the Germanic language, or an English philologist, who will be readily distinguishable from a historical linguist who studies what you can call 'principles of historical linguistics'. He will draw examples, of course, from all over the place, but will be attempting to give some general and comprehensive account of how languages may change in time. Do you think this is a workable definition?

GREEN: Yes, I would accept that distinction, but I still hold to the view that 'linguistic' and 'linguists' should be looked at as carefully as David and I are going to do with 'paganism' in the future.

BALZARETTI: Could I introduce something that we really have not talked about as a slightly different approach? It is the very faddish subject of gender which I mention because I think it was implicit in what several people have said. Can males and females, men and women, be identified as groups? Did that change as the people migrated? Perhaps we could say something about that or think about it, because it must have been important, at least biological things must have been important, actual physical reproduction, if you have got, which we may or may not have, groups that are biologically identified. So, we have Lombards moving into a place where there are non-Lombards, do they interbreed? What happens? And that is something we could have said more about. The reason we could have discussed it more is that methodologically speaking it is a very big problem: how do we find out about it? Also because archaeologically we are not able always to identify the physical remains of men and women. I know there has been some work by historians, but it is one of those basic assumptions. The fact that there are men and women in the world is a basic assumption.

TURTON: Let me give a personal example very quickly. I've made five films on the Mursi with a documentary film-maker, Leslie Woodhead. In all of them we've concentrated on what might be called a male view of Mursi society. This wasn't for arbitrary or chance reasons but because of the way I've done my research. When I showed our second film in the States in 1982, a woman in the audience got up afterwards and asked: "Are there any women in this society?"

This was a perfectly valid criticism, but we tried to deal with it in our subsequent films by the absurd technique of simply interviewing more women—as though the fact that we had ignored them in the past was an unfortunate oversight, rather than a function of the way I've done my fieldwork. During the shooting of our last two films on the age set ceremony in 1991, I went up to some older women, on the last day of the ceremony, and tried to get them to give a 'woman's point of view' to the camera. Much to my annoyance, they'd have none of it: "Why should we talk to you?" they said. "You've been paying no attention to us; you've spent all your time with the men".

At the time I treated this as yet another example of women being 'difficult', failing to 'cooperate' like the men. By the time we got to the cutting room, however, I realised that the only way to deal adequately with the criticism that our films had ignored women was to leave this sequence in the final film—to let the women make the point themselves. The confrontation between me and these 'difficult' women was in fact quite revealing, especially when seen on film. It showed dramatically that the women were characters to be reckoned with—not the marginal creatures our films had, unintentionally, made them out to be.

In trying to focus on medieval women, historians are clearly limited by the available evidence. But the relative invisibility of women in the historical record, as in our films, is obviously not a true reflection of their actual social role and significance. Could it be that their 'invisibility' at this meeting is not entirely due to the shortage of women scholars in the fields of early medieval history and archaeology?

HINES: You are faced with a comparable situation in attempting to study this medieval period; a similar set of problems in trying to study gender in the early Middle Ages comprehensively as your problems in trying to study the economy of northern Italy. We are the prisoners of our sources. That gender differences are a persistent and a variable feature of culture is hardly an unfamiliar point now. Nor could it really be called a neglected topic, for there have been some rather exaggerated attempts made to drag information on gender out of a whole symbolic cultural record which pretty consistently leaves that information out in certain areas.

WOOD: I think you mentioned Kenya and migration.... Even a short bibliography of the anthropology of migration would be very helpful.

DUMVILLE: It would, it would indeed.

HINES: My general opinion on the exercise we have been engaged in here has largely been expressed already by others in this discussion, indeed already by Morten in opening this discussion. There is, I perceive, a very strong consensus in this meeting.

If there is anything that I think I would like to underline once again, it would be to repeat the point of how useful, interesting and regrettably unusual, it is to be in a forum where we are confronted with historical, linguistic and archaeological evidence, and indeed see these categories of evidence confront one another. If you go some way back into the history of scholarship you find closer links between people working in these areas; this is a connection that has been lost to a very large degree. Simply to recognise the value of these links is something that I think and hope will eventually bear fruit as more people come to take it seriously. In particular what we really need is to encourage philologists—there are plenty of archaeologists around, but philologists are not so numerous—as the difficulties a young philologist would face in getting a job (certainly in Britain) are even more immense than those facing aspiring archaeologists. Any encouragement that can be given to a recognition of the value of the trade or expertise of the philologist would be very welcome; in Britain, philologists have to find jobs in language or literature departments where philology is perceived as outdated and negligible.

DUMVILLE: I think that among weak-minded or trendy academics there is widespread belief that philology is not something useful, or is politically unsound.

HINES: It has, however, to be said, as in most cases, the blame does not lie entirely on one side. There are linguists who have insisted too much on the autonomy of their field: presenting language as a hermetically sealed system that can only be studied by linguists on their terms—which means too that their findings can only be evaluated and applied in this same charmed circle. In fact this whole situation seems quite bizarre given the importance of language in general philosophical thought in the twentieth century: the way in which linguistic science has replaced natural science as the provider of paradigms for theories relating to all sorts of phenomena—as in the case of structuralism. There are cultural theorists who constantly refer to linguistic theory as a justification or model for their own systems of thought. Yet the amount of what I would recognise as real linguistic knowledge that they reveal and use is very small indeed. I find it a strange, strange paradox that they can use the systems or grammars of linguistics without the actual linguistic data that inform those grammars.

GREEN: But, in just the same way as linguistics has permeated other disciplines in the twentieth century, and I am in full agreement with you there, so has it permeated the study of language to the detriment of historical philology. I grant you historical philology has a lot of responsibility for this, but what I think we have to do is demarcate our frontiers between the study of language which takes on board the historical dimension, and linguistics which does not....

HINES: Yes. I fully agree with that.

I am making one further point, I do not want to make us restart a terminological discussion that has already been aired; I will, however, throw out a view in case anybody thinks it worth commenting on.

One of Giorgio's opening questions was, in a sense: "What is the name of what we are engaged in? Is there a name for what we are doing?" Some of the formulations we have thought of have been ever more complex compounds: historical anthropology, historico-ethnographical archaeology, etc. [laughter]. The point that I would make is that I think this is cultural history and that I am a cultural historian. I say this on the basis of what seems to be a perfectly justifiable, broad view of human culture, as everything that people do which is not strictly biologically determined. In this sense there is virtually no human history that is not cultural history. One can specialise within cultural history and write economic history, social history, etc. But when a group is meeting to try to build bridges between such divisions of cultural history—which become represented as separate disciplines of cultural history—it is really trying to find a way of re-integrating culture; and this, I think, has very substantial implications for advancing the general understanding of the nature of culture itself. These implications ought to be kept to the fore to initiate and encourage structured study of this very big issue. This would put into proper perspective the (one hopes) instructive experience of trying to study 'culture' empirically.

And so back to the question of possible names: terms like 'historical anthropology', 'ethnoarchaeology' ought to refer to just very slightly different versions of the same thing. I really wonder whether the constant division of cultural studies into different '-ologies' isn't something that hinders rather than aides understanding. For this reason I continue to be unashamed, if not aggressive, in using the term 'cultural history' to refer to this sort of exercise.

TURTON: Since I am leaving now I would like to say how much I have enjoyed our discussions. I found them much more rewarding than I had expected. It has been for me a salutary reminder that we are all—historians, archaeologists, philologists, linguists and anthropologists—working away at the same task: that of understanding other cultures, other ways of thinking, in order to learn more about ourselves. My thanks go to all of you. [Recess]

DUMVILLE: In seeking a working name for the method being proposed we need to bring together the meaning of the proposed name with the definition offered. If it is going to be archaeoethnology, the definition needs to shift somewhat.

AUSENDA: Was it defined in the paper I sent you, or during the discussion?

DUMVILLE: No, just a few moments ago, only you did not have the tape on [laughter].

SCHÜTTE: Palaeoethnobotany.... [Laughter]

DUMVILLE: Yes, that is the impression it conveys, but there is no reason why it should, because palaeography is the study of 'old writing'.

GREEN: Good company indeed.

AUSENDA: Well, I prefer 'archaeo' to 'palaeo', because 'palaeo' seems more remote, whereas 'archaeo' is less drastic. And, after all, archaeology is important, I would say that archaeology represents the eyes of the ethnographer in this case, because archaeology is directly in touch with the remains of what those people did. Therefore, archaeology is involved to a considerable extent. The second part of the compound implies that an ethnological method is brought to bear, in the sense that one would try to understand everything one could of a particular society at a given time, rather than specialising in one aspect alone of that society. This is why I believe the proposed 'archaeoethnology' is the combination of terms most suitable to express this kind of approach. New combinations of these same terms for interdisciplinary endeavours emerge every ten to fifteen years and some have been preempted already. I believe the term 'palaeo' has two minuses, it does not imply the primary importance of archaeology, and it points to a more distant past, which is not our case.

GREEN: No further back in the past than palaeography.

RICHARDS: What you are trying to define is not really any different from cultural anthropology, because, after all, most of the societies about which one can read ethnographies now are, in fact, extinct.

AUSENDA: Why is it different from anthropology? Because anthropology is predicated on the method of participant observation. We cannot apply this method to what those people were doing, we can presumably observe some of the results of what they did through the eyes of archaeologists. In theory archaeologists have the scientific means to do it. In practise they can be greatly helped by other historical disciplines. They have to reconstruct the communicational backgroud, that is where philologists come in, they have to rely on ethnologists in some way to obtain an idea of methodology, something that has been exemplified here, they have to rely on historians to put them in the right time context and, as Ian said, historians have to tell them what was going on at the same time around the society whose remains the archaeologists have recovered in order to reconstruct the historical perspective of that period.

RICHARDS: I think you are looking at it from a European perspective only.

AUSENDA: Definitely.

RICHARDS: But that causes problems in North America, where the dividing line between archaeology and anthropology is very much more difficult to draw. As you know, there is no such thing as an archaeology degree in North America. There is only a degree in anthropology for the very reason that the societies that were being studied by archaeologists were surviving.

AUSENDA: Yes, I agree entirely with you and I think this approach should be limited to Europe, and maybe in future to Asia. I do not think many other regions and periods can use this kind of approach. There weren't many societies which were poised on the threshold of history and left little trace of their sociocultural background. One cannot do the same thing with American Indians. In the first place the study would have to reconstruct their history; in fact, the first step in their case is what has become known as ethnohistory, and the approach which is being discussed here would be a subsequent step. A further difference concerning North American aborigines is that there are several reports on their customs and subsistence base at the time of contact, probably because they were different enough to be interesting to the European immigrants who associated with them, whilst there are very few and questionable reports on the customs and subsistence base of European barbarian populations at the time of contact. Obviously barbarian customs were not that strange to the Romans because many rural populations within the Empire may have lived at similar levels of complexity. Is there a description of a barbarian encampment?

WOOD: Yes, Priscus on the Huns. It is available in translation in Gordon, *The Age of Attila*, or in R. C. Blockley, *The Fragmentary Greek Historians*.

DUMVILLE: Or the Arab who travelled among the Rus in the early tenth century—Ibn Fadlan.

HINES: My impression is that 'ethnology' is not a very familiar term in Britain, and it would be welcome to have a clear statement of what it were to mean in this context.

AUSENDA: Would you prefer 'archaeoanthropology'?

HINES: No, no, I would not. Perhaps, largely, I suppose, because 'ethnology' conveys to me more of the sense of a focus upon the group rather than on undifferentiated mankind; also, I think, because 'anthropology' carries for me those connotations of fieldwork and participant observation you mentioned just before.

AUSENDA: All right, let us turn this argument around. Let us start with a definition. You have the floor.

HINES: I suppose that the sensible way to proceed would be to start with my perception that (1) 'ethnology' is a reasonable description of what you were hoping we would talk about—or at least a useful framework we could talk within—and (2) that 'ethnology' deals with the human group, with an agglomeration of people who are connected by all sorts of different factors and not just by the fact that they live in some definable single area at the same time: it may be that they behave in perceptibly similar ways, or we may see that the behaviour of one person or group of people affects in some way the life of another group of people who, in this sense, are located somewhere within a common system. The study of the phenomena that are peculiar to this particular situation—that are not absolutely universal, characteristic of all groups of people, wherever and whenever they live—is the study of their culture; and cultural history must be interested in the systems in which these inter actions take place. In contemporary situations one can describe this study as 'ethnology', and one distinguishes ethnology from cultural anthropology by criteria that are not known to me though I imagine that once again the difference between the particular and the general is likely to be involved. That doesn't seem to be my problem.

'Archaeoethnology' will then refocus such study on a context at some significant remove in the past. I don't see that this distance has to be precisely (arbitrarily) defined by, say, a minimum number of years; perhaps all one needs is a certain level of breakdown in the transmission of knowledge between ourselves and the people we are studying. Perhaps we don't really need to draw a line between archaeoethnology and ethnology at all.

AUSENDA: Yes, I meant to forget for the time being the question of the title, and try instead to come to a definition which is....

HINES: ...a statement of what we want to do.

AUSENDA: That's right.

HINES: I think I would say that what we want to do is to work towards an understanding of the connectedness of the experiences and behaviour of agglomerations of people.

RICHARDS: That is not sufficient in itself because that then could be anthropology. We must qualify it by saying that it is on societies that one cannot study by participant observation, because then it becomes anthropology.

GREEN: I would like to add another point to what John has said, particularly latching on to this use of the word 'conglomerations' or 'agglomerations' because I would like to stress the rise and fall of such agglomerations, both from within, by means of fission and fusion, and from without by contact with other cultures and other peoples. I think we can stress two complementary aspects of the same changing dimensions of your agglomerations.

AUSENDA: From without by means....

GREEN: By contact with other peoples and cultures, and that surely is what we should be doing a lot of the time. Does that make you unhappy John?

HINES: No, it does not make me unhappy; I was, perhaps exaggeratedly, trying to be abstract, and not to build into a definition my own views on what the major actual features of this sort of connectedness within agglomerations are.

GREEN: Yes, that may be justifiable in abstract, but is it justifiable in the light of what we have been talking about?

HINES: It may very well not be in the context of medieval Europe, and I do not deny that for a moment; it is indeed a topic I am particularly interested in. I simply wanted to try to avoid building into the definition of the general topic my beliefs about what was going on in the specific context in which I am most interested to apply whatever general insights I can gain.

A different point: I am a great believer in the functional character of culture. Something which I think has not been discussed as thoroughly as it might have been here was the topic of the first paper, which was, however, discussed in some detail in respect of that case study, and this is the question of adaptation to the natural environment. In comparison with the exhaustive degree to which some other general points have been discussed, this seems not to have been approached here in any comprehensive way.

AUSENDA: David [Dumville], you seem to have been thinking long enough to have collected your thoughts.

DUMVILLE: My thinking has been going in some rather different directions. I should rather hold off for a moment. I have a few words I want to say about interdisciplinarity which I think may set us off in a different direction.

WOOD: I come to a position much closer to John's than to the position that, as I understand it, you are taking. In English anthropology there is a tradition which allows for historical anthropology. It is certainly within the area studied by Mary Douglas. Mary Douglas talks about the Maccabees, for instance. If the Maccabees in the second century BC are room for the field of the anthropologists, then the fifth, sixth, seventh, and eighth centuries AD are too. I do think that in a sense we are trying to do something like an anthropology of this period. Obviously we are not trying to do a total anthropology, but then nor does any anthropologist try to do a total anthropology of his individual, or her individual tribe. And I want to register the idea that if one is making distinctions between archaeologists and anthropologists and so on, at some point in the preface a distinction should be made between different types of historians. There are historians who can work in a very intertextual way, being basically concerned with evidence as text; there are historians who are concerned much more with reconstruction and there are those of us who move from one to the other according to what our particular problematic is on any one day, or any one issue. But certainly British anthropology also allows for intertextuality. So, within the lines of British anthropology I would want to say that we are trying to do an anthropology of the early medieval period, and that is what I hope we were doing. I am not necessarily saying that that should determine our title, but it seems to me that what British anthropology has done really covers most of the things, if not all of the things, that I think that we want to do here.

AUSENDA: Could I just add a note to your observations? What I think we should aim for is not only to get historians, philologists, and archaeologists, but anthropologists interested as well. So far anthropologists, at least those I have talked to, did not seem to be interested in the idea that they could contribute to the study of ancient populations. My impression is that when David [Turton] came over, he began to realise that it was something he could usefully put his experience to.

WOOD: Absolutely. For that reason I would rather like to have 'anthropology' in the title, and *An Anthropology of the Early Middle Ages* is exactly what I would like to see.

AUSENDA: Do you prefer 'anthropology' to 'ethnology'?

WOOD: Personally, but that is because I am used to thinking of 'ethnology' in terms of museums, seeing lots of masks hanging in Victorian cases, but that is just my personal reading of the word.

AUSENDA: 'Archaeoanthropology' sounds much worse than 'archaeoethnology'.

WOOD: I am quite happy to have *An Anthropology of the Early Middle Ages*, without 'archeo' at all.

SCHÜTTE: As a German I have a problem with 'anthropology' because in Germany 'anthropology' is used in a different way, as 'physical anthropology'. The discipline we are describing is called 'ethnology'. I would still agree as to the sense of using the other term, but leave 'archaeo' out because we have different methods even if we are working on the same problem. If you include 'archaeo' you should include all these fragment words. I think it is better for the area we are working on with different methods to use a different term. even 'anthropology' would be agreeable to me. I think this would be a good idea, the question is: will it be recognised and have some effect outside this circle or is it a fiction we are building up at the moment?

HINES: Can I express a worry about the term 'anthropology' that is, I think, akin to my understanding of 'linguistics' as a general linguistics: one of the reasons why British Anthropology attempts a complete range of physical, cultural, social anthropology, etc., is, I imagine, that the specialised anthropologists see their individual contributions as feeding into a total, global, complete anthropology which is a general science of humanity, just as linguistics attempts to understand language as a totality. I may very well be wrong, but I would have thought that, if one claimed to be writing an anthropology of the early Middle Ages, it would be putting forwards a claim to be producing that sort of total science that would run the whole gamut from physical anthropology to cultural anthropology and so on; at the very least this would risk appearing pretentious and be claiming too much.

SCHÜTTE: I see the danger as well. I think you are quite right, this could be somewhat pretentious.

WOOD: It depends on the anthropological school you are looking at.

AUSENDA: I think John [Hines] is right in this sense. You can say that a book contains an 'ethnography' of a given population, but you normally do not say that it contains an 'anthropology' of a population. Also the term 'ethnology' refers to specific populations. As John remarked 'anthropology' is a generalising term, it defines a discipline. You do not write the anthropology of something as you do not write the linguistics of something.

We need as few words as possible to characterise this approach. They should become a kind of label. You can define these clusters of words any way you want, so we should have a definition. I rather prefer 'ethnology' to 'anthropology'.

WOOD: Can you have an 'ethnology' of a period rather than a people?

AUSENDA: You can have an 'ethnology' of a people during a given period.

DUMVILLE: Yes, *An Ethnology of the European Early Middle Ages*.

WOOD: *Studies in Early Medieval Ethnology*, I would go along with something like that, because I think that ethnology of specific peoples presents me with various difficulties. I can understand something like *The Ethnology of the Anglo-Saxons*. It seems to me that 'ethnology' actually implies a people. So, if you say ethnology of a period, I think the category does not work.

DUMVILLE: We have a problem anyway between the relationship of etymology and what we are thinking to define anyway at the moment we use an element like 'archaeo' as, of course, the first part of a compound where it has to mean archaeology and, yet, it does not mean archaeology; you are relying on that sound conveying something apart from its meaning. It may be fine, but the moment we start analysing the term, or talking about it, it starts becoming controversial, it starts getting picked apart. Then it becomes a term of questionable value.

AUSENDA: Why should it be picked apart if one defines it well and it just remains as a label? The term 'ethnoarchaeology' has not been picked apart.

DUMVILLE: It is simply a question of whether it is of sufficient interest for people to start discussing it. And, on the assumption that it will be, then....

AUSENDA: Interest is also built up on contradiction.

DUMVILLE: On shock-value.

GREEN: At the risk of introducing a further word into whatever title we agree upon, if we agree upon any title, I would like to come back to what Ian [Wood] suggested. He started off by saying *Studies in....* I would be in favour of something like *Studies in...,*

Approaches to.... not for more wordiness, but because I share John's worry at the possible impression of pretentiousness and a totality which is not there and is not meant to be there.

DUMVILLE: There are two different things being talked about. Something like that would be fine for a series-title, but not a book title.

GREEN: It is true, I have shifted from definition to title, and that is because Ian did that, and I wanted to support that while it was still in my mind.

AUSENDA: In my experience, the shorter the title and the better chance of survival it has if it is well defined. It looks as if the sum of suggestions for a series title is *Studies in Historical Archaeoethnology.*

DUMVILLE: If you start using it more, especially if you start using it as some kind of disciplinary name, that is when people will start thinking.

WOOD:...and criticising it with reason which I might say they'll do.

DUMVILLE: Only, after all, in various subjects and disciplines that we hold conferences in, we tear one another to pieces on just such a word.

RICHARDS: I am amazed that historians have not suggested just 'history'.

DUMVILLE: It is the 'archaeo' which bothers me, because for three hundred years, in English, 'archaeology' meant knowledge of and study of the past, and then it was hijacked by people who study physical objects, that kind of thing. So, the etymology indicates a rather broader meaning than current usage. But when you detach 'archaeo-' (that is, 'old'), it cannot by itself convey the sense which 'archaeology' now has. 'Archaeo-ethnology', in other words is not a compound of 'archaeology' and 'ethnology'. If the title were 'Studies in (something)...' compound with 'archaeology', I would be a lot more sympathetic to it.

AUSENDA: You can not call it 'ethnoarchaeology', the term already stands for a well defined field of research.

DUMVILLE: Can you not simply hybridise 'anthropology'—'archaeoanthropology'?

AUSENDA: No, for the reason that John [Hines] pointed out. Anthropology is more generalising than ethnology.

HINES: It seems to me that the choice between 'historical ethnology' and 'archaeoethnology' is virtually an aesthetic one. I think I slightly prefer the 'historical', though probably it means just the same as 'archaeoethnology'.

WOOD: I just wonder how many people understand the word 'archaeoethnology'?

AUSENDA: I accept David's suggestion that this should be downgraded to a series title. The definition for this series title can be given at the end of the discussion.

GREEN: What then happens not if, but when our qualifications of your definition all head off in different directions, as they undoubtedly will?

AUSENDA: In which sense?

GREEN: In the sense that they may not be reconcilable with one another, just as they have not been reconcilable yet, if I am not mistaken.

AUSENDA: You mean the definitions?

GREEN: No, I mean, if you agree on something and then submit it to us, we then qualify it. It would be simple for you if all our qualifications moved in the same direction, but will they?

AUSENDA: I can put the definition together from your considerations. Your observations may be incorporated in the final definition or, if in complete disagreement, quoted separately.

GREEN: We have all said different things, so far.

AUSENDA: My impression is that your remarks were additive.

GREEN: We have not yet agreed on a title.

AUSENDA: We are coming to the title now. So far we talked about the series title. Someone rightly said: "Do not put it in the title, because no one will understand what it is and they might think it has something to do with Amazonia". So, I shall leave this as the series title mentioned inside the cover. It should not be difficult to put together a definition as there were three or four eminent scholars who suggested several parts of the definition.

GREEN: Who are they, by the way? [Laughter]. [The discussion for a title and subtitle took up some twenty additional pages. It was interesting, not so much from an epistemological point of view, but as a document on the motivations and processes that come into play in the choice of titles and subtitles for the disciplines concerned. The final choice was *After Empire: Towards an Ethnography of Early Medieval Europe*. This was subsequently changed to *After Empire: Towards an Ethnology of Europe's Barbarians* more in line with the subsequent titles in the series].

Editor's Postscript

The kind of meetings we have all attended many times in the past are intra-disciplinary and inter-paradigmatic: within the ambit of one discipline, they bring together people with differing theoretical credos. Paradoxically, or perhaps purposely, the result makes for greater differentiation by feeding, rather than dampening, rivalries and contrasting modes of interpretation. Competing paradigms come out from these meetings strengthened rather than harmonised.

The 'interdisciplinarity' of this symposium was made possible by the fact that the objective of the meeting was common to us all: to try better to understand a period of transition which lies at the base of modern Europe. We recognised the importance of this common objective and, at the same time, the feasibility of approaching it from the viewpoint of different disciplines. In this sense the meeting was cohesive, because, rather than producing a confrontation of paradigms it evoked points of mutual interest and common theoretical assumptions.

I believe everyone saw the advantages of inter-disciplinarity in that—for some at least for the first time—they had to scale down their interventions to the common denominator of all the disciplines represented, thereby making them more intelligible and to the point.

An important benefit which one participant noted—probably because it is also present in traditional symposia—was due to 'internationality'. In traditional symposia this is often obscured, however, because different theoretical approaches are themselves international and because there isn't always a common objective.

Finally, a very important ingredient which contributed immeasurably to the favourable outcome of the meeting was the 'informality' which is clear even from the minutes of the discussion. Very quickly titles were dropped and first names adopted. This made for greater openness and allowed for strong disagreements to be aired, as they were alleviated by the lightness, but not frivolity, of the atmosphere. The informality also engendered cohesiveness, as all participants gathered for meals together even though they had the option of attending different places, and even during those periods of relaxation discussions and exchanges went on.

Based on the opinions expressed by the participants and on the constraints of the circumstances, I believe that the project upon which this research centre is embarking should be called 'historical archaeoethnology'.

Taking the three components of this expression in sequence, the attribute 'historical' owes its presence to the importance of historical disciplines in this project. Indeed, it is historians and philologists of the early Middle Ages who need to widen their diachronic perspective in order to escape from the culturo-centric and chrono-centric views which are characteristic of Western scholarship. Among historical disciplines, philology in particular has an important role to play. It is, in fact, the only discipline for which past reality is not mediated by human subjectivity, because the linguistic evidence it focusses on depends on 'langue' rather than 'parole'. For this reason philological correspondence may be considered the ultimate validation of a model. Furthermore, the historical approach is also predicated on written evidence, the correct interpretation of which makes up, perhaps, at least half of the information one has on the populations of the early Middle Ages. Finally, the attribute 'historical' signifies a period during which those populations came onto the scene of history—it is, of course, possible to conceive of a prehistoric archaeoethnology.

The second term, 'archaeo', recognises—albeit without etymological justification—the importance of the discipline of archaeology in this study. Among scholars who study the period, archaeologists are the most numerous 'in touch' with the remains of past 'reality'. They too must shed their biases and adjust their theoretical approaches to envisage with the necessary openness and imagination the unveiling of past secrets. Again, 'archaeo-', has a double meaning: it also signifies a distant but not a remote past.

The third term, 'ethnology', refers to a discipline which is a newcomer to the field. Ethnologists are scholars who have been individually trained through the process of fieldwork in societies of 'others', this being a fundamental formative characteristic of the discipline. A practitioner of 'anthropologie historique' (see Introduction) who has not been in the field for at least one year remains inevitably an historian. There is a similarity here with the requirement that someone who wants to practise psychoanalysis must first undergo a full analysis to realise how one feels on the opposite side of the desk.

Ethnology, seen as a subdivision of the discipline of anthropology, can bring several benefits to our project. First of all, 'ethnoarchaeological' observations (see Introduction), especially about artefacts, economics and the technology of simple societies, can bring into better perspective previously poorly understood aspects of a past society. A second benefit which can be derived from ethnology-anthropology is the realisation that one has to be cautious when interpreting historical sources that describe populations comprising hundreds of thousands, or formidable 'armies'.

The perspective of anthropology seems to be the best suited to defeating culturo-centrism and chrono-centrism. Even David Turton, despite his cautious approach, had to admit that he was struck by the similarity between the situation described for early medieval Europe by some of the participants and that within which anthropologists have worked in Africa. For myself I can say that I did not understand the gist of the Langobard oath-taking procedure, set out in Rothari's Edict, until I read abaut the oath-taking procedure of the Sinai Bedouin. I am not saying that present-day anthropological information can fill historical gaps, but it certainly can orient one in the right direction and warn one if one is going the wrong way.

Finally, why 'ethnology' rather than 'anthropology'? Because ethnology is based on a holistic approach, that is, it attacks a problem from all possible angles: not solely myth, or kinship, or power-relations but everything from subsistence to religion. Since the available information is so fragmentary, we must set the limits of the puzzle as wide as possible so as to offer many different points of attack. A traditional 'ethnological' approach will allow one to see what is certain, what is doubtful and what is still unknown of the various aspects of the population studied.

Paradoxically, while information at the disposal of contemporary anthropologists on simple societies is constantly on the wane because they are gradually becoming more complex, that which pertains to early medieval societies is constantly increasing, because of the increasing sophistication of historical research and the growing contribution of archaeology. In a hundred years, we may know more about those populations than what their imperial contemporaries did.

Having listed the characteristics and benefits deriving from this new approach, and based on what was suggested during the discussion, we may attempt to define it: *Historical archaeoethnology* is a study predicated on an interdisciplinary approach by historians and philologists, archaeologists, and anthropologists aiming to understand the connectedness of the experiences and behaviour of agglomerations of people (Hines, p.298, this vol.), in particular historical societies which one can no longer study by participant observation (Richards, p.298, this vol.), and the rise and fall of such agglomerations, both from within, by means of fission and fusion, and from without by contact with other cultures (Green, p.298, this vol.), bearing in mind that ethnology implies the study of a given people (Wood, p.300, this vol.), and is directed at the study of populations which settled in the forrner Roman Empire during the early Middle Ages.

References in the conclusion

Blockley, R. C.
    1981/83   *The Fragmentary Classicising Historians of the Later Roman Empire*, Vol. 1 & 2. Liverpool: Liverpool University Press.
Gordon, C. D.
    1960   *The Age of Attila*. Ann Arbor, MI: Michigan University Press.
Henige, D. P.
    1974   *The Chronology of Oral Tradition*. Oxford: Oxford University Press.
Needham, R.
    1975   Polythetic classification: convergence and consequences. *Man* (NS) 10: 349-369.
Schlee, G.
    1989   *Identities on the Move*. Manchester: Manchester University Press.
Thompson, P.
    1978   *The Voice of the Past: Oral History*. Oxford: Oxford University Press.
Whitehead, A. N.
    1929   *Process and Reality*. Cambridge: Cambridge University Press.

INDEX

Acculturation; of Germanic populations 12
Adam of Bremen 255
Adornment; uniformity in supra-regional - 83
Aedui; patriotism of - 211
Aegidius 182, 206, 208, 209
Aetius 180, 182
Affinal; links 20, 23
Agathias 259
Age; among A.-S. 68; and livestock bone deposits and decoration 67; differences as a basis of structure 101; formation of a new - set 104; grade(s) 25, 32, 101, 109; mean - at death for men 239; of cremated person 73; of deceased 61; organisation 95, 289; set 25, 32, 101, 109; set ceremony 105, 111, 294; set members as agents of force 102, 103; set systems connected with warfare 103; sets among women 109; span of an - set 101; system 100
Ageing; to construct symbolic systems 99; use of physiological - to organise social action 96
Agilmund 34
Agilulf 34
Agitium; British appeal to - 184
Agnates; patrilineal - 36
Agnatic; clan or lineages 15, 16, 17; kinship 18; understanding of term - 49
Agrarian; history 76; life 115
Agriculture(al) 38, 121, 138; and pastoralism 20, 28; changes in - methods under Roman influence 225; exploitation 119; foods in pastoralists' diet 28; history 138; in Lombardy 136; land allotment 37, 38, 48; laws on - 31; practices 76, 138; production 120; reorganisation of - 228; surplus 121; underdeveloped

- systems 119; under-represented in models 117; world 135
Alahis; duke of Brescia 122
Alamans 217, 259
Alans 146
Alboin 34, 35
Alcuin 255, 256,258-260,262
Alfred the Great 218
Altfrid's, '*Life of Liudger*' 255, 260
Ambrose, St, 196
Ambrosius Aurelianus 182, 184, 187, 198, 206
Ammianus Marcellinus 147
Amphorae 157, 158
Amulets 260-263, 270
Anastasius; Emperor 157
Ancestor; divine 232
Aneirin 199, 209
Angeln; peninsula 245
Angles(i) 33, 80, 244, 245
Anglian English; cemetery at Spong Hill 78; dress-style 83
Anglicisation 93
Anglo-Saxon(s); building types in - settlements 57; burial 56, 57, 139, 272; cemeteries 139; cities in - England 138; cremation burials 57; cremation urns 61, 62; early - social development 79; economy 117; England 285; glass- and enamel-working and bead-making 77; helmets 152; history 245; in Kent 180; invasions as origin-myth 72, 73; kingdoms 83, 232, 264; kingship and overkingship in - England 246; language 149, 159; names of months 259; pagan religion 85, 92, 276; pagan temples 256, 271; relations bw British and - 215; royal genea-logies 248; Surrey 139; tide 182
Animal; bones in cremation urns 58
Animism; term - 273
Animistic; Christianity 277
Annales; school in France 2, 97

Anno 164
Anskar 222, 257
Anthropological; account of cultures 107; interpretations 116; results of - research 106; synchronic - approach 110
Anthropologie historique 2, 303
Anthropologists('); disregarded all history 250; job to question cultural assumptions 290; prepared by fieldwork to getting at 'native' point of view 107; structural functionalist - 97
Anthropology('s) 96, 296; anti-historicism and modern - 98; boundaries and symbolic - 98; dividing line bw archaeology and - 297; history and - 95, 97, 289; in Germany problem with term - 299; models of - 281; more generalising than ethno-logy 301; of migration 294; perspective of - 303; stimula-ting new approaches 290; term - 300; written from a sedentary point of view 250
Antiquarianism 289
Ara Ubiorum 174
Archaeoethnology 296, 298, 303
Archaeological; culture 288; filtering of - evidence 52; sources 284
Archaeology 303; dividing line bw - and anthropology 297; hermetic 283; New - 55; philo-logy and - in eastern Europe
Arian; treason 184
Arimanni 32
Aristocracy(ts); consumption by theft or plunder 126; demand for luxuries 123; in ancient and feudal mode of production 116; in cities or countryside? 134, 135; urban - 123
Armies; equipment of whole - in bog deposits 224

305

Pope Gregory III (*cont.*)
  people of Germany 256; on
  sooth- saying, auguries and
  sorcery 260
Pope Gregory the Great('s) 256,
  271; letter to Mellitus 269; letter
  to Byzantine commander 32, 34;
  permission to the Angles 33
Pope Leo the Great; language of - 150
Pope Zacharias; Boniface's letter
  to - on auguries and phylacteries
  in Rome 261; letter of - 33
Population; movement 71, 290
Post-marital; residence 36, 40
Post-processualist(s) 52, 54, 115
Potlatch 139
Pots; similarity bw - and brooches 62
Potters; women - in kin group 67
Pottery; and annular brooches 71;
  and bronze metalwork 67; firing
  69; glazed - 168; Merovingian -
  168; Pingsdorf- 164; Roman - in-
  dustry 76; urns & household - 74
Practices; condemned by
  Indiculus superstitionum 254
Praise; poems 122, 136
Pre-capitalist; economies 119
Pre-Carolingian; period 134
Pre-circulation 281
Pressure(s); ecological & political -
  20; towards sedentarisation 29
Prestige; Frankish - style 81; goods
  117, 227; material production in
  Migration period 78
Priest(s); absence of comments on
  - 257; all members of a certain
  clan may be - 274; etymology of
  - 276; mediator bw community
  and external power 274, 275;
  Mursi - 's presence in community
  guarantees its success 275; pagan
  - 258; Tacitus on - casting lots
  258, 262; terms for pagan - 269;
  word for high - 270
Priesthood 268, 269, 274
Priestly; absence of - figure at
  Marklo 258; functions when
  satraps meet at Marklo 269;
  rites 258
Priorities; research - 285
Priscillianist; tracts 211
Priscus; on the Huns 297
Prisoners of war; conversion of
  Goths by - 215
Processualist; approach to archaeo-
  logy 70
Procopius; on Franks sacrificing
  Goths 151, 259, 270; on Gothic/

Lombard wars 123; on *Heruli* and
  Danoi 218
Production; craft - 121; issues of -
  and consumption 118; salt and
  glass - 121; textile - 70
Prophets 270; diviners and - 260;
  in response to outside threats &
  incursions 273; Widukind compared to more recent - 263
Provisor mercatorum; in Cologne
  and in Paris 174
Pyre(s) 57-59, 69
Pytheas 80

Queen Margrethe's Bridge 222

Radbod('s) 262; in priestly role
  260; King - 258, 260; near
  conversion 263
Radcliffe-Brown, A. R., 18, 97,
  289
Raid(s) 24, 46, 112, 179
Rampart(s); around Århus & Ribe
  220; as territorial boundaries 224;
  inspired by Roman *limes* 224;
  linking Danevirke & Hedeby 220;
  Olgerdiget and 'Æ vold' 223
Ratchis 33
Ravenna 283
Reciprocity 115, 117, 141
Redistribution 115, 228
Redistributive; mechanisms 119
Redwald 152, 256, 268
Regimental; age set members can
  form - organisations 102
Region; explanatory model 119
Regional; differentiation in Migra-
  tion period 81; exchange networks 113; supra-regional uniformity in personal adornment 83;
  system unit of analysis 88
Regionality 89
Regnum Romanorum 182, 206
Religion; A.-S. pagan - 92; aspect
  of community life 274, 278;
  changed in parallel with state
  structure 268; definition of - 278;
  distinction bw - and superstition
  261, 273; east of the Rhine 292;
  indigenous - 273; moral activity
  273; organised - 274; Tacitus on
  Germanic - 264
Religious; concept of - obedience
  149; cults 228; history 253;
  public - activities 231; zones 261
Renders; and rents 135
Residential; units 23
Revolution; Kuhnian type - 292

Rhein; Vorstadt 172
Rhenish; cattle 167; tufa stones 171
Rhine 163, 164, 167, 171; Britain
  not east of the - 285; Caesar's
  bridge across the - 39; campaign
  across the - 16; Christianity and
  religion of peoples east of the -
  264; Constantine's - bridge 165,
  171; frontier 145; human sacrifice
  attested east of the - 259; pagans
  east of the - 254; religion east
  of the - 292; Valley 137
Ribe 167, 170, 171, 222, 229, 232,
  240, 242, 249, 281; & market
  finds in Cologne 243; rampart
  around Århus & - 220; silver coins
  in eighth century layers at - 222
Rimbert; bishop of Bremen 257
Ring-fort(s) 220
Riothamus 181, 206, 207; contrast
  with Ecdicius of Clermont 208
Ripuarian; law codes 89
Ritual(s); a kind of language 106;
  as explanation used by archaeologists 72; boys condemned to -
  drowning 260; centres for pagan
  - 82; deposition 78, 227, 241;
  initiation 111; linguistic evidence
  for open air - 271; male - activity
  associated with age 103; power
  of - to do things 106; warfare is -
  103, 104
Ritualisation; of male violence 96
Road; Broskov - 239; construction
  prompted by Roman influences 225
Roman; activities of - veterans 239;
  Austrasia 173; bridge in Cologne
  165; bronze vessels 227, 229;
  Broskov road built like - road
  239; building complexes 164;
  buildings 172; cattle 167;
  Church, heir to Roman imperialism 85; *ciuitas* boundaries
  168; coins 224, 226; continuity
  173; decorations in bog deposits
  226; élite establishing its status
  around middle of - Iron Age 228;
  floor 172; Germanic gods and
  rituals seen in - terms 254; glass
  to demonstrate élite status 227;
  helmet in bog deposits 226;
  image of the - army 184;
  Imperial - economy 117; imports
  228; influence 153,225; influence
  of - paganism 254; large-scale
  movement across the - frontiers
  244; law 150, 165; lettering on
  coins 82; mercenaries from

Jacket photo by *Claudio Pollini, Ravenna (Italy)*: "Mausoleum of Theoderic in Ravenna"
Page setting: Bene e Presto, I - 20144 Milano
Phototypesetting: *Fotoedit srl (R.S.M.)*
Printers: *Studiostampa S.A. (R.S.M.)*